Full details of all our publications can be found on http://www.multilingual-matters. com, or by writing to Multilingual Matters, St Nicholas House, 31-34 High Street, Bristol BS1 2AW, UK.

Linguistic Landscape in the City

Edited by
Elana Shohamy, Eliezer Ben-Rafael
and Monica Barni

MULTILINGUAL MATTERS
Bristol • Buffalo • Toronto

Library of Congress Cataloging in Publication Data
A catalog record for this book is available from the Library of Congress.
Linguistic Landscape in the City/Edited by Elana Shohamy, Eliezer Ben-Rafael and
Monica Barni.
Includes bibliographical references and index.
1. Multilingualism. 2. City dwellers–Language. 3. Languages in contact. 4. Sociolinguistics.
5. Immigrants–Language–Social aspects. 6. Linguistic minorities. I. Shohamy, Elana Goldberg.
II. Ben-Rafael, Eliezer. III. Barni, Monica.
P115.L565 2010
306.44'6091732–dc22 2010021282

British Library Cataloguing in Publication Data
A catalogue entry for this book is available from the British Library.

ISBN-13: 978-1-84769-298-6 (hbk)
ISBN-13: 978-1-84769-297-9 (pbk)

Multilingual Matters
UK: St Nicholas House, 31-34 High Street, Bristol BS1 2AW, UK.
USA: UTP, 2250 Military Road, Tonawanda, NY 14150, USA.
Canada: UTP, 5201 Dufferin Street, North York, Ontario M3H 5T8, Canada.

The policy of Multilingual Matters/Channel View Publications is to use papers that are natural,
renewable and recyclable products, made from wood grown in sustainable forests. In the
manufacturing process of our books, and to further support our policy, preference is given to
printers that have FSC and PEFC Chain of Custody certification. The FSC and/or PEFC logos
will appear on those books where full certification has been granted to the printer concerned.

Typeset by Datapage International Ltd.
Printed and bound in Great Britain by the MPG Books Group.

Contents

Contributors vii

Introduction
Eliezer Ben-Rafael, Elana Shohamy and Monica Barni xi

Part 1: Linguistic Landscape Multilingualisms
1 Linguistic Landscape and Language Vitality
   Monica Barni and Carla Bagna 3
2 Language and Inter-language in Urban Irish and Japanese
   Linguistic Landscapes
   Jeffrey L. Kallen and Esther Ní Dhonnacha 19
3 'The Holy Ark in the Street': Sacred and Secular
   Painting of Utility Boxes in the Public Domain in a Small
   Israeli Town
   Yael Guilat 37

Part 2: Top-down, Power and Reactions
4 Decorating the City of Tel Aviv-Jaffa for its Centennial:
   Complementary Narratives via Linguistic Landscape
   Shoshi Waksman and Elana Shohamy 57
5 Bloemfontein/Mangaung, 'City on the Move'. Language
   Management and Transformation of a Non-representative
   Linguistic Landscape
   Theodorus du Plessis 74
6 Chinese on the Side: The Marginalization of Chinese
   in the Linguistic and Social Landscapes of Chinatown in
   Washington, DC
   Jia Jackie Lou 96
7 Linguistic Landscape under Strict State Language
   Policy: Reversing the Soviet Legacy in a Regional Centre
   in Latvia
   Heiko F. Marten 115
8 Linguistic Landscape of Kyiv, Ukraine: A Diachronic Study
   Aneta Pavlenko 133

Part 3: Benefits of Linguistic Landscape

9   Life in the Garden of Eden: The Naming and Imagery
    of Residential Hong Kong
    Adam Jaworski and Simone Yeung. 153

10 Selling the City: Language, Ethnicity and Commodified
    Space
    Jennifer Leeman and Gabriella Modan 182

11 Showing Seeing in the Korean Linguistic Cityscape
    David Malinowski 199

Part 4: Perceptions of Passers-by

12 Multilingual Cityscapes: Perceptions and Preferences
    of the Inhabitants of the City of Donostia-San Sebastián
    Jokin Aiestaran, Jasone Cenoz and Durk Gorter 219

13 Linguistic Landscape in Mixed Cities in Israel from
    the Perspective of 'Walkers': The Case of Arabic
    Nira Trumper-Hecht. 235

14 Responses to the Linguistic Landscape in Memphis,
    Tennessee: An Urban Space in Transition
    Rebecca Todd Garvin 252

Part 5: Multiculturalism in Linguistic Landscape

15 Linguistic Landscape and Language Diversity
    in Strasbourg: The 'Quartier Gare'
    François Bogatto and Christine Hélot. 275

16 Marking France's Public Space: Empirical Surveys
    on Regional Heritage Languages in Two Provincial Cities
    Robert J. Blackwood 292

17 Linguistic Landscape as Multi-layered Representation:
    Suburban Asian Communities in the Valley of the Sun
    Gerda de Klerk and Terrence G. Wiley 307

18 Diaspora and Returning Diaspora: French-Hebrew
    and Vice-Versa
    Eliezer Ben-Rafael and Miriam Ben-Rafael 326

Epilogue. 344
Index 347

Contributors

Jokin Aiestaran is Lecturer of Research Methods in Education at the University of the Basque Country in Spain. His research focuses on bilingual and multilingual education, and he has published papers on bilingual education, the linguistic landscape and language attitudes.

Carla Bagna is a Researcher in Educational Linguistics at the Università per Stranieri di Siena (University for Foreigners of Siena, Italy). She focuses on language teaching – especially L2 Italian – and on new methodologies for collecting and analysing data on immigrant languages in Italy.

Monica Barni is a Professor in Educational Linguistics at the Università per Stranieri, Siena. Her research focuses mainly on issues of language policy in education, specifically in relation to immigrants, and in purilingual societies. She publishes on the analysis of the impact of national and European language policies in educational contexts and of the conditions of plurilingualism and linguistic contact in Italy.

Eliezer Ben-Rafael is a Professor Emeritus of Sociology and former holder of the Weinberg Chair of Political Sociology at Tel-Aviv University. He is Past President of the International Institute of Sociology. He has done research and published in the areas of transnationalism, the comparative study of modernities, identity and culture.

Miriam Ben-Rafael holds a PhD in French Linguistics and is a freelance researcher who has studied and published on the French (*Franbreu*) of francophone immigrants in Israel, the influence of English in French comics and processes of language attrition, and the linguistic landscape of transnational diasporas.

Robert Blackwood is a Lecturer in French at the University of Liverpool, UK. He has published on sociolinguistic questions pertaining to Corsica. He is currently working on two linguistic landscape projects; both focused on France, one of which is a collaborative study of the linguistic landscape of French and Italian Mediterranean towns.

François-Xavier Bogatto is a PhD student at the University of Strasbourg, France, and a teaching assistant in the Department of Dialectology. His research interests include the linguistic landscape and urban sociolinguistics. His PhD dissertation focuses on the linguistic landscape of Strasbourg.

Jasone Cenoz is Professor of Education at the University of the Basque Country. Her research focuses on bilingualism and multilingualism. She is co-editor of the *International Journal of Multilingualism*. Her recent publication focuses on multilingual education in the Basque country in an international perspective.

Gerda de Klerk is a researcher/and instructor at Arizona State University where she analyzes demographic data and teaches statistics, and runs workshops on using the internet and social media in language teaching. She is also affiliated with the University of California Los Angeles as program director of the First International Heritage language conference.

Theodorus du Plessis is a Professor in Language Management and Head of the Department for Language Management and Language Practice at the University of the Free State and is involved in language planning activities in South Africa. He is editor-in-chief of the Van Schaik series, *Language Policy Studies in South Africa* and is co-editor of books on language politics in South Africa. He is a member of the International Academy of Linguistic Law.

Rebecca Garvin earned her MA in TESOL from Murray State University, Kentucky. The chapter is based on her PhD study in the composition and TESOL Program at Indiana University of Pennsylvania. Her interests include visual literacy and emotional responses to multilingualism.

Durk Gorter is Ikerbasque Research Professor at the Faculty of Education of the University of the Basque Country in San Sebastian/ Donostia. He conducts projects and publishes on multilingualism, European minority languages and linguistic landscapes.

Yael Guilat is a Senior Lecturer and Head of the Art Institute at Oranim Academic College. Her major fields of study are culture identity, visual memory and landscape as a culture construction in contemporary art.

Christine Hélot is a sociolinguist working in the area of educational linguistics and bilingual studies. She is Professor of English at the University of Strasbourg in the Teacher Education Faculty (IUFM Alsace) and a member of the research group GEPE/LILPA-EA1339 (Groupe d'études sur le plurilinguisme européen).

Adam Jaworski is Professor at the Centre for Language and Communication Research, Cardiff University. His research interests include discourse and tourism, non-verbal communication and multimodality. He is co-editor of the book series *Oxford Studies in Sociolinguistics*.

Jeffrey L. Kallen is a Senior Lecturer in Linguistics and Phonetics and a Fellow of Trinity College, Dublin. He has published widely on the English language in Ireland (Hiberno-English), and is co-director of the Irish component of the International Corpus of English (ICE-Ireland). He is also active in teaching and research on language variation and change, discourse analysis, and English as a world language.

Jennifer Leeman is an Associate Professor of Hispanic Linguistics at George Mason University. Her recent research focuses on ideologies of multilingualism in the USA, the linguistic racialization of Latinos and the sociopolitics of language education.

Jackie Jia Lou is an Assistant Professor in the Department of English, City University of Hong Kong. Her primary interest lies in the discursive and semiotic construction of place and the ways in which cultural, economic and political forces underpin such constructions. She is also engaged in investigating creative language use mediated by new communication technologies. She received her doctoral degree from the Department of Linguistics at Georgetown University.

David Malinowski is a PhD Candidate at the Graduate School of Education at the University of California at Berkeley. In addition to conducting studies of linguistic landscapes both local and virtual, he is researching the social effects of new media and digital technologies in the foreign language classroom.

Heiko F. Marten holds a PhD in English Linguistics from Freie Universität Berlin. After his PhD, he worked at Rēzekne University College in Latvia and currently has a position at the Chair of German at the University of Tallinn, Estonia. His research interests include linguistic landscapes, language policy, minority languages and attitudes and motivation in language learning.

Gabriella Modan is an Associate Professor of Sociolinguistics at Ohio State University. Her work focuses on discursive constructions of place and the intersection of language, ethnicity and urban identity from an ethnographic perspective.

Esther Ní Dhonnacha is a graduate of Fitzwilliam College, Cambridge, where she studied Archaeology and Anthropology. She has done field-work with gibbons in Borneo, and later studied Japanese at the Fukuoka

University of Economics. She currently works in Dublin as a freelance copy-editor.

Aneta Pavlenko holds a PhD in Linguistics from Cornell University. She is a Professor at the College of Education, Temple University, Philadelphia. Her research focuses on sociolinguistic and psycholinguistic aspects of bilingualism and second language acquisition.

Elana Shohamy is a Professor and Chair of the language education program at the School of Education, Tel Aviv University, where she teaches, researches and writes about multiple issues relating to multilingualism: language policy, language testing, language nights and languages in the public space.

Nira Trumper-Hecht is a research student at Tel-Aviv University, School of Education; she also teaches at Kibbutzim College of Education, Technology and the Arts. Her major scholarly interest lies in the study of linguistic landscape analysis with a special focus on mixed Jewish-Arab cities in Israel.

Shoshi Waksman is a Lecturer at Levinsky College and Kibbutzim College of Education, Technology and the Arts in Israel. Her main interests are social and cognitive aspects of literacy, and specifically multimodality in the process of meaning construction.

Terrence G. Wiley is Professor of Applied Linguistics in the Department of English at Arizona State University. His research and teaching focus on language policy, adult literacy-biliteracy, immigrant and heritage-community language education, societal multilingualism, language demography, TESL and English as an international language, and language and identity.

Simone Yeung is a published poet, researcher and musician. She strives to pursue an MPhil (Language and Law) in the University of Hong Kong and was called to the HK Institute of Vocational Education where she teaches English.

Introduction: An Approach to an 'Ordered Disorder'

ELIEZER BEN-RAFAEL, ELANA SHOHAMY and MONICA BARNI

Linguistic Landscape and Urban Spaces

This book focuses on the study of linguistic landscapes (LL) in present-day urban settings. This new area of study has developed in recent years as a field of interest and cooperation among applied linguists, sociolinguists, sociologists, psychologists, cultural geographers and several other disciplines. The common interest of all is the understanding that the LL as the scene where the public space is symbolically constructed (Ben-Rafael *et al.*, 2006; Shohamy & Gorter, 2008). The means of this construction are the marking of objects – material or immaterial – with linguistic tokens. These tokens may be analyzed according to the languages utilized, their relative saliency in the LL, as well as syntactic and semantic aspects. Analysts contend that these facts of language that illustrate the widest range of variation relate to cultural, social, political and economic circumstances.

In a seminal paper, Landry and Bourhis (1997) include in those linguistic objects, road signs, names of sites, streets, buildings, places and institutions, as well as advertising billboards and commercial shop signs. An important characteristic of the LL is that it comprises both 'private' and 'public' signs: signs issued by public authorities (like governments, municipalities or public agencies), and those issued by individuals, associations or firms acting more or less autonomously in the limits of authorized regulations. Landry and Bourhis maintain that the LL functions not only as an informational indicator, but also as a symbolic marker communicating the relative power and status of linguistic communities in a given territory. Focusing on Canada, Landry and Bourhis also emphasize the role of the LL in language maintenance using the framework of ethnolinguistic vitality research in bilingual settings. On the other hand, Spolsky and Cooper (1991), who focus on Jerusalem, emphasize the influence of political regimes on the LL. While both approaches are fruitful, they also manifest shortcomings requesting further elaborations.

The Landry-Bourhis approach, indeed, sees the LL as a 'given' context of sociolinguistic processes and does not pay attention to the dynamics of the LL as a field of its own. The Cooper-Spolsky approach addresses aspects of change more clearly, but still ignores the complexity of the LL and the numerous actors that participate in its moulding. Moreover, while both approaches do emphasize the interest of the LL as deserving study and research, they provide only a limited grasp of the far-reaching importance of the LL.

It is our own contention that LL facts constitute a field characterized by dynamics of its own, contingent on the nature of its linguistic, social, cultural and political context. This assessment has already been established by three recent books – edited by Durk Gorter (2006) and Elana Shohamy and Durk Gorter (2008), and authored by Peter Backhaus (2007). While Gorter's collection represented the first general coverage of the field from a variety of disciplinary perspectives, Shohamy and Gorter's volume aspires to crystallize the field through an emphasis on its limitations, borders and possibilities of expansion. Backhaus's work in this context represents a sociolinguistic investigation of a case-study, Tokyo, revealing the rich reality of the contemporary LL of a metropolitan city (see also Bairoch, 1988).

These works are the starting point of this volume, which attempts to analyze systematically – despite the multidisciplinarity of this set of contributions – the formation and essential aspects of today's urban spaces. Spaces of this kind constitute the major human and social settings of our era, and this collection aspires to bring out what LL investigations teach us about present-day cities – in general as well as in different and specific circumstances. This ambition should enable us to contribute theoretical statements, building up the field of the LL as a pertinent area of study where different disciplinary preoccupations meet and formulate common questions, if not identical answers.

The notion of public space (see Jaworski & Thurlow, 2010), we recall, refers to areas that are open and accessible to the 'crowd', i.e. the public at large. They include streets, town squares, parks, as well as built premises of official agencies or public libraries (Miles, 2007). Moreover, in today's metropolitan cities, one observes a constant increase of outdoor advertising on walls and billboards aimed at the wide public. Participating in the production of LL items – as designers, sponsors or first-hand manufacturers – are professional designers and producers, employees of municipal bodies, national agencies or corporate organizations, and individual entrepreneurs or shopkeepers. The physical setting is socially constructed, as limitations are imposed in the space, and this frame constitutes the scene where LL-related public interaction takes place.

Today, the urban space takes the form of a city: a relatively large and permanent settlement endowed with a particular administrative, legal or historical status. In Christian Europe, a city possesses a cathedral in addition to its systems for sanitation, housing and public transportation. A big city, or metropolis, consists of quarters and also has a variety of suburbs and smaller satellite cities surrounding it. Large cities indeed illustrate urban sprawl toward its periphery conjunctively with its commercial, touristic or industrial development. At the limit, we speak of a conurbation or megalopolis. In cases where the population achieves what is nowadays called a 'large population', i.e. it numbers millions of inhabitants, one often also observes rising crime rates and sharp differentiation between quarters, by socioeconomic status and ethnicity (Childe, 2007; Pacione, 2001; Pile, 1999; http://en.wikipedia.org/wiki/City-cite_note-2).

As a rule, large modern cities, like New York or London, contain huge central business districts and constitute global financial arenas, as well as the podium for presenting the latest innovations to the world. Applied to such cities, the term 'global city' means a city of enormous size, power and influence (Sassen, 2000). This term is bound to an image of 'container', encompassing a concentration of skills and resources warranting the city's power and capability to expand further. At a more descriptive level, today's urban LLs refer principally to areas where large businesses, department stores, supermarkets, coffee houses, libraries, public institutions and offices of associations of all kinds are concentrated. All these are found in given spaces of the urban territory – a set of streets, boulevards or squares – where 'the crowd' is particularly dense (except for closing days). City centers are also poles of attraction for residents of quarters far from the center, who live on the outskirts or in rural areas: old-timers rub shoulders with immigrants and tourists there.

It is in these areas that the LL expresses most clearly its multilingualism (Backhaus, 2007): values like patriotism and national pride directly impact on the use of official languages, ethnic allegiances that may find their paths to the public scene through tokens stemming from community vernaculars, commercial competition and allegiances to globalization that are imprinted in the use of the present-day recognized *lingua franca*, i.e. English. It is here that one also finds expressions of conflicts between groups, and attempts by political bodies to 'maintain some order' by enforcing strict regulations.

In brief, we know that LLs are moulded by different circumstances – historical, social, political, ideological, geographic and demographic – and at the same time, illustrate processes that are inherent to their own dynamic, which, in turn, participate in the melding of the wider social and cultural reality. It is in this context and by investigating a variety of such urban settings that this volume attempts to elicit the convergences and divergences of contemporary urban LLs, and to propose some general assessments. With this purpose in mind, we focus here on the relevant dimensions of the notion of urban LL.

Defining the Linguistic Landscape as a Field: Between Chaos and Gestalt

Looking at urban LLs from the viewpoint of the social sciences, one cannot ignore the contribution of the Chicago School of urban sociology, which as early as the 1920s and 1930s evinced the differentiation of affluent quarters and slums. As Adam Jaworski and Simone Yeung remind us, in their contribution to this volume, the sociologists of Chicago already pointed out the social heterogeneity of the city's population (see Mac Giolla Chriost, 2007) and addressed its invisible boundaries and gates. From this angle, Adam Jaworski and Simone Yeung address LLs as scenes of confrontation between different codes of meaning-construction. Spaces are constructed not just through the objects and boundaries that surround us and the habitual ways we conceive of them, but also through interaction with others operating in the 'same' space (Scollon & Scollon, 2003).

From these insights, it follows that the notion 'linguistic landscape', which refers to linguistic objects that mark the public space, i.e. inscriptions – or LL items – includes any written sign found outside private homes, from road signs to names of streets, shops and schools. The study of LLs focuses on analyzing these items according to the languages utilized, their relative saliency, syntactic or semantic aspects. These language facts which landmark the public space are social facts that, as such, relate to more general social phenomena. In this light, the study of the LL focuses on the articulation by actors of these linguistic symbols that mould the public space.

The notions of *public space* or (in an earlier formulation) *public sphere* are associated with the work of Jürgen Habermas (1989) who sees them as buffers between the state and the private sphere. In this area of activities, civil society crystallizes. In present-day mass society, the institutions that make up that sphere – from coffee houses to charities – tend to be absorbed by the commercial sector that, as Habermas also shows (Delanty, 2007), becomes more and more cosmopolitan under the increasing influence of globalization.

The public space includes every space in the community or society that is exposed to the public eye – streets, parks, billboards, shops, stores and offices. The core of the public space in this era, however, consists principally of areas designated as 'center' or 'downtown', i.e. the group of streets and squares where one sees 'a crowd' when most people are not at work (see also Eder, 2005; Kögler, 2005). These notions do not generally encompass major governmental bodies, factories and storehouses, which in many cities tend to be located in specialized areas. In the central area, by contrast, one now finds fashion boutiques, workshops of tailors and locksmiths, cafés, restaurants, fast-food places, offices, municipal buildings, theaters, movie houses and above all, huge department stores. All this heterogeneous whole is marked by a multitude of LL items mostly offering the image of a genuine jungle of signs – a jungle that is the LL of contemporary urban-metropolitan spaces.

To passers-by, however, who are accustomed to this kind of LL as the 'natural' decor of the urban space, it carries emblematic significance: the languages of LL items and the symbols they display landmark this space and represent its symbolic construction. It is here, downtown, that new fashions are launched, standards of consumption proposed, social services dispensed and ongoing cultural events advertised (Ben-Rafael *et al.*, 2006).

At first glance, this jungle is, as the term indicates, an extreme example of disorder. New LL items sprout incessantly with the inauguration of new institutions and stores, with the launch of new gadgets and products, and changing window displays. Old LL items disappear just as rapidly, when businesses close down or a department store changes hands. This instability is instantly visible in any central area of a transglobal metropolis and, to a lesser degree, is also discernible in more provincial cities. Participating in this dynamism are countless actors whose motivations and horizons are as numerous as their number (Ben-Rafael *et al.*, 2006). Personal preferences and inclinations, fashions originating from the outside, new local styles, linguistic innovations and borrowings from diverse tongues, all influence LL actors in their choices of sizes, colors, phrasings and wordings. These actors include professional designers, of course, but also independent professionals, shopkeepers, public relations officers, marketing experts, employees in public administrations, school principals and many others. Nothing warrants the coherence of their LL melding as they mostly ignore each other, contributing individually to the overall LL and in this very manner, giving it the usually chaotic aspect.

Chaos, indeed, seems to us quite an appropriate term in the present context. This notion has recently gained a new popularity in social science. *Chaos*, which originates from Χάος in Greek, typically refers to situations dominated by unpredictability (Gleick, 1987). The antithesis of law and order, it designates unrestrictiveness – both creative and destructive. A chaotic reality can hardly be the object of systematic analysis as its very principle implies incoherence (Urry, 2005). It should be added though that where chaos designates incoherent situations because of the inconsistencies of the amalgam they are composed of, as far as it still illustrates some degree of permanence, that chaotic principle does not necessarily imply orderlessness – at least in the way actors perceive it. Once given chaotic aspects of reality become recurrent, they also become familiar to actors who perceive them. By becoming humdrum, the perception of the disorder may then leave room in the participant's mind for a notion of commonly known configuration where the respective locations of objects vis-à-vis each other is – more or less – constant. The diverse and intrinsically incoherent and independent 'contributions' to the totality of the LL may then be perceived by actors as 'one whole', that is, as a *gestalt* ('configuration' in German). Individuals accustomed to a given LL may come to view it as 'the center', 'downtown' or something else, i.e. as a configuration. As shown by Gestalt theory (Scholl, 2001), the set of constituents of such config-urations come to be viewed as illustrating structural–systemic properties that pertain to none of these constituents individually. In this sense, gestalt and chaos are but two sides of the same reality. Passers-by generally come to crystallize a general landscape-like picture of the space – in the very manner that visitors capture as a single picture a sharply diversified natural landscape – such as one made conjunctively of mountains, valleys, rivers, forests and houses.

Unlike natural landscape, the LL is of course an entirely human-made phenomenon that pertains to social reality. It typically qualifies for Durkheim's (1964/1895) definition of a 'social fact', that is, a reality pertaining to and marking social life, independently from *a priori* individual velleities. LL items appear to passers-by as 'givens' of the space. As such, the disorder reigning in this space – different languages, humorous interjections, incoherent slogans, a jumble of colors and writings – is taken for granted and viewed as 'a whole'. It is in this sense, and despite its chaotic disparity, that the LL is a *gestalt* (Breidbach & Jost, 2006). As in other relevant cases, the *gestalt* effect draws from the items' appearing *ensemble* ('together', in French) that tend as such to be perceived as *un ensemble* (one whole).

This *ensemble* may, as such, become the emblem of societies, commu-nities or regions. Representations of the chaotic Champs Elysées and its LL are emblematic of Paris and France, and the same is true of Times Square for New York and the USA or Piccadilly Circus for London and England.

The Structuration of the Linguistic Landscape

Moving ahead by applying the structuralist methodology (see Levy-Strauss, 1958), we can now embark on deciphering the disorder reigning in an LL by trying to single out given structuration principles accounting for its moulding – however chaotic it appears on the surface. The singular, autonomous and uncoordinated perspectives of such principles might then, in the final analysis, be held responsible for that chaos, to the extent that all are relevant to the creating of LL items and, at the same time, represent different, even contrasting, exigencies. As developed in previous works (Ben-Rafael, 2008; Ben-Rafael *et al.*, 2006), we find in the social science literature several major relevant approaches to social action that diverge from each other, but do not exclude each other.

A first tradition is attached to the name of Bourdieu (1983, 1993), contending that social reality consists primarily of power relations between categories of participants in given fields (another word for space) of social facts. Each field endeavors its own dynamics and affects and is affected by other neighboring fields. Power relations refer to the extent to which given actors are able to impose patterns of behavior on others – even against their will (see Weber's formulation in Bendix, 1960). With respect to LLs, this structuration principle may transpire in the stronger party's capacity to impose limitations on weaker actors' use of linguistic resources. Moreover, this approach is relevant to LL studies, as it pays particular attention to the differentiation between top-down and bottom-up flows of LL items. The top-down flow originates from public bodies – from governmental or municipal level to public or associative organizations – that produce LL items to designate official agencies and diffuse information. As the actors behind this flow – politicians and public servants – are more powerful than those participating in the bottom-up flow, they may be able to exert some control over them. The question of the role of power in the LL may thus be widely explicated by comparing the two flows from the viewpoint of LL item features. This would show how far bottom-up items are designed by actors who are able to maintain their autonomy.

Another tradition in the social sciences places less emphasis on power *per se* than on interest. This approach is linked to the name of Boudon (1990, 2007; see also Coleman & Fararo, 1992), who stipulates the importance of rational considerations, i.e. *good reasons*, in the accounting of actions by actors. Following this methodological-individualism approach, actors' aspirations – material as well as expressive – are moved by interests in attainable goals. This assumption in the context of the LL in an urban metropolitan environment clarifies the intensive competition that sets actors against each other to attract the attention of passers-by: this imposes some restrictions of its own on the freedom of maneuver by LL actors. Actors, who compete for influence over the same public, are bound to respect the latter's sensibility, its values, propensities and tastes. In our consumerist-cultural context, numerous actors may be similarly induced to emphasize orientations toward comfort, luxury or prestige widely shared by the public, and to make use of the same or similar 'in'-cultural codes. Particularly in contemporary settings, which are generally moved by very instrumental considerations, LL items must 'play on' and anticipate clients' cost-and-benefit considerations. Given the far-reaching pervasiveness of the public space's commercial character, such anticipations may be assumed to play a major part in LL structuration. Actually, against the backdrop of present-day overproduction of the kinds of goods and services that often blurs the clarity of what is more 'reasonable' and what is less so, actors may present themselves as 'guides' to confused clients.

The third tradition is the subjectivist perspective (Goffman, 1963). It analyzes social action as a function of perceptions of one's environment and preoccupations with the presentation of self. This approach is privileged by researchers who investigate the contemporary importance of the subjective dimension of social experiences (for a review, see Abrams & Hogg, 1990). In this perspective and with respect to the LL, one may ask how the 'crowd', i.e. the public of passers-by, perceive and react to the LL. We know from numerous works in social psychology (Myers, 1993; Flick, 1998) that documented facts may be perceived in diverse manners by individuals – according to value biases, *a priori* convictions or cognitive variance in interpretations. Hence, while LL items aspire to seduce passers-by, different individuals or categories of individuals react differently to these efforts. Obviously, the more dense and numerous the LL items, the more one may expect perceptions of the LL to be diversified and heterogeneous, and so also the level of satisfaction or dissatisfaction passers-by draw from the LL. It should be stressed though, that this subjective dimension is a structuration principle of the LL only when and where it is taken as a reference to LL actors themselves – when they, like their potential clients, aspire to illustrate their individual singularity vis-à-vis their competitors in their struggle for the attention of the 'crowd'.

Finally, our fourth perspective refers to the importance of collective identities in our era of globalization and multiculturalism. In such contexts, the design of LL items may also eventually assert – among other interests – their actors' particularistic identities, thereby exhibiting *a priori* commitment to a given segment within the general public. This collective-identity principle, which is bound to regional, ethnic or religious particularisms, should express, in one manner or another, a difference from the all-societal identity. It is this principle that is especially focused on by researchers investigating the contemporary importance of sociocultural communities and their related use of linguistic markers (Calhoun, 1997; Hutchinson & Smith, 1996; Ben-Rafael & Sternberg, 2009). Hence, the study of the prints of the collective identity principle in the LL should reveal the vitality of such societal cleavages. In general terms, we may expect that the more a setting qualifies for the notion of multiculturalism, LLs should comprise items expressing such particularistic identities – in addition to, or on account of, symbols of all-societal solidarity.

In sum, each of these perspectives carries theoretical significance for LL research:

(1) From a 'Bourdieusian' perspective, the relation of different codes in LL should be explainable in terms of power relations between dominant and subordinate groups, and especially with respect to top-down LL items that are much more controlled by the authorities and their policies than bottom-up items.

(2) From the 'good reasons' perspective, one expects that LL actors mould their LL items according to their understanding of the public's instrumental and rational interests, i.e. its good reasons.

(3) From the subjective-perception perspective, one may expect anarchic tendencies from which it transpires that segments of the 'crowd' have differing perceptions of the LL and diversely influence LL actors who aspire to seduce them.

(4) From the collective identity perspective, we expect that LL items may convey meanings in terms of *identity markering*, testifying to the special ties binding *a priori* actors and given categories of clients.

Hence, we have here a system comprising focuses on the relations of groups of LL actors among themselves (in terms of power relations), of LL items to the public in general (in terms of good reasons), of LL items to LL actors (in terms of self-presentation) and of LL actors to given segments of the public (in terms of collective identities). From these principles stem different, even divergent, requests of LL items. However, these principles by no means exclude each other as they project themselves on different aspects of the LL, and do not necessarily represent the same weight in the melding of specific areas of the LL. Only empirical fieldwork can attempt to supply answers to the questions raised by these assessments. It is this space of issues that preoccupies the various contributions that make up this volume.

The Empirical Field

These contributions, we emphasize, were not guided by the theoreticization presented above, which the editors of this volume propose here. Moreover, this introduction is the outcome of debates, and we see in the theoretical approach proposed here, firstly a way of launching a debate on options for developing a theory of LL that till now have been hesitant and scattered. What is proposed here is not, to be sure, the only prospect for LL theoretization in the eyes of its proponents. We believe that the collection of works presented here can be viewed as a systematic multi-faceted investigation thanks to the theoretical approach that guided this volume's structuration.

Part 1: Linguistic Landscape Multilingualisms, consists of three chapters that assess the multilingualism of the LL in present-day urban spaces. With respect to the LL, one may apparently speak of multilingualism in different ways. Monica Barni and Carla Bagna overview several Italian cities and show the diversity of languages related to immigration and other contextual circumstances. The connection they find does not seem to be determined by a direct, one-to-one causal link and they emphasize that, in this respect, one may speak of a whole range of factors. More specifically, the various data confirm that there is no direct relation between the presence of a language in the population of an area, its vitality and visibility. This relationship depends on numerous linguistic, extralinguistic and contextual factors.

Jeffrey L. Kallen and Esther Ní Dhonnacha take the investigation of multilingualism in the LL to a comparison involving Japan and Ireland, and they, too, aspire to reveal the social and cultural determinants of linguistic variation. Multilingualism, in their understanding, not only concerns the conjunctive use of different languages in writing, but also the semiotic functioning of signage. Their argument is that signage in the visual channel opens up ways of transcending the sign's literal message to invoke covert meanings through devices and inter-language expressions. They also argue that this approach allows for an assessment of the ways in which various language communities use the LL in different ways to address the same issues of globalization. The LL itself is nearly limitless in its flexibility, and highly complex in its systems of reference.

Both the Barni-Bagna and the Kallen-Ní Dhonnacha contributions assess the importance of English as the language of globalization in the present era. This importance goes far beyond the impacts of other circumstances; several other contributions to this volume that discuss other aspects of the LL still find it necessary to signal the presence of English. These chapters still refer to the wide occurrence of English in non-English-speaking societies – independent of immigration or the presence of English speakers – and rather relate it to the flows of tourists or the current status of the language in the eyes of locals. Yael Guilat elaborates on a scheme, operated in a peripheral Israeli city, of paintings produced to decorate electricity installations across the city. Inspired by varied visual culture sources, they represent different levels of participation in shaping the public space. Guilat's chapter focuses on the relationship between the LL and visual culture through a particular project of marking the city's singularity through what the author calls a 'peripheral dialect'.

In brief, these chapters represent a range of modes of multilingual practices in contemporary urban spaces. It is by no means an exhaustive range, but well illustrates how far the LL may deviate from standard monolingualism that in many societies has long been a prevailing norm.

Within this multilingual LL, and as shown by Part 2: Top-down, Power and Reactions, a category of items, as mentioned previously, is produced by LL designers on behalf of public institutions. We call this category the top-down flow of LL items, as its major feature is that these items translate the power of authorities. In this vein, Shoshi Waksman and Elana Shohamy discuss the placing of LL items sponsored by the Tel-Aviv-Jaffa municipality, on the occasion of the city's centennial. This chapter analyzes the LL items purposely designed by the municipality and scattered throughout the public space. They comprise new signs, poems and photos displayed here and there on billboards, walls and in squares. These items highlight the national Zionist ideology and Jewish-Israeli identity. In some milieus however, these messages arouse reactions expressed in graffiti and messages posted on internet sites and talk-backs. The data demonstrate that LL policies are able to redefine cities' overall identities in the context of special events like centennial celebrations. This new LL design can also be understood as a means of differentiating various audiences: those who belong to the meanings of the official voice, and others who are excluded. Yet it is this display of explicit and visible authoritative narratives via the LL that creates a negotiable space through which other voices and arguments may be heard.

Theo du Plessis, who focuses on South Africa and addresses the post-apartheid changes of geographical names, analyzes how standardization processes result in a transformation of the LL. In this case, transformation takes place in the context of harsh debates that reveal the pressures and constraints that target language policy in the area of LL; a reality, that allows further theoretical elaborations on language policy as a field of divergent forces and ideological debates of its own. A change in regime can bring about a change in the LL. That landscape then becomes one of the most 'vocal' and concrete indicators of consequential language regime change. In the case investigated (Bloemfontein, South Africa), few changes in the LL have recently been recorded on the surface, but research still points to the emergence of a new English monolingual LL. This Anglicization of public signs can be viewed as a visually public statement on the transformation of the LL of the 'apartheid city' (Krige, 1988: 161). This covert policy contravenes the overt policy of bilingual and multilingual language visibility.

Jia Jackie Lou proposes an additional perspective on the question of language policy in the realm of the LL. Focusing on Chinatown in Washington, DC, she shows how the values granted to varieties of

Chinese in Chinatown are contingent not only on *where* they are practiced, but also on the discursive reconstruction of Chinatown by established LL actors, and their disconnecting the area from its history as an enclave of immigrants. LL policies may also make use of non-linguistic material. Chinatown in Washington is characterized by bilingual signage throughout the neighborhood as the product of urban planning policies jointly administered by a group of Chinese American entrepreneurs and various agencies in the District government. The conceivers of this policy consider this kind of LL as a major achievement in preserving the neighborhood's ethnic identity – which is also respected by non-Chinese businesses in the area. Yet geosemiotic analysis then shows that although Chinese appears on most of the shop signs, it is visually and materially much less significant than corporate logos and other forms of business identities in English, and is systematically de-emphasized. Hence, this chapter argues that while the LL of Chinatown may serve practical, informational functions, it conveys negligible economic value.

Heiko Marten focuses on multilingual Latvian cities where Russian as the strongest – unfriendly – minority language is the object of stigmatization. The determination of the majority brings about the gradual marginalization of Russian in the LL, while English tends to expand in support of LL actors' presentation of self as 'modern' and 'Western'. The importance of this principle is translated in what the author designates as 'legal hypercorrection'. This principle aims to reverse the language shift back from Russian to Latvian, Estonian and Lithuanian, turning upside-down language prestige and linguistic hierarchies. 'Legal hypercorrection' is used to indicate that linguistic behavior follows new language laws more strictly than obliged. This stems primarily from the widespread desire to see the national languages take over the prestigious language uses that belonged to Russian in the past – independent of the fact that speakers of Russian continue using it outside the LL, which is another confirmation that the LL is not a faithful reflection of the linguistic societal reality.

Aneta Pavlenko focuses on Kiev, Ukraine, where she shows how Russian, in contrast to Latvia, illustrates clear signs of survival and vitality, in the context of a similar struggle with the local legitimate language – and despite the government's efforts to relegate Russian to the status of a 'foreign language'. The context of this vitality is Ukrainian Russians' conviction that they represent a cultural and social status that is unbeaten by the Ukrainian majority. This chapter asks why depolonization succeeded in Lvov, making it a Ukrainian-speaking city, while derussification failed in Kiev. A bird's-eye overview of sociolinguistic history reveals that language shifts in the LL are not necessarily a reflection of larger language shifts, and are strongly influenced by political regimes. In contexts where newly imposed languages are incongruent with the languages spoken by large segments of the population, one may expect the emergence of a diglossic situation with one language being used for LL official signage and another for commercial and private signage and everyday interaction.

On the whole, these chapters show a variety of operations of power relations and how far these relations take on forms of their own. Moreover, they also clearly show – at least as far as the cases studied are concerned – that the impacts of top-down power relations may be limited by counter-constraints and contingencies.

The power of top-down LL actors is, indeed, but one factor in the attitudes of bottom-up LL actors. These actors who confront the public of passers-by and aspire to seduce them have their own 'good reasons'. Part 3: Benefits of Linguistic Landscape raises considerations that tend to revolve around the issue of the economic and/or social benefits of LL strategies by autonomous actors. Adam Jaworski and Simone Yeung, who led a LL study in Hong Kong, point out the importance of this issue in the shaping of the LL in given neighborhoods of the city. The focus here is on the linguistic makeup and composition of signage on buildings, and the authors consider different patterns of bilingualism, monolingualism and semantic fields that serve to decorate, name and valorize buildings and, more generally, the neighborhood as a whole. This chapter concerns a selective and relatively random set of semiotic objects, cohering around their task of indexing residential buildings. Unlike other chapters of this volume, it focuses on residential signage. The major argument is that language/discourse creates buildings' functionality, power and symbolic value, as well as a sense of community and privacy; it transforms 'space' to 'place'.

Jennifer Leeman and Gabriella Modan argue that the understanding of urban linguistic landscapes requires an in-depth knowledge of the ways in which cities themselves are shaped. Their contextualized, historicized and spatialized approach to linguistic landscape highlights how material manifestations of language interact with other features of the built environment. Drawing on research from urban studies, tourism studies and sociology to offer new insights on linguistic landscapes, they utilize the notion of 'symbolic economy' to theorize material manifestations of language in downtown revitalization projects and themed ethnic enclaves. Written language works as a visual index of ethnicity that, when linked to various products, places and experiences, contributes to the commodification of culture. Anchored in territory in this way, written language helps to turn neighborhoods themselves into commodities.

David Malinowski discusses the economic viability of the LL from the viewpoint of corporations as well as individual consumers, and the impact of technologies of visualization. His field of study consists of digital maps as a mechanism by which the LL is commoditized. His argument, based on a case study of the digitized linguistic landscape in the city of Seoul, Korea, is that this commoditization is detrimental to the vibrancy of urban space in that it imposes fixed regimes of seeing. The use of digital maps to visualize urban scenes has been steadily expanding across the world, allowing virtual tourists to 'walk' up and down its roads, giving remotely located language learners access to millions of authentic texts embedded in lived urban spaces. Yet, scholars have begun to critique the ways in which the signed landscape has been commoditized in this way. The author's discussion of these approaches leads to the conclusion that users of freely available, economically viable and personally compelling technologies of contextualization for LL imagery must learn to recognize ways in which the LL is *iconicized*, or rendered into a decontextualized form, ready for commodification.

In brief, the chapters in this section deal with the issue of the rationality of LL actors as a function of how they perceive the considerations of their clients. While top-down actors, on the one hand, and their bottom-up counterparts, on the other, target the 'crowd' (or the 'public'), the question that arises is how individuals within that crowd effectively feel about the LL, and if they share any particular expectation. This is the debate at the center of Part 4: Perceptions of Passers-by. In their study of perceptions and preferences of the inhabitants of Donostia-SanSebastián, Jokin Aiestaran, Jasone Cenoz and Durk Gorter question – in terms of sheer monetary cost – people's preferences for LL items. The authors' research technique, inspired by environmental economics, is intended to estimate the economic value of languages in the LL, in the eyes of inhabitants (cities in the Basque country). More specifically, this chapter asks – by means of a survey – about passers-by preferences for given languages in the urban space and their modes of appearance (monolingual, bilingual or multilingual). This work represents an innovative approach to the LL derived from environmental economics. Basque speakers on average are ready to pay a higher amount for more Basque signs than Spanish speakers are ready to pay for more Spanish items. They seem to have a greater commitment for 'reversing language shift'. For their part, Spanish speakers are aware that their language is not threatened and very few of them support a monolingual Spanish LL. They seem to prefer a multilingual cityscape over an all-Spanish one. This can be interpreted as acquiescence with the current autonomous status of the Basque country, but it could also be an expression of support for a positive view of multilingualism.

Nira Trumper-Hecht also focuses on inhabitants' feelings and aspirations about the LL. Her work takes place in the context of Israeli mixed Jewish-Arab cities. Her LL findings show that there exist significant differences in the images of Jews and Arabs, and that these images may often bluntly contradict the reality of the LL as documented by an objective camera. This chapter analyzes the diverse perceptions, preferences and attitudes held by walkers vis-à-vis the degree of saliency of the majority and the minority languages in the LL. The cases under study are Arab and Jewish residents in three mixed cities in Israel. Each of these cities tells a different story of co-existence, but together all three tell something about the complexity of the relationships between two groups caught in an intractable conflict. While the minority shows optimism, in the context of its demographic growth in the cities investigated, the majority appears to be worried about its status, for the very same reason. These attitudes are expressed in appreciations of the LL and the roles it imparts to Arabic and Hebrew.

Rebecca Garvin also investigates passers-by perceptions, but she works in a different arena – Memphis, USA – using a different methodology, what she calls the 'postmodern walking tour interview'. From this qualitative research perspective, her chapter examines resident's self-reported emotions and visual perceptions of the LL. With interviews conducted onsite during 'walking tours' of selected streets, this qualitative study focuses on self-reported understandings. The question posed was: in what ways do individual residents understand, interpret and interact with their communities' LL? The findings illuminated a dynamic process of negotiation and co-construction of meanings through interactions between interviewer and participants in the context of the LL. Results showed that the LL served as a stimulus text mediating visual perceptions and eliciting emotional statements of belonging and identity in time and place.

What primarily puzzles passers-by confronted with the LL is, however, the imprint left on it by the multiplication of pluralisms in this era of globalization. Hence, Part 5: Multiculturalism in Linguistic Landscape, explicitly or implicitly deals with the roles, in linguistic terms, of collective identities in present-day urban spaces where numerous communities of immigrants and regional populations often illustrate a high sociocultural and linguistic vitality. François Bogatto and Christine Helot's study of the 'Quartier Gare' (Strasbourg) focuses on this multiculturalism and shows how it may impact on LLs. The research concentrates on the surroundings of the main railway-station, using both quantitative and qualitative methodologies. The setting they investigate leaves room for both endogenous and exogenous linguistic varieties. All in all, their research underlines the importance of the LL in the markering of collective identities bounding LL actors to given segments of the population. This LL markering of collective identities also indicates the diffusion of diglossia communities as a wide scope phenomenon that concerns more than a few communities. The authors thus unquestionably show that the city of Strasbourg, although officially monolingual, is not impervious to the process of language contact. The production and display of messages are in no way trivial and mark symbolic spaces where LL actors present themselves as *different*, expressing their identity in various ways and through different processes.

Robert Blackwood investigated Rennes (Brittany) and Perpignan (French Catalonia). Interestingly, in France the state recognizes only one language and is very reluctant to allow heritage languages to achieve legitimacy. Hence, Breton and Catalan are used only in informal speech and domains (by those who know them and who are quite a minority in their respective populations). It remains that even here – and in given circumstances – these languages, which designate specific regional ethnolinguistic communities, tend to surface in the LL. In France, the long-standing pursuit of language management strategies to manipulate language practices in favor of French has always distinguished it vis-à-vis its European neighbors. This research of the LL in Rennes and Perpignan adds some nuances to these assessments. Although both cities are unquestionably francophone, an individual is twice as likely to encounter Catalan in the LL of Perpignan as Breton in Rennes. In Rennes, the minimal use of Breton in the public sphere is warranted by top-down agencies; in Perpignan, it is the shop-owners, small companies and individuals who are largely responsible for using Catalan. Bilingualism in the Perpignan LL is a top-down phenomenon, and it may be hypothesized that the tolerance of Breton is economically or politically beneficial to official decision makers, while the use of Catalan stems rather from grass-roots attitudes that by-pass the longstanding – and not updated – rigorous regulations.

The complex contact between minority languages – including immigrant languages – and the national language is the focus of Gerda De Klerk and Terrence Wiley's chapter, which deals with a very different reality, that of Arizona, in the USA. They present a case-study of two suburban communities contiguous with the Phoenix metropolitan area. In a political and regulatory climate, they see English engaged in a zero sum game against other languages that show resistance and vitality and retain their anchorage in the LL. Arizona, the authors contend, illustrates negative attitudes toward immigrants, and its elites want to keep English as both the dominant and sole recognized language in the LL. However, the authors elaborate on examples – especially the Chinese residents – who have developed a number of strategies for staying connected over distance, and for keeping their languages vibrant and relevant. Commercial endeavors and trading of goods and services play an important role here, and success means that heritage languages do show remarkable resilience.

Eliezer Ben-Rafael and Miriam Ben-Rafael add another case of multiculturalism – communities that were created by 'returning diasporas'. The case investigated consists of French Jews who have settled in Israel in the last 20 years and continue to form a special entity there. They insert themselves in today's multicultural Israel and, as such, represent a shift in the condition of the same immigrants prior to their immigration. The diasporic code appears to persist – even though via the inversion of ethnic and national identities – and to express itself quite bluntly in the LL. The chapter also compares the case of French Jewish immigrants in Natanya, Israel, with one of its original communities (Sarcelles, France). *Returnees*, they show, are moved by a transnational model and a notion of dual homeness: the roles granted to French and Hebrew in the LL point to an orientation asserting a Jewish future in Israel while maintaining allegiance to French culture. This characterization converges with the results of the research conducted in France, where the uses of French are also conjunctive with Hebrew and Jewish markers. This convergence indicates that both populations participate in one and the same transnational diaspora – though the primary role endowing Frenchness related to Jewishness in Sarcelles, is inverted in Natanya where Israeli Jewishness is granted the first part. It remains that, as discernible in the LL of both places, the very fact of 'returning' does not equate, in this case, with the negation of the diasporic condition itself. This does not prevent the case where the very 'return' and insertion (or re-insertion) in society makes them different in many respects from what they were on departure. One major line of differentiation is that French and Hebrew in Israel – unlike the case in France – become allied with both English, which symbolizes Israel's globalization endeavor, and Russian, which is indicative of this country's multiculturalism.

To conclude this volume, our epilogue briefly demonstrates our overall theoretical edge.

Bibliography

Backhaus, P. (2007) *Linguistic Landscapes: A Comparative Study of Urban Multilingualism in Tokyo*. Clevedon: Multilingual Matters.

Bairoch, P. (1988) *Cities and Economic Development: From the Dawn of History to the Present*. Chicago: University of Chicago Press.

Ben-Rafael, E. and Sternberg, Y. (eds) (2009) *Transnationalism: Diasporas and the Advent of a new (dis)order*. Leyden and Boston: Brill.

Ben-Rafael, E., Shohamy, E., Amara, M.H. and Trumper-Hecht, N. (2006) Linguistic landscape as symbolic construction of the public space: The case of Israel. *International Journal of Multilingualism* 3, 7–30.

Boudon, R. (1990) *La place du désordre. Critique des théories du changement social*. Paris: Quadrige.

Boudon, R. (2003) *Raison, bonnes raisons, Paris, Puf, 2003*.

Bourdieu, P. (1983) *La distinction: Critique sociale du jugement*, Paris: Les Editions de Minuit.

Bourdieu, P. (1991) *Language & Symbolic Power*. Edited by J.B. Thompson. Translated by G. Raymond and M. Adamson. Cambridge: Polity Press.

Breidbach, O. and Jost, J. (2006) "On the gestalt concept" *Theory in Biosciences* 125 (1), 19–36.

Calhoun, C. (1997) *Nationalism*, Buckingham: Open University Press.

Childe, V. G. (2010) "The Urban Revolution." *Town Planning Review* 21 (1), 3–19. doi:10.1068/d5307.

Coleman, J.S. and Fararo Th. (1992) *Rational Choice Theory: Advocacy and Critique*. Newbury Park, Calif: Sage.

Delanty, G. (2007) "Public Sphere." In Ritzer, George (ed.) *Blackwell Encyclopedia of Sociology*. Oxford: Blackwell Publishing.

Gorter D. (ed.) (2006) *Linguistic Landscape: A New Approach to Multilingualism* (pp. 7–30). Clevedon: Multilingual Matters.

Durkheim, E. (1964 [1895]) *The Rules of Sociological Method*. New York: The Free Press of Glencoe.

Eder, K. (2005) *Making Sense of the Public Sphere*. In: G. Delanty (ed.) *Handbook of Contemporary European Social Theory*. London: Routledge.

Gleick, J. (1987) *Chaos: Making a New Science*. London: Cardinal.

Goffman, E. (1963) *Behavior in Public Places*. New York: Free Press.

Habermas, J. (1989) *The Structural Transformation of the Public Sphere*. Cambridge: Polity Press.

Hutchinson, J. and Smith, A.D. (eds) (1996) *Ethnicity*. Oxford: Oxford University Press.

Jaworski, A. and Thurlow, C. (eds) (2010) *Semiotic Landscapes: Text, Image, Space*. London: Continuum.

Kögler, H.H. (2005) *Constructing a Cosmopolitan Public Sphere*. European Journal of Social Theory? 8, 207–20.

Landry, R. and Bourhis, R.Y. (1997) Linguistic landscape and ethnolinguistic vitality: An empirical study. *Journal of Language and Social Psychology* 16 (1), 23–49.

Levi-Strauss, C. (1958) *Anthropologie Structurale*. Paris: Plon.

Mac Giolla Chríost, D. (2007) *Language and the City*. Basingstoke: Palgrave Macmillan.

Miles, M. (2007) *Cities and Cultures*. London: Routlegde.

Pacione, Michael (2001) *The City: Critical Concepts in The Social Sciences*. New York: Routledge.

Pile, S. (1999a) What is a city? In D. Massey, J. Allen and S. Pile (eds) *City Worlds* (pp. 3–52). London: Routledge.

Sassen, S. (2000) Whose city is it? Globalization and the formation of new claims. In F.J. Lechner and J. Boli (eds) *The Globalization Reader* (pp. 70–76). Oxford: Blackwell.

Scholl, B.J. (2001) Objects and attention: The state of the art. *Cognition* 80 (1–2), 1–46.

Scollon, R. and Wong Scollon, S. (2003) *Discourse in Place: Language in the Material World*. London: Routledge.

Shohamy, E. and Gorter, D. (eds) (2008) *Linguistic Landscape: Expanding the Scenery*. New York: Routledge.

Spolsky, B. and Cooper, R. (1991) *The Languages of Jerusalem*. Oxford: Clarendon Press.

Urry, J. (2005) The complexity turn. *Theory, Culture & Society* 22 (5), 1–14.

Part 1
Linguistic Landscape Multilingualisms

Chapter 1

Linguistic Landscape and Language Vitality

MONICA BARNI and CARLA BAGNA

Introduction

The objective of this chapter is to reflect on the relationship between linguistic landscape (LL) and language presence and vitality (Extra & Yağmur, 2004; Barni, 2008) in urban spaces. Recent decades have witnessed the arrival of an increasing number of immigrants who have decided to settle in urban spaces, and this has been among the reasons for the emergence of linguistic and cultural diversity within these spaces. To an ever-increasing extent, cities are places where different cultures, languages and identities interact; they are also places where this interaction can be observed (Goffman, 1963; Lefebvre, 1991). In this chapter, our interest lies in examining the impact that different languages can have in different urban territories on the LL, as well as in exploring the factors that can influence its configuration.

Our data and analyses focus on a number of cities in Italy where immigrant communities have settled. Although all the cities analysed are places where immigration is present, they differ among themselves in terms of various factors, including geographical position, size and linguistic space. Our investigation has concentrated on Rome, the capital of Italy, as well as other, smaller, cities that represent other urban realities in which immigrants have chosen to live and work.

Socio-demographic data show that about 4,330,000 immigrants currently reside in Italy (Caritas, 2009), approximately 7.2% of the Italian population. It is obvious that this presence can have an influence on linguistic realities. The immigrant groups that have settled in different areas of Italy have imported their languages to the communities where they reside, at a time when the dynamics of collective and individual variation in language use are changing in form and structure. Italianisation is gradually spreading within the country, but the linguistic situation, which includes dialects and historic minority languages, is still composite and of great complexity. Immigrant communities are adding a new element of plurilingualism to what is already a composite linguistic situation. In this chapter, we define a language as an *immigrant language* when it is used by a community that is not only present in an

3

area in 'quantitative' terms (i.e. number of foreign residents), but also strong in 'qualitative' terms, and used in social interaction and maintained by its speakers (Bagna *et al.*, 2003; Barni, 2008). This latter aspect brings us back to the need for detailed studies on the types of language use within an area where a group has settled. This is because simply identifying the languages present within a country or area in quantitative terms does not provide us with any information about the relations between the languages observed and their uses in a given place. This, in turn, implies the need to monitor the possible outcomes of linguistic contact, such as language maintenance and loss, and new language variety formation through contact and linguistic assimilation of differing degrees according to the generation in question. For these reasons, we need a multi-level observation built on a theoretical and methodological basis, taking into account the linguistic and extra-linguistic variables that can influence linguistic uses.

In this sense, understanding, documenting and analysing specific areas' LL offers one of the levels of the research: linguistic use in contexts of social communication, defined here as language 'visibility'. This complements language presence, the socio-demographic weight of speakers, and language vitality, the declared uses of languages within familial contexts (Bagna *et al.*, 2007; Barni & Bagna, 2008). The relationship with the local linguistic situation and the possibilities of interaction between the local language and linguistic dynamics coming from outside should also be examined.

The Role of Cities in Language Contact

In our search for a link between LL and language vitality through analysis of language presence, use and visibility, we have chosen urban spaces as our places of observation. Given that urbanisation is one of the most important characteristics of today's world (*State of the World*, 2007), 2008 marked a turning point, in which for the first time the world's population became predominantly urban (Lee, 2007: 6). Furthermore, due to their social, ethnic, religious, economic and, we would also add, linguistic diversity, nowadays there are cities that 'are the world', as Augé (2004: 20) has noted (see also Vertovec, 2007). The most recent research shows that urban contexts provide more interesting and significant sources for the reading and interpretation of linguistic dynamics (Chríost, 2007). Using LL analyses, this fact has already been observed in the more traditional contexts of the coexistence of regional minority languages in a given area (Bourhis & Landry, 2002; Extra & Gorter, 2001, 2008; Williams, 2007). Specifically, it has been shown that the LL is used for the purposes of handling and governing these areas. LLs are also gaining importance in those contexts affected by recent or long-standing immigrant settlement

(Gorter, 2006; Shohamy & Gorter, 2008). Urban spaces are therefore increasing in importance as 'showcases' and, above all, environments where languages weave together and linguistic destinies and expectations are 'played out'. Within the city, or at least some of its neighbourhoods, languages can find or carve out sufficient space to manifest their vitality as well as their visibility (Mondada, 2000).

The aim of our research is to understand the roles played by the different factors influencing the visibility of languages in LLs, such as the linguistic situation of the area, the size of the city, the extent of the immigrant communities, their degree of 'rootedness', employment opportunities in the area, migration channels and migration status, community organisations, local public policy towards immigrants, etc. We know, for example, that, far more than in smaller cities, linguistic dynamics in a large city move within two different poles and often lead to opposing outcomes in terms of linguistic contact. On the one hand, we observe a tendency towards a pole of monolingualism, insofar as the city is the centre where the unitary linguistic model is the strongest, for both its permanent inhabitants and the new arrivals, because the dominant language is a necessary and indispensable tool for interaction, as well as a symbol of integration, assimilation and full citizenship (De Mauro, 1963, 1989). On the other hand, however, there is also a tendency towards a plurilingual pole, insofar as big cities are places where there is much contact between groups and where the cohesive forces of collective groups, and hence their linguistic visibility, are least impeded by the social and linguistic closure of historic groups. A big city with a strong multi-ethnic component can therefore be a place where collective and individual identities are enabled to express themselves, since spaces that are more open to creativity, change and relations between social and linguistic groups are also more dynamic (Bagna & Barni, 2006; Barni, 2008).

The Surveys

The research presented here had as its goal the analysis of language visibility and vitality of some of the immigrant languages present in various Italian urban contexts. It is a comparative study that aims to demonstrate how various factors, both linguistic and extra-linguistic, can influence the visibility and vitality of the languages found in these spaces. For our investigation, we selected a number of urban contexts in Italy with a marked presence of immigrant communities. Our research was carried out between 2004 and 2007. As we have suggested elsewhere (Barni, 2008), one of the prime sources for information on the languages spoken by immigrant communities is demographic data regarding country of origin. Statistics document the number of nationalities present in Italy, which are the most numerous immigrant communities, and where in the country they have chosen to live. This statistical information enables us to hypothesise the presence in these areas of the languages used by the communities in question, which come into contact with the autochthonous linguistic substrate of Italian, its dialects and varieties. A second level of analysis involves the study of language use and vitality, which can be observed using methods such as interviews and questionnaires. The LL approach offers us a more detailed exploration of the visibility of immigrant languages in a relatively circumscribed area (Bagna *et al.*, 2004, 2007; Barni, 2006, 2008; Barni & Bagna, 2008). Based on the above criteria, we have chosen the cities of Arezzo, Ferrara, Florence, Monterotondo, Rome and Prato for our survey.

Data Collected

In this chapter, we focus on the abovementioned Italian cities and analyse their LLs in relation to the patterns of use of the specific languages present there. In particular, we examine the following:

- Chinese in Rome and Prato.
- Romanian in the areas around Rome and Florence.
- Russian and Ukrainian in Ferrara and Arezzo.

Chinese in Rome

The dual role of Rome as a city driving diffusion of standard Italian both within itself and for the whole of Italy, while also at the same time being the elective centre of plurilingual and interlinguistic contact dynamics, makes it a laboratory for the reorganisation of expressive uses, as well as the ultimate communicative space. Indeed, Rome's status as the capital of Italy has played an undeniable role in the process of Italianisation of the peninsula. As early as the mid-19th century, 'Italian was considered, and to a great extent truly was, the language in everyday use' in the city (De Mauro, 1989: xvii). At the same time, Rome has always been a centre attracting foreigners, a place of immigration (De Mauro, 1989) for a highly varied range of reasons with a markedly polycentric ethnicity. Apart from motivations of a religious nature, which make Rome unique in character globally, the factors influencing its choice as a place of residence and the composition of its population by nationality of origin include the job market, which is marked above all by a continuous flow towards a single sector, domestic work (as well as construction and commerce). Consequently, the number of languages present in Rome is very high. Villarini (2001: 65) estimates that there are about 64 different languages used in schools in Rome.

The *Municipio I* administrative area in the centre of Rome, which includes the Esquilino neighbourhood, is the area with the greatest number of foreigners (25,004, 11.16% of Rome's total foreign population in 2004, with the ratio remaining constant in subsequent years) as well as the highest percentage of foreigners – 20.4% (22.9% in 2006) – relative to the total number of residents. In other publications, we have focused in detail on a survey of languages in the Esquilino neighbourhood (Bagna & Barni, 2006; Barni, 2006) using statistical and demographic analysis and linguistic landscaping. Twenty-four (visible) languages were identified, scattered unevenly across the area and establishing a variety of relations with Italian and other languages. It was found that the most visible language is Chinese, even though it is not the language of the most numerous immigrant communities, which are from Bangladesh, the Philippines and Romania (Municipality of Rome, 2004, 2005; Caritas, 2005, 2006, 2007a). In the Esquilino neighbourhood, Chinese is the leading language both in terms of dominance (quantitative prevalence of texts observed in the area) and autonomy, i.e. the capacity to be used in the LL without the use of Italian or other languages (Barni, 2006; Bagna *et al.*, 2007). During our survey in the Esquilino neighbourhood, we found 851 LL items in languages other than Italian (in total 24 languages were found), of which 483 contained Chinese in mono- and plurilingual texts (see Figure 1.1 and Figure 1.2). Of the 296 monolingual texts found, 197 were in Chinese only

Figure 1.1 Chinese language in the Esquilino LL

Figure 1.2 Chinese language in the Esquilino LL

with no other languages present. This shows that there is no firm link between the linguistic visibility of a language and the numeric consistency of the ethnic group speaking it. This presence of Chinese is also felt by residents. In a document entitled *Esquilino dei mondi lontani* [*The Distant Worlds of Esquilino*] (Caritas, 2007b: 54), which analyses the processes of urbanisation of the Esquilino neighbourhood from 1970 onwards, it is emphasised that the neighbourhood now feels 'the alienating impact caused by the presence of ideograms [...], an indecipherable language that does not facilitate everyday communication'. Such a statement shows that Chinese is, in this case, a language capable of conserving its autonomy more than other foreign languages are, as is manifested by its visibility in the LL of a neighbourhood characterised by a high level of plurilingualism. It is also worth noting that in Esquilino there were hardly any texts in Chinese produced by Italian institutions, so-called *top-down* texts (Ben-Raphael *et al.*, 2006). Almost all Chinese texts observed were produced by individual Chinese people (e.g. shop owners). It is thus no coincidence that the strong visibility of Chinese is such that it has led to the signing of an agreement between the City of Rome and the Chinese community (11 May 2007). This document emphasised that the Chinese community must 'improve shop signs and fittings, being sure to install signs written in Italian at the top, and in Chinese below'. The same document states that the City of Rome, on the other hand, must 'facilitate the life and integration of the Chinese community by organizing courses to enable them to learn Italian and to understand the requirements of the law, particularly with regards to integration, legality and trade; [... and] make communication between institutions and foreign communities easier by translating laws and regulations into Chinese'. As a result of this agreement, in the three months following May 2007, monolingual Chinese signs became bilingual Chinese-Italian signs. Provisions of this kind clearly recognise the role of Chinese as the language of a minority community for which agreements similar to those established for the defence of historic minorities in Italy (Iannàccaro & Dell'Aquila, 2004) can be drawn up. In the case of Chinese, however, the aims are somewhat different: not so much to maintain an ethno-linguistic identity as to regulate and even limit the use of a specific language. This provision provides us with an element of confirmation as to the visibility of the Chinese language, which has affected an area so strongly that laws have been made regarding its use.

Chinese in Prato

Prato is the Italian municipality with the highest number of foreigners (25,489 people) among its resident population (186,608, data from 31 May 2009, Municipality of Prato). Of these foreigners, 40.64% are Chinese (10,361). The Chinese community began settling in Prato around 1990 and developed businesses in the fields of textile and leather production. In our survey, carried out in 2006, we collected 200 LL items in languages other than Italian in the city centre (Lufrano, 2007). We found 12 languages visible in the LL. As in Rome, Chinese is the most visible language in the urban linguistic makeup (128 LL items contain Chinese; in 39 cases the texts are in 'Chinese only'), but unlike the situation observed in Esquilino, the visibility of the Chinese language is determined not only by individual choices or strategies of a commercial nature, but also by the way communication and public life more generally is handled. Compared to Esquilino, the domains of use of Chinese are broader by far, and the authors/sources of messages in Chinese (or Chinese and Italian) are not only members of the community itself, but also Italian institutions (see Figure 1.3). In other words, the visibility of Chinese is exerted through both *bottom-up* and *top-down* mechanisms, making it a unique case in Italy due to the intensity and range of this balance. The force of Chinese also has a correspondence in its vitality, as it continues to be the language used within Chinese families, despite their long-term residence in Italy (see Ceccagno, 2003, 2004). Italian seems to seek out space within Chinese and vice versa. We may thus affirm that Chinese in Prato is also felt to be an immigrant language by Italian institutions, and is therefore also used top-down.

Figure 1.3 Multilingual top-down sign in Prato

These data describe the situation as it stood before 2009. On 3 August 2009, an article of the *Regulations for Commerce, Retail Activity in Set Premises* (Part VI, article 37, paragraph 3, Municipality of Prato) came into force, which rules: 'Signs or writing inside or outside of shop windows should be accompanied by the equivalent translation in Italian when in a foreign language. Exception is made for signs in foreign languages that have by now entered into common Italian usage'. In the city, 140 signs considered in breach of this regulation as they were written in only one language were discovered and blacked out, and their owners were fined (see Figure 1.4).

Naturally, the first to be affected were Chinese businesses. This ruling extended the social conflict deriving from the global economic crisis to the linguistic level: foreign entrepreneurs, especially the Chinese, are blamed for the problems facing the economy of Prato. The autonomous use of a foreign language is perceived as a distinguishing and isolating factor, and the delicate linguistic equilibrium created over the years is today compromised. It should also be underlined that the formulation of the Prato ruling aims primarily at hitting languages that are immediately perceived as foreign, including those that use writing systems other than the Roman alphabet. It will be interesting to see how this ruling will be applied to less exotic languages like English or French, as well as to analyse the criteria according to which it will be decided which are the

Figure 1.4 Shop sign blacked out in Prato

words entered into 'common Italian usage'. Prato, which has stood as an example for the type of policy chosen with regard to immigrant groups and their languages and is a central pole for Chinese communities in Europe, is thus becoming a place in which groups' linguistic choices become the subject of social clashes and rulings adopted in the name of public order.

Romanian in Rome and the Province of Rome

Immigrants from Romania have been the largest community in the province of Rome since 2004; on a national level, too, their presence has increased considerably in recent years, to the point where they are now the largest immigrant group in Italy as a whole (Caritas, 2009). The data indicate that more than 15% (around 100,000) of the Romanians in Italy (625,278) live in the province of Rome (Caritas, 2008: 297).

The data collected in the Esquilino neighbourhood show few traces of Romanian and few texts in it. The language is contained in only 13 of the 851 texts observed, and dominant in just 3 texts. It never appeared autonomously. Therefore, this proves that Romanian is a language that relies on Italian or other languages. The majority of texts in which Romanian is visible are of a *top-down* type, produced by the Romanian community or other immigrant communities. The texts are posters of a 'political' nature, aimed at inviting immigrant groups to participate in meetings and demonstrations asking for their rights to be recognised. The group's preponderantly 'non-commercial' vocation, and consequent lower visibility in terms of text production for public communication, would appear to explain the results obtained. Nonetheless, these figures are counterbalanced by the linguistic vitality indexes (as against visibility), gathered in part using questionnaires and interviews with families and schoolchildren (Bagna & Barni, 2005). Thus, we found a strong declared vitality, surveyed specifically in the municipalities of Mentana and Monterotondo near Rome, chosen as a new home by families of Romanian origin, who have found this area to have the most favourable conditions for settling (for a total population of some 50,000 people). In these towns, the visibility of the Romanian language is of secondary importance, and is above all a result of a process of vitality and established presence in the area. Indeed, it took at least 5–6 years' stable presence of the Romanian community here before any writing in Romanian was to be observed within the social communication space. As of 2005, Monterotondo in particular has shown elements of visibility of the Romanian community, previously completely absent, which reinforce the role of Romanian as an immigrant language. The very few traces previously observed were top-down, produced exclusively by public bodies (see Figure 1.5), so that the choice to use Romanian came from

Figure 1.5 Top-down sign in Romanian in Monterotondo

above. Here, the maintenance of the language of origin within the family (surveys with questionnaires and interviews) and the stable presence of the Romanian community have led to a broadening of its use in contexts of public communication.

Romanian in Florence

Florence is another city that is particularly attractive to immigrants from Romania, who are the fourth largest immigrant community in the city. With some 3000 people (following immigrants from China, Albania and the Philippines), they account for 8% of foreign residents. The city (370,323 inhabitants), however, seems impermeable to the presence of this community. Our LL survey was conducted in 2006–2007 in Quartiere 1, a neighbourhood in the city centre, stretching from San Lorenzo and Santa Croce. It is one of the most touristed areas of Florence. The neighbourhood was chosen because it (and Quartiere 5) has the largest presence of immigrant groups (around 25% of immigrants in Florence, Municipality of Florence, 2007). Although Quartiere 1 has the second greatest number of Romanian residents, minimal traces of their language were found. The data found in Florence regarding the Romanian language are similar to those from Esquilino and the province of Rome. Out of a total of 114 LL items in languages other than Italian, Romanian was visible in only five (Fortuni, 2007; Massaro, 2007). The space of the central area, and particularly Quartiere 1, is caught between Italian and English, and the weight of these languages of mass communication and mass tourism minimises the visibility of other languages, and thus of immigrant languages.

In the case of the city of Florence, where Romanian is maintained in use in family and intracommunity situations, other contextual factors would seem to contribute to its low level of visibility, such as, for example, the presence of tourist languages in the LL. Out of 114 LL items found, English is present in fully 64 items (Fortuni, 2007).

Russian and Ukrainian in Arezzo and Ferrara

The analysis of these two languages leads our research into immigrant groups in Italy to assume a gender perspective. Russia and Ukraine are the two countries from which we see the greatest imbalance between the sexes, with a marked prevalence of women immigrants. Added to this is the fact that these women are prevalently employed in the home-help field, with living conditions that often involve staying at the assisted person's home. This means that, unlike other groups, the dynamics of maintenance of their language of origin have to find a space outside the domestic environment, since this *is* the work place. For this reason, the vitality of these languages is strictly reserved for time spent outside the house (e.g. in public parks or shopping) and it generates visibility that is defined by the women themselves as they move about the city (Census, forthcoming).

Our LL surveys were carried out in the city centres of Ferrara in 2006–2007 (Mingozzi, 2007) and Arezzo in 2006–2007 (Tellini, 2007). Arezzo and Ferrara are cities in the centre of Italy, where most of the Ukrainian and Russian immigrants have only recently arrived and work as home helps (Municipality of Arezzo, 2008; Municipality of Ferrara, 2009). In Arezzo (98,788 inhabitants), the proportion of Russians and Ukrainians (218 out of 10,246 foreigners, data from 31 December 2008, Municipality of Arezzo) is far lower than in Ferrara (134,464 inhabitants), where the largest immigrant group (alongside Romanians) is that from Ukraine (1,239 out of 8,121 foreigners, data from 31 December 2008, Municipality of Ferrara). In both cases, as has been mentioned, these groups show a prevalently female component (57% in Arezzo, 79% in Ferrara). Consequently, Ferrara has become a showcase of female presence with strong linguistic vitality. In Ferrara and Arezzo, we recorded a dense network of interactions in specific locations within the city. At times it is a monolingual use, and at times it is mixed with Italian and the dialects spoken by the elderly people with whom the immigrants work.

In Arezzo, one of the places with the greatest concentration of immigrant languages is Piazza Guido Monaco, a square in the city centre. Russian and Ukrainian are commonly spoken there, as well the other languages of the main immigrant groups – Romanian, Albanian, Polish, Arabic, Hindi and Chinese. Since the late 1990s, the square, which is large, round in shape and very central, has been divided into several different areas. Each area is occupied by a specific national group. Dominican women occupy some areas, together with eastern European women – Romanians, Poles, Ukrainians, Moldovans and Russians – and Dominican youths, while a quarter of the square has become a meeting place for North African communities, particularly Moroccans and Algerians. On the other side of the street, near a shopping centre and a youth support office, is the place where young Albanians usually meet. In Ferrara, the same role is played by the public gardens in Viale Cavour, in the city centre. In both cities, outdoor spaces become the spaces of maximum vitality, expressed as interaction within the immigrant communities.

The LL data collected in Ferrara and Arezzo have shown that while the use of Ukrainian and Russian is immediately noticeable in the city, and especially in the places where the communities live and socialise, their visibility in the LL remains tied to certain basic services and domains. It is limited to institutional spaces: hospitals, employment centres, offices of voluntary associations, etc. (Mingozzi, 2007). Furthermore, unlike the situation with Chinese, it is far more common in Ferrara to find bilingual texts (Italian-Ukrainian, Italian-Russian) publicising facts and events such as local elections, people seeking work, parties, etc., thus making the message available to more people, including Italians.

Conclusions

The objective of this chapter has been to analyse the relationship between LL and language presence and vitality in specific urban areas in Italy. According to Landry and Bourhis (1997: 34), 'the linguistic landscape may be the most visible marker of the linguistic vitality of the various ethnolinguistic groups living within a particular administrative or territorial enclave'. The various data collected and analysed have confirmed our hypotheses that there is no direct relationship between the presence of a language in an area, its vitality and its visibility. As we have seen, this relationship depends on numerous linguistic, extra-linguistic and contextual factors.

We will only venture here to state that languages that are more visible have a greater potential for vitality and therefore a greater probability of being maintained in an immigration context, since in addition to their use in private and familial contexts, they are also used in public.

However, this connection is not determined by a causal link, rather it is constructed through a range of differentiated factors. Indeed, the conditions that enable languages to become visible in a given area are not due exclusively to positive attitudes towards the use of these languages. There are various conditions for the possibility of a relationship between the visibility of languages within a territory and their potential (and actual) vitality, and they depend on factors including the characteristics of the area in which people settle and the length of time that they stay, as well as the attitude of speakers towards their own language. The linguistic policy choices of the host country and of specific cities within a nation also play a role: in the case of Italy, there are no policies globally aimed at the recognition of immigrant languages, but isolated actions motivated by specific political agendas. The recent array of laws aimed at guaranteeing Italian citizens' safety (Law n. 94, 15 July 2009, in force from 8 August 2009) has as its primary aim the fight against illegal immigration through increasingly restrictive measures (e.g. arrest). In the wake of this law, individual city mayors can adopt different rulings in the name of safety and 'decency'. The rulings adopted in Rome and Prato show that the fight against diversity has widened to include everything that evokes linguistic and cultural diversity. Linguistic diversity, maintenance and visibility are currently the subject of bitter political clashes in a country where the presence of immigrant groups is now a vital structural element for social and economic growth (Caritas, 2009).

References

Augé, M. (2004) Città e surmodernità. In R. Bombi and F. Fusco (eds) *Città plurilingui: Lingue e culture a confronto in situazioni urbane* (pp. 16–32). Udine: Forum.

Bagna, C. and Barni, M. (2005) Spazi e lingue condivise. Il contatto fra l'italiano e le lingue degli immigrati: percezioni, dichiarazioni d'uso e usi reali. Il caso di Monterotondo e Mentana. In C. Guardiano, E. Calaresu, C. Robustelli and A. Carli (eds) *Lingue, Istituzioni, Territori* (pp. 223–251). Atti del XXXVIII Congresso Internazionale di Studi della Società di Linguistica Italiana, Modena 23–25 settembre 2004. Rome: Bulzoni.

Bagna, C. and Barni, M. (2006) Per una mappatura dei repertori linguistici urbani: nuovi strumenti e metodologie. In N. De Blasi and C. Marcato (eds) *La città e le sue lingue: Repertori linguistici urbani* (pp. 1–43). Naples: Liguori Editore.

Bagna, C., Barni, M. and Siebetcheu, R. (2004) *Toscane favelle: Lingue immigrate nella provincia di Siena*. Perugia: Guerra.

Bagna, C., Barni, M. and Vedovelli, M. (2007) Italiano in contatto con lingue immigrate: nuove vie del plurilinguismo in Italia. In C. Consani and P. Desideri (eds) *Minoranze linguistiche: Prospettive, strumenti, territori* (pp. 270–290). Rome: Carocci.

Bagna, C., Machetti, S. and Vedovelli M. (2003) Italiano e lingue immigrate: verso un plurilinguismo consapevole o verso varietà di contatto? In A. Valentini, P. Molinelli, P. Cuzzolin and G. Bernini (eds) *Ecologia linguistica* (pp. 201–222).

Atti del XXXVI Congresso Internazionale di Studi della Società di Linguistica Italiana, Bergamo 26–28 settembre 2002. Rome: Bulzoni.

Barni, M. (2006) From Statistical to Geolinguistic Data: Mapping and Measuring Linguistic Diversity, EURODIV First Conference *Understanding Diversity: Mapping and Measuring*, Milan, 26–27 January 2006. *FEEM Working Papers*, KTHC – Knowledge, Technology, Human Capital, 53.2006. On WWW at http://www.feem.it/Feem/Pub/Publications/WPapers/default.htm.

Barni, M. (2008) Mapping linguistic diversity: immigrant languages in Italy. In M. Barni and G. Extra (eds) *Mapping Linguistic Diversity in Multicultural Contexts* (pp. 217–243). Berlin: Mouton de Gruyter.

Barni, M. and Bagna, C. (2008) A mapping technique and the linguistic landscape. In E. Shohamy and D. Gorter (eds) *Linguistic Landscape: Expanding the Scenery* (pp. 126–140). London: Routledge.

Barni, M. and Extra, G. (eds) (2008) *Mapping Linguistic Diversity in Multicultural Contexts*. Berlin: Mouton de Gruyter.

Ben Rafael, E., Shohamy, E., Amara, M. and Hecht, N. (2006) The symbolic construction of the public space: The case of Israel. In D. Gorter (ed.) *Linguistic Landscape. A New Approach to Multilingualism* (pp. 7–28). Clevedon: Multilingual Matters.

Bourhis, R.Y. and Landry, R. (2002) La Loi 101 et l'aménagement du paysage linguistique du Québec. In P. Bouchard and R.Y. Bourhis (eds) *L'Aménagement linguistique au Québec* (pp. 107–132). Québec: Publications du Québec.

Caritas (2005) *Osservatorio Romano sulle Migrazioni, Primo Rapporto*. Rome: Idos.

Caritas (2006) *Osservatorio Romano sulle Migrazioni, Secondo Rapporto*. Rome: Idos.

Caritas (2007a) *Osservatorio Romano sulle Migrazioni, Terzo Rapporto*. Rome: Idos.

Caritas (2007b) *Esquilino dei mondi lontani*. Rome: Idos.

Caritas (2008) *Romania: Immigrazione e lavoro in Italia*. Rome: Idos.

Caritas (2009) *Immigrazione: Dossier statistico 2009*. Rome: Idos.

Ceccagno, A. (ed.) (2003) *Migranti a Prato: Il distretto tessile multietnico*. Milan: Franco Angeli.

Ceccagno, A. (2004) *Giovani migranti cinesi: La seconda generazione a Prato*. Milan: Franco Angeli.

Censis (forthcoming) *La sicurezza del lavoro domestico*. Rome: Censis.

Chríost, D.M.G. (2007) *Language and the City: Language and Globalization*. New York: Palgrave Macmillan.

De Mauro, T. (1963) *Storia linguistica dell'Italia unita*. Rome-Bari: Laterza.

De Mauro, T. (1989) Per una storia linguistica della città di Roma. In T. De Mauro (ed.) *Il romanesco ieri e oggi* (XIII–XXXVII). Rome: Bulzoni.

Extra, G. and Gorter, D. (eds) (2001) *The Other Languages of Europe, Demographic, Sociolinguistic and Educational Perspectives*. Clevedon: Multilingual Matters.

Extra, G. and Gorter, D. (eds) (2008) *Multilingual Europe: Facts and Policies*. Berlin: Mouton de Gruyter.

Extra, G. and Yağmur, K. (eds) (2004) *Urban Multilingualism in Europe: Immigrant Minority Languages at Home and School*. Clevedon: Multilingual Matters.

Fortuni, F. (2007) Linguaggio e migrazioni: Una mappatura di lingue immigrate nel centro storico di Firenze. Tesi di Master in Genere, cittadinanza e pluralismo culturale, Università di Firenze, in collaborazione con Università per Stranieri di Siena, 2005–2006. Unpublished manuscript.

Goffmann, E. (1963) *Behavior in Public Spaces*. New York: Free Press.

Gorter, D. (ed.) (2006) *Linguistic Landscape. A New Approach to Multilingualism*. Clevedon: Multilingual Matters.

Iannàccaro, G. and Dell'Aquila, V. (2004) *La pianificazione linguistica: lingue, società e istituzioni*. Rome: Carocci.

Landry, R. and Bourhis, R.Y. (1997) Linguistic landscape and ethnolinguistic vitality: An empirical study. *Journal of Language and Social Psychology* 16 (1), 24–49.

Lee, K. (ed.) (2007) An urbanizing world. In Worldwatch Institute *2007, State of the World. Our Urban Future* (pp. 3–25). Washington, DC: Worldwatch Institute.

Lefebvre, H. (1991) *The Production of Space*. Oxford: Blackwell.

Lufrano, F.L. (2007) Le lingue immigrate nello spazio linguistico del territorio della città di Prato. Tesi di Laurea Specialistica in Scienze Linguistiche per la comunicazione interculturale, Università per Stranieri di Siena, 2005–2006. Unpublished manuscript.

Massaro, B. (2007) Le lingue immigrate nello spazio linguistico della città di Firenze: il quartiere di Santa Croce. Tesi di Laurea Specialistica in Scienze Linguistiche per la comunicazione interculturale, Università per Stranieri di Siena, 2006–2007. Unpublished manuscript.

Mingozzi, V. (2007) Plurilinguismo e immigrazione: Un'indagine sulla città di Ferrara. Tesi di Master in Genere, cittadinanza e pluralismo culturale, Università di Firenze, in collaborazione con Università per Stranieri di Siena, 2005–2006. Unpublished manuscript.

Mondada, L. (2000) *Décrire la ville: La construction des savoirs urbains dans l'interaction et dans le texte*. Paris: Anthropos.

Municipality of Arezzo (2008) On WWW at http://www.comune.arezzo.it.

Municipality of Ferrara (2008) On WWW at http://servizi.comune.fe.it.

Municipality of Florence (2007) On WWW at http://www.comune.firenze.it.

Municipality of Prato (2009) On WWW at http://www.comune.prato.it.

Municipality of Rome (2004) *Le condizioni socio-lavorative degli immigrati a Roma: Primo rapporto di sintesi*. Rome: Comune di Roma.

Municipality of Rome (2005) *I numeri di Roma*, Rome: Ufficio Statistico del Comune di Roma, 2.

Osservatorio Sociale, Provincia di Arezzo (2008) *Immigrazione e lavoro dipendente in provincia di Arezzo al 1° gennaio 2008*. Arezzo: Provincia di Arezzo.

Osservatorio sull'Immigrazione della Provincia di Ferrara (2009) *Immigrazione a Ferrara: Rapporto 2009*. Ferrara: Provincia di Ferrara.

Shohamy, E. and Gorter, D. (eds) (2008) *Linguistic Landscape: Expanding the Scenery*. London: Routledge.

Tellini, B. (2007) Le lingue immigrate ad Arezzo: una presenza invisibile. Tesi di Master in Genere, cittadinanza e pluralismo culturale, Università di Firenze, in collaborazione con Università per Stranieri di Siena, 2005–2006. Unpublished manuscript.

Vertovec, S. (2007) Super-diversity and its implications. *Ethnic and Racial Studies* 30 (6), 1024–1054.

Villarini, A. (2001) Gli immigrati in Italia e a Roma: i dati statistici. In M. Barni and A. Villarini (eds) *La questione della lingua per gli immigrati* (pp. 59–67). Milan: Franco Angeli.

Williams, C. (2007) *Linguistic Minorities in Democratic Context*. London: Palgrave.

Chapter 2

Language and Inter-language in Urban Irish and Japanese Linguistic Landscapes

JEFFREY L. KALLEN and ESTHER NÍ DHONNACHA

Introduction

Urban areas often pose acute problems for the linguistic landscape. Their physical design frequently creates competition for spatial dominance, while social diversity in many urban areas – seen both in the resident population and in the transient population of tourists, businesspeople, students and other such groups – brings together different languages and linguistic value systems without necessarily seeking consensus or a common linguistic order. The heightened economic and administrative activity of urban areas often generates large amounts of multilingual signage in a compact space. While it is possible to draw correlations between the linguistic landscape and the city as a geographical and social entity (as in Backhaus, 2007; Landry & Bourhis, 1997; Spolsky & Cooper, 1991; Trumper-Hecht, 2009), our concern in this chapter is with the relationships between the languages of individual units of signage. Our fundamental argument is that since signage uses language in the visual channel, it opens up ways of going beyond the literal message of the sign to invoke covert meanings by the use of visual devices such as fonts and colours and by the use of inter-language expressions and forms of wordplay that could not arise in purely oral communication. While some of these semiotic concerns may appear not to be strictly limited to urban areas, the common occurrence in cities of the kinds of text we examine here suggests that the diversity of the city encourages this kind of linguistic mixing. In comparing linguistic land-scapes from selected urban areas in Ireland and Japan, we argue that both landscapes use the same semiotic properties of signage, but point out that these properties can be used toward very different ends.

The cities that we discuss here prove no exception to the characterisa-tion of the urban linguistic landscape as polyphonous and multilingual. Galway, a coastal city in the west of Ireland, is the third largest city in the Republic of Ireland, with a population of 72,414. Dublin, from which we discuss one example, is the capital city of the Republic of Ireland,

and has a population of nearly 1.2 million people in its metropolitan area (Central Statistics Office, 2007a: 40). Galway is a major tourist centre and a site that attracts considerable foreign investment. The economy of Dublin depends on a greater diversity of enterprises, many of them also involving overseas investment, and the city receives a large number of international tourists each year. Current census figures (e.g. Central Statistics Office, 2007b: 104–105) also demonstrate considerable diversity (as measured by birthplace) within the resident population. As documented in Kallen (2010), this diversity is manifested in the Dublin linguistic landscape, and our experience suggests that linguistic diversity has also increased in the Galway linguistic landscape.

Fukuoka, on the island of Kyushu in the south of Japan, is the eighth largest city in the country, with a population of approximately 1.4 million people. Though it does not have any large non-Japanese communities, it does have a significant tourist industry. According to official figures (City of Fukuoka, 2008), 620,600 overseas tourists, 80% of whom were from Korea and Taiwan, entered the city through its seaport and airport in 2007. Though this chapter will focus on the use of Japanese and English in Fukuoka, our sample, which makes no claims to be exhaustive, also includes official and commercial signage in Chinese and Korean, as well as commercial signage using French, Russian, Finnish and Portuguese.

The signage that we discuss in detail comes from two sets of data. The Galway material dates primarily from 2005, and was collected as part of a study of tourism and language policy in relation to the use of Irish and English: see Kallen (2009). Most of this material was collected in the city centre in places readily accessible to tourists; it has been supplemented in later visits and constitutes a file of 103 photographs. The material from Fukuoka was shaped by the observations of the second author during a year's residence in Fukuoka (2006–2007) and comes from a file of 181 photographs taken by the first author in March 2007. These photographs emphasise the city centre areas of Tenjin and Hakata, yet they also include material from less central urban districts including Asakura-Gaido and Futsukaichi, and give prominence to areas with special attraction for tourists such as the historic Dazaifu area, with its important shrine complex, and the Momochi district, which includes the Fukuoka Tower and SoftBank Hawks baseball stadium. While space limitations preclude a detailed presentation of the complete files, we have ample evidence that the theme of inter-linguistic reference that is explored here is broadly representative of themes found elsewhere: with regard to signage in Tokyo, for example, cf. Vartanian and Martin (2003) and Backhaus (2007, 2009).

Models of Multilingual Signage

Looking at the linguistic landscape purely as a place where information is put into the public domain, a natural expectation might be that multilingual sign texts should convey the same information in each of the languages of the text. Our sample contains many such signs: street and information signs in English and Irish in Galway, and in Japanese and English (or, additionally, Chinese and/or Korean) in Fukuoka. Yet this expectation of textual symmetry is often violated. Asymmetry could represent differential knowledge of particular linguistic codes on the part of the sign creator, or, as Lanza and Woldemariam (2009) point out, attempts to reach different audiences through the use of different languages. In this section, then, we turn our attention to the development of models that attempt to account for the complexity of mappings between message content and linguistic choice.

As a point of reference, we use the model that Reh (2004) proposes in distinguishing four types of relationship between message content and the languages used in signage: (a) *duplicating multilingual writing*, which presents the same information in each language; (b) *fragmentary multilingualism*, where 'the full information is given only in one language, but in which selected parts have been translated into an additional language' (Reh, 2004: 10); (c) *overlapping multilingual writing*, which describes a unit of signage 'if only part of its information is reported in at least one more language, while other parts of the text are in one language only' (Reh, 2004: 12); and (d) *complementary multilingual writing*, 'in which different parts of the overall information are each rendered in a different language' (Reh, 2004: 14). Such a model is intuitively satisfying and accounts for much of the signage that we have observed in Ireland and Japan. Though it is not identical to the models of, for example, Inoue (2005) or Backhaus (2007), it is sufficiently similar to suggest a general consensus on how to categorise the relationships between content and language choice in multilingual signage.

In order to focus on those elements of plurilingual signage that are not well accounted for by such models, we develop here an argument based on three main points, outlined as follows.

(1) *Writing systems themselves introduce choices that generate meanings independently of the message content.* The Irish linguistic landscape makes particular use of two related, yet distinguishable, writing systems. One is the modern Roman orthography that is now generally used for both English and Irish. A second system is based on Irish language manuscript tradition and has been used in print for Irish since the 17th century (see McGuinne, 1992). This system has been adapted into a stylised font for use in

English – what we refer to here as Celticised English. In Japan, the linguistic landscape is dominated by the Japanese language, which employs three writing systems: *Kanji* (the pictographically derived system based on Chinese orthography), *Hiragana* (a phonetic syllabary used to spell out Japanese words without using Kanji and to represent certain grammatical features of the language) and *Katakana* (a second, visually distinct syllabary generally used for non-Japanese loanwords). The Roman alphabet (referred to as *Rōmaji*) is also used for transliterations of Japanese. As Inoue (2005) points out, the co-existence of these systems, and the elements of choice between them, are highly significant in the shaping of the Japanese linguistic landscape.

(2) *Signage plays on linguistic awareness to create linguistic hybrids that accomplish specific purposes apart from the literal meaning of the text.* What we refer to here is a notion similar to *metaphorical codeswitching* as discussed originally by Blom and Gumperz (1972). For Blom and Gumperz, metaphorical codeswitching relies on a contrast between two codes, each of which is normally available for communication within a distinctive context of use. The normal pairing of code and context leads to associations in which, as Blom and Gumperz (1972: 425) put it, 'the context in which one of a set of alternates is regularly used becomes part of its meaning'. Metaphorical usage arises when a form is 'employed in a context where it is not normal', since the unexpected use of the code 'brings in some of the flavor of this original setting'. Though the Blom and Gumperz model is developed for spoken language, the material we consider below demonstrates that multilingual signage also relies on the metaphorical invocation of frames of discourse associated with specific languages.

(3) *Linguistic landscapes show varying reactions to modernity and globalisation.* A contrastive study of urban and rural landscapes would lie outside the scope of this chapter, yet we suggest that urban environments that function as centres for tourism, international economic activity, immigration and inward migration, public administration and competition for space are especially conducive to the development of signage that reflects debates of nationhood and national identity (associated with modernism) and changing definitions of identity arising from globalisation. Ireland and Japan are both countries with national languages that predate industrialisation and the growth of cities.

Use of the Irish language in Ireland extends back at least 2300 years. English was introduced in the 12th century, but remained a minority language associated from the late middle ages with urban areas, while Irish continued as the first language of the overwhelming majority of the population (apart from certain areas in Ulster) into the late 18th century. Today the so-called *Gaeltacht* areas in the Republic of Ireland, where Irish is maintained as a community language, are all rural. (For further details see Kallen, 1994; Ó Cuív, 1986; Ó Giollagáin & Mac Donnacha, 2008.) It is crucial to note, then, that while current census figures in the Republic show that just over 40% of the population over the age of three can speak Irish (Central Statistics Office, 2006c: 12), estimates based on linguistic surveys show that no more than 5% of the population 'use Irish as their first or main language' (Ó Riagáin, 2007: 229). Against this historical background, Irish is now often used to reference cultural authenticity and a look backwards to an essentially rural tradition, real or invented, but can also be used to look forward, pointing to Ireland's status as a nationally conscious player in the cultural and economic marketplace of globalisation. English, by contrast, can be seen variously as the legacy of colonialism, the modernising response of the majority of the Irish population to the economic and political developments of the late 18th century onwards, or the utilitarian adoption of an international language of wider communication, accelerated by large-scale emigration to English-speaking countries in the 19th century.

The introduction and development of Japanese in Japan (see Rozycki, 2003) dates to roughly the same time as Irish in Ireland, but since Japan has not undergone a comparable language shift, Japanese maintains an unchallenged position as the language of cultural authenticity and national unity. (See, however, Gottlieb, 2005: 18–38 for a review of language diversity in Japan.) Many commentators (e.g. Backhaus, 2007, 2009; Inoue, 2005; Tanaka, 1994) have noted that English in Japan is often associated with modernity and internationalisation. Our sample supports this view: while there are instances where English simply fulfils a communicative role for English speakers, we see many signs in which the use of English is best understood as a general signifier of modernity that is oriented to native speakers of Japanese and is anomalous or even incomprehensible to monolingual speakers of English.

We thus point out that while the Irish and Japanese linguistic landscapes both use linguistic diversity to index values pertaining to national identity in the (post)modern world, Irish as the national language, now spoken as a first language by a minority population, fulfils a very different role from English as a global language used in Japan. Though these linguistic hierarchies are not themselves intrinsically urban phenomena, we suggest that the urban linguistic landscape, whether putting Irish into the city or bringing Japanese-English hybrids into the everyday lives of native speakers of Japanese, brings such ideological references into particularly sharp focus.

Ireland: Irish and English, Old Roles and New Relationships

We start with a consideration of what Reh's (2004) taxonomy refers to as 'complementary multilingual writing', in which the messages displayed in two languages are entirely different. We analyse Figure 2.1 as a single unit that presents the public face of a shop known as 'An Taiscín' (or 'The Little Treasure') by using two sets of messages in two languages. The sign over the door welcomes customers to the shop in Irish, using a traditional Irish font. On the left hand side is a statement in English on the value of customers, which uses a modern Roman font. An internet

Figure 2.1 An Taiscín shop front, Galway

search shows that this text has been adapted and used by a variety of healthcare providers, community groups and businesses around the world. It is frequently attributed to Mahatma Gandhi, though our search of standard references (e.g. CWMG website) provides no evidence to support this attribution. On the right hand side, we find three proverbs using the Irish language and orthography: *Is beag an rud is buaine ná an duine* ('Any little thing may serve as a reminder of someone'), *Is buaine clú ná saol* ('Fame lasts longer than life') and *Bíonn siúlach scéalach* ('Travellers have tales to tell').

Useful though it may be to categorise the signage of Figure 2.1 solely by reference to the relationship between message content and language choice, we suggest that this categorisation is incomplete. There is no obvious reason why a tourist-oriented shop in Galway should express philosophy or proverbial wisdom in any language. The value of these messages can only be understood as part of a self-presentation strategy to influence consumer behaviour. The customer relations statement on the left is based on a globally circulated text and speaks to a modern marketing concept. The proverbial wisdom on the right, however, takes an entirely different tack. The use of traditional Irish orthography may make the message obscure even to the younger generation of Irish people, and will be doubly opaque to the international visitor. Assuming, however, that the signage as a whole is intended to communicate something relevant to the reader, we can only infer that it is the juxtaposition of the two messages – one global and consumer oriented, the other local and perhaps semantically problematical but nevertheless visually salient – that makes for a single unit of signage. The complementary messages are not addressed to different audiences, but have the effect of indexing the shop's claim to be simultaneously global and modern as well as local and traditional.

Turning to a more linguistically complex case, we consider Figure 2.2. The sign in this figure was photographed in Dublin, though its occurrence on a van means that it is not tied to a single location. Since the van belongs to a company that offers window installation and repairs, we assume that the intended audience is purely local and the tourism element of Figure 2.1 does not come into play.

The advertising material on this van, which offers a 'complete design and instalation [sic] service' and 'fast repair service', could easily be translated into Irish. The word *Brishta*, on the other hand, looks more like Irish and is certainly not English. On these grounds, we could classify this signage as an example of complementary multilingual writing. Yet this description would miss the important role of hybridity and language awareness in the sign. In fact, the company name *Brishta* is not a word of English or Irish. The Irish word *briste* 'broken' is phonetically ['brɪʃtʲə], and is a high-frequency word that would probably be learned by most

Figure 2.2 Brishta Glass service, Dublin

Irish children in primary school. The anglicised spelling <Brishta> is a transliteration that would thus be recognised by most of the target audience. This Irish-like coinage could not be translated to provide a matching English expression: writing 'Broken' in the signage, for example, would convey a message at the literal level that would be detrimental to the image of the company as one that fixes, rather than breaks, windows. The word-form *Brishta* thus does not simply provide information, but rather catches the eye in presenting a linguistic puzzle that can be resolved with a small amount of effort by anyone with sufficient awareness of the Irish language and the English orthographic system. The language used here indexes the shared experience of learning the Irish language in school: the playful use of metaphorical codemixing is not designed to convey literal content, but to achieve indexicality by presenting an anomalous use of Irish in an unexpected setting.

Figure 2.3 also relies on the linguistic awareness of the intended audience. Ostensibly, the shop front here is a simple example of complementary multilingual writing, since the name of the business and the list of services available are given only in English, while two additional lines of text appear only in Irish. The business name, Claddagh Laundrette, is written in a Celticised English, straddling the two languages. This element incorporates a further semiotic reference in its picture of the Claddagh ring (featuring a heart held by two hands and topped by a crown), which is traditionally associated with the Claddagh area of Galway. The Irish orthography in the rest of the signage is based on, though not completely consistent with, the traditional Irish system.

Figure 2.3 Claddagh Laundrette

When we analyse the use of the two languages in this shop front, however, we again find that the complementary text analysis does not fully account for the signage. The greeting on the left, *Fáilte isteač*, 'welcome in', is conventional and is a common Irish phrase that a tourist or occasional visitor might learn. Since this laundrette is located close to tourist areas and a university, this conventional greeting could be directed both to overseas visitors and more local audiences. The Irish writing on the right, however, is anything but conventional. The phrase *slán agus beannacht* is conventionally used as a farewell and literally means 'health and blessing'. It too is a phrase that may be casually encountered by visitors or those with only a passing knowledge of Irish. The word *glan* in Irish, however, means 'clean', and the phrase *glan agus beannacht*, literally 'clean and blessing', is neither grammatical nor idiomatic in Irish. Like <Brishta> in Figure 2.2, the use of the word *glan* here has general relevance to the business that is being advertised, but creates an intentional violation of the rules of the language. Some effort must be expended by the reader to make sense of this linguistic anomaly, but this effort yields a reward in the decoding of a linguistic puzzle. As a type of metaphorical codeswitching, the sign thus reaches out to readers who understand the sign's linguistic humour, while retaining the appearance of authentic Irishness even for those who do not.

Figure 2.4, from the shop front of the Galway branch of the Schuh chain of shoe shops, focuses our attention on the use of Irish in contemporary globalisation. The Schuh chain opened in 1981 in Edinburgh and operates in the UK and Ireland (see Schuh website for a history). Despite the German name, it has nothing to do with Germany. This use of a foreign language metaphorically does not index tradition, but rather the commercial activity of a multinational company within a multilingual Europe. As we will see below, Figure 2.4 is thus more comparable to the use of European languages in the Japanese linguistic landscape.

Apart from the Schuh name partially shown at the top of Figure 2.4, the main message on the right of the figure looks like a simple case of what Reh (2004) calls duplicating multilingual writing, since the Irish *éadach do chosa* is equivalent to the English 'clothing for feet'. This use of equivalent

Figure 2.4 Schuh shoe shop, Galway

messages, however, does not arise from language policy (as with the duplicating multilingual writing on street signs) or communicative necessity. Rather, we point to the signage as a whole and suggest that the use of language here invokes a metaphorical reference to Irish as the national language of Ireland in an international, postmodern context in which Scottish-based shoe shops use the German language to advertise goods that have no necessary connection to any German-speaking country.

Japan: Repurposing English for Local Meanings

Turning to our material from Japan, we first consider Figure 2.5, a poster from a commuter train, which shows a purposeful and extreme degree of Reh's 'fragmentary multilingualism'.

The full name of the company, *Melon Bridal Counter*, is given in English much more prominently than it is in Japanese. The Japanese name is written in Katakana only in a small font in the first line of the paragraph in the middle of the sign. It would be wrong to assume, though, that the company is advertising to English speakers: there is no other English text in the sign. Variation within the Japanese language is exploited to index many non-Japanese referents. Many of the services offered in the

Figure 2.5 Melon Bridal Counter on commuter train

advertisement are described using loanwords written in Katakana – dresses, hairdressing, nails, dessert buffets and a 'wedding school'. Since most of these concepts could have been described using native Japanese words and written in Kanji, the use of Katakana makes a metaphorical reference to the West. The model provides a further point of exotic reference, since she is wearing a Western wedding dress. Western-style weddings are now more popular in Japan than traditional Shinto weddings, and a whole industry has developed to provide this service (see, e.g. BBC News, 2006). Thus, Figure 2.5, while functionally aimed at a Japanese clientele, accomplishes its task by the use of an English name, Japanese that is markedly rich in foreign loanwords, and Western imagery. A model of bilingual signage needs to incorporate these additional references in order to understand ways in which English, rather than being simply imported into Japan, has been repurposed to suit contemporary Japanese culture.

In Figure 2.6, we see a quintessentially Western symbol placed in a novel context that is as much Japanese as American. This poster comes from a shopping centre near the Fukuoka Tower and advertises a limited-edition teriyaki egg burger that was available at McDonald's during spring 2007.

Noticing and celebrating the four seasons of the year has long been an essential aspect of Japanese traditional high culture and aesthetics (see, e.g. De Mente, 2006: 104–105). In modern times, Japanese businesses often hold special promotions to go with the seasons. The seasonal element is prominent in Figure 2.6, where the most salient images are the cherry blossom and the hybrid Japanese-American *teritama* (coined from *teriyaki + tamago* 'egg' and denoting a teriyaki burger with an egg on top). The cherry blossom is the classic traditional symbol of spring in Japan, and cherry-blossom imagery is ubiquitous at this time of year. The legend at the right announces that 'Spring comes in together with teritama' and uses the traditional top-to-bottom, right-to-left orientation of writing in Japanese in order to index traditional orthography and culture (much like the use of Irish orthography in our earlier examples). The McDonald's logo also appears in the bottom corner, along with the slogan 'I'm lovin' it', which in Europe appears on McDonald's packaging in several European languages, but here appears in English alone. Semiotic hybridisation reaches its peak in the stylised cherry blossom at the top of the poster, which contains the kanji 春 *haru* 'spring' and, in Roman letters, the English word 'mac', used here as shorthand for a McDonald's product (as in McMuffin, McNugget, and so on). The resulting hybrid word, *harumac*, is not a real word in either language (just as *Brishta* in Figure 2.2 is neither Irish nor English), but is filled with associations pertaining both to Japanese culture and to Western consumer culture. English is thus used not to communicate concrete information,

Figure 2.6 Teritama, near Fukuoka Tower

but as a reference to the McDonald's brand. One could argue that this poster as a whole thus reflects the cultural hybridity that accompanies globalisation – a point that goes beyond the scope of this chapter.

Figure 2.7, from the Shintencho shopping area in central Fukuoka, appears comprehensible to the European at first glance. 'Lotteria' is (or closely resembles) the word for a lottery in several European languages, so an outsider might readily guess that this shop sells lottery tickets or scratch cards.

In fact, Lotteria is a fast-food chain based in Japan, which also operates in South Korea, Taiwan, China and Viet Nam. Its product range includes

Figure 2.7 Lotteria, Shintencho district

Western-style fast food such as burgers and chips, more Asian-style food such as squid rings and tongue stew, and fusion foods including shrimp burgers and green tea ice cream. The name Lotteria comes from the parent corporation, Lotte, which in turn is named after the character Charlotte in *The Sorrows of Young Werther* by Goethe. Though the name 'Lotteria' in this setting is uninformative to anyone unfamiliar with the Lotte brand history, there is no doubt that the original intention of the brand name is to appeal to ideas of European high culture and literature: the Lotte website states that the company is named after Charlotte because she is 'a character who stays in the memory for a long time and is deep in the hearts of many people around the world'. Adding to the specific historical references of the Lotte company, we can see a more general global reference in the *-eria* ending of *Lotteria*. As pointed out by Barni and Bagna (2009), this word form has taken on a life of its own in international signage, combining not only with Italianate roots (*pizzeria*, *gelateria*, etc.), but with a wide range of other elements. Thus, while the sign in Figure 2.7 is linguistically very simple, its multiple systems of reference express far more than its referential meaning.

Figure 2.8 shows a poster for a 390-yen shop in the Daimyo area of Fukuoka, which includes a number of 'cool' shops aimed at a young clientele. The English text here, *Thank You Mart*, while composed of legitimate English words, does not convey a particularly meaningful message. This phrase is in fact a pun directed solely at Japanese speakers. Many Japanese speakers pronounce the expression *thank you* as ['saŋkju], which sounds exactly like the Japanese words *san* 'three' and *kyuu* 'nine'.

Figure 2.8 Thank You Mart, Daimyo district

Thus, *san kyuu* 'three nine' is a reference to the fact that everything in this shop costs 390 yen. Though the shop name is also transliterated in Hiragana at the bottom of the poster, the main effect of the sign is to create a message in which English words are divorced from their original meanings, yet still trade on the popularity of English as a branding device.

Conclusions

In this investigation of signage in two urban areas widely separated by geography, language and culture, we have focused on the ways in which multilingual signage can be indexical of more than the literal message of the sign. Our observation is that notions such as *duplicating multilingual writing* or *complementary multilingual writing* account for the relationships between languages in multilingual signs when the analysis focuses on linguistic codes and literal meanings alone. We would go one step further, though, and suggest that *metaphorical reference* in the linguistic landscape – whether achieved by language choice, choice of font or writing system, or complementary relationship to other semiotic systems – must also be fully accounted for.

We also argue that the approach we have developed here allows for an assessment of the ways in which language communities use the linguistic landscape in different ways to address issues such as globalisation. We see that in the Irish linguistic landscape – particularly in the city, where Irish is not the expected language of everyday communication – Irish can be used to refer both to tradition and to globalisation when juxtaposed with other languages. In Japan we see that while the use of English is often indexical of modernity and postmodern hybridity, metaphorical references to modern globalisation can also be accomplished by multi-linguistic reference to an 18th-century German Romantic character. We further hypothesise on the basis of our urban evidence that the recontextualisations of language that we have seen here are more typical of urban environments, with their social diversity and cross-cultural encounters, than of rural settings. Further contrastive research may be needed on this point as the field of linguistic landscape continues to develop.

References

Backhaus, P. (2007) *Linguistic Landscapes: A Comparative Study of Urban Multilingualism in Tokyo*. Clevedon: Multilingual Matters.

Backhaus, P. (2009) Rules and regulations in linguistic landscaping: A comparative perspective. In E. Shohamy and D. Gorter (eds) *Linguistic Landscape: Expanding the Scenery* (pp. 157–172). London: Routledge.

Barni, M. and Bagna, C. (2009) Italian language and LL in the market of languages. Paper presented at the Linguistic Landscape Workshop, Siena.

BBC News (2006) Faking it as a priest in Japan. Online news, 2 November. On WWW at http://news.bbc.co.uk/1/hi/world/middle_east/6067002.stm.

Blom, J. and Gumperz, J.J. (1972 [1986]) Social meaning in linguistic structures: Code-switching in Norway. In J.J. Gumperz and D. Hymes (eds) *Directions in Sociolinguistics: The Ethnography of Communication* (2nd edn) (pp. 407–434). Oxford: Blackwell.

Central Statistics Office (2007a) *Census 2006: Principal Demographic Results.* Dublin: Stationery Office.

Central Statistics Office (2007b) *Census 2006: Volume 4, Usual Residence, Migration, Birthplaces and Nationalities.* Dublin: Stationery Office.

Central Statistics Office (2007c) *Census 2006: Volume 9, Irish Language.* Dublin: Stationery Office.

City of Fukuoka (2008) City of Fukuoka website. On WWW at http://www.city. fukuoka.lg.jp/english/index.html. Accessed 15.3.09.

CWMG website (n.d.) Collected works of Mahatma Gandhi. On WWW at http:// gandhiserve.org/cwmb/cwmg.html. Accessed 13.7.09.

De Mente, B.L. (2006) *Elements of Japanese Design.* Rutland, VT: Tuttle.

Gottlieb, N. (2005) *Language and Society in Japan.* Cambridge: Cambridge University Press.

Inoue, F. (2005) Econolinguistic aspects of multilingual signs in Japan. *International Journal of the Sociology of Language* 175/176, 157–177.

Kallen, J.L. (1994) English in Ireland. In R. Burchfield (ed.) *The Cambridge History of the English Language* (Vol. 5) (pp. 148–196). Cambridge: Cambridge University Press.

Kallen, J.L. (2009) Tourism and representation in the Irish linguistic landscape. In E. Shohamy and D. Gorter (eds) *Linguistic Landscape: Expanding the Scenery* (pp. 270–283). London: Routledge.

Kallen, J.L. (2010) Changing landscapes: Language, space, and policy in the Dublin linguistic landscape. In A. Jaworski and C. Thurlow (eds) *Semiotic Landscapes: Language, Image, Space* (pp. 41–58). London: Continuum.

Landry, R. and Bourhis, R.Y. (1997) Linguistic landscape and ethnolinguistic vitality: An empirical study. *Journal of Language and Social Psychology* 16 (1), 23–49.

Lanza, E. and H. Woldemariam (2009) Language ideology and linguistic landscape: Language policy and globalization in a regional capital of Ethiopia. In E. Shohamy and D. Gorter (eds) *Linguistic Landscape: Expanding the Scenery* (pp. 189–205). London: Routledge.

Lotte website (2009) On WWW at http://www.lotte.co.jp/english/. Accessed 14.7.09.

McGuinne, D. (1992) *Irish Type Design.* Blackrock, Co. Dublin: Irish Academic Press.

Ó Cuív, B. (1986) Irish language and literature, 1691–1845. In T.W. Moody and W.E. Vaughan (eds) *A New History of Ireland, Volume 4: Eighteenth-Century Ireland 1691–1800* (pp. 374–423). Oxford: Clarendon Press.

Ó Giollagáin, C. and Mac Donnacha, S. (2008) The Gaeltacht today. In C. Nic Pháidín and S. Ó Cearnaigh (eds) *A New View of the Irish Language* (pp. 108–120). Dublin: Cois Life.

Ó Riagáin, P. (2007) Irish. In D. Britain (ed.) *Language in the British Isles* (pp. 218–236). Cambridge: Cambridge University Press.

Reh, M. (2004) Multilingual writing: A reader-oriented typology – with examples from Lira Municipality (Uganda). *International Journal of the Sociology of Language* 170, 1–41.

Rozycki, W. (2003) When did the Japanese language come to Japan? In O. Toshiki and A. Vovin (eds) *Perspectives on the Origins of the Japanese Language* (pp. 451–461). Kyoto: International Research Center for Japanese Studies.

Schuh website (n.d.) On WWW at http://www.schuhstore.co.uk/about/. Accessed 29.12.08.

Shohamy, E. and Gorter, D. (eds) (2009) *Linguistic Landscape: Expanding the Scenery*. London: Routledge.

Spolsky, B. and Cooper, R.L. (1991) *The Languages of Jerusalem*. Oxford: Oxford University Press.

Tanaka, K. (1994) *Advertising Language: A Pragmatic Approach to Advertisements in Britain and Japan*. London: Routledge.

Trumper-Hecht, N. (2009) Constructing national identity in mixed cities in Israel: Arabic on signs in the public space of Upper Nazareth. In E. Shohamy and D. Gorter (eds) *Linguistic Landscape: Expanding the Scenery* (pp. 238–252). London: Routledge.

Vartanian, I. and Martin, L.A. (2003) *Graphiscape: Tokyo*. Mies: Rotovision.

Chapter 3

'The Holy Ark in the Street': Sacred and Secular Painting of Utility Boxes in the Public Domain in a Small Israeli Town

YAEL GUILAT

Introduction

This chapter focuses on the relationship between linguistic landscapes (LL) and visual-culture research by conducting a case study in *Migdal ha-'Emeq*, Israel. *Migdal ha-'Emeq*, founded as a place for the settlement of Jewish immigrants from Morocco in the 1950s and now a small city comprising multi-ethnic groups, is hosting a project of decorative paintings on electricity and telephone boxes.

The 268 painted utility boxes in *Migdal ha-'Emeq* may be interpreted as landmarks that signify and 'explain' the city, weave stories of local identity and create a sense of the town's 'little own place'. The project also raises questions about the role of official popular art with the LL as a sociolinguistic domain. If the social dimension is a social product, as Lefebvre (1974: 35) claims, popular art in the public domain may be considered a sociocultural product. Moreover, the understanding of images as social practice also involves seeing images as part of power struggles among opposing social groups. Therefore, visual-culture study of this urban decoration project may illuminate the way in which power is exercised through the institutions of government as well as other influential groups.

In presenting my empirical findings about *Migdal ha-'Emeq*, I argue that the painted boxes in a neighborhood tenanted by religiously observant people of north African origin have given this particular group of people a sense of place and, concurrently, reflect their attitude toward Israel's hegemonic national narrative.

Theoretical Framework: Text/Image and the Urban Linguistic Landscape

In *The Language of Images*, Mitchell (1974) compiled various perspectives that had been developed in semiotic research over the past century, ever since Pierce's and de Saussure's seminal works. Mitchell's writings focused on what was then called 'the linguistic turn' in arts, which dealt with the 'almost' total adoption and application of semiotic methods to visual images. In terms of visual-cultures studies, Mitchell's book was considered a breakthrough. Later, in his *Iconology: Image, Text and Ideology*, Mitchell (1986) took up the question of what images are, how they differ from words, and the ideological significance of this struggle between pictorial and linguistic signs throughout cultural history. Two decades after his original study, Mitchell wrote in *Picture Theory* that the answer to those early questions must include:

> reflections on texts, particularly on the ways in which texts act like pictures or incorporate pictorial practices and vice-versa... It doesn't mean that there is no difference between words and images: only that the differences are much more complex that they might seem at first glance, that they crop up within as well as between media and they change over times as modes of representation and cultures change. (Mitchell, 1994: 4)

Gradually, visual studies transferred the focus from the text–image relationship to the visual as a place where meanings are created and contested. The visual has attained such a proliferation today that one may argue, after Mirzoeff (1999: 1), that in 'this swirl of imagery, seeing is not just a part of everyday life, it is everyday life'. Furthermore, visual culture, according to Slater (1997: 164) 'involves understanding images in terms of how they are slipped into people's daily rituals rather than as self-contained texts'. As Rogoff (1998: 26) says, in large cities as well as in small towns, individuals create unexpected visual narratives in everyday life from 'the scrap of an image which connects with a sequence of a film and with the corner of the billboard or the window display of the shop we have passed by'.

The public sphere that Rogoff and others refer to is where the LL and visual culture share certain themes of language and daily life. Written texts on signs in the public domain provide us with information on everyday urban life and also symbolize the social and linguistic identity of a given region (Landry & Bourhis, 1997), but they do so within a complex visual context. According to Duncum (2002), this context (no less than the image as a text) is the aim of visual-culture research that concerns the social conditions of image production and the distribution and use of the images in the public sphere.

Recently, the LL has been viewed in its expanded form, addressing the topic of language and public space within a broader range of related topics such as multimodality, text–image and other forms of text types (Shohamy & Gorter, 2008). There is reason to regard the LL and visual culture as having the shared goal of studying the traces of cultural texts in everyday life and tracing the confrontation between consumers' internal images and the aims of the designers of the public LL, especially in the urban space.

It is the realization that spectatorship (the look, the gaze, the glance, the practices of observation, surveillance and visual pleasure) may be as deep a problem as various forms of reading (decipherment, decoding, interpretation), and that visual experience or visual literacy might not be fully explicable on the model of textuality (Mitchell, 1994: 16).

The focus on practice and, even more, on public practice is critical for understanding the growing interest in how texts/images play a role specifically in the urban landscape. As Mitchell (1994: 5) points out, the differences between visual and written signs are actually 'the differences in practice between the self (speaking) the other (seen), between telling and showing; between "hearsay" and "eyewitness" testimony'.

There, in the urban space, the 'seen' text (of signs, advertising, billboards, graffiti, etc.) and the 'shown' image (of buildings, monuments, posters, cinema announcements, shop windows and also decorated utility boxes) conjoin and together construct the LL, yielding a cultural multimodal construction. Therefore, like other visual items, painted utility boxes serve as signifiers in the textual urban array (urban path) that is visually read in everyday life. Beyond the focus on the urban visual culture, one may recognize the city as a dynamic social domain that reflects the nexus of ideology and everyday life.

In sum, the major aim of visual culture, as Evans and Hall (1999) note, is to focus on images as a social practice rather than mere objects of textual analysis. This, in turn, entails attention to three dimensions: the lived experience of people, socioeconomic issues and the history of images including their production and reception. Thus, the purpose of this chapter is to analyze how a specific project – painting utility boxes in a small and peripheral town (*Migdal ha-'Emeq*) – may be understood and explained in terms of visual culture, in two senses: as the creation of urban visual texts and as a social exercise in the practice and power of ideology.

Research Methodology

Visual-culture research is basically a multidisciplinary field of study that entails the use of different approaches. This study brings a qualitative ethnographic approach to the gathering and analysis of data and invokes extensive historical, iconological and visual-culture research as well. Interviews were conducted with the municipal officials and the painters involved in the project. Photographs of all 268 decorated boxes were taken and official press releases about the project were collected. I then classified the boxes by the different visual motifs that corresponded to the streets (the neighborhood) and by the painters,

Rami Tayib and Sergei Ivchenko, who were hired to carry out the project. The classification of the motifs led to a search for the artistic and popular sources of the pictures on the boxes and their interpretive analysis.

From first glance (the picture-taking tour of the city) and *a fortiori* after examination of the data after classification, it became clear that this large and distinctive group of painted utility boxes constituted a consistent array of images that appear only in neighborhoods tenanted by religiously observant Jews and, especially, in the ultra-Orthodox neighborhoods of Migdal Or and Ramat Eshkol. It is important to note that ultra-Orthodox Jews (who account for 30% of the town's population according to official municipal reports and the Israel Central Bureau of Statistics)[1] may regard figurative images in the public realm as contrary to their way of life and even as affronts or attacks on them by the secular Israeli Zionist apparatus. I discuss this point in detail below.

Thus, the study concentrated on understanding the lived conditions in which the images on the decorated boxes were produced and used. This brought a central question to the fore: May these images be viewed, in terms of both LL and visual culture, as a kind of local-identity narrative, or do they mark 'symbolic boundaries' between different subcultural groups in the city? This chapter focuses on the study of 70 painted utility boxes in the religious neighborhoods of *Migdal ha-'Emeq*, 26% of all boxes painted in the project.

The data

Migdal ha-'Emeq

Migdal ha-'Emeq is situated on the Haifa–Nazareth highway, bordering the Lower Galilee hills and the Jezreel Valley. Ringed today by high-tech factories, it was founded in 1953 as a town for the settlement of Moroccan-Jewish families that had arrived in Israel amid the mass immigration that followed the establishment of the State of Israel. Before reaching *Migdal ha-'Emeq*, those families had been settled in a provisional camp and awaited the establishment of 'development towns' that, according to the governmental policy of population dispersion, would absorb them. Most of these towns, like *Migdal ha-'Emeq*, were tenanted by Jewish immigrants from Arab countries, mainly in northern Africa (known as *Mizrahim*, i.e. 'easterners'), who suffered from economic backwardness and deprivation (Tzfadia, 2004: 124). The new towns were established in the national periphery. In the case of *Migdal ha-'Emeq*, even though the physical setting was shared with cooperative and collective settlements (moshavim and kibbutzim) founded by the Zionist Labor Movement, the population of this small town was perceived as a hinterland of the hegemonic veteran society of Israel. Religious customs, ethnic affiliation, low socioeconomic level and political leanings led to the emergence of a sense of place that was a 'non-place', trapped on the margins of Israeli-Jewish society (Ben Zadok, 1993; Tzfadia, 2004: 125).

Granted municipal status in 1988, today *Migdal ha-'Emeq* has a population of about 24,700, comprising native and foreign-born Israelis (30%), immigrants from Morocco, Tunisia and Iraq, a small group of immigrants from South America, Russia and the Caucasus, and a few immigrants from Ethiopia. Most of the population is traditional in its religious observance, but there are also distinctly ultra-Orthodox neighborhoods and 30% of the population is ultra-Orthodox (municipal reports and Central Bureau of Statistics, 2007). The socioeconomic status of the town, according to the statistics, is medium-low.

Importantly, *Migdal ha-'Emeq* is the center of a very broad religious educational network, known as Migdal Or, founded by the Ashkenazi chief rabbi of the city, Yitzhak David Grossman. At the time the research was conducted, the city was governed by a coalition of the Likud (the right-wing ruling party, to which the mayor belonged) and Shas[2] (an ultra-Orthodox Sephardi party). In the most recent municipal elections (2009), Shas emerged as the largest party (28%), followed by Yisrael Beitenu, the largely Russian-immigrant party (23%), Likud (13%), a local and religious list (10%) and three small local lists (approximately 7% each).[3]

The combination of topography (low hills and valleys – the word ha-'emeq in the town's name denotes the Jezreel Valley) and the gradual growth process gave rise to an urban array of circling streets and neighborhoods. Although the city is not very large, its social and physical conditions created over the years a distinctive urban landscape in different parts of town, such as the spacious secular neighborhood of Nof ha-'Emeq and the old area inhabited by a traditional and ultra-Orthodox population, Ramat Eshkol.

The painting project

Itzik Rozilio, the initiator of the idea and the municipal official in charge of it, described the background and framework of the project:

> Let there be no mistake—we were the first in Israel to do this. The idea was born here in *Migdal ha-'Emeq* in the need to fight vandals of utility boxes. We sat together, I as a municipal director and my deputy, and decided to paint them. During our meeting on the question of the boxes, the director the municipal immigrant-absorption department asked me to help some immigrant artists,

and the representative of the immigrants in the municipality told me that there were funds from the Ministry of Immigrant Absorption that he could give me to employ them. We then decided to link the problem with the contribution and asked Sergei [Ivchenko] to paint the three boxes at the entrance to the municipal amphitheatre for a start. I am sure that one of the reasons that we received a five-star commendation was because of those paintings on the boxes. It gave us a wonderful feeling for two reasons. One was that we initiated an idea that all other cities have adopted, and the second is that we don't have problems about pasted-up notices, legal writs, and fines anymore.[4]

The project took place in 2003 and lasted four months. Participating in this project were two artist painters, Sergei Ivchenko and Rami Tayib, who were contracted by the Municipality.[5] Tayib, whose parents had come from Tunisia *to Migdal ha-'Emeq*, is an amateur autodidact artist. Ivchenko, aged 51 when interviewed, immigrated to Israel from USSR; an educated artist and a qualified muralist, he is familiar with traditional themes and motifs in Christian art as well as Russian folklore art.[6]

Many municipalities have followed the example of *Migdal ha-'Emeq* (Chazak, 2003). In recent years, the presence of painted utility boxes in the public domain has become a familiar sight in Israeli cities. Some towns show off the projects on their official websites.[7]

The kind of street painting that has emerged is much different from the graffiti art of subways or British urban art as described by Pennycook (2008) and others (see Hanauer's chapter in this volume). Unlike these radical responses to social and artistic authority and canons, the *Migdal ha-'Emeq* initiative began as a conformist enterprise of a peripheral establishment. The *Migdal ha-'Emeq* Municipality, as the pioneer of this sort of visual design in the public scene, was involved in a different pattern of official intervention or control: it sometimes proposed a motif with retroactive consent in the choice of artists and even encouraged neighborhood discussion and requests by residents.

Themes and motifs of the painted electricity and telephone boxes

Motifs

Analyzing the themes of the utility-box paintings at large, we may identify the following topics in accordance with different social environments:

Boxes	Social environment		
Topics	Neighborhood	Religious customs	Ethnic origin
1. Quotations and echoes of art history	Nof ha-'Emeq; Ya'arat ha-'Emeq; Pninat ha-'Emeq	Traditional and secular	Mixed
2. Paintings of flowers, animals and children	Nof ha-'Emeq; Ya'arat ha-'Emeq	Traditional and secular	Mixed
3. Jewish religious and Jewish-Israeli religious-national themes	Ramat Eshkol; Migdal Or	Ultra-Orthodox	North African majority (Mizrahim)[8]

While the first two categories are common in the other cities, the third is presented only in *Migdal ha-'Emeq*. Elsewhere, one may encounter one or two of the same 'ritual' representations, but the dimension of this phenomenon, e.g. sacred and ritual-based images in the public city sphere, is strictly a local one.

The paintings exhibit various repetitive motifs. Two motifs are the most popular: the Star of David and the menorah. It is important to note the motifs that are absent among the street paintings but commonly found in the homes of residents of these neighborhood, such as images of tombs of the pious, priestly blessings, kabbalistic letters or amulets, and portraits of sages, rabbis or pious men. These are all general characteristics of the Mizrahi-Jewish visual home environment.

Several additional motifs that were very popular in official visual projects in the 1950s or later, but are absent in the *Migdal ha-'Emeq* project are, for example, visual symbols of Zionist agricultural settlement and Zionist landscape images with plowed fields, kibbutzim and water towers. Two motifs from that era – 'blue boxes' (classical Jewish National Fund donation boxes) and the Israeli flag – are exceptions; they appeared on various city streets in combination with ritual artifacts.

Motif	Frequency	Style	Iconological (pictorial and historical) sources
Star of David (see Figure 3.1)	15	Graphic (4); decorative (5); symbolic-allegoric (6)	New Year's (Rosh Hashana) greetings; early Israeli art; official national celebratory posters of the 1950s, motifs in Jewish ritual embroidery and decorations of Jewish ritual artifacts from Morocco
The menorah[9]	11	Graphic (2); decorative (2); symbolic-allegoric (7)	New Year's (Rosh Hashana) greetings; decorations of Jewish ritual artifacts; decorated windows (vitraux); early art in Israel (Bezalel School of Art, 1906–1929)
Tree of Life (resembling a menorah but with candles shaped like the Star of David)	2	Decorative; symbolic; fantastic	Popular stamps and New Year's greetings from the 1950s to the present
Jewish visages	2	Figurative; realist; symbolic	Russian-Jewish painting in the 20th century; referring also to Bezalel iconography
Jewish still life	3	Figurative; realist; symbolic	20th-century Russian-Jewish painting after the still-life motif in western art
New Year's greetings (see Figure 3.2)	3	Graphic	Popular stamps and New Year's greetings in Israel from the 1950s to the present
Holy arks	3	Graphic-symbolic; fantastic	Popular stamps and New Year's greetings from the 1950s, crafted receptacles of ritual artifacts from the Moroccan-Jewish community, and the Bezalel style

(Continued)

Motif	Frequency	Style	Iconological (pictorial and historical) sources
Flying Torah scrolls, Torah crown and lions (see Figure 3.3)	4	Graphic; symbolic; fantastic	Popular stamps and New Year's greetings from the 1950s to the present, and Jewish ritual artifacts (Succot [Feast of Tabernacles] decorations)
Lubbock illustrations (recitation of the Haggadah)	1	Graphic; symbolic	Russian-Jewish popular art
Rachel's Tomb, Jerusalem and others holy places	5	Graphic; figurative; realist; symbolic	Early Israeli art (Bezalel School of Art)
Noah's Ark	1	Graphic; symbolic	Popular stamps and New Year's greetings from the 1950s
The Burning Bush	1	Graphic; symbolic; fantastic	Popular stamps and New Year's greetings from the 1950s, early Israeli art (Bezalel School of Art)
Symbols of the Twelve Tribes	2	Graphic; symbolic	Early art in Israel (Bezalel School), official national celebratory posters from the 1950s and stamps
The Temple	1	Graphic; symbolic	Early art in Israel (Bezalel School), official national celebratory posters from the 1950s and stamps

(Continued)

Motif	Frequency	Style	Iconological (pictorial and historical) sources
Kiddush Cup	1	Graphic didactic (illustrative)	Illustrations of readers for Jewish religious public schools in Israel
Prayershawl (see Figure 3.4)	1	Graphic; didactical (illustrative)	Illustrations of readers for Jewish religious public school in Israel
The Israeli Flag (including (1) on the JNF 'blue box')[10]	4	Graphic	Official national celebratory posters from the 1950s
Doves of peace	3	Graphic	Official national celebratory posters from the 1950s
Decorated windows, frames (including view of palms) and shapes of arks	11	Decorative (5); symbolic (6)	Early art in Israel (Bezalel School); decorative receptacles of ritual artifacts from the Moroccan-Jewish community
Hamsa (hand extended in blessing)	1	Decorative	Ritual artifacts from the Moroccan-Jewish community

Figure 3.1 Rami Tayib, Aliya St. Sapir

Style and iconographical sources

The style varies between the realistic and the symbolic. The style reflects the different iconographical sources, such as stamps, posters and postcards, from the early days of statehood as well as the Bezalel style of the early pre-independence period.[11] One may also see reminiscences of crafted and decorated ritual artifacts from the Moroccan-Jewish community. In some cases, the images are copied directly from the graphic realm; they include imitations of stained-glass windows (vitraux) and imitations of postcards of Jewish paintings commonly found among Jewish painters in the former USSR in the 1960s and 1970s, when they waited for permission to emigrate to Israel (Mishori, 2000: 268–290).

Figure 3.2 Sergei Ivaczenko, Hagefen St. Migdal Or

Discussion

Visual text functions

The painting of electricity and utility boxes as a deliberate and official attempt to embellish the public sphere with significant visual signs and turn the city into a kind of meaningful visual text provides us with different levels of interpretations and views.

A painting requisitioned by persons who wield public authority differs from other private or public *objets d'art* and, when it concerns an entire city, one may even speak of an urban discourse in the sense expressed by Lefebvre (1974). Even in such a requisitioned project, the 'anonymous' and modernistic urban domain should reveal its potential of promoting identity at the individual and communal-minority levels, beyond and behind the official enterprise.

Basically, this visual text can fulfill two basic functions, one practical and the other symbolic. The practical function was defined by the official promoter as 'preventing the pasting of notices such as obituaries, advertisements, and posters on electricity and telephone boxes in the streets, causing public blight and vandalism'.[12] This may be seen as a kind of forewarning that is meant to avoid the necessity of imposing fines

Figure 3.3 Sergei Ivaczenko, Hagefen St. Migdal Or

and to enforce municipal bylaws. It replaces the conventional text with a decorative image that warns against such illegal actions.

The second practical function is the decorative one. 'If there were paintings on the boxes that people could identify with and enjoy, it might not only solve the problem but might even contribute to the appearance of the city'.[13]

The practical decorative function, however, might be prohibited according to a rigid interpretation of the Second Commandment ('You shall not make for yourself a graven image': Exodus 20:4) in an area populated by religiously observant people. Religious Jews, especially the ultra-Orthodox, live by the rules of *halacha* (rabbinical law) and follow the guidance of rabbis and religious authorities. Thus, it seems that the decorative function (e.g. providing aesthetic pleasure) should satisfy some other purposes for the town's religious authorities. The reason for this may be that most inhabitants of the ultra-Orthodox neighborhoods were raised in public schools (in Israel or elsewhere) and have become more observant under the influence of Shas and Migdal Or. Both organizations practice relative tolerance in order to enlarge their membership and also use certain tools, such as visual images, with which people are already familiar. In most cases, they stress the denotative function of

Figure 3.4 Rami Tayib, *Tephilim*, Kadesh St. Ramat Eshkol

the images, e.g. realistic emulation of ritual artifacts or holy places. By using established symbols that are carefully painted for didactic purposes, they skirt the potential injunction against visual images.

Interpretation: Linguist landscape and the visual urban discourse

De Certau (1980: 29) writes that the city is 'understood' as a place in consciousness 'which has to be marched through'. One may see this in *Migdal ha-'Emeq*, where the 'box art' provides neither a panoramic view nor a particular perspective, but an interweaving of time and place, a 'conversation' between interlocking fields. The urban discourse exists for the viewer only as a reading text, and here lies the strength of the structure of a signified urban domain that is imaginary and elusive, but also permanent and recurring. The repetition of motifs in the streets of the neighborhoods contributes to this impression.

An urban discourse may also be thought of as the popular visual manifestation of a 'folkloristic' array of images. In cultural research terms, the 'popular' is portrayed as having 'fallen from the heights' (cf. Jakobson & Bogatyrev, 1971 [1986]: 280) as opposed to the way it is perceived by researchers of late 19th-century folklore and Romantic nationalism, as a source of authenticity transmitted from one generation to another.

The fact is that popular visual culture in Israel had never been planned or developed as a culture continuous with the abandoned popular Jewish culture in the immigrant Jews' countries of origin. In particular, the urban discourse of the towns founded soon after the establishment of the State of Israel was invented, as was the 'authentic' popular Zionist visual culture of posters, greeting cards, stamps, etc. The melting pot of that era seems to have been a shallow one because it was very selective (Efrat, 2000) Although the quoted and reproduced artworks, the Jewish motifs, the sacred ritual artifacts (Figure 3.4) and even the few symbols of Zionist sovereignty have undergone a prolonged evolution of popular transmission originating mainly in early 20th-century posters and postcards, they were invented and 'used' in ideological terms for the sake of an Israeli identity under construction. They produced a meta-visual language that was, in fact, an invented popular visual language.

At this stage, the question is why and how these motifs were adopted in *Migdal ha-'Emeq* in religious neighborhoods that are populated mostly by people from northern Africa. The influence of early Israeli art iconography (the Bezalel school) is easily recognized in three motifs: gates and windows, the Star of David and the menorah. The merging of menorahs and Stars of David, however (Figure 3.3), with emphasis on light and sometimes a praying figure, is definitely new. The signifiers of messianic redemption, represented as light and heavenly harmony, are stronger than those of the practical redemption of a people returning to its land for the sake of labor (as in the Zionist praxis of the new Jew as a muscular Hebrew worker), so typical of the Bezalel school and paintings and graphics of the 1950s.

In the utility-box paintings in *Migdal ha-'Emeq*, the adoption and transformation of the motifs took place in the realm of what had been defined as popular in the early statehood period – a realm that did not, at the time, include the repertoires that the north African immigrants had brought with them. Nevertheless, there is little remembrance of Moroccan-Jewish embroidery and ritual artifacts and of the influences of Russian-Jewish painting. The *Migdal ha-'Emeq* project exhibits a 'neighborhood melting-pot' pattern similar to the mainstream pattern in the pre-statehood and early statehood years. *Migdal ha-'Emeq* gives the appearance of an encapsulated Zionist era that has ended. The erstwhile 'mainstream center' has now passed into the privatization of post-modernist identities while the struggle for a sense of place in a non-place is confined to the margins of society.

The marginal culture in which the encounter of the popular arts (e.g. the Zionist, the Jewish-religious and -ritual, and the Moroccan and the Russian) takes place and where a 'fallout of motifs' both communal and traditional occurs, has 'melted' or 'merged' into a shallow kind of general Israeli culture. How is this peripheral-marginal aspect expressed? Does it mirror a local identity that is more peripheral than religious, communal or social? Which kind or sense of place can one identify? Metaphorically, one may notice a vague recollection of what was once perceived as the official state Zionist culture. What was then unobtainable for the recently landed immigrants, however, is no longer obtainable today because it has disintegrated. Yet it still exists by adjustment to, by selective adoption by, the geographical and social margins of the state as a yearning for the center, for acceptance. And as Dahan (2006) argues in regard to local officials and leadership as well as functionaries like Rozilio, whose political culture was shaped within the framework of dependent paternalism, there is certainly an aspiration for institutional integration and the acceptance of hierarchy. What we witness in *Migdal ha-'Emeq*, then, is a process of marginalization and displacement of previous repertoires from the center to the periphery.

The peripheral nature of the box-painting project may also be understood through the character of the Shas party, which is showing a gradual increase in electoral strength in the ultra-Orthodox neighborhoods of *Migdal ha-'Emeq* that host the box-painting project. Much research has been done on whether Shas is a pro-integration or pro-segregation movement or a religious or a communal one. The residents of *Migdal ha-'Emeq* who vote for Shas share a Mizrahi culture that they mingle with the shadow of fading Israel state symbols that they once wished to embrace but could not due to rejection. As Horowitz (2000: 30) remarks, among those in Israel's peripheral regions, both physical and mental protest and a kind of return to religion (as in *Migdal ha-'Emeq*) joined forces with a sense of deprivation and abandonment to their socioeconomic fate: 'Shas is an Israeli phenomenon that merges social protest with the creation of an alternative identity that is oriental [Mizrahi], religious and conservative in the State of Israel'.

In conclusion, the cultural mix that emerges from the iconography of the utility-box paintings creates a peripheral segregation that is in itself integrative: a small Israeli-religious place within the larger Israel social space. The identity of a low-income town of immigrants and their descendants who did not participate in the ethos of the new Zionist identity, but were caught up in the Jewish melting pot of Israeli statehood that also absorbed new waves of immigrants, has created a kind of 'second-hand' melting pot. While the center undergoes a process of postmodern liberalism and globalization, the periphery maintains a hierarchic and institutional religious-national statehood filled with symbols of sacred and secular Jewish-Israeli sovereignty.

The influence of this project on other municipalities that followed *Migdal ha-'Emeq*'s lead does not take the national-religious motifs into account. As Bourdieu (1984) notes, peripheral tensions should lead to the same changes in the central culture but are usually appropriated by being disentangled from their potential 'threat' to the mainstream. The Israeli public domain has embraced the presence of decorated utility boxes as were pioneered in *Migdal ha-'Emeq*, but the visual language that developed in that town remains 'a peripheral dialect'. *Migdal ha-'Emeq*, then, created a distinctive LL based on visual cultural signifiers: a Holy Ark in the Street.

Acknowledgements

This chapter is part of a research study conducted under my supervision in 2005/2006 with the participation of MA candidates in multidisciplinary graduate studies at Oranim College. I thank them for their important contribution, especially Esther Chen and Hila Mashali, who edited the findings.

Notes

1. On WWW at http://www.migdal-haemeq.muni.il. Accessed 1.1.09.
2. An acronym for the Talmud, adopted by and abbreviating the name of the party: Sephardi Torah Guardians or Torah Observant Sephardi Jews.
3. City Elect, the Center of Municipal Elections. On WWW at http://www.cityelect.org.il/Opening.asp. Accessed 20.5.09.
4. Interview with Itzik Rozilio, *Migdal ha-'Emeq*, 19 October 2005.
5. Rami Tayib had a slightly different version of who promoted the enterprise: 'I was one of the first to initiate the idea. I applied to the Migdal ha-'Emeq Municipality and they applied to a company that contacted me to launch the project. They [the Municipality] teamed me up with Sergei, who had studied art and was experienced and knowledgeable about it'. Interview with Rami Tayib, 20 May 2005.
6. Interview with Itzik Rozilio, 19 October 2005.
7. On WWW at www.jerusalem.muni.il/pages/jerusalem-Presentation2.ppt. Accessed 20.5.09.
8. In these neighborhoods, Shas, the ultra-Orthodox Sephardi party, had a majority and represented itself as a voice of the Mizrahim. See notes 3 and 4.
9. The seven-branched candelabrum from the Temple in Jerusalem, not to be confused with the eight-branched Hanukka menorah.
10. The JNF blue box. On WWW at http://www.kkl.org.il/kkl/english/main_subject/about_kkl/box/land%20in%20the%20box.x#tdTitle4. Accessed 10.8.09.
11. For further explanation of these styles, consult Shilo-Cohen (1982) and Arbel (1996).
12. Itzik Rozilio, interview 19 May 2005.
13. Itzik Rozilio, interview 19 May 2005.

References

Arbel, R. (1996) *Zionist Iconography 1897–1947*. Tel Aviv: Beth Hatefutsoth and Am Oved (in Hebrew).

Ben Zadok, E. (1993) Oriental Jews in the development towns: Ethnicity, economic development, budgets and politics. In E. Ben Zadok (ed.) *Local*

Communities and the Israeli Policy (pp. 91–123). New York: State University of New York Press.

Bourdieu, P. (1984 [2005]) *Questions of Sociology* (A. Lahav Hebrew trans.). Tel Aviv: Resling.

Chazak, H. (2003) Painting on electricity boxes. On WWW at ynet.co.il, July 17, 2008.

Dahan, Y. (2006) *Political Cultures in Development Towns.* Jerusalem: Floersheimer Studies, The Hebrew University of Jerusalem (in Hebrew).

De Certau, M. (1980) *The Practice of Everyday Life (1984)* (S. Rendall English trans.). Berkeley, CA: University of California Press.

Duncum, P. (2002) Visual culture art education: Why, what and how. *Journal of Art and Design Education* 21 (1), 15–22.

Efrat, Z. (2000) The plan. *Theory and Criticism* 16, 203–211 (in Hebrew).

Evans, J. and Hall, S. (1999) What is visual culture. In J. Evans and S. Hall (eds) *Visual Culture: A Reader* (pp. 1–8). London: Sage.

Israel Central Bureau of Statistics (2007) *Statistical Abstract of Israel.* Jerusalem: State of Israel.

Horowitz, N. (2000) Shas and Zionism: A historical analysis. *Kivunim Hadashim* 2, 30–60.

Jakobson, R. and Bogatyrev, P. (1971 [1986]) On the boundary between studies of folklore and literature. In G. Tori and I. Even-Zohar (eds) *I. Semiotics, Linguistics and Poetics* (pp. 276–284). Tel Aviv: Hakibbutz Hameuchad and Porter Institute, Tel Aviv University (in Hebrew).

Landry, R. and Bourhis, R. (1997) Linguistic landscape and ethnolinguistic vitality: An empirical study. *Journal of Language and Social Psychology* 16 (1), 23–49.

Lefebvre, H. (1974) *La Production de l'espace.* Paris: Editions Economica.

Mirzeoff, N. (1999) *An Introduction to Visual Culture.* London: Routledge.

Mishori, A. (2000) *Look Around and See: Icons and Zionist Visual Symbols in Israeli Culture.* Tel Aviv: Am Oved (in Hebrew).

Mitchell, W.J.T. (ed.) (1974) *The Language of Images.* Chicago, IL: University of Chicago Press.

Mitchell, W.J.T. (1986) *Iconology: Image, Text and Ideology.* Chicago, IL: University of Chicago Press.

Mitchell, W.J.T. (1994) *Picture Theory.* Chicago, IL: University of Chicago Press.

Pennycook, A. (2008) Linguistic landscape and the transgressive semiotic of the graffiti. In E. Shohamy and D. Gorter (eds) *Linguistic Landscape: Expanding the Scene* (pp. 302–312). London: Routledge.

Rogoff, I. (1998) Studying visual culture. In N. Mirzeoff (ed.) *The Visual Culture Reader* (pp. 24–37). London: Routledge.

Shilo-Cohen, N. (1982) *Bezalel of Shatz, 1906–1929.* Jerusalem: Israel Museum (in Hebrew).

Shohamy, E. and Gorter, D. (eds) (2008) *Linguistic Landscape: Expanding the Scene.* London: Routledge.

Slater, D. (1997) *Consumer Culture and Modernity.* London: Polity Press.

Tzfadia, E. (2004) Trapped sense of peripheral place in frontier space. In H. Yacobi (ed.) *Constructing a Sense of Place—Architecture and Zionist Discourse* (pp. 119–136). Cornwall: Ashgate Publishing Company.

Part 2
Top-down, Power and Reactions

Chapter 4

Decorating the City of Tel Aviv-Jaffa for its Centennial: Complementary Narratives via Linguistic Landscape

SHOSHI WAKSMAN and ELANA SHOHAMY

> April 2009 will mark the 100th anniversary of the city of Tel Aviv. The City will celebrate this milestone with worldwide events reflecting Tel Aviv's unique place in the history of the Jewish people, as the first Hebrew city established in more than 3,000 years. (http://www.telavivfoundation.org/Tel_Aviv_100.htm)

Introduction: Focus on the City

Multiple theories and perspectives have been put forward to define and theorize what Lefebvre (2003) termed the 'urban phenomenon' and its relationship to spaces such as nations, neighborhoods and countries. The 'global city' has gained much focus in recent years, referring to places anchored in other spaces 'beyond the nation'. One aspect relates to the constituency of the residents of global cities, consisting of diverse groups of 'others', often 'different' from those residing in the city in its early days. This refers to immigrants, refugees, asylum seekers and transnationals perceived as those who continuously change the homogenous nature of the city while importing 'foreign' cultures and turning the city into a heterogeneous entity. Hence, the city is perceived and interpreted as a place that does not reflect the 'original' nation. Sayings such as 'Berlin is not Germany' or 'New York is not the US' are often used in reference to cities, thus placing them in a complex relationship with global, national and local entities. Fenster and Yakobi refer to this phenomenon as:

> The social and demographic dimensions of the global economy change urban landscapes and at the same time contradict, and even "endanger" national ideologies. (but)... urban space, which is dynamic and socially produced, is also shaped by the daily experiences of those who are excluded, "illegal" and "transparent" in the city. (Fenster & Yakobi, 2005: 208)

57

In their view then, this change in the nature of the city should be taken into account while planning and designing cities. McQuire (2006: 1) refers to the phenomenon as 'relational spaces', implying that constant changes and belongings to multiple narratives and discourses 'demands new ways of thinking about how we might share space to constitute collective experience'.

The shaping and perceptions of cities are also influenced by the way policy makers decide to market the cities' identities. Avraham (2004) points to the various devices that policy-makers of cities employ in order to redefine them. He demonstrates how cities attempt to change their unfavorable identities and improve them, especially those that are marked as 'bad cities', using devices such as new names and logos, so to deliver counter-stereotypical messages.

Focus on Temporal Markers

Dates and other types of temporal markers provide special opportunities for remarking and rewriting cities along specific ideologies. Zerubavel (1981: 70) argues that 'Temporal arrangements are closely interlinked to group formation... it clearly contributes to the establishment of intergroup boundaries'. He also refers to different types of temporal arrangements and demonstrates the close connection that those arrangements have with group cohesion and solidarity. A related idea is expressed by McDonald and M'ethot (2006), who refer to the special meaning attributed to arbitrary points in time, such as anniversaries, centennials and jubilees. They show how people find something mystical about numbers, 'especially those that end with zeros' (McDonald & M'ethot, 2006: 307). It is the adoption of the decimal system, they argue, that has given importance to such dates. Thus, centennials, for example, are used as opportunities to foster and consolidate nationalism and/or remind residents of past achievements, particularly in the process of nation building. Thus, 'points in time' are often used for ideological purposes, such as redefining, perpetuating, re-educating, contesting and displaying unification and solidarity.

Another facet of temporal arrangements refers to the meaning attributed to specific points in time. According to Hatuka (2008) the 'moment', either arbitrary, initiated or caused by some traumatic event, might be marked and framed as a new imagined space via various devices, such as logos, signs, newspaper articles, advertisements and other types of decors. Thus, it is the shift of the 'moment' to a new imagined space that creates the illusion of a new order that is instrumental in the construction of a collective narrative (Lefebvre, 1984). One example of such a moment is the Twin Towers' destruction in New York in 2001, which interrupted the regular order and redefined a new symbolic space of imagined cohesive community (Greenspan, 2005). This new redefinition is often being imposed on the community. Yet, at the same time, it might invite or suggest responses that resist it and could thus create a 'third space' in which the dichotomy between the oppressor and the oppressed is blurred (Bhabha, 1994).

These multiple marks of the city of Tel Aviv-Jaffa in relation to its global, national and local identities in a specific point – its centennial – drew our attention and are the focus of this chapter.

Focus on Tel Aviv-Jaffa

As of April 2009, the city of Tel Aviv-Jaffa celebrated its centennial; the event was marked by various activities such as concerts, conferences, workshops, excursions, street shows, guided tours, exhibits and lectures displaying the city's history and various displays of past achievements. The event was also marked by new *decor* of the public space, which included signs, photographs, announcements, poems and a new logo.

Yet, at this point in time, a number of debates regarding the nature and perceived identity of the city emerged and were echoed in the media and in the public space. For example, the specific day chosen to mark the centennial, 9 April 1909, is a contested issue as there are those who claim that the establishment of the city should be marked when 66 Jewish families gathered on the sand dunes north of Jaffa to participate in a lottery to purchase plots to establish the new *Ahuzat Bayit* neighborhood. On the other hand, there are those who prefer to relate to 1867, when plots were purchased by Jews in the area of *Neve Tzedek* neighborhood. Related to that is the contested topic of Tel Aviv as a city that 'rose from the sands', reinforced by a familiar photograph (Figure 4.1) displaying the gathering of the buyers of the plots in the sandy area and thus pointing to the emptiness of the surrounding. The photograph portrays Tel Aviv as a 'new city' where the new settlers created 'something' out of 'nothing', detaching themselves from the past and symbolizing the emergence of the 'new Jew'. Yet, this very photograph is being contested by those who claim that it ignores the Arab villages that existed in the area at the time.

Moving along the Global-National-Local Continuum

The city of Tel Aviv has always been connected to international and global spaces, being a town near the seashore where a multitude of newcomers first arrived. This was captured by Akiva Weiss, one of the founders of the city, in 1906, regarding the aspiration of the city: 'In the same way that the city of New York is marked as the central gate to

Figure 4.1 The lottery on the dunes, 1909

America, so we ought to create our own city; it should turn into the New York of the land of Israel' (Azaryahu, 2005: 158).

Yet, at the same time, there was very strong pressure as well as active campaigns to market Tel Aviv as a city that symbolizes Zionist ideology and the revival of the Hebrew language, especially in its early years. It is in those very years that the Jewish and Hebrew identities were strongly enhanced, mostly in order to differentiate it from the neighboring cosmopolitan city of Jaffa, populated by Arabs and a vibrant commercial and cultural city on its own at the time. The active campaigns to ensure that Tel Aviv was designed and defined as a *Jewish* and *Hebrew* city inhabited by Jews only, included the extensive use of Jewish and Hebrew symbols in various public spaces. These included the selection of Jewish figures as names of streets, active campaigns to promote residents to speak Hebrew in public spaces while eliminating other languages, especially Yiddish and German (Gelber, 1990), and the creation of schools where Hebrew was the language of instruction.

Over the years, Tel Aviv developed into a big, modern and cosmopolitan urban center incorporating both national Jewish symbols as well as a global identity. According to Azaryahu (2005), it was after the establishment of the state of Israel in 1948 that a more international vision and ideologies were enhanced. He points to 1959, when Tel Aviv celebrated its Jubilee, as a marker of Tel Aviv as a modern and

cosmopolitan city (e.g. establishing the first supermarket and department store and the erection of a number of skyscrapers). At the end of
the 1980s, the slogan 'a city that never sleeps' was introduced to
indicate the city's energy and global flavor mostly in order to attract
visitors and tourists and associate it with pleasure and leisure. At
present, Tel Aviv is a city that includes both national and global
symbols, as can be deduced from various sources such as its bilingual,
Hebrew and English signs on most shops, street writings as well as the
names of buildings (Ben Rafael *et al.*, 2006). Yet, the current flavor often
meets criticism and controversies, especially in relation to its 'global
flavor', which is viewed by many as symbolizing distance and
detachment from the national Israeli ideology. Tel Aviv is often referred
to as a 'bubble', or 'the state of Tel Aviv', pointing to its alienation from
the main national Zionist ideology. Moreover, its liberal and open nature
in relation to other cities in Israel associate it with hedonism and
exclusion from the rest of the country. The local demography of the city
reveals great diversity, consisting of multiple groups of distinct 'others':
Jews of Middle Eastern origin, residing mostly in the south of the city; a
small minority of religious Jews and a growing number of foreign
workers, refugees and asylum seekers, residing mostly in rundown
neighborhoods of the city.

The main aspect of diversity is the relation with the Arab population
of Jaffa, as Tel Aviv is officially considered a 'mixed city', along with
Jaffa; 'Tel Aviv-Jaffa' is indeed the official name of the city. As noted
earlier, Tel Aviv emerged as a settlement for Jews outside the city of Arab
Jaffa and it was during the 1948 War of Independence and the
establishment of the state of Israel that Jaffa was conquered by the
Israeli military, resulting in a situation whereby most of its 70,000 Arab
residents left the city while 3,900 remained. By 1950, two years after the
establishment of the state of Israel, Jaffa was officially annexed by the city
of Tel Aviv and during the same year it was decided to change its name
to 'Tel Aviv-Jaffa', so that Jaffa became marginalized and was granted a
status of 'secondary' in relation to Tel Aviv. Thus, the city of Tel Aviv was
officially declared a 'mixed town' by the Ministry of Interior, along with
the status of seven other cities in Israel that are made up of both Jews and
Arabs (Monterescu & Rabinowitz, 2007). Demographically speaking, it
means that while the Arab population of the Tel Aviv part constitutes
4.3%, the Jaffa part consists of 25% Arabs, 80% of whom reside in one
neighborhood named 'Adjami'.

In *White City, Black City*, Rotbard (2005) demonstrates the hierarchy of
the two cities whereby Jaffa is referred to as 'the black city' – with its
neglected neighborhoods, low-income populations, low-achievement
schools, rundown infrastructure and services for its mostly Arab
population – in stark contrast to 'the white city' of Tel Aviv, which is

generally prosperous, developed and modern. Yet, while these two entities are run under one municipality, that of 'Tel Aviv-Jaffa', each of the entities is treated differently. Not surprisingly, the relationship between these two areas is interpreted as an act of appropriation, occupation and marginalization (Monterescu & Rabinowitz, 2007).

Linguistic Landscape

The display of languages in the public spaces of Tel Aviv-Jaffa reflects, to a large extent, many of the issues and debates mentioned above regarding the city's identity. During the early decades of the establishment of Tel Aviv, with its strong Zionist and Hebrew ideologies, fierce campaigns for the revival of Hebrew took place. There is ample evidence of militant organizations, such as the *Gdud Meginei Ha-Safa* (the Groups for the Defense of the Hebrew Language), employing aggressive and oppressive methods to ensure that Hebrew was displayed and used in public spaces and events (Segev, 1999; Shohamy, 2008). During the period of the British Mandate (1917–1948), the names of the streets in Jaffa were still in Arabic, following the official laws of the time of three languages – Arabic, the language of the Arab population; Hebrew, recognized as official by the British in 1923, and English as the language of the British authorities.

The official laws were changed once Israel gained its independence in 1948, when the official status of English was removed, while Hebrew and Arabic remained official, a situation that continues today. Yet, the official status of the two languages is not reflected in *de facto* practice, which is mostly Hebrew and English with only marginal representation of Arabic, even in Jaffa (Ben Rafael *et al.*, 2006). The only exceptions are the signs that resulted from the Supreme Court decision of 1999, which came about as a response to an appeal by *Adalah*, an activist Arab group, stipulating that Arabic should be included in all street signs of mixed towns in Israel (Trumper-Hecht, 2009; Shohamy, 2006). This brought about the inclusion of Arabic on certain street signs in the city, most often along with English and Hebrew. However, there is very little representation of Arabic in any other signs not included in the court decision, such as storefronts, names of buildings, public notices, etc. Another initiative to change the languages of the signs took place in 2004 when Zohar Shavit, a council member, requested that all store signs should include Hebrew, symbolizing a need to reinforce the value of the language as a symbol of national identity; a campaign that targeted mostly the dominance of English. While this request was approved by the city council, it has not been carefully implemented. Over the years, various patterns of the linguistic landscape (LL) emerged – in some periods signs were displayed in 'Hebrew only', at others these were accompanied by English and at others, Arabic was included on some street signs as well. As to street names, these primarily represent people and events closely associated with the Zionist history with very little mention of any others. Thus, the LL can provide an important indication of the authoritative identity of the city.

In sum, Tel Aviv consists of multiple identities – its 'global' identity places it with other global cities elsewhere; its 'national' Israeli identity is manifested in relation to the Zionist collective ideology of a home for the Jews. At the same time, its 'local' identity, consisting of many 'other' ethnic and social groups residing in the city, is marginalized. In the next part of the chapter, we will describe how these very identities are being manifested and negotiated during the centennial year.

The Study

In the period preceding the centennial celebrations and during the centennial year itself, massive planning of festive events and various operations took place. One of the main features was the reorganization of the city by decorating the public space with new writings and images. Thus, Tel Aviv-Jaffa dressed itself up with a new *decor* of the public space, which included texts, signs, photographs and sculptures intended to tell and retell the story of the city during its 100 years of existence. The focus of our data is on the collection of LL items within an expanded view, including not only written signs, but also a variety of multimodal text types of various genres, such as images, signs, poems and photographs (Shohamy & Waksman, 2009).

The data for the study were collected during the year preceding the centennial festivities as well as during the centennial year itself. The documentation took place in a number of central places: two main streets (*Ibn Gvirol* and *Dizengoff*), three main boulevards (*Rotchild, David Ha-Melech* and *Ben Gurion*) and four leisure and shopping areas (*Rabin Square*, the *Ha-Tayelet* promenade near the beach, the *Ha-Namal* area near the old port of Tel Aviv and *Basel Square*). The data collection yielded three sets of LL data: (1) designs and writings of street names, (2) displays of poems and other text types, and (3) displays of the private photograph collection.

Decorating the City from the Top Down

Design and writings of street names

The street signs in the city of Tel Aviv-Jaffa usually appear on the corner of each street in two types of layout: illuminated signs displayed on posts at the corner of the streets (Figure 4.2a) and signs posted on corner houses (Figure 4.2b).

Figure 4.2 (a) Illuminated corner sign; (b) design of sign in corner house

As noted, as a result of the 1999 Supreme Court decision, Arabic was added to the street signs at the corners of the streets. Yet, a gradual decision was made regarding the street signs, where at the center of the signs, between the Hebrew and the English transcripts, Hebrew texts were added. These texts provide a description of persons or events associated with the name of the street and they provide an explanation of the connection of the name of the street with an historical episode related to the city and/or some aspect of the state of Israel.

One case illustrating this is a street sign named 'Bracha Fuld', located at the center of Tel Aviv just by the *Rabin* Square. The sign describes the significant role that a woman named Bracha Fuld played as a heroine who died in 1946 in an operation against the British soldiers during the Mandate years. The text is quite elaborate for such a short passage and includes the affiliation of Bracha Fuld with the

Palmach (the Jewish underground military organization that operated prior to the establishment of the state), the coined name of the event in which she died ('the night of Wingate') and mention of different types of dates – the year of her birth and the year of her death according to both Jewish and Christian calendar systems. The information provides the reader with ample details of evidence of her participation and sacrifice for nation building.

This same pattern can be observed on a large number of signs around the city; in each case, the person whose name is used to mark the name of the street is being connected and associated with some elements in Jewish and/or Israeli history. Thus, all signs foreground these historical aspects, either ancient or modern, while specific traits of the person herself/himself are either marginalized or ignored. Interestingly, this relates also to people who are not Jewish, as can be seen in Figure 4.3, a street named after George the VI, the King of England. The description of King George in Hebrew marks the fact that 'in his days the Balfour declaration was written', referring specifically to the event when the British government supported the establishment of a homeland for the Jews in Palestine in 1917.

Figure 4.3 The street sign of King George

The display of the Hebrew calendar system appears on almost all signs and is thus in line with Zerubavel's (1981) claim that calendar systems represent a means to sustain and form group cohesion and belonging. The choice of the Hebrew calendar system can be considered a method of appropriating the non-Jewish personas by 'placing' him/her in Jewish history along with other Jewish markers.

The analysis of these signs provides evidence of how the design of street names and texts are used to create connections of the city to Zionist ideology and history. Thus, Tel Aviv is being connected to its Zionist heritage by the use of 'Hebrew only' in the supplementary texts that accompany the names of the streets. They include the use of concepts, words, events, dates and the display of the Jewish calendar anchored in Jewish history and nation building.

The facets just described gain special meaning when these signs are placed in close proximity to the illuminated signs (Figure 4.2a), where the name of the street in Arabic transliteration was added to the Hebrew and English, as per the Supreme Court decision; these other signs, in Hebrew and English, can also be interpreted as a 'response' to this decision.

Displaying poems and other text types

Additional sources of the centennial landscape consist of text types that are displayed in central places in the city, such as poems, historical anecdotes and sayings accompanied by historical photographs and drawings. Poems and songs have always been part of consolidation processes of collective identity in Israeli society, portraying themes such as hard labor associated with nation building (Azaryahu, 1995). One example is the poem 'Shir HaNamal' (Song of the Port, Figure 4.4a) displayed in the port area of Tel Aviv, built in the 1930s and symbolizing the commitment of the new city to the creation of an independent economic and political entity outside the Jaffa port. The Hebrew poem describes the hard work invested in building the port so that the territory of the port is being appropriated and 'conquered' with hard labor. Another example is the Hebrew poem 'The White City', displayed in *Rotchild* Boulevard, pointing to a mythology of Tel Aviv emerging 'from the foam of waves and from the clouds'.

The LL of Tel Aviv is also manifested through historical accounts displayed in various places, which include different types of short texts accompanied by historical photographs, scattered in various locations around the city. One such example is the sign displayed at the entrance to a large parking lot in *Basel* square, which includes a text about the location of the first Zionist conference in 1897 (Figure 4.4b).

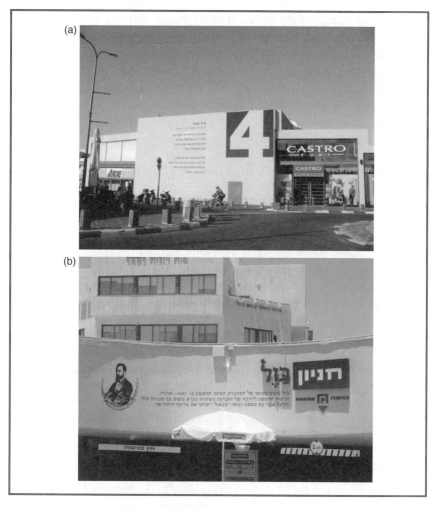

Figure 4.4 (a) The poem *Shir HaNamal*; (b) reference to Herzl and the first Zionist conference

The Hebrew description refers to Basel as the city where the first Zionist conference took place. The text ends with the saying of Theodor Herzl (the visionary of Zionism) displayed in Hebrew. It reads: 'In Basel I founded the Jewish state', accompanied by his portrait as the visual icon of Zionism.

One additional example is the new logo of the city of Tel Aviv as part of the centennial celebration and its inclusion on all documents, from posters to public announcements to city tax forms, to storefronts and buildings.

Displays of the private photograph collection

Another source of LL data designed specifically for the centennial, originated by the municipality of Tel Aviv is the project entitled Revealing the Hidden City (http://www.tlv100.co.il/EN/Events/Pages/RevealingtheHiddenCity.aspx). At the beginning of the year, the municipality requested that residents donate photographs associated with the city's history, found in their personal albums. The selected photographs were displayed in shop windows, bus stations, leisure centers, shopping areas and community centers. The themes of these photographs included scenes from the everyday lives of people such as small children and babies in their daily routines, taking baths, playing with toys, wedding parties, holiday activities and school ceremonies. Included in these pictures were scenes from the history of the city, famous buildings and houses of the early days of Tel Aviv. These private photographs are being appropriated into the collective memory of the city so that the very act of collecting and displaying the photographs under the heading of the 'centennial of the city' can be interpreted as a means of recruiting private 'faces', resources and memories to the collective meaning attributed to the city's centennial.

In conclusion, the texts displayed in the public spaces of the city are anchored in Zionist history. The visibility of such genres in public spaces, the choice of Hebrew only, the themes depicted and the frequent use of the Jewish calendar, aim to mark Tel Aviv as inherent in the national ideology while minimizing its global and local natures and overlooking its demographic diversity, portraying it in very homogenous colors.

Contestation: Talking Back

The centennial authoritative LL just described originated primarily by the municipality of the city; yet, it activated alternative voices that turned the LL into an arena of contestation and negotiation, as could be expected given its wide visibility, attention and displays in the public spaces of streets, media and on the internet. Data of these alternative narratives have been found in street signs, graffiti, 'talk-backs' over the internet and in newspapers. There were also reactions to the global-national-local dimensions, specifically as to the lack of representation and exclusion of other groups residing in the city, such as immigrants, foreign workers, 'green' groups, immigrants residing in the southern part of the city and Arabs residing in Jaffa; in fact, Jaffa was almost totally absent from the celebrations. These signs of resistance displayed around the city included writings such as: '...and who is not included in the party'; there were ample internet 'talk-backs' in reaction to media articles describing the festivities as belonging to a very defined bourgeois groups and leaving many others behind.

The most dominant contestation originated by the *Zochrot* ('remembering' in Hebrew) group, consisting of activists whose main agenda is to highlight the Palestinian historical narratives in the area. The actions of the group consists of designing maps of the city of Tel Aviv marking the Palestinian villages that used to exist in this very area at the time of the British Mandate and long before the establishment of the state of Israel and the city of Tel Aviv (Figure 4.5a). These maps rewrite the map of Tel Aviv as a city built in the place where other people used to live. The map is accompanied by texts that read: 'The city of Tel Aviv was built in the area of eight Palestinian villages; their names are absent from travel-guides and city signs do not show how to reach them. This map challenges readers to rethink the landscape of their city'. The map appears in various flyers and is displayed on their website (http://www.zochrot.org). Some of this information is also part of new history textbooks written by the group and offered to the educational system. The map and the texts that accompany the books challenge the notion of Tel Aviv as a city that 'rose from the sands'. In this way, they attempt to replace the current image with the notion of a city that 'deleted' the lives and existence of others and is deleting them from the physical space and from displayed representations. This message is reinforced by guided tours organized by the group on various occasions, including one for the centennial as well as at exhibitions, public talks and museums.

Other contestation and optional rewriting of the city's history can be observed in various installations and art works. For example, in July 2009, in the leisure space near the old port of Tel Aviv, an exhibition by another activist group called *Parrhesia* (public space in Hebrew) initiated the art exhibition *kama yagib* (which is the Arabic translation for this commercial space called *comme il faut*). In this exhibition there was a 'graffiti dictionary' sprayed on the walls that consisted of words in two of Israel's official languages – Hebrew and Arabic. The displayed words are part of the conflicted vocabulary such as the word 'return' referring to the 'right of return' of Palestinian refugees to their old homes in Israel. This exhibition is aimed at contesting the deletion of the Arabic language, history and Palestinian narrative from the public space. This event is joined with previous activities, such as the installation called *Hassan Beck Street on the corner of Abu Lughud*, where the streets names of what used to be the Arab *Manshia* quarter were rewritten on the green lawns of the current *Charles Clore* Park, thus creating an act of reminding the public that the Arab neighborhood was replaced by a park and a nearby military museum (http://www.jaffaproject.org/events).

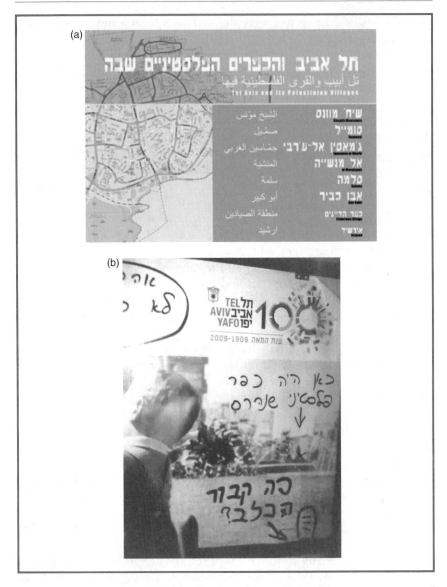

Figure 4.5 (a) Map designed by *Zochrot*; (b) graffiti writing over a poster of the photograph collection

Other types of alternative narratives include graffiti writings around the city depicting words and ideas that contest the deletion of its past. Figure 4.5b depicts an example of graffiti written over one of the photographs displayed near the campus of Tel Aviv University where one of the Palestinian villages used to exist. This graffiti reads: 'Here once existed a Palestinian village that has been destroyed'.

Conclusions

The LL writing and designs displayed by the municipality of the city for its centennial foregrounds LL resources related primarily to the national Zionist history and ideologies via different designs such as street signs, text types and images. Most of these texts are anchored in national identity where Tel Aviv is presented as a central 'actor', agent and symbol in the process of nation building. The use of Hebrew in all these signs accompanied by Jewish and Zionist lexical items and the use of the Jewish calendar, mark the city as an integral part of the national space. In this context, even the 'private' faces and scenes 'revealed' through the displayed photographs can be interpreted as recruiting private acts, images and memories into the collective 'repacking', reframing and marketing of the city through its belonging to the national space. These themes and topics are in stark difference to the dominant image of Tel Aviv as described in the media, common discourse and tourist guidebooks of a city 'of its own', as the Mediterranean 'New York', with its unique character that can be integrated and connected to other global cities sharing common characteristics, and detached from national agendas. It is via these different types of LL that such patterns and directions can be observed as tools attempting to change, redefine and construct new ones.

This new LL design can also be interpreted as a means of differentiating among various audiences (Shohamy & Waksman, 2010), those who belong to the official voice and others who are either excluded or even ignored by it; somehow in the LL of this diverse city there is no mention of the 'others'. It is interesting to note that in some cities in the world, those others are a source of pride where diversity is welcomed. Yet, in Tel Aviv and in Israel in general, 'otherness' of non-Jews is not accepted or welcomed since it 'interrupts' the notion of a homogenous 'Jewish' state. This notion is also in contrast to current views of cities as places that are being promoted as 'just' places that offer a truer representation of 'otherness', especially within global cities. This notion is strongly advocated by Fenster and Yakobi (2005: 209), who claim that 'Urban planning and management... requires the development of different conceptual tools that will bridge over the different perceptions and knowledge of urban places and spaces' and thus incorporate 'the multilayered identities of the residents of globalized cities'.

As Coulmas (2009) notes, it is this display of explicit and visible authoritative narratives via the LL that creates contested and negotiable spaces that are instrumental in differentiating between those who 'belong' and the others. In a way, this mono vocal nature of the new *decor* invites all groups to react and for their voices to be heard. Coulmas (2009: 14) refers to the writings in public spaces as: 'It is a genie let out of the bottle. In the long run it cannot be controlled'. In our case, the explicit design of Tel Aviv's narrative 'invites' other voices to gain access to the public sphere through other spaces and genres like cyber space, walking tours, art works and graffiti. All those voices craft another type of geography and history of a city that deprives, deletes and destroys those who do not fit into the authoritative narrative. Thus, the framework of this chapter takes into account the role played by the LL of a city in promoting and creating an ecology that is not neutral, but rather is used as an activist space where multiple narratives can be heard, discussed and negotiated in dynamic ways. Further discussions of these other voices are echoed in Shohamy and Waksman (2010).

References

Avraham, E. (2004) Media strategies for improving an unfavorable city image. *Cities* 21 (6), 471–479.

Azaryahu, M. (1995) *State Cults, Celebrating Independence and Commemorating the Fallen in Israel 1948–1956*. Beer Sheba: Ben Gurion University Press (in Hebrew).

Azaryahu, M. (2005) *Tel Aviv – The Real City*. Beer Sheba: Ben Gurion University Press (in Hebrew).

Ben Rafael, E., Shohamy, E., Amara, M.H. and Trumper-Hecht, N. (2006) Linguistic landscape as symbolic construction of the public space: The case of Israel. *International Journal of Multilingualism* 3 (1), 7–31.

Bhabha, H.K. (1994) *The Location of Culture*. London: Routledge.

Coulmas, F. (2009) Linguistic landscaping and the seed of the public sphere. In E. Shohamy and D. Gorter (eds) *Linguistic Landscape Expanding the Scenery* (pp. 13–24). New York and London: Routledge.

Fenster, T. and Yakobi, H. (2005) Whose city is it? On urban planning and local knowledge in globalizing Tel Aviv Jaffa. *Planning Theory & Practice* 6 (2), 191–211.

Gelber, Y. (1990) *A New Homeland – The Immigration from Central Europe and its Absorption in Eretz Israel 1933–1948*. Jerusalem: Leo Baeck Institute and Yad Izhak Ben-Zvi (in Hebrew).

Greenspan, E. (2005) A global site of heritage? Constructing spaces of memory at the World Trade Center site. *International Journal of Heritage Studies* 11 (5), 371–384.

Hatuka, T. (2008) *Revisionist Moments Political Violence, Architecture and Urban Space in Tel Aviv*. Tel Aviv: Resling (in Hebrew).

Lefebvre, H. (1984) *Everyday Life in the Modern World*. London: Transaction Publishers.

Lefebvre, H. (2003) *The Urban Revolution*. Minneapolis and London: University of Minnesota Press.

McDonald, T. and M'ethot, M. (2006) That impulse that bids people to honour its past: The nature and purpose of Centennial Celebrations. *International Journal of Heritage Studies* 12 (4), 307–320.

McQuire, S. (2006) The politics of public space in the media city. On WWW at http://firstmonday.org/htbin/cgiwrap/bin/ojs/index.php/fm/article/view/1544/1459. Accessed 9.9.09.

Monterescu, D. and Rabinnowitz, D. (eds) (1994) *Mixed Towns/Trapped Communities: Historical Narratives, Spatial Dynamics and Gender Relations in Jewish-Arab Mixed Towns in Israel/Palestine.* London: Ashgate.

Rotbard, S. (2005) *White City Black City.* Tel Aviv: Babel Publishing House (in Hebrew).

Segev, T. (1999) *Palestine Under the British.* Jerusalem: Keter Publishing House (in Hebrew).

Shohamy, E. (2006) *Language Policy: Hidden Agenda and New Approaches.* London: Routledge.

Shohamy, E. (2008) At what cost? Methods of language revival and protection: Examples from Hebrew. In K. King, N. Schilling-Estes, L. Fogle, J. Lou and B. Soukup (eds) *Sustaining Linguistic Diversity: Endangered and Minority Languages and Language Varieties* (pp. 205–218). Washington, DC: Georgetown University Press.

Shohamy, E. and Waksman, S. (2009) Linguistic landscape as an ecological arena: Modalities, meanings, negotiations, education. In E. Shohamy and D. Gorter (eds) *Linguistic Landscape: Expanding the Scenery* (pp. 313–331). New York and London: Routledge.

Shohamy, E. and Waksman, S. (2010) Building the nation, writing the past: History and textuality at the Ha'apala memorial in Tel Aviv-Jaffa. In A. Jaworski and C. Thurlow (eds) *Semiotic Landscapes: Language, Image, Space* (pp. 241–255). London: Continuum.

Trumper-Hecht, N. (2009) Constructing national identity in mixed cities in Israel: Arabic on signs in the public space of Upper Nazareth. In E. Shohamy and D. Gorter (eds) *Linguistic Landscape: Expanding the Scenery* (pp. 238–252). New York and London: Routledge.

Zerubavel, E. (1981) *Hidden Rhythms: Schedules and Calendars in Social Life.* Chicago, IL: University of Chicago Press.

Zochrot, retrieved from http://www.nakbainhebrew.org/index.php?lang=english/

Chapter 5

Bloemfontein/Mangaung, 'City on the Move'. Language Management and Transformation of a Non-representative Linguistic Landscape

THEODORUS DU PLESSIS

Introduction

A change in regime can bring about a change in the linguistic landscape (LL). The LL then becomes one of the most 'vocal' and concrete indicators of consequential language regime change. As Backhaus (2005: 104) indicates, the LL plays an important role in any study of the transformation of a language regime.

South Africa moved from a language dispensation in 1910 (with the establishment of the first unified state) where English and Afrikaans enjoyed official status at the national level, to a dispensation in 1961 (with independence from Britain) where nine African languages received official status in the Bantustan territories and then to a policy whereby all eleven of these languages could enjoy equal official status. Thus, since 1994, the country has no longer been officially 'bilingual' (1910–1994), where bilingualism is defined in terms of competency in English and Afrikaans, but officially multilingual. In terms hereof bilingualism is still a minimum requirement, but no longer defined, and multilingualism is cherished as an overall ideal. Further, no longer does the principle of 'equal treatment' of official languages apply (1910–1994), but instead there is a rather complex set of language treatment norms, e.g. 'parity of esteem' and 'equitable treatment' (cf. RSA, 1996).

These changes in the language regime are significant and it stands to reason that the LL will not be left unchanged. A feature of the pre-1994 English/Afrikaans official bilingualism was its strong correspondence with the equally bilingual LL. If it is to be consistent, the post-1994 LL needs therefore to signal the change from a strictly defined bilingual public space to a 'not-so-well-defined' bilingual or multilingual one.

In comparison to other prominent cities and towns in South Africa (cf. Jenkins, 2007: 133ff.), relatively few LL changes have been recorded since 1994 in Bloemfontein (cf. Loftus, 2008), South Africa's most central city. As a historically 'Afrikaans' city, one would have expected Bloemfontein to be at least targeted for name changing (of street names, especially), a popular mechanism of transformation in South Africa. The case of language visibility in respect of utilities accounts would bear out such an expectancy. Mangaung Local Municipality (MLM), of which the city of Bloemfontein forms part, elicited attention with a controversial decision taken during 1999 henceforth to print municipal accounts for services in English only, as opposed to the previous policy of English/ Afrikaans bilingual accounts (cf. Venter, 2007: 145–146). This decision raised questions about the MLM's approach to the new multilingual reality in terms of which additional languages were now declared official. The accounts saga suggested that the MLM was following the route of other governmental agencies and urban centres and opting for English as the primary medium of communication (cf. Giliomee, 2003), even in the public space.

In this chapter, we will investigate language policy development in the MLM after 1994, specifically in relation to the LL. Our intention is to establish whether this municipality considers the Anglicisation of the LL as a major step in transforming the bilingual LL from the pre-1994 era to a LL that can 'speak' to all its citizens.

Bloemfontein after 1994

Since space does not allow for a detailed overview of the history of the city of Bloemfontein, suffice it to remark that different political dispensations since the city's establishment in 1846 (cf. Schoeman, 1980: 1) have resulted in changes to the city's language regime (Table 5.1).

Early LL features, such as names on important buildings, have been captured in old photographs taken around the city centre between 1860 and 1910 (cf. Schoeman, 1987). These photographs reflect the dominance of English in both top-down and bottom-up signs. Dutch signs are not prominent and neither are Afrikaans signs.

The establishment of the first democratically elected government in South Africa in 1994 set in motion a process of socio-political transformation that continues to impact every aspect of South African life. One of the immediate challenges as far as local government is concerned and that has had a significant impact on Bloemfontein has been the integration of the former racially separated structures. The *Local Government Transition Act* (LGTA) of 1993 (RSA, 1993) initiated the establishment of Local Transitional Councils (TLCs), which were elected largely on a proportional basis in a way that recognised minorities (cf. Pycroft, 1996: 238). The final phase of restructuring was initiated hereafter through the *White Paper on Local Government* (RSA, 1998) that

Table 5.1 Different language regimes of Bloemfontein up to 1994

Period	Language era	Languages
British protectorate (1846–1854)	Monolingual era	English
Boer Republic (1854–1900)	Bilingual era	*English*/Dutch
Anglo-Boer War (1900–1907)	Monolingual era	English
Pre-unification (1907–1910)	Bilingual era	*English*/Dutch
Union of South Africa (1910–1948)	Bilingual era	*English*/Dutch > Afrikaans
Republic of South Africa (1948–1994)[1]	Bilingual era	*Afrikaans*/English

Note: Dominant languages in language combinations have been italicised
[1] So-called apartheid era.

was published in 1998. The *White Paper* resulted in six different acts dealing with local government (cf. Van Donk & Pieterse, 2006: 114), of which the *Local Government Municipal Systems Act* (RSA, 2000) is the most important. With the municipal elections of 2000, the transformation of local government in South Africa into a sphere of authority that represented and served all citizens on an equitable basis was drawn to a conclusion. From this date onwards, the TLCs were replaced by Local Municipalities.

As with other political changes in the history of Bloemfontein, the restructuring of local government after 1994 again impacted on the language dispensation of the city. Local government was transformed almost overnight by the amalgamation of three former 'white' municipalities (Bloemfontein City Council, Bloemspruit Local Authority, Bainsvlei Local Authority), and four former 'non-white' municipalities (the coloured Heidedal Management Committee, Mangaung Black Local Authority, Thaba Nchu Town Council and Botshabelo Black Local Authority). Thus, a new multiracial municipality came into being, erasing the 'apartheid city' of Bloemfontein (Krige, 1988: 161). Bloemfontein became the seat of an enlarged local government authority, representing a much more diversified population. Of the 645,437 inhabitants of the MLM, the majority are black (82.8%). The other population groups (white, coloured and Asian) are clearly minorities. Another important demographic feature is that more than half of the inhabitants of the MLM (389,828) live in Bloemfontein. The racial composition of the 'new' Bloemfontein effectively corrects its apartheid image.

Although most of the 11 official languages are spoken by the inhabitants of the MLM, three African languages are prominent home

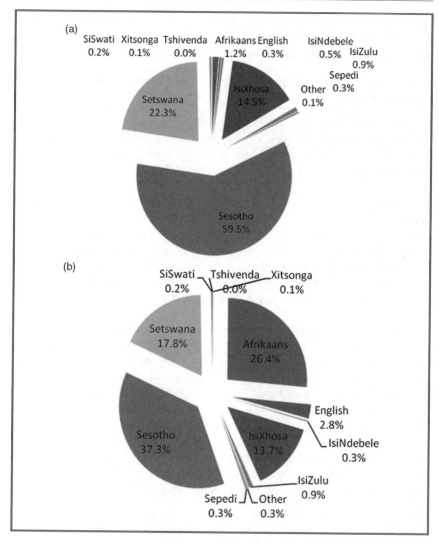

Figure 5.1 (a) Language spread of the MLM (Census 2001); (b) language spread of the city of Bloemfontein (Census 2001)

languages, Sesotho (59.5%), Setswana (22.3%) and IsiXhosa (14.5%) (cf. Figure 5.1a). English is the home language of a very small minority. Its spread as the most common second language is not reflected. The language spread of the city of Bloemfontein, on the other hand, reflects a relatively more even spread. As can be seen in Figure 5.1b, Sesotho remains the largest language, but Afrikaans is more prominent owing to the historic origins of the city.

The rather insignificant presence of English speakers in Bloemfontein is most striking in comparison to the alleged widespread use of English as the second language (cf. Pelser & Botes, 2002: 56).

Language Policy and Planning for Local Government in South Africa

Since 1994, language policy in South Africa has been managed at national, provincial and local government level and informed by section 6 of the constitution (cf. RSA, 1996). Language management is further informed by the National Language Policy Framework (NLPF) (DAC, 2002).

Section 6 of the constitution makes a distinction between the role of national government and the nine provincial governments on the one hand, and local government on the other. National and provincial governments are required to function in at least two official languages (section 6(3)(a)), but are to elevate the status and extend the use of the previously marginalised languages (section 6(2)). Official languages are to be managed by means of a language policy (see section 6(4) and Schedule 4).

Local government, on the other hand, does not seem to have a similar constitutional mandate. It is merely required to 'take into account the language usage and preferences' of the residents (section 6(3)(b)). The second part of Schedule 4 lists local government competencies. Notably, language policy is not listed here. Furthermore, Schedule 5 of the constitution includes a section on the exclusive functions of local government. Language policy is also not listed here.

The *Local Government Municipal Systems Act* (RSA, 2000) further strengthens the constitutional mandate of local government and links the constitutional mandate to a specific area of application, i.e. providing information and also taking into account:

(1)   Language preferences and usage in the municipality.
(2)   The special needs of people who cannot read or write.

Section 21 actually compels local government authorities to 'determine official languages' and ensure that public notifications 'must be in the official languages determined by the council, having regard to language preferences and usage within its area'. In terms of this provision, official languages are determined on the basis of the constitutional directives.

All government structures are also subject to the provisions of the NLPF (section 2.4.1). Section 2.4.3 specifically instructs local government regarding language policy:

Local governments will determine the language use and preferences of their communities within an enabling provincial language policy framework. Upon determination of the language use and preference of communities, local governments must, in broad consultation with their communities, develop, publicise and implement a multilingual policy. (DAC, 2002: 12)

Language Policy and Planning in the Mangaung Local Municipality

Overt local government language policy before 1994 was largely informed by the overall national policy of official bilingualism (English/ Afrikaans) in all areas, except for the former Bantustan areas where additional indigenous official languages were recognised. According to Joubert (2008) *de facto* policy favoured the two primary official languages: Afrikaans in the former white and coloured areas, and English in the former black areas – a clear racial divide in sociolinguistic terms.

According to Joubert (2008), 1994 ushered in a totally new language regime. The language issue was at the forefront of the amalgamation of the different local authorities that made up the MLM. He ascribes this partly to the complete change in the language profile of the amalgamating entities 'from overall Afrikaans speaking to overall non-Afrikaans speaking'. The pre-1994 language policies of the different local authorities were largely continued. Internally, the use of all post-1994 official languages was tolerated. Inputs at meetings were 'summarised', many times by the chairperson. No interpreters were made available, which led to the practice that the chairperson of the meeting took it upon himself/ herself to 'interpret' contributions in a language other than English, assuming of course superior knowledge of all the languages of the meeting. In reality, however, English soon became the *lingua franca* of the amalgamating structures.

The MLM language policy provides for three official 'municipal' languages, Sesotho, Afrikaans and English. Provision is made for two further 'administrative' languages, Setswana and IsiXhosa, to be used under special circumstances, but not as official languages. The policy foresees the equitable use of the three municipal languages, even for internal use. Records of official municipal meetings, however, should always include a summary in English. Significantly, the policy also includes a section on 'identification signs', an attempt at regulating the LL (cf. MLM, 2003). The language policy and implementation plan were approved by Council on 27 November 2003 and duly published in the Provincial Gazette in 2004 (cf. MLM, 2008: 3–5).

By 2004, the stage was set for significant changes regarding language visibility and the urban public space of Bloemfontein. Not only had the city's racial and language composition changed from a predominantly white and Afrikaans city to a predominantly multicultural and multilingual city, but the language policy of the city had also changed. Instead of requiring equal treatment for two official languages, the MLM language policy now required the use of three official languages. The LL would become the foremost space where the new official language dispensation would be displayed publicly.

Regulating the Linguistic Landscape of Bloemfontein

Visitors to Bloemfontein will be struck by the difference between official (top-down) public signs and non-official (bottom-up) public signs, not only in terms of volume (non-official signs by far outnumber official signs), but specifically the level of standardisation. Official signs are public signs that the municipality has to erect. Hence, they appear to be more 'organised' and systematic.

Altogether three sets of legislation are particularly relevant for Bloemfontein's LL, namely, the *South African Manual for Outdoor Advertising Control* (DEAT & DoT, 1998), the *South African Roads Traffic Signs Manual* (DoT, 1999) and the *Mangaung Municipal Language Policy* (MLM, 2003, as amended, 2004). Once finalised, the *Policy and Procedural Guidelines for the Naming and Renaming of Geographical Features* (MLM, 2005a), will also play a role.

South African Manual for Outdoor Advertising Control

The *South African Manual for Outdoor Advertising Control* (DEAT & DoT, 1998) is a national manual that broadly covers all signs visible from public roads and streets. Consequently, the concept of 'advertising' is described in broad terms. Even the display of street and suburb names is included (DEAT & DoT, 1998: 5–6, 55). However, the manual contains no stipulations on the linguistic profile of these signs or the language requirements of geographical names. The manual largely applies to signs erected by non-municipal institutions, primarily regulating bottom-up signs while refraining from giving directives regarding language use other than on the avoidance of profanity.

Based on the *South African Manual for Outdoor Advertising Control*, the MLM's *Outdoor Advertising Control Policy* (MLM, 2008) also contains no provisions on language.

South African Roads Traffic Signs Manual

The *South African Roads Traffic Signs Manual* (DoT, 1999) is also a national manual that regulates road traffic signs at national, provincial and local government levels. This manual requires road signs to be in harmony with the *Southern African Development Community Road Traffic Signs Manual* (DoT, 1997), contributing to predominantly English road traffic signs. The display of geographical names is to be done in accordance with the approved names lists of mandated authorities. Road traffic signs in the MLM area are regulated in terms of this manual (cf. Loftus, 2008).

It is notable that both national manuals do not seem to be aligned with the national language policy requiring state institutions to function in at least two official languages. This requirement could be interpreted as a form of official bilingualism, albeit one where bilingualism is not prescribed in strict terms (as before 1994). Cowling (2003: 109) therefore sees it as a qualitative rather than a quantitative requirement, but nevertheless argues 'that bilingualism is the bottom line in any language dispensation in South Africa as a whole or any part of it' (Cowling, 2003: 84). For Cowling (2003: 88), the essential difference with the past is the move 'from colonial bilingualism to representative multilingualism'. In the next section, I will elaborate on the way that the MLM deals with this minimum requirement.

Mangaung Municipal Language Policy

The *Mangaung Municipal Language Policy* includes a section on 'identification signs'. This particular section reads as follows:

Identification signs

(1) If an institution of the Municipality identifies any of its offices or facilities by way of sign boards, or if it can reasonably be expected of the relevant institution to do so, such sign boards, as well as street names and directions, shall be displayed in at least two of the municipal languages, and the administrative languages, in accordance with the language preferences of the specific community concerned.

(2) At least two municipal languages shall be used in identifying municipal assets and vehicles.

(3) Where required administrative languages shall also be used in identifying municipal assets and vehicles.

This provision deals with public signs that the MLM itself produces or has direct jurisdiction over. Bilingual visibility is required, a provision that does not seem to support the MLM's trilingual policy. Another weakness of the MLM policy on language visibility is the confusing requirement regarding the display of administrative languages.

A follow-up circular to municipal officials by the City Manager rectifies the above anomaly. The circular, entitled *Compliance with the Municipal Language Policy: Signage and notices placed at municipal buildings* (MLM, 2005b), requests 'full compliance' with the MLM language policy. It specifically instructs officials to take steps 'to ensure that parity of esteem is accorded to all three municipal languages' and to 'elevate the status and advance the use of all three municipal languages' on notice boards. Incidentally, the circular was necessitated after complaints about the 'absence of visible language signs'.

The MLM's 'signage' policy addresses language visibility on three types of public signs:

- Signs on municipal property or municipal signs (in and around municipal buildings, on vehicles, etc.).
- Street name signs.
- Direction signs (including tourist signs – cf. Anonymous, 2007).[1]

Language visibility on *municipal signs* is, according to Mahoko (2008), the responsibility of the originator of the sign who has to comply with the MLM's language policy. However, Mahoko concedes that despite the clear trilingual policy, a tendency does exist towards English signs, as the circular discussed above indeed confirms. Apparently, this tendency can be ascribed to an earlier decision by the MLM Council to replace Afrikaans as the language of business of the MLM with English. No evidence for such decision could be provided.

Language visibility on *street name signs* used to be the responsibility of the now defunct Street Names Committee. This committee functioned as an advisory committee on street names to the previous city council, but became dysfunctional during the amalgamation of local government structures (cf. Loftus, 2008). According to Loftus (2008), in the absence of such a committee, the responsibility currently falls on the urban development agency operating in a certain area. However, at this stage no attention is being given to unnamed streets, negatively affecting informal settlement areas. A proposal for a new policy on geographical names (cf. MLM, 2005a) has not yet been approved. According to Mothekhe and Matiase (2008), the Council has decided to re-establish its Street Names Committee, but has not done so yet.

Language visibility on *direction signs* is the responsibility of the Traffic section, subject to the *South African Roads Traffic Signs Manual* (cf. Anonymous, 2007). Tourist signs fall partly under Environmental Management (cf. Naidoo & Shakwane, 2008) and partly under Communications (cf. Khedama, 2008). According to Khedama (2008), a Communication Task Team has been established to improve liaison between the different sections mentioned above. However, no meetings have taken place since May 2008. According to Mothekhe and Matiase (2008), this may be ascribed to instability within the Municipality as a result of political infighting in the ruling party.

We have seen that language visibility on public signs in the urban space of Bloemfontein is regulated by a variety of policies. These policies are not always aligned, nor do they necessarily correlate to the official bilingualism of the South African constitution. Also, a variety of municipal role players are responsible for regulating the different categories of signs under their jurisdiction. This leads to a lack in consistency regarding the realisation of the MLM's language requirements for public signs.

Changing Language Visibility in Bloemfontein

Given the language policy context outlined above, we will now turn to describing a number of examples of changes in the LL of Bloemfontein since 1994 within the three categories of signs under the jurisdiction of the MLM. They are municipal signs, street name signs and direction signs.

Changes in municipal signs

Samples of municipal signs were gathered at the ground level of the MLM head office in Bloemfontein city centre, officially named 'Bram Fischer Building'. As a bilingual (Afrikaans/English) official plaque inside the foyer indicates, the building was inaugurated in 1992. The ground level was chosen as this is the area where all citizens have to enter in order to do their business with the municipality. This is also the area where the information desk is situated.

All permanent as well as non-permanent signs at the ground level of the building were photographed on two occasions, 6 November and 8 December 2008. A second recording was required as some signs had been overlooked during the first encounter. Altogether 58 separate signs were identified during these photographic sessions. (A separate sign is taken as a sign that 'stands' on its own.)

The majority of the recorded signs are 'new' signs (44) originating after 1994. Standardised 'old signs' were affixed at the completion of the building and are identifiable by their unique bilingual formatting, in accordance with the pre-1994 policy. Less than a quarter (14) of the current signs are 'old' signs. The collected signs have been categorised as name signs (signs displaying the building name), directional signs (leading to specific locations), information signs (i.e. information on office hours, etc.), labels (for different counters), municipal adverts, notices (on meetings, gatherings, etc.), plaques (a unique permanent sign affixed to buildings and conveying information on the inauguration of the building, usually a copper mould) and warning signs (not to smoke, what not to bring into the building, etc.). The majority of the 'old' signs are information signs.

As Table 5.2 indicates, most of the former bilingual signs are information signs. No monolingual or trilingual signs from the pre-1994 era could be found at the ground level of the Bram Fischer Building. In comparison, the public signs from the post-1994 era show a much larger degree of variation in terms of their sociolinguistic profile (cf. Table 5.2).

Table 5.2 Sociolinguistic profile of post-1994 bilingual municipal signs at the ground level of the Bram Fischer Building of the MLM as at 12 August 2008

Type of sign	Monolingual		Bilingual		Trilingual		Symbol		Total	
	N	%	N	%	N	%	N	%	N	%
Building names	2	8.0	0	0.0	0	0.0	0	0.0	2	4.5
Directional	0	0.0	0	0.0	1	12.5	0	0.0	1	2.3
Information	3	12.0	3	37.5	6	75.0	0	0.0	12	27.3
Labels	0	0.0	0	0.0	0	0.0	0	0.0	0	0.0
Municipal adverts	2	8.0	0	0.0	0	0.0	0	0.0	2	4.5
Notices	0	0.0	2	25.0	1	12.5	0	0.0	3	6.8
Notices (temporary)	13	52.0	3	37.5	0	0.0	1	33.3	17	38.6
Plaques	0	0.0	0	0.0	0	0.0	0	0.0	0	0.0
Warning	5	20.0	0	0.0	0	0.0	2	66.7	7	15.9
Total	25	56.8	8	18.2	8	18.2	3	6.8	44	100.0

More than half (56.8%) of the new signs are monolingual signs. Three of these (temporary notices) are monolingual Afrikaans signs, the rest are monolingual English signs. Some of the new signs (18.2%) are still bilingual Afrikaans/English and the same percentage are trilingual signs (adding an African language). The high incidence of monolingual signs is related to the large number of temporary notices – 38.6% of all the new signs fall within this category. Even when temporary signs are left out of the count, the largest percentage of signs remain monolingual. Of the recalculated total of 27 permanent signs, 44.4% (12) are monolingual English signs. However, proportionally more of the permanent signs (29.6%) are then trilingual signs and fewer (18.5%) are bilingual signs. The format of the eight bilingual signs is interesting, as displayed in Table 5.3.

Almost two-thirds of the current bilingual signs on the ground level of the Bram Fischer Building are of a permanent nature. Of these permanent bilingual signs, the majority maintain the former bilingual Afrikaans/English format with one third displaying a new format, English/Sesotho (cf. Figure 5.2).

In Figure 5.2, the example on the left is of a pre-1994 bilingual sign and the example on the right is of the new generation multilingual public signs required by the MLM language policy.

Table 5.3 Bilingual format of post-1994 municipal signs at the ground level of the Bram Fischer Building of the MLM as at 12 August 2008

	Permanent signs		Temporary signs		Total	
Bilingual format	*N*	*%*	*N*	*%*	*N*	*%*
Afrikaans/English	3	60.0	1	33.3	4	50.0
Afrikaans/Sesotho	1	20.0	0	0.0	1	12.5
English/Sesotho	1	20.0	2	66.7	3	37.5
Total	5	62.5	3	37.5	8	100.0

Figure 5.2 Examples of old and new public signs in the foyer of the MLM main building

Changes in street name signs

According to Loftus (2008), no significant street name changes occurred after 1998 apart from the renaming of the main street of Bloemfontein from the bilingual 'Voortrekker Straat/Street' to the bilingual 'Nelson Mandela Avenue/Rylaan' in 2001, in honour of the first president of the democratic South Africa (also see Lubbe, 2003). All old signs were subsequently replaced. For the purposes of this section of the chapter, the display of the new street name on street name signs alongside the entire length of the main street was photographed on 5 and 8 December 2008. The display of the adjoining street names was also photographed in order to be able to position the Nelson Mandela sign accurately alongside the main street.

The recording revealed that the changed name is displayed on 23 signposts of which 13 are considered 'non-official' signposts (erected by advertisers) and the remaining 10 'official' signposts (erected by the

Figure 5.3 Examples of non-official (left) and official (right) street name posts

Municipality), as displayed in the left and right photographs in Figure 5.3, respectively.

Bilingualism in these particular signs is determined by the street name suffix: English as in 'Avenue' and Afrikaans as in 'Rylaan', and not by the name itself. However, a distinction needs to be made between the linguistic profile of the entire signpost and the linguistic profile of the individual street name sign. Each signpost carries individual sign plates that display the street name. In the signpost on the left in Figure 5.3, the individual name plate displaying the name of the main street can be categorised as an 'Afrikaans sign' because of the suffix *-rylaan* (Afrikaans for *avenue*), whilst the name plate to its right can be categorised as 'English' because of the English suffix *–square*. In the signpost on the right, both individual name plates of the signpost can be categorised as 'English signs' because of their English suffixes (respectively, *-street* and *-drive*). Each of the individual street name signs can now be categorised as either 'monolingual Afrikaans' or 'monolingual English', as they do not simultaneously display a bilingual street name suffix on the same side of the plate as in the case of the pre-1998 example in Figure 5.4.

The individual street name signs on the right represent the 'new generation' type of monolingual street name signs erected after 1998. We can therefore categorise the entire signpost on the left in Figure 5.4 as a 'bilingual' signpost as it carries an individual street name plate in two languages. The signpost on the right can also be classified as a 'bilingual' street name signpost, but for a different reason. Here the language of the flipside sign alternates (in other words, the flipside signs in this case display 'Kellner Street' and 'Melville Rylaan', respectively). Official bilingualism is less visible in the latter case.

Figure 5.4 Example of a pre-1998 'bilingual' street name sign (left) and its post-1998 'monolingual' equivalents (right)

Table 5.4 Linguistic profile of official and non-official street signs displayed in Bloemfontein's main street

Language profile	Official street name sign				Non-official street name sign			
	Main street		Adjoining street		Main street		Adjoining street	
	N	%	N	%	N	%	N	%
Monolingual	6	60.0%	9	90.0%	6	46.2%	4	30.8%
Bilingual	4	40.0%	1	10.0%	7	53.8%	9	69.2%
Total	10	100.0%	10	100.0%	13	100.0%	13	100.0%

Table 5.4 contains a comparison of the linguistic profile of the individual street name signs displayed in Bloemfontein's main street.

The comparison suggests a greater tendency towards monolingual language visibility in official individual street name signs. In the case of bottom-up individual signs, there is a greater tendency towards bilingual visibility. However, the linguistic profiles of the signposts are equally monolingual and bilingual. This is brought about by the language combinations of the individual street name signs on each signpost and thus, it can be observed that almost 85% of non-official signposts are bilingual.

The most striking feature of the examples collected for this comparison is that no single individual street sign includes a street name suffix in Sesotho, the third municipal language.

Changes in direction signs

The Municipality is responsible for two types of direction signs, signs displaying information regarding tourist destinations and directional signs displaying information regarding public services.

The signs that were recorded for the purposes of this survey are all located within the Central Business District (CBD) of Bloemfontein. As this area houses several important tourist sites and information venues, it was decided to record all relevant directions signs located here. Again, all relevant signs along the streets within the CBD have been photographed (in total 20). The targeted signs are easily identifiable as tourist signs have a brown background (and white letters) and direction signs a white background (and blue letters). Table 5.5 contains a summary of the classification of the recorded signs in terms of their linguistic profile. The use of symbols instead of text (in the case of 4 signs) and of symbols in combination with text (10 signs) is in accordance with the *SADC Road Traffic Signs Manual* (DoT, 1997).

None of the signs are bilingual and where a combination of destinations is displayed on the sign, they are largely in the official language of the name of the destination. However, where a translation in an alternative language is possible, as in Figure 5.5, the destination is still displayed only in one language. (The Afrikaans equivalent for the sign on the left is 'Stadsaal' and the English equivalent for the sign on the right is 'Station building'.) This would suggest that the signs cater for the international tourist.

Incidentally the monolingual English direction signs are all from the post-1998 era, also signalling a possible move away from the 'bilingual' practices of the past. However, a larger sample needs to confirm this observation.

Discussion

The comparison between the pre-1994 and post-1994 public signs in the samples discussed suggests some changes in the LL of Bloemfontein in so far as municipal signs are concerned. Some of our findings regarding these changes are:

- Not all former, permanent bilingual signs (including the alternating type) have been replaced at once or in a systematic way.
- Where signs have been replaced, a new generation of predominantly monolingual English signs has been introduced, but the replacement has been quite selective. In comparison, Sesotho is largely absent from new public signs.
- In some cases, new permanent signs still maintain the former bilingual format, particularly those flowing from a partnership between the MLM and the private sector (as is the case with

Table 5.5 Linguistic profile of official direction signs displayed in Central Bloemfontein

Type of tourist and information sign	Symbol		Symbol + Afrikaans		Symbol + English		Symbol + A & E		Afrikaans		English		Combination (Afrikaans, English)		Total	
	N	%	N	%	N	%	N	%	N	%	N	%	N	%	N	%
Public services	0	0.0%	0	0.0%	0	0.0%	0	0.0%	0	0.0%	2	100.0%	0	0.0%	2	10.0%
Tourist destinations	4	22.2%	4	22.2%	5	27.8%	1	5.6%	0	0.0%	0	0.0%	4	22.2%	18	90.0%
Total	4	20.0%	4	20.0%	5	25.0%	1	5.0%	0	0.0%	2	10.0%	4	20.0%	20	100.0%

Figure 5.5 Examples of translatable monolingual direction signs in Central Bloemfontein

signposts in the main street). Attempts at developing a new bilingual (or trilingual) format seem to be lacking.
- Temporary signs are largely monolingual and English, although some are (still) Afrikaans.

By and large, these tendencies point towards non-compliance with the MLM's explicit signage policy (which as noted before requires visibility in at least two of the municipal languages). On the other hand, where there is compliance, the bilingual format of signs ironically still largely reflects pre-1998 Afrikaans/English language combinations. Although not technically contravening MLM language policy, the latter is not really contributing to transforming the LL of Bloemfontein with a new form of bilingualism (i.e. Afrikaans/Sesotho or English/Sesotho, etc.).

The tendency towards monolingual English signs vindicates the City Manager's call (mentioned above) for compliance with the MLM language policy. This tendency seem to be suggesting that a certain tension exists between what the overt policy requires and what officials perceive to be 'the real' (covert) policy. English has thus become the 'general language of business' in the Municipality (cf. Mahoko, 2008) and, as such, a strong symbol of change. Ironically, the regime change after 1994 may have re-introduced an English-dominant LL to Bloemfontein, reflecting the pre-1948 situation. The languages of the indigenous peoples that have been ignored by previous regimes have still not been elevated. A regime change does not always consequentially advantage the previously subordinate mother tongues of the new regime.

The anomaly alluded to above could be explained against the background of language politics in the MLM. The adoption of a multilingual overt policy that added a local language as third official language followed the pre-1994 tradition of language prescriptivism. Its purpose, however, was not necessarily to establish a new prescriptive framework as such, but rather to play a role in the process of restructuring local government in the MLM. Its role was to appease the powerful Afrikaans-speaking section of the community and elicit their peaceful cooperation in the process of transformation. According to Joubert (2008), speakers from this community have been making language demands from the start of the amalgamation process. A second explanation is that the inclusion of Sesotho as the MLM's third language was of symbolic importance, but not necessarily of instrumental value. By elevating the language to official status, the MLM gave a strategic signal about the 'home-coming' of the previously marginalised black residents. The actual official use of the language on par with Afrikaans and English was not really intended; in fact, no serious demands have been made for the official use of the language since amalgamation (cf. Joubert, 2008). Given the language requirements of the previous regime, Sesotho was also not a language that was entrenched in the former local government structures as in the case of Afrikaans. A third explanation relates to the prestige of English. It is well known that English is seen as the 'language of liberation' in South Africa and thus closely related to the new rulers after 1994, who are considered liberators from the point of view of black South Africans. English is also the language preferred in black education and generally the language of black mobility. A language like Afrikaans, on the other hand, is closely associated with the oppressive apartheid past. Consequently, the removal of this language from the public space becomes an important act of 'redress', as does the erection of new English-only public signs.

One could also explain the anomaly against the background of urban change in 'cities off the map' such as Bloemfontein (cf. Marais & Visser, 2008: iv) or change in 'secondary cities' (cf. Marais & Visser, 2008: 116). Given also what these authors call the 'historically marginal position' of the Free State province at large, one could expect a greater role for English in future. According to Khedama (2008), the English logo for the MLM, 'City on the move', precisely confirms the importance accorded to English as 'international language', in other words as a symbol of progressiveness. It also underlines the direct association made between the 'modernisation' of Bloemfontein (as part of the MLM) and English, the language of the 'outside world'. Marais and Visser (2008: 119) indeed emphasise that tourism has become one of the key drivers of the local economy of Bloemfontein. The display of increasingly more English-only public signs becomes an important public communications mechanism in countering the inferiority complex associated with Bloemfontein and in repositioning it as a city that is indeed on the move – moving away from its apartheid image, from its Afrikaans image, from its 'backward' image; and moving forward as a historical tourist destination, as a modern, progressive city of the 'new' South Africa. The logo 'City on the move' essentially becomes a metaphor for breaking out of isolation and entering the global sphere. Localised languages like Afrikaans and Sesotho consequently fall short in their instrumental value to assist with this outward drive.

Conclusions

The case study presented here joins other studies on the relation between language policy and the LL in urban settings contained in the two important LL volumes preceding this one (cf. Gorter, 2006; Shohamy & Gorter, 2009). These studies stress the significance of the differences between top-down (or official) public signs and bottom-up (or non-official) public signs, the struggle that may arise because of these differences and the role of these public signs in constructing or even reconstructing the public space (cf. Backhaus, 2005; Ben-Rafael *et al.*; Cenoz and Gorter – in Gorter, 2006; Trumper-Hecht – in Shohamy & Gorter, 2009).

The present case study has confirmed how the LL can become a site of struggle for power and how language choice for new public signs of the incoming regime is determined by power relations. Our case study also confirms how an overt language policy, which is intended to unite contending speech communities and legitimise a previously marginalised language, can get neutralised and lose its value and impact. Whereas change in the LL often happens from below, particularly in dynamic and evolving urban settings, the MLM case documents change from above, in other words, orchestrated and engineered change. But it highlights a second aspect that emanates from the studies mentioned above, the creeping influence of English as a global language and the vital role that the LL plays in cultivating and reinforcing this notion. Although this form of globalisation would not necessarily constitute a change from above, it would indeed appear to be so in the Bloemfontein case because of the intricate relationship the new ruler has with the English language.

The MLM case study further confirms the need to extend our understanding of language policy not only in terms of its overt form, but also in terms of its covert form, as Shohamy (2006) so aptly argues. Our findings suggest that the engineers of the LL of an urban setting seeking to redefine itself is more prone to respond to (dynamic) covert top-down stimuli regarding language use in the public space than to (cumbersome) bureaucratic directives.

More data on the LL of Bloemfontein will confirm whether the tendencies highlighted above will continue and what the possible impact will be of overt intervention in regulating language use in the public space of a city struggling with the challenges of social integration.

Note

1. The source, a high-ranking MLM official, requested to remain anonymous.

References

Anonymous (2007) Interview with an official from Metropolitan Transport Planning, 9 March 2007, Mangaung Local Municipality (MLM) Headquarters, Bloemfontein.

Backhaus, P. (2005) Signs of multilingualism in Tokyo – A diachronic look at the linguistic landscape. *International Journal of the Sociology of Language* 175/176, 103–121.

Ben-Rafael, E., Shohamy, E., Amara, M.H. and Trumper-Hecht, N. (2006) Linguistic landscape as symbolic construction of the public space: the case of Israel. *International Journal of Multilingualism*, 3 (1), 7–30.

Cenoz, J. and Gorter, D. (2006) Linguistic landscape and minority languages. *International Journal of Multilingualism* 3 (1), 67–80.

Cowling, M. (2003) The tower of Babel – language usage and the courts. *EHRR* 36 (2), 84–111.

Department of Arts and Culture (DAC) (2002) *National Language Policy Framework* (NLPF). Pretoria: Department of Arts and Culture.

Department of Environmental Affairs and Tourism (DEAT) and Department of Transport (DoT) (1998) *South African Manual for Outdoor Advertising Control.* Pretoria: Department of Environmental Affairs and Tourism.

Department of Transport (DoT) (1997) *Southern African Development Community Road Traffic Signs Manual* (3rd edn). Pretoria: National Department of Transport.

Department of Transport (DoT) (1999) *South African Roads Traffic Signs Manual.* Pretoria: National Department of Transport.

Giliomee, H. (2003) *The Rise and Possible Demise of Afrikaans as a Public Language.* PRAESA Occasional Papers No. 14. Cape Town: Project for the Study of Alternative Education in South Africa (PRAESA).

Gorter, D. (ed.) (2006) *Linguistic Landscape: A New Approach to Multilingualism.* Cleveland: Multilingual Matters.

Jenkins, E. (2007) *Falling Into Place: The Story of Modern South African Place Names.* Cape Town: David Philip Publishers.

Joubert, N. (2008) Interview with Natie Joubert, Special Adviser: Committee Service, Mangaung Local Municipality, 23 September 2008, MLM Headquarters, Bloemfontein.

Khedama, Q. (2008) Interview with Qondile Khedama, General Manager: Communications, MLM, 16 October 2008, MLM Headquarters, Bloemfontein.

Krige, D.S. (1988) Afsonderlike ontwikkeliking as ruimtelike beplanningstrategie: 'n toepassing op die Bloemfontein – Botshabelo – Thaba Nchu-streek. Doctoral dissertation, University of the Free State, Bloemfontein.

Loftus, W. (2008) Interview with Willie Loftus from Metropolitan Transport Planning, MLM, 30 October 2008, MLM Headquarters, Bloemfontein.

Lubbe, J. (2003) Van heilige tot ikon: Die geskiedenis van naamgewing van een van Bloemfontein se strate. *Nomina Africana* 17 (1), 5–19.

Mahoko, L. (2008) Interview with Lebo Mahoko, Manager: Facilities, 29 October 2008, MLM Headquarters, Bloemfontein.

Mangaung Committee Service (2007) Language Unit working documents. Meeting with Chief Operations Officer, 6 March 2007, MLM Headquarters, Bloemfontein.

Mangaung Local Municipality (MLM) (2003) *Manguang Local Municipality Language Policy.* Approved by Council on 27 November 2003 under Item 51A3, and further amended by Council on 27 May 2004 under Item 27A1. Bloemfontein: Mangaung Local Municipality.

Mangaung Local Municipality (MLM) (2004) *Mangaung Local Municipality Language Policy.* Approved by Council on 27 November 2003 under item 51A3 and further amended by Council on 27 May 2004 under item 27A1. Bloemfontein: Mangaung Local Municipality.

Mangaung Local Municipality (MLM) (2005a) *Policy and Procedural Guidelines for the Naming and Renaming of Geographical Features.* Draft policy. Second edition, 9 March 2005. Bloemfontein: Mangaung Local Municipality.

Mangaung Local Municipality (MLM) (2005b) *Compliance with the Municipal Language Policy: Signage and Notices placed at Municipal Buildings.* City Manager Circular No. 7 of 2005.

Mangaung Local Municipality (MLM) (2008) *Mangaung Local Municipality Outdoor Advertising Control Policy.* Approved by the MLM Council on 26 September 2008. Bloemfontein: Mangaung Local Municipality.

Marais, L. and Visser, L. (2008) *Spatialities of Urban Change. Selected Themes from Bloemfontein at the Beginning of the 21st Century.* Stellenbosch: Sun Press.

Mothekhe, M. and Matiase, S. (2008) Interview with Motete Mothekhe, Manager: Committee Services and Sam Matiase, Head: Language and Translation Service Unit, 4 November 2008, MLM Headquarters, Bloemfontein.

Naidoo, R. and Shakwane, T. (2008) Interview with Roger Naidoo, General Manager: Environmental Management and Tumelo Shakwane, Head: Outdoor Advertising, 25 September 2008, MLM Headquarters, Bloemfontein.

Pelser, A. and Botes, L. (2002) *Language Needs and Preferences in the Mangaung Local Municipality Area: Findings of a Survey Assessment.* Bloemfontein: Centre for Development Support and Unit for Language Facilitation and Empowerment, University of the Free State.

Pycroft, C. (1996) Local government in the new South Africa. *Public Administration and Development* 16, 233–245.

Republic of South Africa (RSA) (1993) *Local Government Transition Act*, Act No. 209 of 1993. Pretoria: Government Printers.

Republic of South Africa (RSA) (1996) *Constitution of the Republic of South Africa*, Act No. 108 of 1996. Pretoria: Government Printers.

Republic of South Africa (RSA) (1998) *White Paper on Local Government.* Pretoria: Department of Provincial and Local Government.

Republic of South Africa (RSA) (2000) *Local Government Municipal Systems Act*, Act No. 32 of 2000. Pretoria: Government Printers.

Schoeman, K. (1980) *Bloemfontein: Die Ontstaan van'n Stad, 1846–1946.* Kaapstad: Human & Rousseau.

Schoeman, K. (1987) *Bloemfontein in Beeld, 1860–1910.* Kaapstad: Human & Rousseau.

Shohamy, E. (2006) *Language Policy: Hidden Agendas and New Approaches.* London and New York: Routledge.

Shohamy, E. and Gorter, D. (2009) *Linguistic Landscape. Expanding the Scenery.* New York and London: Routledge.

Southern African Development Community (SADC) (1999) *SADC Protocol on Transport, Communication and Meteorology.* On WWW http://www.sadc.int/english/documents/legal/protocols/transport.php. Accessed 22.1.07.

Trumper-Hecht, N. (2009) Constructing national identity in mixed cities in Israel. Arabic signs in the public space of Upper Nazareth. In E. Shohamy and D. Gorter (eds) *Linguistic Landscape. Expanding the Scenery* (pp. 238–252). New York and London: Routledge.

Van Donk, M. and Pieterse, E. (2006) Reflections on the design of a post-apartheid system of (urban) local government. In U. Pillay, R. Tomlinson and J. Du Toit (eds) *Democracy and Delivery: Urban Policy in South Africa* (pp. 107–134). South Africa: HSRC Pretoria: Press.

Venter, S. (2007) *'n Plek in die son vir die Afrikaner. Jubileum-gedenkboek van Die Afrikanerklub van Bloemfontein 1957–2007.* Danhof: Die Afrikanerklub van Bloemfontein.

Chapter 6

Chinese on the Side: The Marginalization of Chinese in the Linguistic and Social Landscapes of Chinatown in Washington, DC

JIA JACKIE LOU

Introduction

This chapter addresses the complexity of the linguistic landscape in a complex urban environment through a multi-level analysis of the bilingual commercial signage of Chinatown in Washington, DC. Drawing from a larger study (Lou, 2009) that combines the geosemiotic analysis of shop signs, with ethnographic fieldwork, observation of community meetings and interviews with neighborhood residents, the chapter argues that a wide array of social actors with competing political and economic interests and resources contribute to the collective shape of Chinatown's linguistic landscape and that the social significance of this linguistic landscape emerges through its embedding in a complex, multilingual urban space (Blommaert *et al.*, 2005; Scollon & Scollon, 2003). Findings from this multi-methodological approach suggest an alternative view to earlier observations of Chinatown's linguistic landscape as a symbolic means to commodify the neighborhood (Leeman & Modan, 2009; Lou, 2007; Pang & Rath, 2007). Rather, this chapter points to the linguistic landscape as a product of competition and negotiation among multiple stakeholders, including corporations who see little value in putting up Chinese signs, government agencies who have shifted priorities from neighborhood preservation to urban development, and community organizations that rely on Chinese shop signs to maintain a visible presence. Further, by ethnographically situating Chinatown's linguistic landscape in its complex urban environment and the everyday life of neighborhood residents, the chapter interprets the significance of the linguistic landscape, not simply from the perspective of the researcher, but also as grounded in the lived experiences of the researched. Hence, the chapter is also an empirical response to two growing concerns that have emerged in the expanding body of research on linguistic landscapes: the complexity of authorship (Malinowski, 2009) and the complexity of urban space (Blommaert *et al.*, 2005; Shohamy & Waksman, 2009).

I begin the analysis by applying the geosemiotic framework (Scollon & Scollon, 2003) to shop signs. Results from quantitative analysis indicate that although the Chinese language appears on most of these shop signs, it is visually and materially much less prominent than corporate logos and other markers of business identity that are displayed in English. Following this analysis, I investigate the micro-level interactional process at the approval meetings for the signage design of the flagship store of *AT&T* (the largest telecommunication provider in the USA) in Chinatown, during which both spoken and written Chinese were accorded lower commercial and cultural values than English. This marginalization of the Chinese language in Chinatown's linguistic landscape is mirrored by the geographic distribution of Chinese away from the commercial center of Chinatown and by the spatial movements of Chinese residents on the periphery of the neighborhood.

Linguistic Landscape of Chinatown in Washington, DC

Like many Chinatowns in North America, the one in Washington, DC, took shape in the urban center in the late 19th century, when the first wave of immigrants from China settled in the District (Chow, 1996). Although this Chinatown is substantially smaller than some of its better known and historically more significant counterparts (e.g. the Chinatowns in New York City, San Francisco and Vancouver), it boasts a unique visual appearance, fronted by the largest single-span Chinese archway in the world (Cultural Tourism DC, 2007) and bilingual signage on most Chinese (about 82% as of 2007) and non-Chinese businesses (about 69% as of 2007) throughout the neighborhood (Lou, 2009).

This largely bilingual linguistic landscape is the product of a set of urban planning policies jointly designed and administered since the late 1980s by a group of Chinese American entrepreneurs and various agencies in the District government, particularly the Office of Planning (Pang & Rath, 2007). Even though the original conceivers of this policy consider it as a major achievement in the ongoing struggle to preserve the neighborhood's ethnic identity (Lou, 2009), it has provoked much sarcastic criticism in the local press, which has either straightforwardly evaluated such bilingual signage as 'fake' (Gillette, 2003) or more thoughtfully questioned whether it is simply a layer of 'varnish' on a 'vanishing' neighborhood (Moore, 2005). Meanwhile, the linguistic landscape of Washington, DC's Chinatown has also captured the attention of sociologists (Pang & Rath, 2007) and sociolinguists (Leeman & Modan, 2009; Lou, 2007). These studies concur in their analyses that the presence of Chinese writing in commercial signage serves mainly a symbolic rather than an informational function (Leeman & Modan, 2009; Lou, 2007; Pang & Rath, 2007; also see Landry and Bourhis's (1997) seminal paper on this distinction). Moreover, Leeman and Modan (2009: 333) argue that Chinatown's linguistic landscape is an example of symbolic means employed to turn the neighborhood into a commodity, to sell Chinatown as a destination of cultural tourism. Pang and Rath (2007) have pointed to the complex nature of the authorship of the linguistic landscape by considering the different roles played by entrepreneurs and regulators in the making of urban planning policy, and Leeman and Modan (2009) have contextualized Chinatown's linguistic landscape in the histories of urban development in Washington, DC. However, both studies as well as my own earlier study (Lou, 2007) have tended to overstate the amount of agentive control the Chinese community and the government agencies exert over Chinatown's linguistic landscape and, by extension, have overestimated their power to 'sell' the neighborhood as a cultural destination. While the analysis presented in this chapter does not claim neutrality, it attempts to provide a more well-rounded understanding of the significance of Chinatown's linguistic landscape by adopting multiple, complementary research methods (Scollon & Scollon, 2004).

This chapter will suggest that commodifying the neighborhood through bilingual signage is only one of the motivating factors that has led to the current linguistic landscape of Chinatown. In fact, it is a policy that non-Chinese businesses in the area, especially the newer ones, comply with rather unwillingly. As the following analysis shows, Chinese writing on the shop signs of non-Chinese stores is systematically marginalized, as is the use of spoken Chinese during community meetings approving shop signs, the geographic distribution of Chinese businesses and the everyday activity space of remaining Chinese residents in the neighborhood.

Semiotic Marginalization of 'Chinese' on the Linguistic Landscape

My analysis begins by investigating the linguistic landscape of Chinatown in a *geosemiotic* framework (Scollon & Scollon, 2003). Although such a bilingual linguistic landscape seems homogeneous, a close examination of its geosemiotic features reveals subtle variation and the semiotic marginalization of Chinese in the signage of most non-Chinese businesses.

The quantitative analysis presented in this section shares many methodological similarities with the growing body of research on linguistic landscapes (e.g. Gorter, 2006; Shohamy & Gorter, 2009), but with a focus on the multimodal design of shop signs. A common method adopted in many of these studies is to note the number of occurrences of each linguistic variety on photographed signs. In this chapter, however, I would like to suggest that, in addition to counting the number of occurrences, researchers can gain deeper insights by looking more closely at *how* linguistic varieties are *designed visually* and *placed materially* in relation to each other on the signs, as these multimodal resources contribute to the overall significance of the linguistic landscape (Malinowski, 2009). Hence, I find the geosemiotic framework (the study of the physical placement of the sign in the material world; Scollon & Scollon, 2003) particularly useful for such analytical purpose.

Distribution of Chinese Signage Features

The first similarity between the shop signs of non-Chinese and Chinese businesses is, quite evidently, their different ways of using bilingual Chinese-English shop signs. In Figure 6.1, the photograph on the left shows one sign of the *MCI* sports center (which changed its name to the *Verizon Center* in 2006), a 20,000-seat multifunctional arena. Its Chinese name, 體育中心 (*tiyu zhongxin*, 'sports center'), is written in traditional Chinese characters in calligraphic typeface. The photograph on the right is of the sign at the *Goethe Institute* in Washington, DC's Chinatown.

Similar to the *MCI Center*, a number of other non-Chinese stores have adopted the vertical text vector in their signage. As illustrated in the banner of the *Goethe Institute* located in the Chinatown area (Figure 6.1, right), the vertical text vector is read from the bottom up. Although

Figure 6.1 *MCI Center* (now *Verizon Center*), Chinatown, Washington, DC (left); *Goethe Institute*, Washington, DC (right)

this inverted text vector is not uncommon nowadays in China, it is the top-to-bottom text vector that is more frequently associated and used with traditional Chinese writing.

Another example of a vertical text vector is found in the *Starbucks* sign in 2 (left), which also serves as an illustration of transgressive emplacement. Its Chinese name, 星巴克咖啡 (*Xingbake Kafei*, 'Starbucks Coffee'), is inscribed in Chinese characters in modern sans-serif font. A green circle surrounds each character. Six such circles are vertically ordered and fixed by black steel poles to the maroon brick siding of the row house. Such placement of shop signs is uncommon in other parts of Washington, DC, but it seems to become legitimatized when situated in Chinatown, as 85.3% of the Chinese stores in the neighborhood carry this geosemiotic feature. As we have also seen, not only Chinese restaurants but also non-Chinese business, such as the *MCI Center* (Figure 6.1), have adopted this practice.

Finally, it is noticeable that many non-Chinese stores have used symmetrical layouts in their Chinese shop signs. In the sandwich franchise *Subway*'s shop sign (Figure 6.2, left), its Chinese name, a clever transliteration, 赛百味 (*Saibaiwei*, literally meaning 'most tasty among a hundred delicacies'), is repeated on both sides of its logo displayed in English, so that the shop sign is symmetrical in layout.

Table 6.1 summarizes the geosemiotic features that have spread from Chinese to non-Chinese stores' shop signs. About 69% of non-Chinese stores have installed Chinese signage; 34.5% of non-Chinese stores' signs also appear in symmetrical composition; a similar percentage of them carry signs that extend conspicuously away from the store's own building

Figure 6.2 *Starbucks* (left) and *Subway* (right), Chinatown, Washington, DC

Table 6.1 Spread of Chinese signage's geosemiotic features to non-Chinese stores

	Bilingual		*Symmetrical*		*Transgressive emplacement*	
Chinese stores' shop signs	28/34	82.4%	16/34	47.1%	29/34	85.3%
Non-Chinese stores' shop signs	38/55	69.1%	19/55	34.5%	19/55	34.5%

toward the street space. In the following section, I discuss the main subtle differences between Chinese and non-Chinese store's signage.

Visual and Material Minimization of Chinese in non-Chinese Stores' Signage

Although most non-Chinese businesses comply with the municipal zoning regulation to adopt Chinese signage, they also minimize the visual prominence of Chinese on their signs through several geosemiotic strategies.

First, in contrast to the visual prominence given to Chinese in the shop signs of Chinese stores, non-Chinese stores often place English in a more visible position. For example, *Subway* (Figure 6.2) has its corporate logo in the center of the sign. On the storefront of some other retail businesses, the Chinese sign is not only in a less preferred position, but is also de-emphasized through other visual means.

In Figure 6.3, the photograph on the left shows the storefront of *Urban Outfitters*, an international fashion chain. To the left of the store's name, the Chinese phrase says, 男女服装 (*nannü fuzhuang*, 'men and women's clothing'), and to the right, the phrase says, 家庭用品 (*jiating yongpin*, 'household goods'), describing the variety of commodities sold in the store. These Chinese components of the sign are posted flatly against the wall in a *post hoc* manner. The Chinese is faint and hardly noticeable. In stark contrast, the English store name, *Urban Outfitters*, is inscribed in a specially designed typeface, all capitalized and on large three-dimensional plastic blocks.

Also illustrated in this example is another difference in the content of shop signs adopted by non-Chinese businesses. *Urban Outfitters* and a number of other businesses, including an Irish bar and another sandwich chain, do not have translated or transliterated Chinese names such as *Saibaiwei* for Subway. Rather, the Chinese words on the signage of these stores are generic nouns that describe the types of commodities sold at

Figure 6.3 *Urban Outfitters* (left) and *Chinatown Garden* (right), Chinatown, Washington, DC

the store. By contrast, all Chinese businesses have proper Chinese store names, such as *Da Hsin* or *Taishan Restaurant*.

The last subtle difference lies in the color scheme of the signs. Non-Chinese businesses in the Chinatown area maintain corporate identities by using the same color scheme in the English and Chinese components of their shop signs. To name a few examples, the Chinese sign of the *Goethe Institute* is printed in white characters against a background of their institutional light green (Figure 6.1), and the characters in the *Starbucks* shop sign are placed inside green circles just as their mermaid logo (Figure 6.2). The Chinese signage on *Urban Outfitters'* storefront shares the same blue color with its English store name (Figure 6.3). By comparison, the color of Chinese stores' shop signs is not chosen specifically for the display of individual corporate identity. Green, red and gold or yellow are the common colors adopted by Chinese-run restaurants and stores, as illustrated in the shop sign and also exterior decoration of the restaurant *Chinatown Garden* in the photograph on the right in Figure 6.3. Below the roof, their Chinese store name is inscribed in gold with each character inside a green circle, the frames of the windows and door are painted red, and the decorative roof over the extension on the first floor is covered with green tiles. Table 6.2 summarizes the comparison between non-Chinese stores' shop signs with those of the Chinese stores in terms of code preference, content and color scheme. We can see that less than 2% of the non-Chinese stores display their Chinese store names in prominent positions, only about 38% of them have proper nouns as store names and less than 15% chose the color scheme typical of Chinese businesses in the area.

In summary, through a comparison of the geosemiotic (visual and material) features of Chinese and non-Chinese stores' shop signs, we

Table 6.2 Geosemiotic features minimizing the appearance of Chinese in non-Chinese stores' shop signs

	Chinese in preferred positions		Store/brand name in Chinese proper noun		Chinese color scheme	
Chinese stores' shop signs	18/34	52.9%	32/34	94.1%	33/34	97.1%
Non-Chinese stores' shop signs	1/55	1.8%	21/55	38.2%	8/55	14.5%

have found that although more than half of the non-Chinese stores in Washington, DC's Chinatown have incorporated Chinese into their signage design and adopted several Chinese geosemiotic features, most of them also de-emphasize the Chinese language visually and materially, by placing Chinese characters in less visually prominent positions, by using generic description rather than proper names in the Chinese signs (which is a much less expensive solution than having store names translated into Chinese brand names) and by maintaining corporate color schemes and reducing the contrast between Chinese characters and background colors. Was such geosemiotic marginalization of Chinese on Chinatown's linguistic landscape intentional or coincidental? How has it become this way and why? In order to answer these questions, it was necessary to go beyond the surface of the linguistic landscape and to investigate the range of participants and resources involved in its production. In the second section of this chapter, I will turn to a case study of the approval meetings where *AT&T*'s flagship store's signage was presented and will discuss how the Chinese language, in its spoken and written forms, was also marginalized during the micro-level interactional process, which led to the visual and material marginalization of Chinese in the final individual shop sign that eventually became part of Chinatown's linguistic landscape.

Interactional Marginalization of 'Chinese' in Meetings

As the linguistic landscape of Chinatown is the aggregate of all types of visual signage, in order to investigate how it came to have its current shape, it was necessary to learn how individual shop signs were designed. Although I was not able to observe the graphic design process of the shop signs, which is typically contracted to independent signage design companies located outside Washington, DC, I was able to observe the process of design review by attending several Chinatown Steering Committee (CSC) monthly meetings in early 2008 and by collecting relevant policy documents and signage designs. The design review is critical, because any new business in Chinatown must receive approval in order to obtain a building permit. The main data that inform my analysis in this section are the field notes and video recordings from two CSC meetings, during which the design of a new *AT&T* store was presented, reviewed, rejected and finally approved.

Participant Framework during *AT&T* Design Review

In the summer of 2007, *AT&T* rented a prime retail location, the *Gallery Place* complex (a multifunctional retail, entertainment and luxury condominium complex) at the corner of 7th and H Street, right next to the archway in the heart of Chinatown. During renovation, its shop windows were completely covered with vinyl bearing the logo of *AT&T* and the words 'Opening Soon'. But before the store could open, its design had to pass the *Chinatown Design Review*. After the initial design was rejected by the Design Review Sub-Committee of the CSC for its lack of Chinese writing, *AT&T* submitted a revised design to the CSC in December 2007, which was scheduled to be reviewed in the subsequent monthly CSC meeting on 7 January 2008 and was further discussed during the meeting on 4 February. Although these meetings are announced as 'open to the public', only committee members of the CSC, staff of the Office of Planning and the applicant (i.e. *AT&T* in this case) were on the recipient list of meeting announcements. I learned about these meetings after volunteering for about a year at the Chinatown Community Cultural Center, which also served as the meeting place for the CSC. I obtained permission from the meeting attendants to record the meetings on video. I also took observation notes from the corner of the meeting room. These meetings provided rich opportunities to examine the complex authorship involved in the making of the linguistic landscape of Washington, DC's Chinatown, as many visual and material aspects of the shop sign (as analyzed in the previous section) were actually points of contention among various stakeholders at the meeting.

Specifically, I will discuss two kinds of shift in the production format that I observed during these meetings. These shifts can be fruitfully analyzed using Goffman's distinction between the *author, principal* and *animator* (Goffman, 1981). First, the *authors* of the *1989 Chinatown Design Guidelines Study*, that is, Alfred Liu and his company AEPA, are not members of the CSC and do not attend these public meetings. As the Chairman of the CSC, Mr. Wang, once informed me, Alfred Liu was one of the 'new' people when he came to Chinatown, whereas the founders and the key members of the CSC were from families that had been in Chinatown for many years before the *1965 Immigration Act*. Thus, the *author* of this policy that proposed bilingual signage as a measure to preserve Chinatown is not the *principal* who implements it now. In the *1989 Chinatown Design Guideline,* bilingual commercial signage was only a small part of the overall design of Chinatown, whereas for the CSC, it has become the only measure that is still in force. The second consequence of this shift is the unfamiliarity with the document, especially among the new members of CSC, which creates a rather fragmented *front* (Goffman, 1959) of the Chinese community organization to the commercial developers and business applicants with whom they are negotiating.

The second change in the participant framework took place between the two meetings, when the Office of Planning representative, Ted,[1] switched from the *mediator role* to speak *on behalf* of the business applicant. During the first meeting, *AT&T's* design was presented by two higher-level employees from *Akridge* (the building management corporation that runs *Gallery Place*). In other words, *AT&T's* design proposal was *animated* by their landlord. Ted's role was mainly to introduce the presenters, and he prefaced their presentation with an explanation of why the first submission had been rejected. *Akridge* representatives then presented the revision and argued their case. However, the full committee again rejected the revision, including the initially approved banners, for the incorrect translation of the slogan, minimal appearance of Chinese writing on the signage and the broken image of the dragon that was included in the design.

During the February meeting, however, *Akridge* representatives did not attend the meeting. Instead, Ted presented the second revision, urging the committee to join him 'in the effort to expedite the process' and suggesting, 'Chinese characters don't work with that new store (*AT&T*) concept well' (CSC Meeting, February 2008). His second comment, positioning Chinese orthography in opposition to novel concepts such as an Apple store can be seen as reversed synchronization (Blommaert, 2005), which may also be called diachronization. In other words, despite the continued use of the Chinese writing system in our contemporary world, it was historicized as an old feature that detracted from the new design. At this point of the meeting, Ted's role was questioned by a more outspoken committee member, who asked, 'Why are they (*Akridge* and *AT&T*) not here today?'

Ted's shifted position is to some degree analogous to the change in the District's urban planning policies over the past 20 years, when the municipal government shifted planning priority to the commercial development of urban neighborhoods. This change in participant framework, on the other hand, can also be seen as a loss of political resources for the Chinese community. This observation was further confirmed when a long-term committee member nostalgically recalled,

'The old director of the Office of Planning was really nice to us, but he retired a long time ago'.

Distribution of Communicative Resources during *AT&T* Design Review

Linguistic and communicative resources were also unequally distributed during these two meetings. First, all these meetings were conducted in English, and the presentation was delivered in a format that did not seem familiar to the older members of the committee, both of which prevented them from participating fully during the meeting. Second, none of the second-generation Chinese American members of the committee were able to read or write Chinese, even though they were all conversationally fluent in Mandarin and some in Cantonese as well.

During the presentations at these meetings, most members of the committee listened quietly, and if there was a problem or question, they tended to talk among themselves on the side rather than directly to the presenter. On 7 January 2008 when the *AT&T* store design was first presented, *AT&T*'s slogan 'Your world delivered' was translated incorrectly into Chinese as '您的世界被交付' (Figure 6.4). When the banner appeared on the projection screen in front of the committee, there was a quiet unease among the older members. Looking puzzled, two meeting participants whispered to each other about how bad the translation was. There are several issues with '您的世界被交付' (*nin de shijie bei jiaofu*; literally, 'your world is in the custody of'). First, rather obviously, *jiaofu* does not mean 'deliver'. Also grammatically, the passive construction *bei* is usually used with undesirable actions, as in *wode zixingche bei tou le* ('my bicycle was stolen'). Finally, if the agent of action (i.e. *AT&T*) has to be elided as in the English slogan 'Your world delivered', the verb will have to come before the object – *nin de shijie*. Despite the audience's awareness of this unacceptable translation, they did not raise the issue. Before the presentation moved on to the next slide, Cindy, one of the *Akridge* representatives, interjected to call the audience's attention to the dragon on the top of the banner as evidence for their compliance with the *Chinatown Design Review*.

As an observer, I was waiting to see if anyone would raise the question about the translation. Unfortunately, nobody did. I raised my hand when Ted asked if anybody had any questions about the presentation. Many in the audience echoed my critique of the translation. Amy added that the translation sounded to her like a will, 'very unlucky'. Then, another man pointed out that even the dragon lacked a tail, was incomplete, and thus was also inauspicious. At that point during the January meeting, the complete proposal, including the banners, was rejected. Once the meeting was over, more outrage and disbelief was expressed among

Figure 6.4 The original problematic translation of 'Your world delivered'

the older members of the committee in their familiar tongue – Chinese. At the same time, many of the second generation Chinese Americans in the committee teased each other about their own lack of Chinese literacy. Rather ironically, the Design Review Sub-Committee of the CSC, which functions as the first gatekeeper in the review process, consists of these younger Chinese Americans, the sons and daughters of the founders of the CSC. Although it is quite common for the second generation in immigrant families not to speak or be literate in their parents' language, what this entails for the CSC is the loss of a valuable communicative resource, which would have enabled them to evaluate the signage designs in a more critical and confident manner.

Despite its unanimous rejection during the first meeting, the same translation appeared on the presentation slide during the second meeting, in which Ted pushed for the timely approval of the design. In the end, the CSC compromised, and Mr Wang wrote to the Office of

Planning to grant their approval. When the banners were finally installed, however, the translation of the slogan was abandoned and replaced by a straightforward translation of 'telephone company' in thin white strokes, placed rather indiscernibly against a bright orange background, *AT&T*'s corporate color. Thus, this case study shows how the lack of both political and communicative resources in approval meetings has contributed to the semiotic marginalization of the Chinese language on Chinatown's linguistic landscape. This marginalization is further paralleled by the geographic locations of Chinese businesses, which also aggregate at the edges of the neighborhood.

Geographic Marginalization of Chinese Businesses

In 2008, the Chinatown Community Cultural Center applied for a small grant from the Humanities Council of Washington, DC, to produce a map and brochure highlighting Chinese businesses and organizations in the neighborhood. The map, in return, also provides a clear overview of where the remaining Chinese businesses and organizations are located (Figure 6.5).

At its peak in 1939, there were about 60 Chinese restaurants in Chinatown, in addition to many other stores (Lim, 1991). As of 2008, there are only about 22 restaurants owned by Chinese and Asian Americans, as indicated by dots 1 to 21 on this map (Figure 6.5). Dots 23 to 44 represent other Chinese businesses and service organizations, respectively.

It should be noted here that the intersection of 7th and H Street, indicated by a star, is the busiest intersection in Chinatown and arguably the busiest in the entire downtown Washington, DC area. It has even been compared to Times Square in terms of the high volume of its foot and vehicle traffic and as a tourist destination. The glistening Friendship Archway stands on top of this crossroad, above the subway station, and across the street from a *Starbucks* coffee shop and a *Fuddruckers* fast food chain. Most Chinese businesses are located away from this commercial, if not geographic, center of the neighborhood. However, the 7th Street and H Street corridors were once populated with Chinese restaurants. From 2005 to 2008 alone, I have witnessed the closing of five Chinese restaurants and the only supermarket in these busiest sections of the area. As the property values in the neighborhood have risen rapidly in recent years, more Chinese businesses, especially those who do not own the properties themselves, have been bought out by real estate developers for greater profit than running the restaurants themselves, and have been replaced by non-Chinese chains such as *Creative Salad Company* and *Bed, Bath & Beyond*.

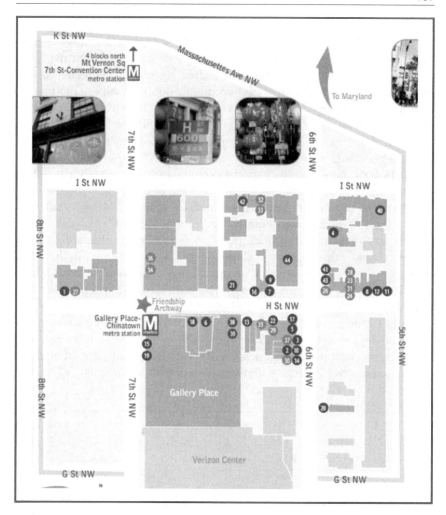

Figure 6.5 Geographic distribution of Chinese businesses and organizations in Chinatown, Washington, DC

Next I will turn to examine how individuals, especially those older Chinese residents who have little knowledge of English navigate the neighborhood.

Marginalization of 'Chinese' Activity Space

In order to observe how individuals move about in Chinatown and what impact, if any, the linguistic landscape of Chinatown has on their activity space, I conducted 18 months of fieldwork as a part-time community volunteer. Through participation in community activities,

I established contacts for further in-depth interviews with 12 individuals. At the end of nine of these interviews, I also asked each interviewee to draw a map of Chinatown on a blank piece of paper and tell me what they were drawing during the task. In this section, I will focus on one map in particular (Figure 6.6), drawn by Liu Bobo, a Chinese man in his eighties, who has lived in Chinatown with his wife, Wu Ayi, for the past 10 years in Wah Luck House, a low-income building. I will also draw supplementary evidence from observations and interviews with other Chinese residents.

Liu Bobo's map has no clear-cut boundary line but has quite a few neighborhood establishments labeled. Five out of these eight place names were written in Chinese using generic place names: 图书馆 (*tushuguan*; library), 大会堂 (*dahuitang*; literally, 'grand meeting hall', i.e. convention center), 邮局 (*youju*; post office), 体育中心 (*tiyuzhongxin*; literally, 'sports center', now the *Verizon Center*), 教堂 (*jiaotang*, church) and 亚裔老年活动中心 (*yayi laonian huodong zhongxin*; Asian Senior Citizen Activity Center). The three places that he indicated with proper nouns in English are CVS (a convenience store), CCCC (Chinatown Community Cultural Center; indicated with a single 'C') and the *Chevy Chase Bank*, but he struggled with the spelling of the last. In the interview, he referred to the *Chevy Chase Bank* in Chinese as 银行 (*yinhang*; bank). He labeled the only Chinese grocery store with a proper noun in Chinese as 大新 (*daxin*;

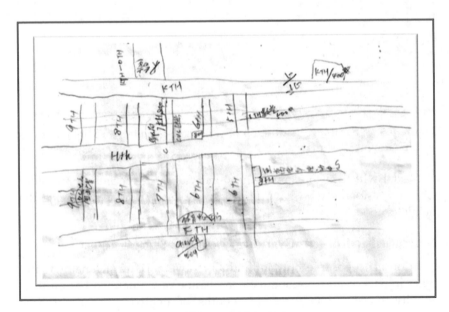

Figure 6.6 Map of Chinatown drawn by Liu Bobo

spelled as *New Da Hsin* on their shop sign). These labeled places are those that Liu Bobo visits frequently in the neighborhood.

If we connect these dots on the map (Figure 6.7), we have the shape of Liu Bobo and Wen Ayi's activity space in Chinatown. Although I have not walked with them throughout Chinatown, they told me during the interview that they prefer to walk on I Street, 6th and F Street, because H Street is 太乱 (*tailuan*, literally 'too messy', but it also means 'unsafe'). Their explanation was further corroborated by my observations of other Chinese senior residents making detours around the center of Chinatown. Many of them often perceive the large number of homeless people, mostly African American, as a threat to safety. Another explanation for their avoidance of the center of Chinatown is simply an economic one. Based on interviews with several of them and visits to their homes, I realized that almost all these elderly residents lived on social security and could not afford to eat at any of the restaurants in the area, including Chinese ones. Even if they could afford to, as one of them (Yan Ayi) told me during an interview, American Chinese food does not taste good. Therefore, the bilingual signage on non-Chinese restaurants on 7th Street means very little to them. Even if there are signs that they could actually understand, their economic status, dietary preferences and lifestyles make these stores and restaurants virtually irrelevant to their everyday lives.

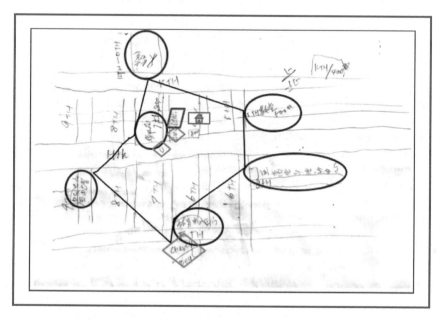

Figure 6.7 Activity space of Liu Bobo

Thus, just as the Chinese signs on the mandatory bilingual landscape of Washington, DC's Chinatown serve a mainly symbolic function for an audience who do not understand Chinese (Leeman & Modan, 2009; Lou, 2007; Pang & Rath, 2007), they are also little more than decoration for the Chinese-speaking residents in the neighborhood. In addition, their marginal activity space is shaped by their geopolitical orientation. Unlike many first-generation immigrants of a similar age, for whom Chinatown was their first home in the USA, a place where they built their businesses and families, Liu Bobo and Wen Ayi immigrated in 1997, after their children had settled in the USA. They moved to Chinatown from their children's suburban houses for its convenient location and the availability of affordable housing.

The interview also revealed that for Liu Bobo, the fact that they live in America is more important than the fact that they also live in Chinatown. When I asked him if he liked living here (*'Ni xihuan zhu zai zheli ma?'*), he answered, 'Yes' and compared life in America with life in mainland China. While I had actually intended to index Chinatown with *zheli* (here) in the question, Liu Bobo's assumption of which place the 'here' in my question indexed suggests that, geographically, he orients more toward the USA on a national scale than toward Washington, DC, on the scale of a city or Chinatown on the scale of a neighborhood.

Conclusions: What about the Linguistic Landscape?

Echoing recent calls for ethnographically informed and multimodal methods in the area of linguistic landscapes (e.g. Malinowski, 2009; Shohamy & Waksman, 2009), the study as reported in this chapter has combined multiple research methods, including geosemiotic analysis of shop signs, observations of community meetings, interviews with neighborhood residents and ethnographic fieldwork as a methodological solution to unravel the complexity involved in both the production and the interpretation of the linguistic landscape.

In this chapter, I have observed that the visual and material prominence of Chinese characters on shop signs is systematically minimized in contrast to prominent corporate logos and color schemes. Such semiotic marginalization can, in part, be traced back to the signage approval meetings, during which the Chinese language is also a devalued communicative resource. Expanding the scope of analysis beyond the linguistic landscape reveals that the peripheral geographic space of Chinese businesses and the activity spaces of Chinese residents also mirror the semiotic marginalization of Chinese on the shop signs. Therefore, by examining the linguistic landscape on multiple temporal and spatial scales, this chapter argues that not only does the linguistic landscape of Chinatown serve little practical, informational function, but it also has little economic value as a symbolic commodity within the community. Although this multi-methodological design does not claim the discovery of a single 'true' meaning of the linguistic landscape, it hopefully has brought us a step closer to a rich description of the 'ecological arena' (Shohamy & Waksman, 2009), in which multiple meanings of linguistic landscapes emerge.

Note

1. Except for public figures, all personal names in this chapter are pseudonyms.

References

Blommaert, J. (2005) *Discourse: A Critical Introduction*. Cambridge: Cambridge University Press.

Blommaert, J., Collins, J. and Slembrouck, S. (2005) Spaces of multilingualism. *Language and Communication* 25, 197–216.

Chow, E.N. (1996) From Pennsylvania Avenue to H Street, NW: The transformation of Washington's Chinatown. In F.C. Cary (ed.) *Urban Odyssey: A Multicultural History of Washington, DC* (pp. 190–207). Washington and London: Smithsonian Institute Press.

Cultural Tourism DC (2007) 'Chinatown Gateway Arch'. On WWW at http://www.culturaltourismdc.org/info-url_nocat2536/info-url_nocat_show.htm?doc_id = 44107.

Gillette, F. (2003) Year of the Hooter: The District's Chinese character gets lost in the translation. *Washington City Paper The Fake Issue–Keepin' It Unreal*. http://www.washington citypaper.com/articles/25312/the-fake-issue

Goffman, E. (1959) *The Presentation of Self in Everyday Life*. New York: Anchor Books.

Goffman, E. (1981) Footing. In E. Goffman (ed.) *Forms of Talk* (pp. 124–159). Philadelphia, PA: University of Pennsylvania Press.

Gorter, D. (ed.) (2006) *Linguistic Landscape: A New Approach to Multilingualism*. Clevedon: Multilingual Matters.

Landry, R. and Bourhis, R.Y. (1997) Linguistic landscape and ethnolinguistic vitality: An empirical study. *Journal of Language and Social Psychology* 16 (1), 23–49.

Leeman, J. and Modan, G. (2009) Commodified language in Chinatown: A contextualized approach to linguistic landscape. *Journal of Sociolinguistics* 13 (3), 332–362.

Lim, W. (ed.) (1991) *Chinatown, DC: A Photographic Journal*. Washington, DC: Asian American Arts and Media, Inc.

Lou, J. (2007) Revitalizing Chinatown into a heterotopia: A geosemiotic analysis of shop signs in Washington, DC's Chinatown. *Space and Culture* 10 (2), 145–169.

Lou, J. (2009) Situating linguistic landscape in time and space: A multidimensional study of the linguistic construction of Washington, DC Chinatown. PhD thesis, Georgetown University.

Moore, J. (2005) Beyond the archway: D.C. Chinatown debate: Vanish vs. varnish. *Washington AsiaPress*, p. 1.

Pang, C.L. and Rath, J. (2007) The force of regulation in the land of the free: The persistence of Chinatown, Washington DC as a symbolic ethnic enclave. In M. Lounsbury and M. Ruef (eds) *The Sociology of Entrepreneurship (Research in the Sociology of Organizations, Vol. 25)* (pp. 195–220). New York: Elsevier.

Scollon, R. and Scollon, S. (2003) *Discourses in Place: Language in the Material World.* London: Routledge.

Scollon, R. and Scollon, S.W. (2004) *Nexus Analysis: Discourse and the Emerging Internet.* London and New York: Routledge.

Shohamy, E. and Gorter, D. (eds) (2009) *The Linguistic Landscape: Expanding the Scenery.* New York and London: Routledge.

Shohamy, E. and Waksman, S. (2009) Linguistic landscape as an ecological arena: Modalities, meanings, negotiations, education. In E. Shohamy and D. Gorter (eds) *The Linguistic Landscape: Expanding the Scenery* (pp. 313–331). New York and London: Routledge.

Chapter 7

Linguistic Landscape under Strict State Language Policy: Reversing the Soviet Legacy in a Regional Centre in Latvia

HEIKO F. MARTEN

Introduction

This chapter will present results of a linguistic landscape (LL) project in the regional centre of Rēzekne in the region of Latgale in Eastern Latvia. Latvia was *de facto* a part of the Soviet Union until 1991, and this has given it a highly multilingual society. In the essentially post-colonial situation since 1991, strict language policies have been in place, which aim to reverse the language shift from Russian, the dominant language of Soviet times, back to Latvian. Thus, the main interests of the research were how the complex pattern of multilingualism in Latvia is reflected in the LL; how people relate to current language legislation; and what motivations, attitudes and emotions inform their behaviour.

The Linguistic Situation in Latvia and in Rēzekne

For centuries, the area of today's Latvian State has had a high level of multilingualism. Before Latvia became independent in 1918, Latvian and Latgalian were the vernacular languages of the overwhelming majority of the rural population, while Russian and German were the languages of the elite, and other languages such as Livonian, Polish or Lithuanian were spoken in smaller rural communities. This pattern changed during the Soviet occupation as large numbers of Russians migrated to Latvia from other parts of the Soviet Union and Russian became the main language. The percentage of Latvian speakers fell from 77% before the Second World War to 52% in 1991 (Ozolins, 2003: 218). The dominance of Russian in public life as the language of the occupying power led to a high degree of asymmetric societal multilingualism, as Russians were usually monolingual and Latvians were mostly bilingual Latvian-Russian. Since Latvia regained its independence, Russian has lost its official support and can be considered to be the most widely spoken minority language. At the same time, it is stigmatised as the language of the former Soviet occupying powers, and this results in a climate of partly parallel societies and latent ethnic tensions. In addition to the roughly 60% of the population who speak Latvian as their first language (L1) today and the almost 30% with Russian as their L1, 10% of the population of Latvia speak a different minority language such as Polish, Ukrainian or Belorusian as their L1 (Council of Europe, 2006: 3). Unlike Russian, the smaller minority languages are not stigmatised, but the number of speakers of them is constantly falling. Alongside the other native languages of Latvia is the regional language of Latgalian, spoken in the region of Latgale. Central Latvian attitudes frequently consider it to be a dialect of Latvian, but many speakers are today striving for it to be recognised as a separate language.

The regional administration, culture, business and education centre of Latgale is the town of Rēzekne, which has 36,345 inhabitants (2007). In Rēzekne, Latvian is the high variety and Latgalian the low in a traditional diglossic relationship, although Latgalian today can occasionally be heard in, for instance, the local university. Russians total 49% of the population, outnumbering the 44% who are Latvian/Latgalian L1 speakers. In addition, 2.6% of the town's population are Poles, 1.7% Belorusians and 1.4% Ukrainians (numbers from 2007, Rēzeknes pilsētas dome). The recent *Ethnolinguistic Survey of Latgale* (Lazdiņa & Šuplinska, 2009), based on the self-assessment of more than 9000 respondents, provides a more detailed picture of linguistic competence in Latgale as a whole. As Table 7.1 shows, more than 90% claim competence in both Latvian and Russian, but knowledge of Latgalian is also high. On the other hand, competence in the traditional minority languages and in international languages is quite limited, with only 30% claiming competence in English.

Language Policy in Latvia

As a consequence of the dominant role of Russian in Soviet Latvia, language legislation since the 1990s has aimed to reverse the language shift by reversing language prestige and functions (cf. Schmid, 2008 for an overview of language policy; for language legislation development: Ozolins, 2003). Latvian is the State Language and the only language to be used in all public domains. The only other languages mentioned in the State Language Law are the almost extinct language of Livonian, and Latgalian, which is rather vaguely labelled as a 'historical written variety of Latvian' (Republic of Latvia: State Language Law). The Latvian State takes measures to spread the Latvian language to the non-Latvian parts of the population through language planners, text-books and other teaching material, and is today in the process of integrating Russian and Latvian schools with the aim of ensuring that all students have a reasonable knowledge of Latvian (Ozolins, 2003: 230).

Table 7.1 Language competence in Latgale

Language	Percentage of respondents claiming competence
Russian	93.5
Latvian	90.9
Latgalian	62.1
Belorusian	7.2
Polish	5.2
Ukrainian	3.5
Estonian	0.4
Romany	0.4
English	30.9
German	15.0
French	0.8
Others	1.2

Source: Lazdiņa and Šuplinska (2009)

Latvia has not signed the European Charter of Regional or Minority Languages, and the ratification of the Framework Convention for National Minorities in 2005 contained explicit reservations about languages, stating that no language other than Latvian or Livonian (perceived as the only autochthonous language on Latvian territory besides Latvian) may be used in administration and on topographic signs (Council of Europe, 2006/2008). This shows the general attitude of the Latvian State to written language in the public space. According to the State Language Law, signs, posters, etc., must be in Latvian if they concern State affairs, but in exceptional cases they may also be in other languages. In practice, this rule is used, for instance, for signs showing Latvian traffic regulations for drivers who enter Latvia by road – these signs are notably in Latvian and English, but not in Russian. For private signs, by contrast, the rule is 'at least in Latvian' – signs may additionally be in other languages if the Latvian version is not less prominent than the version in another language (cf. Latvian Language Law §§21.4–21.6, and Cabinet of Ministers of the Republic of Latvia, 2000).

This shows that, despite the strong focus on overcoming the marginalisation of Latvian during Soviet times, Latvian language policy does not entirely ban the use of other languages. Private oral language use is unrestricted, and private companies may use other languages alongside

Latvian for both oral and written functions, including signage. This rule covers not only languages of international business or tourism, but also explicitly includes the minority languages such as Russian. Only in the state sector is a monolingual State language policy enforced.

The Linguistic Landscape in Rēzekne: Linguistic Hierarchies in the Process of Turning

Rēzekne is of particular value for LL research because its balance between speakers of Latvian and other languages reflects Latvian society in miniature, with Latgalian as an additional interesting component. Research was carried out throughout 2008 using the LL method used by, for instance, Cenoz and Gorter (2006) in Ljouwert and Donostia and Edelman (2009) in Amsterdam. The project outline and the interpretation of the results were also influenced by studies of the relation between language policies and the LL, such as Backhaus (2009) on Tokyo and Québec. All instances of written language were collected with digital cameras in clearly defined spaces in five areas of Rēzekne. Atbrīvošanas aleja, the main shopping, tourism and administration street of Rēzekne, served as the point of departure and as the focus. For comparison, two other central roads, the area around the railway station and a small shopping area in a residential district were used. The quantitative research consisted of spontaneous conversations with shop assistants, service staff and passers-by.

Quantitative Results

The quantitative analysis counted 830 signs (124 government, 702 private, 4 unassigned), 504 of which were identified in Atbrīvošanas aleja. Of these, 72.5% were monolingual, 19.5% bilingual, 6.0% trilingual, 1.6% quadrilingual and 0.4% featured more than four languages (Table 7.2).

The first result from the languages displayed – the dominance of Latvian, which is present on 86.4% of all signs – is quite unsurprising. The second result, however, is more unexpected, given that 30.9% of the

Table 7.2 Signs by number of languages displayed

No. of languages per sign	No. of signs	%
1	602	72.5
2	162	19.5
3	50	6.0
4	13	1.6
More than 4	3	0.4

population of Latgale claim linguistic competence in English and 93.5% claim it in Russian: English is used on far more signs (28.9%) than Russian, which appears on only 7.7%. Traditional minority languages are hardly displayed at all, with Lithuanian used on 1.9% of signs, Polish on 0.4% and Ukrainian and Belorusian not used at all, while Latgalian appears on only 0.8%. International languages are used more frequently, with, for example, German on 2.3%, French 1.9%, Norwegian 1.6%, and Estonian and Italian on 1.5% of signs, but all these languages appear far less often than English or Russian (Table 7.3).

On bilingual signs, Latvian is present on 150 of the 162 signs, which means that only 12 (7.4%) signs do not feature Latvian. English appears on 125 (77.2%) of the bilingual signs, and by far the most frequent combination is Latvian-English on 70 (43.2%); when added to the 45 English-Latvian signs, this comes to 71% of all bilingual signs. Latvian as

Table 7.3 Languages on signs in Rēzekne

Language	*Appearances (on 830 signs)*	%
Latvian	717	86.4
English	240	28.9
Russian	64	7.7
German	19	2.3
Lithuanian	16	1.9
French	16	1.9
Norwegian	13	1.6
Estonian	12	1.5
Italian	12	1.5
Latgalian	7	0.8
Spanish	6	0.7
Polish	3	0.4
Swedish	3	0.4
Danish	2	0.2
Finnish	2	0.2
Latin	2	0.2
Japanese	1	0.1

the State language thereby appears more frequently than English as the L1 in this combination. Russian appears on only 26 bilingual signs (16%), of which there are 2 Russian-English and 4 English-Russian signs, and 13 Latvian-Russian and 7 Russian-Latvian signs. No bilingual signs were found with Russian and a language other than Latvian or English, whereas there are a few signs with English and one language, German or Italian, other than Latvian or Russian.

Similarly, Latvian appears on 63 of the 66 signs with three or more languages, followed by English on 55 signs. Of the 11 signs that do not feature English, 8 display the combination of Latvian, Estonian and Lithuanian. Russian was found on 25 signs, while 24 signs had the combination of Latvian + English + a language other than Russian.

Particularly revealing was the investigation of languages on signs published by the Latvian State or a state organisation. By law, these should be in Latvian only, with some limited exceptions. Latvian is indeed present on all state signs, and at 80.6%, the percentage of monolingual Latvian signs is higher than the average of 72.5%, but not nearly all the signs are in Latvian only (Table 7.4).

The exceptions, however, can be explained by looking at the type of signs, most of which are issued by the State but do not concern core state powers. For instance, information from the state tourist agency is frequently in Latvian, English, Russian and German, while instructions in telephone booths of the state-owned telephone company are in Latvian, English and Russian, which are probably in this order so as to avoid the impression that Latvian and Russian might be languages of equal status in Latvia. New road signs are always monolingual Latvian, but occasionally run-down Latvian-Russian signs from Soviet times have not yet been replaced, while some street signs are bilingual because they indicate a company with an English name.

Table 7.4 Signs issued by the State

No. of languages	Government signs	Percentage of government signs	For comparison: Percentage of all signs
Monolingual	100	80.6	72.5
Bilingual	18	14.5	19.5
Trilingual	4	3.2	6.0
Quadrilingual	2	1.6	1.6
More than 4	0	0	0.4
Total	124	100	100

A rare example of Russian-Latvian bilingualism with a Lithuanian element: an advertisement for a telephone company with a Lithuanian name in Rēzekne

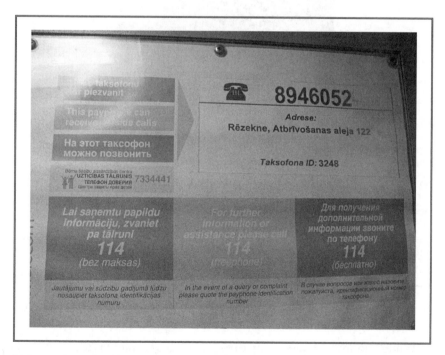

Trilingualism used to avoid the perception of a bilingual society: Latvian, English and Russian in Latvian telephone booths

An increasingly rare example of a bilingual Latvian-Russian public sign in Rēzekne from Soviet days

An exotic touch as a selling point: an advertisement for an Italian restaurant in Rēzekne featuring Latvian, English, Italian and Spanish

While the low frequency of Russian on governmental signs is most probably due to language legislation, it is more difficult to account for its absence on private signs. In this context, it is notable that Russian is more frequently found in locations at the border between the public and private spheres, such as in the stairwells of apartment buildings. People apparently feel safer using Russian when it is not as visible as on the streets. There is also a discrepancy between the inside and the outside of shops and other institutions such as banks, which often use Latvian-only signage in their windows but have multilingual information inside, mostly featuring Russian, but sometimes also with English. This applies more frequently to leaflets and brochures than to information displays about products, which are mostly in Latvian only.

This picture of Russian is confirmed when the overall data from Rēzekne are compared to the data from the most residential district researched, the area around the streets of Maskavas iela and Blaumaņa iela, where 83 (10%) signs were found (Table 7.5). This area has Soviet-style housing blocks that rarely attract tourists or business from outside Rēzekne. The general LL pattern of Rēzekne is confirmed here – Latvian is the strongest language by far, and English is more frequent than Russian. However, Russian is much stronger than in the town in total, with 6 of the total of 12 monolingual Russian signs found in this area, and with Russian appearing on 15.7% of all signs, more than double the 7.7% for the whole of Rēzekne.

English is very frequently used in Rēzekne in advertisements, and sometimes also in the names of shops. Specific information in English, on the other hand, is much less common. Similarly, romance languages enjoy high prestige and are seen as exotic and glamorous. Given the low spread of competence in French, Italian or Spanish, it cannot be assumed that these signs are meant to inform. German, by contrast, is used less for creating a prestigious image, and the quadrilingual tourism information plates reflect the economic potential of German-speaking tourists as well as historical links. Nevertheless, German appears in rather unexpected places, for instance at newspaper stands. It can be assumed, however, that most magazines in German are bought for their illustrations rather than for their language, as visual topics such as interior decoration or gardening predominate.

Table 7.5 Languages in the area of Maskavas/Blaumaņa iela

Language	No.	%	Percentage in all Rēzekne
Latvian	68	81.9	86.4
English	30	36.1	28.9
Russian	13	15.7	7.7
German	2	2.4	2.3
Spanish	1	1.2	1.9

English for prestige purposes in advertisements and company names in Rēzekne

The presence of Scandinavian languages can be explained in yet another way, as they are found mainly in company names or advertisements. The languages of Latvia's neighbours, Lithuanian and Estonian, are found surprisingly rarely, and often feature on advertisements or products by international companies that only have one version for the three countries.

Finally, it is worth noting that there is hardly any written presence of Latgalian in the LL of Rēzekne, as it only appears on seven signs or 0.8%, despite the fact that 62.1% of the population of Latgale report competence in Latgalian (cf. Table 7.1) and that it can frequently be heard in oral use. The instances where Latgalian does occur, however, are often highly marked, such as at a local radio station, a traditional café, a stone commemorating the deportation of part of the local population to Siberia in the 1940s and, very infrequently, in graffiti.

Qualitative Results

The more qualitative results of the research and their interpretation are drawn from spontaneous conversations and loosely pre-structured interviews with people in shops, cafés and other locations, and from the reactions and observations noted during the photographing. The questions asked in these conversations and interviews were related to our main research aims and the concepts underlying them, but were open-ended and didn't initially offer any information about our project, so that they would influence the answers as little as possible. If further asked, however, we were, of course, more than happy to explain our project.

As a point of departure, we were interested in four main categories of linguistic research:

- Linguistic competence – ways in which the signs reflect the linguistic competence of the population as a whole and of the people dealing with the signs.
- Usage/functions – which languages appear in which contexts.
- Attitudes – what opinions of languages and their use the signs reflect, including attitudes to our research.
- Legal provisions – where laws influence linguistic behaviour.

Throughout the research, several reactions reoccurred that may be summarised as follows:

- Significant differences between oral and written language use.
- Positive attitudes, often without further reflection, to a language, reinforcing a positive marketing image.
- A lack of knowledge about legal provisions and the language laws.
- Ignorance of the language(s) on display or a lack of written skills in that language.
- A lack of interest in the linguistic situation or a perceived inability to influence it.
- Anxiety or even hostility, to various degrees, towards us and our research.
- Interest in our research, expressed in open or hidden ways.

Table 7.6 provides an overview of these reactions, with typical situational examples, quotations and a suggested interpretation.

When these categories of reaction are put together with the quantitative results displayed above, the general dominance of Latvian over Russian can be explained by the legal provisions, the insecurity about what they allow, and sometimes directly by negative experiences with the language police, which have caused anxiety and hostility. On several occasions, the researchers were literally chased away when taking pictures of a shop. In many situations, an initially hostile reaction relaxed when we explained our aim and our background as scientists. The ignorance of the rules also explains the difference between oral and written language use. At the same time, occasional genuine interest in the research – such as from local radio and television stations, which were interested in the results for Latgalian – showed that there is a desire for more active discussion of linguistic issues among parts of the population and a desire to raise the currently low-level usage of Latgalian.

One conclusion of the research is that there is very little awareness of linguistic behaviour among the general public. Other answers displayed a superficial perception of languages and names: an employee of a beauty parlour called 'La Femme' reported that the shop owner thought that French was a 'beautiful language', and considered any further contemplation unnecessary. This perception is an instance of the use of

Table 7.6 Qualitative research categories with typical reactions and examples

Research category	Feature	Example of research situation	Quotation	Interpretation
Functions	Difference in oral and written languages used	Oral use of Russian, or Latgalian in a shop – written signs only in Latvian with some English	'Russian shouldn't be visible' / 'Latgalian is for oral, but not for written use'	Official language attitudes on 'good' written language are shared and followed more strictly than necessary
Functions/ attitudes	Lack of interest/ influence	Multilingual advertisements, products, company logos or similar	'I have never thought about which languages are used, why, and what they mean – advertisements are sent by the headquarters'	Lack of interest in language questions because of perceived lack of influence
Competence	Lack of language knowledge	English on display – no awareness what is written	'I don't know what is written there'	Lack of linguistic competence – English used for prestige
Competence/ attitudes	Lack of written competence	Latgalian used orally – no knowledge and/or desire to write it	'I would write Latgalian but I am not sure how to'	Latgalian seen as an oral variety – in line with state ideological traditions
Attitudes	Positive attitudes to a language (marketing)	A French name of a beauty parlour – even if it cannot be understood by many customers	'The owner of the shop thinks that French is a beautiful language'	Exotic languages for prestige/ marketing purposes only – whether the text can be understood is of little importance
Attitudes to research	Open interest in our project	Interest by Latgalian radio and TV station	'How can your research be beneficial to Latgalian?'	Desire to share experience of how to promote a language

Table 7.6 (*Continued*)

Research category	Feature	Example of research situation	Quotation	Interpretation
Attitudes to research	Hidden interest in our project	Bus stops – reading explicitly what we took pictures of	At first non-verbal observation – interest but also distance when academic research is explained	Lack of openness/conflict avoidance and distant attitude to open discussion of language questions
Attitudes to research/legal provisions	Anxiety regarding our agenda	Spontaneous reactions about fulfilment of legal requirements	'Everything here is in Latvian'	Bad experience with language police; little awareness of language laws and how they allow non-Latvian signage
Attitudes to research/legal provisions	Hostility to the research	Threatening and chasing away when taking pictures	'You have no right to investigate what we are doing'	Bad experience with language police
Legal provisions	Lack of knowledge of provisions	Reaction to question why Russian is spoken in a shop but not in advertisements	'But we are not allowed to use other languages!'	Language laws and their underlying ideologies are successfully implemented

languages for prestige purposes – often initiated by central company decisions taken outside the region or even outside Latvia, so that local shop assistants have little influence on the languages on display. This tendency explains the high presence of English and more 'exotic' languages for marketing or prestige purposes, for example in most cases of signs featuring Norwegian. Equally, the few Polish or Lithuanian signs were almost exclusively put up by international companies and were not signs with local information – they can therefore be interpreted as a consequence of globalisation rather than evidence of the presence of these traditional minorities in the region. Russian, on the other hand, features mostly in its local rather than in its global function or as a language of international marketing, as it is mainly used for local private messages, with some exceptions such as for tourist information.

The fact that Russian is more common in situations where specific information needs to be transmitted, i.e. in bilingual job advertisements or in the Maskavas/Blaumaņa iela district, shows that people do want to write in Russian where they can. However, the overall picture remains that people are scared and suffer from a lack of knowledge about the regulations, otherwise Russian might be used much more regularly. This perceived lack of influence might also account for the limited use of Latgalian, and possibly of some local minority languages. Similarly, the lack of knowledge of the legal provisions also corresponds with the lack of Latgalian in the LL, and is in line with attitudes and the limited knowledge of written Latgalian.

Conclusion

From the results presented in the previous sections, it is possible to draw the following conclusions on the hierarchy of languages in the LL of Rēzekne:

(1) Latvian has quantitative and qualitative dominance that is beyond doubt.
(2) English is clearly the second language in frequency, despite relatively low general competence, but it is used mainly for symbolic functions.
(3) Russian is the third language in frequency, and tends to be more present in residential areas and for informative rather than symbolic functions.
(4) Other international languages are present either for prestige purposes or as the result of international marketing.
(5) Latgalian is very rare but is used in some very prestigious contexts like the commemoration stone and the café.
(6) Local minority languages are hardly present at all.

The main conclusions of the qualitative data may be summarised in the following points:

- Language use underlying the LL in Rēzekne is frequently determined by people's attitudes and emotions, including a complete lack of interest in languages.
- Attitudes are also reflected in the reactions to the researchers, both positively in the interest of promoting Latgalian, and negatively in the anxiety or hostility towards language legislation.
- A lack of linguistic competence is typical in other parts of the LL and in reactions to it, i.e. when people don't know the languages that they see in their everyday work.
- In general, the language policy of the State is well reflected in the LL, in particular the dominance of Latvian over Russian and Latgalian.
- The avoidance of 'undesired' varieties as a result of strict language laws and low linguistic awareness resembles the notion of hyper-correction and may therefore be labelled 'legal hypercorrection'.

I will now explain what I mean when proposing the concept of legal hypercorrection. As can be seen from the statistics, Russian is present far less in the LL of Rēzekne than might be expected given the linguistic composition of society and the positive attitudes to the language displayed in the oral behaviour of large parts of the population. Taken alongside the quantitative results, the categories of linguistic behaviour identified in the research indicate that anxiety, hostility and ignorance of the law influence this behaviour. However, as already noted, language laws in Latvia do not prohibit the use of Russian entirely, as language policy and legislation allow the use of languages other than Latvian on any sign that does not concern the immediate sovereign functions of the State, if these languages are not more prominent than Latvian. This means that any information by a private business or any personal note may be in other languages in addition to Latvian. As a conclusion, it is therefore possible to state that the lack of written usage of Russian is the result of people's reaction to the laws rather than of the laws themselves.

The fact that language laws on written language in public in Latvia are followed to a higher degree than necessary may lead to a definition of the concept of legal hypercorrection, in analogy to the classic notion of 'hypercorrection' in sociolinguistics as introduced by Labov in the 1960s, which Bright (2002: 86), for instance, summarises as the way that speakers go 'beyond the highest-status group in adopting new prestige features'. Legal hypercorrection therefore shall denote the fulfilment of linguistic legal norms by language users to a higher degree than required by those who have created the laws.

So, to what extent does this term shed light on the issues discussed here? It contributes to explaining the phenomenon that, although they have the competence and a generally positive attitude to it, people don't use a language because language policy discourages them from using it. This is linked with a lack of knowledge and notions of anxiety and hostility towards legal provisions. In the context of Rēzekne and the post-Soviet reversal of language shift, Russian is regularly used for oral communication, but not in the written LL, although the overwhelming majority of the population received formal education in Russian and is literate in the language.

At the same time, legal hypercorrection in Rēzekne affects not only the use of Russian, but it also applies to Latgalian: because of ignorance about the status of Latgalian in language laws that recognise it but not in a clearly defined way, people feel insecure about using it in the written public space. In contrast to the lack of use of Russian, however, this is more difficult to interpret, since the misperception of the regulations is compounded by a lack of written competence since literacy in Latgalian has not been systematically promoted since the 1930s.

A major reason for the remarkable lack of consciousness about language legislation is a prevailing Soviet-legacy attitude among parts of the population that decisions are taken from above, as is reflected by those respondents who claimed a lack of influence, interest or knowledge of provisions about languages. At the same time, for historical reasons, State language policy neither openly encourages the use of Russian or Latgalian, nor explicitly spreads information about how languages other than Latvian may be used in public signage. The defensive attitude of the population to State authorities is a main explanation for the fear of the language police, as experienced through the hostile reactions during the research. It may therefore be concluded that legal hypercorrection in Latvia is based both on the desire to participate in prestigious domains that are associated with English and other Western European languages rather than with Russian, Polish or Latgalian, and on a lack of knowledge about the law and a fear of punishment by the authorities.

Finally, it may be assumed that the linguistic behaviour as identified through the LL research actually corresponds to the interests of official Latvian language policy, as life without knowledge of Latvian is made difficult. The results regarding the use of Russian beyond public signs show that the shaping of the LL does not prevent the speakers of Russian using Russian in less exposed contexts. At the same time, because of the use of English mainly for prestige purposes and the population's relatively low competence in English, there is currently little fear that English might take over any domains from Latvian. Additionally, as concerns Latgalian, centralised language planning authorities in Riga are arguably not unhappy to see that there is a certain level of confusion about how it may be used on signs and that its speakers have not started to use their language more frequently in the written public domain. Traditional patterns of prestige and of people's insecurity in using the oral language of their choice in written signage thus prevail, despite the language legislation being more favourable towards such use.

Acknowledgements

A warm 'Thank you!' to Sanita Lazdiņa for her help in planning and conducting the research, to the students of the Master's of Philology course at Rēzekne University College for their interest and for making the research excursions very enjoyable – in particular to Solvita Pošeiko, Sandra Murinska, Reǵina Paegle and Daina Rutkovska – and to Rēzekne University College for its financial support. I am also deeply grateful to Loulou Edelman (Amsterdam) for sharing her list of LL parameters with us.

References

Backhaus, P. (2009) Rules and regulations in linguistic landscaping: A comparative perspective. In E. Shohamy and D. Gorter (eds) *Linguistic Landscape: Expanding the Scenery* (pp. 157–172). London: Routledge.

Bright, W. (2002) Social factors in language change. In F. Coulmas (ed.) *The Handbook of Sociolinguistics* (pp. 81–91). Meldan and Oxford: Blackwell.

Cabinet of Ministers of the Republic of Latvia (2000) *The Usage of Languages in Information Issued in accordance with Paragraphs 5 and 6 of Article 21 of the State Language L, Regulations No. 292, 22 August 2000.* On WWW at http://www.minelres.lv/NationalLegislation/Latvia/Latvia_LangRegInformation_English.htm. Accessed September 2009.

Cenoz, J. and Gorter, D. (2006) Linguistic landscape and minority languages. In D. Gorter (ed.) *Linguistic Landscape: A New Approach to Multilingualism* (pp. 67–80). Clevedon: Multilingual Matters.

Council of Europe (2006) *Report submitted by Latvia pursuant of article 25, paragraph 1 of the Framework Convention on the Protection of National Minorities.* On WWW at http://www.coe.int/t/e/human_rights/minorities/2._framework_convention_%28monitoring%29/2._monitoring_mechanism/3._state_reports_and_unmik_kosovo_report/1._first_cycle/PDF_1st_SR_Latvia_en.pdf. Accessed September 2009.

Council of Europe (2008) *List of Declarations Made with Respect to Treaty No. 157.* On WWW at http://conventions.coe.int/Treaty/Commun/ListeDeclarations.asp?NT=157&CM=1&DF=5/27/2008&CL=ENG&VL=1. Accessed September 2009.

Dal Negro, S. (2009) Local policy modeling the linguistic landscape. In E. Shohamy and D. Gorter (eds) *Linguistic Landscape: Expanding the Scenery* (pp. 206–218). London: Routledge.

Data Serviss (2006) *The Influence of Language Proficiency on the Standard of Living of Economically Active Part of Population: Survey of the Sociolinguistic Research.* Riga: Talsu tipogrāfija.

Edelman, L. (2009) What's in a name? Classification of proper names by language. In E. Shohamy and D. Gorter (eds) *Linguistic Landscape: Expanding the Scenery* (pp. 141–154). London: Routledge.

Euromosaic (2004) *Latvia Country Profile*. On WWW at http://ec.europa.eu/ education/policies/lang/languages/langmin/euromosaic/lat_en.pdf. Accessed September 2009.

Gorter, D. (ed.) (2006) *Linguistic Landscape: A New Approach to Multilingualism*. Clevedon: Multilingual Matters.

Lanza, E. and Woldemariam, H. (2009) Language ideology and linguistic landscape: Language policy and globalization in a regional capital of Ethiopia. In E. Shohamy and D. Gorter (eds) *Linguistic Landscape: Expanding the Scenery*. (pp. 189–205). London: Routledge.

Latvijas statistika (2008) Pieejamo tabulu saraksts tēmā: Iedzīvotāji. On WWW at http://data.csb.gov.lv/DATABASE/Iedzsoc/Ikgad%C4%93jie%20statistikas% 20dati/Iedz%C4%ABvot%C4%81ji/Iedz%C4%ABvot%C4%81ji.asp. Accessed September 2009.

Lazdiņa S. and Marten, H.F. (2009) The "Linguistic Landscape" Method as a Tool in Research and Education of Multilingualism: Experiences from a Project in the Baltic States. In A. Saxena and Å. Viberg (eds) *Multilingualism. Proceedings of the 23rd Scandinavian Conference on Linguistics, Uppsala, 1–3 October 2008* (Acta Universitatis Upsaliensis, Studia Linguistica Upsaliensa 8) (pp. 212–225). Uppsala: Studia Linguistica Upsaliensis.

Lazdiņa, S., Pošeiko, S. and Marten, H.F. (2008) Lingvistiskās ainavas metode – netradicionāls celŠ multilingvisma jautājumu izpētē un mācīŠanā. *Tagad* 1. Zinātniski metodisks izdevums, 43–49.

Lazdiņa S. and Šuplinska I. (eds) (2009) *Valodas Austrumlatvijā: pētijuma dati un rezultāti. Languages in Eastern Latvia: Data and Results of Survey. Via Latgalica: humanitāro zinātņu žurnāla pielikums 1*. Rēzekne: Rēzeknes Augstskola.

Marten, H.F. (2008) Misunderstandings about minorities: Notes on Language policy theory and debates from a Western European-Baltic perspective. In *'Etniskums Eiropā: socialpolitiskie un kulturas procesi'/'Etniskums Eiropā: socialpolitiskī i kulturys procesi' Starptautiskā zinātniskā conference, 2007.gada 24.-26. maijs/ International Conference 'Ethnicity in Europe: Sociopolitical and Cultural Processes'* (pp. 78–91). Rēzekne: Rēzeknes Augstskola.

Ozolins, U. (2003) The impact of European accession upon language policy in the Baltic States. *Language Policy* 2, 217–238.

Republic of Latvia (1999) *State Language Law*. On WWW at http://www.minelres.lv/ NationalLegislation/Latvia/Latvia_Language_English.htm. Accessed September 2009.

Rēzeknes pilsētas dome (2008) *Skaitli un fakti*. On WWW at http://www.rezekne. lv/index.php?id=368. Accessed September 2009.

Schmid, C. (2008) Ethnicity and language tensions in Latvia. *Language Policy* 7, 3–19.

Shohamy, E. and Gorter, D. (eds) (2009) *Linguistic Landscape: Expanding the Scenery*. London: Routledge.

Chapter 8

Linguistic Landscape of Kyiv, Ukraine: A Diachronic Study

ANETA PAVLENKO

Introduction

To date, the study of the linguistic landscape, i.e. public uses of written language, has focused predominantly on the here-and-now of the urban linguistic mosaic. And yet, the linguistic landscape is not a state but a diachronic process and the meaning of the present day's arrangements cannot be fully understood without considering those of the past. This past, however, may be difficult to recover, given the field's current dependence on the researchers' own pictures. The purpose of the present chapter is to explore other sources that can help us reconstruct linguistic landscapes of the past.

The focal point of the study is the city of Kyiv,[1] the capital of independent Ukraine. A unique characteristic of today's Kyiv is the discontinuity between the language of the cityscape (predominantly Ukrainian) and the language of everyday interaction (predominantly Russian). To understand demographic, social and historic factors that have shaped this discontinuity, I will travel back in history. My inquiry will be guided by two questions: (a) what were the languages of the linguistic landscape and spoken interaction in different periods in Kyiv history? (b) what factors shaped language change in the linguistic landscape of Kyiv?

Research Method

My interest in Kyiv is not accidental. It is the city where I was born and lived until 1989 and where I have been conducting data collection annually since 1997. Once I started seeing the city as a visitor, I was struck by the changing nature of its visual landscape and I decided to explore the nature of these changes. The approach adopted here relies on two types of materials. Primary materials consist of (a) photographs of linguistic landscapes proper (from the 19th century onward) and (b) photographs of traces of past linguistic landscapes (e.g. inscriptions on old frescoes). These pictures are culled from digital photographic archives, photograph and postcard collections, and historic monographs. I have also used my own corpus of pictures of Soviet and post-Soviet signage and of tombstones in Kyiv's oldest cemetery, Baikovoe. Second-ary materials include historic, archeological, epigraphic and linguistic studies and memoirs of travelers and the city's inhabitants. To ensure a balanced presentation, I have examined claims about language use in Kyiv made in Ukrainian-, Russian- and English-language sources and selected only interpretations on which the majority of the sources agree and for which there is sufficient evidence. The contents of the corpus are listed in Table 8.1.

Predictably, the limitations of the available data led to variation in terms of the scope of the inquiry. Discussion of pre-19th-century linguistic landscapes will involve all types of signage. Discussion of the 19th- and 20th-century landscapes will be limited to traditional units of linguistic landscape inquiry, such as signs on governmental buildings or shop signs. I will also consider the languages of tombstone inscriptions. Throughout, I will differentiate between *official signage*, that is signs placed by authorities (e.g. street signs), *commercial signage*, that is signs displayed by commercial enterprises (e.g. store signs) and *private signage*, that is signs placed in public spaces by individuals (e.g. graffiti or tombstones). Where relevant, I will also discuss religious and political signage.

Since all the sources of information in this inquiry are selective and thus limiting, the approach adopted here undoubtedly lacks the sampling rigor that Backhaus (2007) deems necessary for a scientific and hence quantitative investigation of the linguistic landscape. Never-theless, it is unavoidable if we are to understand factors that affect changes in the linguistic landscape. The advantages of this approach include reliability and transparency ensured by the use of publicly available photographic corpora.

From Kiev to Kijów to Kyiv: A Sociolinguistic History

Where should a history of a city's linguistic landscape begin? Clearly, starting points may vary and will depend on the available evidence and on individual preferences. Some may begin with the appearance of public signage, while others may favor the point at which advances in literacy education make such signage comprehen-sible to the general population. In the case of Kyiv, I have decided to begin with the emergence of Slavic literacy in 860s, because this starting point allows us to place competing claims about the visibility and legitimacy of Russian and Ukrainian in a historic context. In what follows, the discussion will be divided into five historic periods, each involving a partial transformation of the city's linguistic landscape and repertoires.

Table 8.1 Sources of information on Kyiv linguistic landscapes in different historic periods

Period	Primary sources	Secondary sources
9th to 13th centuries	Fresco/mosaic inscription pictures (70) Graffiti pictures (18) Coin inscription pictures (8) Sword-blade inscription pictures (2) Helmet inscription pictures (1) Seal inscription pictures (1) Jewelry inscription pictures (1)	Evdokimova (2008) Franklin (2002) Nikitenko (2008) Rybakov (1982) Smolij (2008)
14th to 17th centuries	Manuscript and document pictures (24) Fresco/mosaic inscription pictures (2) Graffiti pictures (1) Coin inscription pictures (20) Seal inscription pictures (20) Church bell inscription pictures (1)	Lukowski and Zawadzki (2006) Nikitenko (2008) Rusina *et al.* (2008) Smolij (2008) Snyder (2003)
17th to 18th centuries	Manuscript and document pictures (10) Fresco and icon inscription pictures (10) Portraits with captions (2) Church bell inscription pictures (1)	Nikitenko (2008) Smolij (2008)
19th century to 1918	Street signage pictures (87) Kiev postcards with text (564) Author's corpus of cemetery pictures (11)	Anisimov (2003, 2007) Arutiunian (2005) Hamm (1993) Konchakovskii and Malakov (1993); Makarov (2005); www.oldkiev.info; www.nostalgia2.kiev.ua
1918–1991	Street signage pictures (26) Political banner pictures (5) Author's corpus of cemetery tombstone pictures (21)	Anisimov (2003, 2007) Smolij (2008) www.oldkiev.info www.nostalgia2.kiev.ua
1991 to present	Author's corpus: Official signage pictures (14) Commercial signage pictures (75) Pictures of commemorative signs (9)	Besters-Dilger (2008) Bilaniuk (2005) Bilaniuk and Melnyk (2008)

Table 8.1 (*Continued*)

Period	Primary sources	Secondary sources
	Private ads pictures (multiple ads in each) (7) Graffiti pictures (13) Pictures of cemetery tombstones and signs (5)	

Source: For pictures of and information on the mosaic and fresco inscriptions at St. Sophia, see also http://www.iconart.info/location.php?lng = en&loc_id = 148&mode = mos

Kievan Rus: 9th to 13th century

One of the largest cities of medieval Europe, by the year 1200 Kiev had approximately 50,000 inhabitants (Hamm, 1993). This growth was mainly due to the fortuitous location of the city. High on the banks of the river Dnieper, Kiev was situated in the middle of the river route that led 'from the Varangians to the Greeks', i.e. from the Viking North down to the Black Sea and across to Constantinople. The location on a major trade route allowed Kievan rulers to strengthen and extend their reach and in the 880s the city became capital of a new polity, Kievan Rus. This polity was composed of several principalities, inhabited by Slavic and non-Slavic tribes, and ruled by the Kievan princes. At the time of its greatest territorial extent, Kievan Rus included almost all of present-day Belarus, much of European Russia and almost half of present-day Ukraine (Magocsi, 2007). Consequently, most historians see Kievan Rus as a precursor of all three modern East Slavic nations: Russian, Ukrainian and Belarusian (Magocsi, 2007; Rybakov, 1982; Smolij, 2008; Snyder, 2003; Wilson, 2000).

The origins of Slavic literacy are commonly traced to 863, when brothers Constantine (Cyril) and Methodius arrived in Moravia from Byzantium to teach the Christian faith in Slavic. The brothers used Old Church Slavonic, a written language based on Bulgaro-Macedonian Slavonic spoken in the 9th century, to translate texts from Greek and invented a special script to do so. When Moravia rejected Slavonic in favor of Latin, the language found a warmer reception in Bulgaria, where the script was transformed into what is now known as the Cyrillic alphabet (Franklin, 2002). In 988, when Vladimir the Great made Kievan Rus adopt Christianity, Old Church Slavonic, modified to incorporate typically Kievan features (and hence often called Russian Church Slavonic), became the language of the liturgy, religious writing, translation and historiography (Vlasto, 1986).

East Slavonic is a name commonly given to a variety of mutually intelligible dialects spoken by Slavic tribes inhabiting the territory of

Kievan Rus; alternative terms for this conglomerate of dialects include 'Rusian' (the language of the Rusians), 'ancient Russian' and 'old Russian' (Press, 2007). At times, East Slavonic not only co-existed but also intersected with Old Church Slavonic. A common core of grammar and vocabulary facilitated the mixing of the two, and some texts were written in a mixture of Old Church Slavonic and East Slavonic (Press, 2007; Vlasto, 1986). At the same time, sentence structure of Old Church Slavonic was much more complex and elaborate than that of East Slavonic and untutored East Slavs may have found the language difficult to understand (Franklin, 2002).

While Kievan Rus was not yet a literate society in the modern sense of the word, by the late 11th century, reading and writing for a variety of purposes were commonplace among the urban population (Franklin, 2002; Rybakov, 1982) and, in this context, it becomes legitimate to talk about the linguistic landscape. What constituted the linguistic landscape in ancient Kiev? The first place where people from all walks of life were likely to encounter linguistic signs was the city's religious establish- ments, where inscriptions were placed over doors and also as captions on mosaics and frescoes. To date, such inscriptions are best preserved in St. Sophia Cathedral, built in the early 11th century, and in the remaining mosaics of the Church of St. Michael. The captions on these mosaics and frescoes appear in Old Church Slavonic, a written lingua franca of the Slavs, and in Greek, an international lingua franca of the period (Franklin, 2002; Nikitenko, 2008; see also http://www.icon-art.info/ location.php?lng = en&loc_id = 148).

Commercial signage, if such signage indeed existed in ancient Kiev, would have been made of wood. Given the destruction and burning of the city by the Tatar-Mongols in 1240, it is not surprising that we do not have any evidence of such signs. Preserved commercial signage involves secondary writing, that is objects where writing is integral but not the main purpose: inscriptions on coins, personal seals and jewelry, and artisans' names on sword-blades, helmets and household objects (Franklin, 2002; Rybakov, 1982). The dominant language of this signage is East Slavonic, which is consistent with the finding that East Slavonic was the language of commercial and personal writing in Kievan Rus (Franklin, 2002).

Interestingly, we also have evidence of private signage from that period, namely graffiti. The biggest collection of graffiti, counting hundreds, is preserved on the walls of St. Sophia Cathedral. Some of these inscriptions include dates and the earliest are from the period in which the cathedral was built, 1019–1037 (Nikitenko, 2008). The majority of inscriptions from the Kievan Rus period appear in East Slavonic (see Figure 8.1).

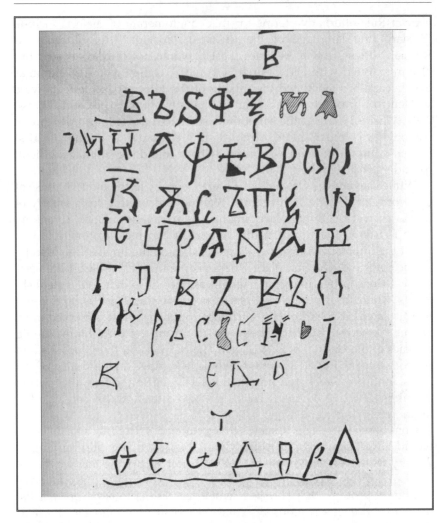

Figure 8.1 Graffiti on the wall of St. Sophia Cathedral announcing the death of Prince Yaroslav the Wise, 20 February 1054 (reproduced from Rybakov, 1982)

At the same time, 80 of the St. Sophia graffiti are in Greek and a few display a mixture of both languages (Evdokimova, 2008). This is not surprising, since Kiev was a major international center of religion and trade, and languages used by its visitors and inhabitants included other Slavic languages, Scandinavian and Turkic languages, and Armenian, German, Greek and Hebrew (Magocsi, 1996). Archeological evidence revealing the presence of these languages in the linguistic landscape includes foreign-made coins bearing inscriptions in Norse runes, Latin,

Kufic, Arabic and Greek, princely seals and amulets sporting Greek or bilingual Greek-Slavonic inscriptions, and a stone mould with an inscription in Arabic (Franklin, 2002; Franklin & Shepard, 1996; Rybakov, 1982).

What we see then is that the earliest period of Kievan history already displays a discontinuity between the languages of official signage, Old Church Slavonic and Greek, and the language of commercial and private signage and of everyday interaction, East Slavonic. This discontinuity can be understood as a form of diglossia, with Greek and Old Church Slavonic functioning as languages of the church and East Slavonic as the language of civil administration, commerce and everyday interaction (Franklin, 2002; Franklin & Shepard, 1996; Press, 2007).

Grand Duchy of Lithuania and the Polish-Lithuanian Commonwealth: 14th to 17th century

The next period of the city's history begins with the near-total destruction of Kiev by Tatar-Mongols in 1240. Its churches and buildings ruined and its population decimated, Kiev lost its significance as a political, economic, religious and cultural center and its population dwindled to 8,500–10,000 inhabitants (Hamm, 1993). Eventually, northern Rus united around Moscow and Novgorod, becoming the land of Muscovy, while southern Rus came under control of the Grand Duchy of Lithuania (Kiev in 1363) (Snyder, 2003). The separation of the former territories of the Kievan Rus led to divergence between East Slavic dialects and to the emergence of a new vernacular, *ruski* (Ruthenian), on the southern territory of the Grand Duchy of Lithuania.

Due to repeated Tatar-Mongol invasions, very few material traces remain of the Lithuanian period in Kievan history. The main information comes from manuscripts and documents of the era and from written testimonies of travelers, such as Martin Gruneveg (1584), Erich Liasota (1594) and Abraham von Vesterfeld (1651), with the latter also producing very detailed drawings of mid-17th-century Kiev (Nikitenko, 2008; Rusina *et al.*, 2008). What is known, however – and is highly unusual – is that the Grand Duchy of Lithuania, Rus and Samogitia did not put its linguistic stamp on the newly conquered territories. Instead, it adopted as its official language the literary version of Ruthenian, written in Cyrillic and also known as Chancery Slavonic; Latin and Polish were also used as official languages in the Grand Duchy, while Lithuanian did not play an important role in the state and was spoken by a small number of people (Magocsi, 1996; Rusina *et al.*, 2008; Smolij, 2008; Snyder, 2003).

Consequently, the linguistic landscape of Kiev did not change much with its incorporation into the Grand Duchy and the public writing continued to be in Cyrillic, as seen in manuscripts and documents, captions on church frescoes and inscriptions on church bells, personal seals and coins (Rusina *et al.*, 2008; Smolij, 2008). The maintenance of the vernacular is confirmed by the graffiti on the walls of St Sophia Cathedral, where 75 inscriptions come from the 13th and 14th centuries and 24 from the 15th to 17th centuries (Nikitenko, 2008). Polish and Latin also began to appear in public writing, in particular on seals and coins (Rusina *et al.*, 2008; Smolij, 2008).

The Lublin Union of 1569 led to the formation of the Polish-Lithuanian Commonwealth and the redistribution of the territories, whereby Lithuania retained the territories of present-day Belarus, while the Polish crown acquired most of present-day Ukraine (Smolij, 2008; Snyder, 2003). The separation of the territories led to gradual divergence between varieties of Ruthenian, opening the path for the eventual emergence of Belarusian and Ukrainian.

The transition also affected the linguistic landscape in Kiev, now Kijów, where public uses of written language became dominated by Polish (Snyder, 2003; Wilson, 2000). Based on the language of documents and manuscripts of the era, we can speculate that Polish may have been the dominant language of public signage in Kijów, but the signage itself has not been preserved. The relentless polonization led to the addition of Polish to the repertoires of Ruthenian elites (Subtelny, 1994) and to the significant influence of Polish on the local variety of Ruthenian (Ogienko, 2004). Old Church Slavonic was, nevertheless, preserved in religious establishments, as seen in the signs placed in St Sophia Cathedral during the reconstructions completed in the early 17th century (Nikitenko, 2008: 52). The languages of everyday interaction in polonized Kijów were Polish and Ruthenian; other languages spoken there include Armenian, German, Greek, Hebrew and Italian (Hamm, 1993; Magocsi, 1996; Snyder, 2003; Subtelny, 1994).

Russian empire: 17th to 19th century

The 1648 Cossack uprising against the Polish overlords, led by Bohdan Khmelnitsky, marks the beginning of the third major period in Kievan history. The rebels took over much of present-day Ukraine, and then sought an alliance with Russia, helping Russians wage war on the Polish-Lithuanian Commonwealth. Following the Treaties of Pereyaslav (1654) and Andrusovo (1667), Ukraine was split along the river Dnieper and left-bank Ukraine, including Kiev, was incorporated into the Russian empire. Integration into the Russian empire led to the replacement of Polish with Russian as the language of administration, education and the linguistic landscape. Polish also disappeared from public use, because Poles who were not slaughtered by Khmelnitsky's troops were either expelled or migrated willingly to the Polish territories.

Meanwhile, the inhabitants of Kiev and the rest of left-bank Ukraine slowly began to shift their self-identification from Ruthenians, Rusyns or Malorossy (Little Russians) to Ukrainians. The latter term gained currency in the 19th century, with the rise of Ukrainian nationalism and the establishment of modern literary Ukrainian, commonly linked to the 1798 publication of Kotliarevsky's play *Eneida* (Magocsi, 1996; Ogienko, 2004; Press, 2007; Subtelny, 1994; Vlasto, 1986). The imperial Russian government attempted a number of reforms to curtail the rise of Ukrainian nationalism, including the 1876 Ems Decree that banned publication of works in Ukrainian (Magocsi, 1996: 372–373). Yet these measures affected only a small proportion of the Ukrainian population, namely, the intellectual elite who now had to rely on works published in western Ukraine. The majority of Ukrainians at the time (93% in 1897) were peasants who were not taught in either Russian or Ukrainian and remained illiterate (Magocsi, 1996; Wilson, 2000).

The real russification of Kiev took place not through enforced administrative measures, but through demographic changes in the city's makeup brought about by the industrial revolution. In the 19th century, the city's population swelled from 19,000 residents in 1797, to 50,137 in 1845 to 626,000 in 1914, due to a massive influx of Russian workers brought in from the north as factory laborers and miners (Hamm, 1993; Magocsi, 1996, 2007; Subtelny, 1994). Factory owners found it more efficient to 'import' skilled Russian workers than to rely on unskilled local labor, while Ukrainian peasants avoided the city, migrating instead to the Northern Caucasus, Kazakhstan, Siberia or the Far East in search of land (Liber, 1992; Magocsi, 1996, 2007; Subtelny, 1994). As a result, in 1897, ethnic Russians constituted 54% of the city's population; the proportion of Russian speakers was even higher due to russification of linguistic minorities and of Ruthenian elites who were switching from Ruthenian and Polish to Russian and French, attracted by advancement opportunities in the imperial service (Subtelny, 1994; Wilson, 2000). In 1917, Ukrainian speakers represented only 16% of the city's population (Liber, 1992).

It is not surprising then that by the 19th century Russian became the dominant language of the Kievan linguistic landscape. In the 1890s, a visitor to Kiev noted that the city was 'not Ukrainian in character, but rather Moscovite. Russian script and Russian words appeared on street signs, storefronts, restaurants, and taverns. And when we said that we neither spoke nor understood Russian, people tried to speak to us in Polish. Here and there a villager spoke Ukrainian, as did a few from the working poor' (cited in Hamm, 1993: 102–103). This observation is borne out by the photographs in my corpus, which show that Russian dominated public signage. A few pictures display official signs, such as *Okruzhnoi voennyi gospital* (Regional military hospital) (Konchakovskii & Malakov, 1993: 286), but the majority are of commercial signage, as illustrated in Figure 8.2. The signs on these pictures announce hotels such as *Natsional'naia gostinitsa* (National Hotel), stores such as *Moskovskij mehovoi magazin* (Moscow fur store) and other service establishments such as *Fotografia* (Photography) or *Parikmaher* (Hair salon). Russian dominates the signage but one can also find signs in French, such as *Coiffeur, Hotel Belle Vue* or *Hôtel François*, in German and Polish, and, as in Figure 8.2, signs of owners' names spelled in the Latin alphabet (Anisimov, 2003, 2007; Arutiunian, 2005; Hamm, 1993; Konchakovskii & Malakov, 1993; Makarov, 2005; Mashkevich, 2006). The dominance of Russian and the importance of French are also replicated in the city's representation of itself. Thus, Arutiunian's (2005) comprehensive collection of turn-of-the-20th-century Kiev postcards contains 496 postcards of which 97% (480) display inscriptions in Russian, 30% (151) are bilingual in Russian and French and only 3% (16) are in Ukrainian.

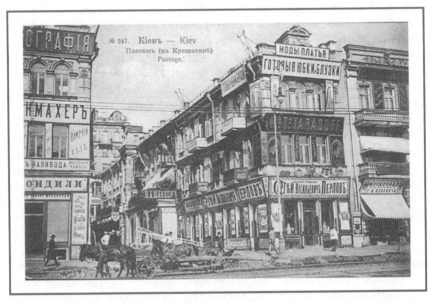

Figure 8.2 Kiev's main street, Kreshchatyk, at the turn of the 20th century (www.oldkiev.info)

We also have material evidence of private signage from that period, namely, cemetery tombstones. Anisimov (2007: 230–232) provides evidence of Russian-language epitaphs from the 17th, 18th and 19th centuries. In my own corpus from the Baikovoe cemetery, late 19th- to early 20th-century epitaphs are mostly in Russian, the other two languages being Polish and Hebrew, which is consistent with the fact that before 1918 the cemetery had Polish, German and Jewish sections. Anisimov (2007: 231) also mentions epitaphs in Ukrainian from the same period.

The renewed presence of Polish in commercial and private signage is a result of the 18th-century incorporation of the right-bank Ukraine into the Russian empire. Subsequently, many Polish landowners moved to the city; thousands more came each winter for the Contract Fair (Hamm, 1993). After the unsuccessful insurrection of 1863, the Polish influence in the city had waned, yet by the turn of the 19th century, Poles still made up about 8% of the total population of Kiev and constituted a lively and thriving community (Hamm, 1993; Lukowski & Zawadzki, 2006).

To sum up, by the end of the 19th century, Kiev was a Russian-speaking city with Russian-language signage. At the same time, the city maintained its multilingual character and alongside Russian, one could see signs in French, Polish, German and Hebrew. One could also hear a variety of languages, including Armenian, Belarusian, French, German, Greek, Polish, Romanian, Serbian, Tatar, Ukrainian and Yiddish (Hamm, 1993).

Soviet Union: 1918–1991

The next period of Kievan history begins when the 1917 October Revolution and the end of WWI led to the dissolution of the Russian empire. The emergence of the Soviet Union led to a new change in the linguistic landscape of the city: the appearance of Ukrainian. This change can be best understood in the context of the overall Soviet policies of the era. To remake the country in a new image, Bolsheviks needed to convey their ideas to people who spoke over a hundred different languages and were often illiterate to boot (Liber, 1992). To mobilize this wary population for socialism, Lenin and his followers initiated a massive literacy campaign and a large nation-building program, known as *korenizatsia* (nativization), which divided the country into stable na-tional-territorial units and supported national elites and their languages and cultures (Liber, 1992; Pavlenko, 2008a).

As a result of this nativization campaign, in 1922–1933, Ukraine had experienced an unprecedented period of Ukrainianization, accompanied by a dramatic rise in literacy levels (Liber, 1992; Magocsi, 1996, 2007;

Masenko, 2004; Ogienko, 2004; Smolij, 2008; Subtelny, 1994). The Soviet government initiated Ukrainian-language standardization efforts, established a comprehensive Ukrainian-language educational system, subsidized publication of Ukrainian books, journals and newspapers, expanded Ukrainian theater, and founded Ukrainian radio, film and opera, sparking an artistic and literary renaissance (Liber, 1992; Masenko, 2004). Ukrainian speakers were favored for promotions, and Russian-speaking officials had to attend Ukrainian-language courses and pass a series of examinations to keep their jobs (Liber, 1992). Linguistic and cultural ukrainianization of Kiev was reinforced by the large influx of Ukrainian peasants who entered the urban labor force. The city population nearly doubled from 366,396 in 1920 to 560,000 in 1934, and by 1926 Ukrainians had become a dominant (42%) ethnic group (Liber, 1992; Masenko, 2004).

It is not surprising then that pictures of the city from the 1920s and early 1930s feature predominantly Ukrainian-language signs. Among these are official signs, such as *Proletars'kyi sad* (Proletarian garden [park]) (1932; Anisimov, 2003: 182), and political signs typical of the era, such as a big banner displayed on the façade of the Anti-Religion museum *'Bezvirnyts'ka kul'tura znyshchyt' religijni zabobony'* (Atheist culture will destroy religious superstitions) (1934; Anisimov, 2003: 27, 331, 336; Anisimov, 2007: 101). And yet, ultimately, Ukrainian did not come to occupy the hegemonic position in Kyiv. In the early 1930s, the Soviet government's concerns about bourgeois nationalism and low levels of Russian competence among non-Russians led to a wave of repressions, purges of national elites and reversal of some *korenizatsiia* policies. The ensuing russification took a three-pronged approach that involved status planning (i.e. promotion of Russian as a language necessary for a true Soviet citizen), acquisition planning (i.e. efforts to make Russian an obligatory language in non-Russian schools) and corpus planning (i.e. efforts to bring grammars and lexicons of national languages closer to Russian) (Pavlenko, 2008a; for details on Ukraine, see Bilaniuk, 2005; Masenko, 2004).

The return of Russian to its dominant position, however, did not mean the disappearance of Ukrainian, rather, throughout the history of the USSR, Ukrainian signs co-existed with Russian ones. Pictures from the 1920s and 1930s also show Russian-language commercial signs, such as *rabochij kooperativ* (workers' cooperative) or *sorabkop* (abbreviation of the 'Soviet workers' cooperative') (see Figure 8.3; also see Anisimov, 2003: 338). In turn, pictures from the 1950s and 1960s display some Ukrainian-language signage (www.oldkiev.info, www.nostalgia2.kiev.ua). For instance, a 1962 picture of the city's largest farmer's market sports Ukrainian-language store signs, such as *bakalia* (grocery) and *ovochi* (vegetables) (Anisimov, 2007: 133).

Figure 8.3 Worker's cooperative store, 1930 (www.oldkiev.info)

Tombstone inscriptions at the Baikovoe cemetery show that during the Soviet period the choice of language 'to die in' was mostly a matter of personal preference and of changing demographics. Hebrew and Polish lost their prominence and appear only in bilingual arrangements: my corpus contains only two Soviet-era pictures with Russian-Hebrew tombstone inscriptions from 1929 and 1933 and one with an inscription in Polish and Ukrainian, on the monument for a Polish writer Wanda Wasilewska (1964) (Figure 8.4). Many of the signs between 1918 and 1991 are in Russian, others are in Ukrainian, including all inscriptions on monuments erected for prominent members of the Ukrainian intelligentsia, such as Maksym Rylsky (1964), Volodymyr Sosura (1965), Pavlo Tychyna (1967), Iurii Smolych (1976), Mykola Bazhan (1983) and Natalia Uzhvii (1986).

All in all, Soviet Kiev, neither fully Russified nor completely Ukrainianized, existed in a state of asymmetrical bilingualism. Official signage often appeared in both languages and commercial and private signs in one of the two, but more commonly in Russian, the language of everyday interaction.

Independent Ukraine: 1991–present

In 1991, Ukraine declared its independence from the USSR. Ukrainian was proclaimed the only state language, and the government initiated the processes of language shift to Ukrainian, derussification and replacement of Russian with English. The derussification took place across all areas of language use, including the linguistic landscape. Bilaniuk (2005) who did her ethnographic fieldwork in Ukraine in 1991–1992 recalls that, at first, Kyiv authorities did not replace bilingual and

Figure 8.4 Grave monument for Wanda Wasilewska, with the tombstone inscription in the back in Ukrainian and Polish (author's picture, August 2008)

Russian-language signs with Ukrainian-language signs, but opted to modify letters in existing signs, thus changing Russian words into Ukrainian as quickly and inexpensively as possible. She also notes that businesses were among the first to display Ukrainian-English signs, in accordance with the new fashion for English.

Eventually, new signage replaced the old, and three changes became evident: the establishment of Ukrainian as the dominant language of the linguistic landscape, the erasure (albeit not complete disappearance) of Russian and the emergence of English as the global

Figure 8.5 Billboard advertising a new magazine issue, with Russian in the main text, Ukrainian on the frame and English in the website address (author's picture, June 2009)

language. In today's Kyiv, official signs and commemorative plaques appear mainly in Ukrainian, commercial signs in Ukrainian, but also in Russian and English, and private signage, such as graffiti and advertisements posted on public billboards, in all three languages. Figure 8.5 illustrates a multilingual arrangement frequently encountered in commercial signage: (a) the text in the red frame appears in Ukrainian (a magazine with Tetyana Ramus – note! Already being sold), (b) the text on the magazine page appears in Russian, as this is a Russian-language publication and (c) the website address above the bar code in the lower right corner appears in English.

While the rise in the visibility of English is easily explained by its prestige and global significance (e.g. Backhaus, 2007), the perseverance of Russian is explained by the fact that Russian remains the dominant language of everyday interaction in Kyiv, even though the city's institutions and educational establishments function in Ukrainian (Besters-Dilger, 2008; Bilaniuk & Melnyk, 2008; Zalizniak & Masenko, 2001). The ukrainianization efforts resulted in the rise in visibility, prestige and use of Ukrainian in Kyiv but not in language shift. The city's inhabitants remain bilingual and Russian retains its prestige and popularity even among members of the youngest generation educated in Ukrainian-language schools (Besters-Dilger, 2008; Bilaniuk & Melnyk, 2008; Marshall, 2002; Masenko, 2004). Many reasons account for this language maintenance, including emotional attachment to the language of childhood, continuous attraction held by Russian-language publications and media, and economic advantages, offered by Russian as the lingua franca of commerce in the post-Soviet space and the language of labor migration to Russia (Besters-Dilger, 2008; Masenko, 2004; Pavlenko, 2008b).

Conclusions

The main purpose of this chapter was to examine the languages used in the linguistic landscape and spoken interaction in different periods in Kyiv history and to consider factors that shaped language change in the Kyiv linguistic landscape. The bird's-eye overview of Kyivan sociolinguistic history reveals that language change in the linguistic landscape is not necessarily a reflection of a larger language shift. Rather, it is a direct outcome of changes in political regimes. In Kyiv, every new administration, with the exception of the Grand Duchy of Lithuania, made a mark on the city's linguistic landscape, initiating a top-down change, from Slavonic used in the Kievan Rus and the Grand Duchy of Lithuania, to Polish in the Polish-Lithuanian Commonwealth, to Russian in the Russian empire, to Ukrainian and Russian in the USSR, and, now, to Ukrainian in independent Ukraine. In cases where the newly imposed languages were incongruent with the language or languages spoken by the population, the changes led to a diglossic situation where one language would be used for official signage and another for commercial and private signage and everyday interaction. The city also has a thousand-year-old multilingual tradition that goes back to the days of its founding as a trade post.

Given Kyiv's centuries-long history as a Russian-speaking city, the prestige of Russian as a regional lingua franca and the bilingualism of the city's population, it is not surprising to see that the new Ukrainian government – just like the administrations of centuries past – has failed to create a homogeneous monolingual population. For now, Kyiv remains unapologetically bilingual, and perhaps even trilingual and triglossic, with English functioning as a global language, Ukrainian as the official language, the language of administration and education, and Russian as the dominant language of everyday interaction, commerce and cultural consumption.

Note

1. Throughout, I will use alternative city names in accordance with the dominant usage in particular historic periods.

References

Anisimov, A. (2003) *Portret v interiere vechnosti: Moi Kiev* [*A Portrait in the Context of Eternity: My Kiev*]. Kiev: Zhnets.

Anisimov, A. (2007) *Kiev i kievliane* [*Kiev and Kievites*]. Kiev: Telegraf.

Arutiunian, A. (2005) *Kiev na pochtovoi otkrytke kontsa XIX – nachala XX veka: Fotoal'bom* [*Kiev on Postcards from the End of the 19th – Beginning of the 20th Century: Picture Album*]. Kiev: Kniga.

Backhaus, P. (2007) *Linguistic Landscapes: A Comparative Study of Urban Multilingualism in Tokyo*. Clevedon: Multilingual Matters.

Besters-Dilger, J. (ed.) (2008) *Movna polityka i movna situatsiia v Ukraïni* [*Language Policy and Language Situation in Ukraine*]. Kyiv: Kyiv-Mohyla Academy.

Bilaniuk, L. (2005) *Contested Tongues: Language Politics and Cultural Correction in Ukraine*. Ithaca, NY: Cornell University Press.

Bilaniuk, L. and Melnyk, S. (2008) A tense and shifting balance: Bilingualism and education in Ukraine. *International Journal of Bilingual Education and Bilingualism* 11 (3&4), 339–372.

Evdokimova, A. (2008) Iazykovye osobennosti grecheskih graffiti Sofii Kievskoi [Linguistic Particularities of Greek Graffiti in St. Sophia of Kiev]. Doctoral dissertation, Russian Academy of Sciences. On WWW at http://www.iling.spb.ru/dissovet/old-abstracts/evdokimova/abstract.pdf. Accessed 18.8.08.

Franklin, S. (2002) *Writing, Society, and Culture in Early Rus, c. 950–1300*. Cambridge: Cambridge University Press.

Franklin, S. and Shepard, J. (1996) *The Emergence of Rus: 750–1200*. London/New York: Longman.

Hamm, M. (1993) *Kiev: A Portrait, 1800–1917*. Princeton, NJ: Princeton University Press.

Konchakovskii, A. and Malakov, D. (1993) *Kiev Mikhaila Bulgakova: Fotografii, dokumenty i otkrytki iz gosudarstvennyh i chastnyh arhivov* [*Mikhail Bulgakov's Kiev: Photographs, Documents, and Postcards from State and Private Archives*]. Kiev: Mystetstvo.

Liber, G. (1992) *Soviet Nationality Policy, Urban Growth, and Identity Change in the Ukrainian SSR 1923–1934*. Cambridge: Cambridge University Press.

Lukowski, J. and Zawadzki, H. (2006) *A Concise History of Poland*. Cambridge: Cambridge University Press.

Magocsi, P. (1996) *A History of Ukraine*. Seattle, WA: University of Washington Press.

Magocsi, P. (2007) *Ukraine: An Illustrated History*. Seattle, WA: University of Washington Press.

Makarov, A. (2005) *Malaia entsiklopedia Kievskoi stariny* [*Little Encyclopedia of Kiev Antiquity*]. Kiev: Dovira.

Marshall, C. (2002) Post-Soviet language policy and the language utilization patterns of Kyivan youth. *Language Policy* 1, 237–260.

Masenko, L. (2004) *Mova i suspilstvo: Postkolonialnyi vymir* [*Language and Society: A Postcolonial Dimension*]. Kyiv: Kyiv-Mohyla Academy.

Mashkevich, S. (2006) Iazyk do Kieva dovedet, a v Kieve? [Your Tongue will Get You to Kiev, but What About in Kiev?] *Zerkalo nedeli* 43 (622), 2006. http:// www.zn.ua/3000/3050/55014/. Accessed 30.4.10.

Nikitenko, N. (2008) *Sviataia Sofia Kievskaia* [*St. Sophia of Kiev*]. Kiev: Gorobets.

Ogienko, I. (2004) *Istoriia ukraïn'skoï literaturnoï movy* [*History of Ukrainian Literary Language*]. Kyiv: Nasha kul'tura i nauka.

Pavlenko, A. (2008a) Multilingualism in post-Soviet countries: Language revival, language removal, and sociolinguistic theory. *International Journal of Bilingual Education and Bilingualism* 11 (3&4), 275–314.

Pavlenko, A. (2008b) Russian in post-Soviet countries. *Russian Linguistics* 32 (1), 59–80.

Press, I. (2007) *A History of the Russian Language and its Speakers*. Muenchen: LINCOM Europa.

Rusina, O., Svarnyk, I., Voitovych, L., Vashchuk, D., Blanutsa, A. and Cherkas, B. (2008) *Ukraïna: Litovs'ka doba* [*Ukraine: The Lithuanian Period*]. Kyiv: Baltia-Druk.

Rybakov, B. (1982) *Kievskaia Rus' i russkie kniazhestva XII-XIII vv.* [*Kievan Rus and Russian Principalities in XII–XIII Centuries*]. Moscow: Nauka.

Smolij, V. (2008) Istoria Ukrainy [*History of Ukraine*]. National Academy of Sciences of Ukraine. Moscow: Olma.

Snyder, T. (2003) *The Reconstruction of Nations: Poland, Ukraine, Lithuania, Belarus, 1569–1999*. New Haven/London: Yale University Press.

Subtelny, O. (1994) *Ukraine: A History*. Toronto: University of Toronto Press.

Vlasto, A. (1986) *A Linguistic History of Russia to the End of the Eighteenth Century*. Oxford: Clarendon Press.

Wilson, A. (2000) *The Ukrainians: Unexpected Nation*. New Haven/London: Yale University Press.

Zalizniak, H. and Masenko, L. (2001) *Movna sytuatsiia Kieva: den' siogodnishnii ta priideshnii* [*Language Situation in Kyiv: Today and Tomorrow*]. Kyiv: Kyiv-Mohyla Academy.

Part 3
Benefits of Linguistic Landscape

Chapter 9

Life in the Garden of Eden: The Naming and Imagery of Residential Hong Kong

ADAM JAWORSKI and SIMONE YEUNG

In the past few decades, space has been theorized in terms of the geography of social networks, as a product and consequence of social interrelations, coexisting heterogeneity and multiplicity, and as a contingent and emergent process (e.g. Yi-Fu Tuan, 1974; Massey & Jess, 1995; Massey, 2005). For David Harvey, the key to understanding space as a social construction lies in human practice:

> The problem of the proper conceptualization of space is resolved through human practice with respect to it. In other words, there are no philosophical answers to philosophical questions that arise over the nature of space – the answers lie in human practice. The question "what is space?" is therefore replaced by the question "how is it that different human practices create and make use of different conceptualizations of space?" (Harvey, 1973: 13, cited in Harvey, 2006, 125–126)

Harvey's view of space echoes Henri Lefebvre's (1991: 39) now well-known approach to space as a (social) product and his notion of *lived* or *representational* space, which 'overlays physical space, making symbolic use of its objects' through its inhabitants' or users' concrete and subjective actions. *Lived* spaces are manifestations of ideological conflicts and tensions, distinct from but contingent upon the representations of space through our cognitive and sensory 'knowing' of space.

Human practice in relation to space may involve physical manipulation through agriculture, architecture and landscaping, and symbolic activities of representation such as depicting, narrating and remembering. These activities transform spaces into places that we come to 'know' both sensually and intellectually (Entrikin, 1991). They are also known discursively. Speaking, writing and other semiotic codes found *in* space index particular localities, orient us through different levels of territorial and societal stratification including identity claims, power relations and their contestations (Johnstone, 2004). This social construction of space is inextricably linked with the idea of a *sense of place*, arising from the cultural meanings people actively give to their lives (see Harvey quoted above), their claims to belong to a place, drawing boundaries and keeping those who do not belong, the outsiders, at a distance (Rose, 1995). These are acts of power aimed at controlling people by controlling an area, for example through economic restructuring headed by multi-national corporations, 'gentrification' of inner-city locations driven by property developers, or more individualized, though no less powerful, 'politics of identity', which transforms socially marginalized people into *geographically* marginalized people (Rose, 1995); for some, social and territorial exclusion finds its culmination in the aggressive enclosure, privatization and territorialization of urban spaces represented by 'gated communities' (see Mills, 1993; Low, 2001; McLaughlin & Muncie, 1999 in Mac Giolla Chríost, 2007: 31; Winchester *et al.*, 2003: 81–84).

Although sociolinguists have long associated different ways of speaking with territorially defined identities of speakers (through association of linguistic variables with neighborhoods, cities, regions or nations), it is only relatively recently that they have been influenced by cultural geographers and have started making more explicit connections between speech variation and place as a more dynamic concept replacing the traditional view of place as a static and neutral location of persons and objects in space. For example, Johnstone (2004) relates the idea of creating a *sense of localness* through the 'local' forms of speech, their development, cultivation and folk-linguistic mythologies, particularly in response to the globalizing processes increasing contact between 'old' and 'new' ways of speaking. In her detailed ethnographic study of Mt. Pleasant, an area of Washington DC, Modan (2007) examines discourse as a form of spatial rather than social action, and demonstrates how the residents' spoken and written, private and public discourses and interactions create different conceptions of the neighborhood and spatialized identities across ethnic, gender and socio-economic boundaries. Written from the position of language policy and planning, Mac Giolla Chríost's (2007) study takes a macro-sociolinguistic approach to theorizing urban spaces with regard to power relations and identity formation through the lens of place-naming, multilingualism and linguistic vitality.

Linguistic and Semiotic Landscapes

An important stimulus for the study of linguistic/semiotic landscapes (e.g. Shohamy & Gorter, 2008; Jaworski & Thurlow, 2010a) has come from Scollon and Wong Scollon's (2003: 110) work on *geosemiotics*, i.e. 'the study of the social meaning of the material placement of signs in the world'. As they explain:

Whether a sign is an icon, a symbol, or an index, there is a major aspect of its meaning that is produced only through the placement of that sign in the real world in contiguity with other objects in that world. This is the focus of the field of geosemiotics. (Scollon & Wong Scollon, 2003: 30)

In their approach, Scollon and Wong Scollon (2003: 146) are primarily concerned with the *indexability* of the material world through discourse, i.e. how the meaning of signs is predicated on their placement in the material world, which includes the situated meaning of social actors' position in space in relation to the semiotic environment and in relation to one another (Goffman's, 1971 *interaction order*). More recent work on linguistic and semiotic landscapes (cf. Leeman & Modan, 2009; Jaworski & Thurlow 2010b) has also adopted the view of human and cultural geographers (e.g. Cosgrove, 1985; Mitchell, 2000) of landscape as a '*way of seeing* the external world' (1984: 46) and 'a visual ideology' (1984: 47; see also Berger, 1982).

In his work, Cosgrove traces the (Western) idea of landscape to its roots in the scientific and artistic developments of the Italian Renaissance in the 15th and 16th centuries and the formulation of the geometric principles of *linear perspective* – a technique through which the artist determines the viewer's 'point of view', while through framing, the scope of reality revealed is also controlled (Cosgrove, 1985: 48). Linear perspective found numerous applications in cartography, architecture, land survey, map-making, artillery science and the measurement of distance, surface and volume, all pertinent to the early development of commerce, capitalist finance, agriculture, the land market, navigation and warfare, in sum, the early development of an urban, bourgeois, rationalist conception of the world (Cosgrove, 1985). Thus, as Leeman and Modan (2009: 337) observe in their study of the commodification of Chinese language displays in Washington DC's Chinatown, the structuring of linguistic landscapes privileges particular subject positions and points of view, and has material consequences for urban dwellers.

In this chapter, we deal with one particular aspect of 'place semiotics': the socio-cultural 'reading' of space due to the placement of material language, or more broadly discourse, inscribed in space. Here, space is both the physical location or setting for emplaced language and one of the contextualizing forces for the interpretation of inscription. Conversely, by indexing the material world, emplaced language and other visible traces of human activity and interactions with space give space its 'meaning' or create our 'sense of place' (cf. above). Nowhere is this more apparent than in the city.

Cities are large and complex spaces whose origins, significance, development and decline are dependent on a variety of interlinked factors: political (as loci of power), economic (as industrial sites; transportation hubs), cultural (as centers of cultural production), religious ('cathedral cities'), educational ('university cities') and so on. Regardless of their 'character', however, cities are always 'densely populated human settlements' (Miles, 2007: 8). It is particularly in this sense that we propose to consider the linguistic landscape of residential Hong Kong – as a dynamic and multifaceted dwelling place within a global financial center of exorbitant property prices. Our prime concern here, then, is a reflection on the linguistic and other semiotic choices displayed in the signage indexing residential buildings in Hong Kong and their possible consequences for the perception (a way of seeing) of the city as a culturally dynamic, hybrid environment characterized by highly complex asymmetries, and uneven social and power relations (cf. Amin & Graham, 1999: 34; cited in Mac Giolla Chríost, 2007: 22).

Scollon and Wong Scollon's (2003) discussion of place semiotics culminates in their notion of the *semiotic aggregate* – the intersection of multiple semiotic systems, sign complexes or discourses in a dialogical interaction with each other that create a composite meaning of place and shape or accommodate various social activities (performances). For example, a combination of commercial signs in a particular area may be indicative of what sort of shopping can be done there, or a particular arrangement of signage and furniture in a public space (e.g. in a café) may facilitate conversational encounters among individuals. However, semiotic aggregates are rarely, if ever, 'read' (or analyzable) all at once; rather each act of semiotic interpretation is a form of selection of a subset of signs for the social actor's attention (Scollon & Wong Scollon, 2003: 205). Following Lanham (1993), Jones (2005, 2010) refers to the cognitive and social frameworks guiding and attracting our attention to specific semiotic objects in space as 'attention structures':

> Spaces are constructed not just through the objects and boundaries that surround us and the habitual ways we conceive of them, but also through interaction with others who are operating in the "same" space. Scollon and Wong Scollon (2004) call these three elements of social space the *discourses in place* (the physical/semiotic setting), the *interaction order* (the social relationships among participants) and the *historical body* (the life experiences-memories, learning, skills, and plans) of the individuals. Each of these elements helps to determine how we "live" space by structuring our attention in particular ways that make some kinds of social actions possible and others impossible. (Jones, 2010: 153)

Jones' approach proves extremely useful for our understanding of how we experience and interact with space and its semiotic 'signposts'; how our attention structures guide us in the process of identifying and discriminating specific signs and, whether we find them *relevant* (in the sense of Sperber & Wilson, 1986), and when we do, how we ascribe meaning to them. In many ways, these cognitive and social frameworks are akin to Goffman's (1974: 10–11) interpretive frames, i.e. our definitions of social situations, of what goes on in strips of ongoing activities, built up in accordance with our subjective involvement in them (see also below).

Initial forays to the study of linguistic landscapes invoking the notion of discursive frames have been made by Kallen (2010) and Coupland and Garrett (2010). Kallen (2010: 43) rejects the idea of the linguistic landscape as a single system and recommends analyzing it as a confluence of systems or as 'different visual discourse frameworks' observable within a single visual field. His non-exhaustive and non-universal list for the study of discursive frames of linguistic landscapes in Dublin includes the 'civic frame', the 'marketplace', 'portals', the 'wall', the 'detritus zone', the 'community' and the 'school'. In contrast to Kallen's taxonomy of frames based on their emplacement, Coupland and Garrett's analysis of signs containing Welsh language or Welsh cultural references in the Chubut Valley in Patagonia draws attention to the role of the linguistic landscape as part of 'metacultural representation and practice', i.e. invoking cultural difference. This is a view of culture as textual performance (Bauman & Briggs, 1990), whereby diverse discursive resources are engaged in the process of cultural entextualization and recontextualization (also Silverstein & Urban, 1996). In this particular setting, where the dominant language of the community is Spanish, Welsh acts as an index of the past Welsh migration to Patagonia and the present, however distant, association with Wales. Thus, Coupland and Garrett analyze their linguistic and visual data in terms of the 'colonial history frame' (e.g. visible in the faint echoes of Welsh personal names in street signs such as *Miguel D. Jones*), the 'reflexive cultural Welshness frame' (foregrounding Welsh history and 'presence' in Patagonia, e.g. through the visual pairing of Welsh and Argentinean flags on bumper stickers), and the 'Welsh heritage frame' (performed through the celebratory, if exoticized, romanticized and commodified displays of the Welsh language and Welsh iconography, e.g. in the signage advertising *casas de té galesas* 'Welsh tea houses'). It is through this contextually and historically sensitive qualitative approach that Coupland and Garrett demonstrate the usefulness of frame analysis in the study of linguistic/semiotic landscapes for drawing our attention to the nuances of cultural and symbolic values activated, intentionally or otherwise, by emplaced signage, and the meaning potentials of specific indexical displays of languages and iconography.

Our Data

Our reason for invoking interpretive frames and structures of attention here is, in part, to justify our analytic focus in this chapter, which concerns a selective and relatively random set of signs cohering around the task of indexing residential buildings in Hong Kong: a diverse array of 'dwellings' such as tenement houses, housing estates, upmarket apartment blocks, exclusive residential enclaves or 'gated communities', townhouses and villas. The data for this chapter was collected over a two-day period (18–19 April 2007) in eight residential areas of Hong Kong:

- Mong Kok (Kowloon)
- Tsuen Wan (New Territories)
- Sai Wan (Hong Kong Island)
- Shatin Heights (New Territories)
- University (Hong Kong Island)
- Mid-levels (Hong Kong Island)
- Kowloon Tong (Kowloon)
- Victoria Peak (Hong Kong Island)

A photographic record of apartment buildings, residential estates, roads and individual houses was created, roughly amounting to some 260 individual 'addresses', which we take to be our 'units of analysis'. In many cases the inevitable problem of how to 'count' signs cannot be easily resolved, as the names of some buildings/estates were obstructed from view by street market stalls or traffic (hence not visible in our photographs, see Figure 9.1), or they may have been found in more than one place: on the building's gate, on its outer walls and over the driveway to an underground car park (see Figure 9.2). In some cases of bilingual Chinese-English signs, the names of buildings in each language appear separated by a driveway, or some other spatial break, giving an impression of two distinct signs, not one (see Figure 9.5). In some locations (especially the exclusive Victoria Peak, see below), we found (and photographed) several signs together (usually street names and/or house numbers) as they were positioned in close proximity to each other at the foot of a private road leading to otherwise inaccessible residences (see Figure 9.6). Consequently, we refrain from any attempt at a quantitative analysis and focus on a more qualitative approach to the possible meanings and value-systems manifested in the residential signage of Hong Kong. Additionally, we took some photographs of advertisements for new housing developments and estate agents' displays.

As a way of introducing our research site, we group the geographic areas of our data collection into three broad socio-economic categories, in

Figure 9.1 Residential and commercial street, Mong Kong, Hong Kong

terms of the relative cost of property and square footage of 'typical' flats and houses. Table 9.1 overviews these areas, including rough calculations of average square footage of the flats, apartments, town houses and villas (the latter two only to be found in Area 3), and the average prices per square foot. These calculations are highly approximate and based on our survey of a number of websites of Hong Kong property agents.

The three, typically working-class districts in Area 1 (including Mong Kok, Kowloon; Tsuen Wan, New Territories; and Sai Wan, Hong Kong Island) are densely built up with a mixture of relatively low (4–5 storey to high rise) tenement houses, Mong Kok being the most densely populated urban area in the world, with some 120,000 inhabitants per square kilometer. Selective 'gentrification' means that new, high-rise apartment blocks found more typically in Area 2 are also found in Area 1, such as 'Cayman Rise'/'加惠臺' in Sai Wan (see Figure 9.10). In Area 1, residential quarters are thoroughly mixed with a great variety of businesses, shops, inexpensive restaurants and hotels, massage parlors, street markets and so on, making most streets very crowded with traffic and pedestrians. As mentioned above, the narrow entrances to the residential buildings 'blend in' with the many commercial stores, or they may be completely obstructed from view by market stalls, trucks or crowds of people (see Figure 9.1).

Table 9.1 Areas of data collection and their socio-economic differentiation

	Area 1: Mong Kok, Tsuen Wan, Sai Wan	*Area 2: Shatin Heights, University Mid-levels*	*Area 3: Kowloon Tong, Victoria Peak*
Typical square footage of apartments/houses	Below 1000	1000–2000	Above 2000
Typical price per square foot	Below $HK5000	$HK4000–6000	From $HK10,000 (no upper limit)
Typical designation	'Working-class'	'Middle-class'	'Middle- to upper-class'

Area 2 (Shatin Heights, New Territories; University, Hong Kong Island; and Mid-levels, Hong Kong Island) includes predominantly middle-class neighbourhoods in clusters of massive apartment blocks, frequently reaching fifty floors or more, and housing estates with their own driveways, security gates, underground garages, shops or small shopping malls, swimming pools and gymnasia, concierge desks in lavishly decorated entrance halls clad in marble, granite, lit by chandeliers, decorated with fountains, sculptures, paintings, mirrors, bouquets of fresh flowers, and so on. Space permitting, buildings are surrounded by some greenery, and the commercial value of individual apartments increases if they offer uninterrupted city views or, even more desirable, views of Victoria Harbour. However, as with the gentrification of parts of Area 1, in Area 2 one can find 'mixed' neighbourhoods with new style, expensive apartment blocks towering over older, lower tenement houses, or in close proximity to cheap municipal housing projects. Mid-levels is commonly associated with middle-class and expatriate residents.

Area 3 (Kowloon Tong, Kowloon; and Victoria Peak, Hong Kong Island) comprises some of the most exclusive low- and high-rise residential buildings, including small gated communities, rows of town houses on quiet streets and dispersed villas set in opulent gardens, in cul-de-sacs accessible through private roads, often with no pavements, closed off by solid or highly ornate, cast iron gates, secured by barbed wire or CCTV. Of all the areas in our sample, these are the sites of greatest power and prestige due to the degree of commoditization of space and the profile of the residents: many Hong Kong Government officials, influential businesspeople, and top professionals, including wealthy expatriates (Kowloon Tong and Victoria Peak providing the location for many top-ranking, private, international schools).

While we eschew any attempts of a systematic quantitative analysis related to code-choice in the residential signage of Hong Kong, a few remarks about different combinations of languages and types of signs present in our data may be useful by way of foregrounding our subsequent analysis. The signage in our data can be grouped into the following categories:

- Bilingual Chinese-English (regardless of the 'sequence' of languages)
- Monolingual Chinese
- Monolingual English
- Bilingual Chinese-Other (French, Spanish, Italian)
- Monolingual Other (Spanish)
- Street name and number (Bilingual Chinese-English)
- Street name and number (English only)
- Street number only

The first five categories listed above refer to signs displaying the names of buildings with or without the name of the street and street number. For example, the name of the building in Figure 9.2, 'Imperial Court'/'帝豪閣' also includes the street address albeit on a separate plaque and in English only. 'La Noblesse'/'豪福軒' (Figure 9.3) has the

Figure 9.2 Imperial Court/帝豪閣, Mid-levels, Hong Kong

Figure 9.3 La Noblesse/豪福軒, Kowloon Tong, Hong Kong

street numbers of the house integrated with the sign, while '龍旺大廈' (Figure 9.4) includes the name of the house and street address in Chinese only. (We disregard here a small number of signs that display residents' names and/or floor/apartment numbers on or next to doorbells.)

Alongside Chinese (Cantonese), English is an official language in Hong Kong, partly as a reflection of its legacy as a former British colony, partly, and more pertinently today, as a resource for the internationalization of the city epitomized by the Government's branding of Hong Kong as 'Asia's World City' (cf. Flowerdew, 2004). Approximately 2% of the population of Hong Kong are L1 English speakers with another 25% displaying different degrees of fluency in English (Crystal, 1995). Therefore, it would be inappropriate to interpret the presence of bilingual signs in our data as an index of a predominantly (Chinese-English) bilingual population (cf. Coupland, 2010). It is probably more appropriate to suggest that in the residential signage of Hong Kong, as in many other contexts, most notably commerce, advertising, high-end travel, fashion and so on, English and a few other high status languages (see below) are frequently used to bestow on various goods and services symbolic capital associated with globalization, internationalism, sophistication, reliability, etc. (Cheshire & Moser, 1994; Friedrich, 2002; Haarman, 1989; Kelly-Holmes, 2005; Piller, 2001; Thurlow & Jaworski,

Figure 9.4 龍旺大廈, Mong Kok, Hong Kong

2003). In the context of linguistic landscapes, similar observations were made, for example, by Backhaus (2006), Cenoz and Gorter (2006), Huebner (2006) and Lanza and Woldemariam (2009).

As is clear from Table 9.2, in Area 1, approximately one third of all signs are monolingual Chinese, probably in line with the more traditional, mono-ethnic and monolingual Chinese make-up of its residents. On the other hand, Area 3 shows a far greater diversity in the types and linguistic choices of its signage. Most significantly, in our data for Area 3, we find only a small percentage of Chinese-only signs

Figure 9.5 Euston Court/豫苑, Mid-levels, Hong Kong

Figure 9.6 Street numbers, Victoria Peak, Hong Kong

Table 9.2 Language choice in residential signage across Areas 1–3

	Area 1	Area 2	Area 3	Total for all area
Bilingual Chinese-English	16 (61.5%)	109 (87.9%)	24 (21.4%)	149 (56.9%)
Monolingual Chinese	9 (34.6%)	4 (3.2%)	4 (3.6%)	17 (6.5%)
Monolingual English	1 (3.8%)	4 (3.2%)	15 (13.4%)	20 (7.6%)
Bilingual Chinese-Other	0	1 (0.8%)	2 (1.8%)	3 (1.1%)
Monolingual Other	0	0	3 (2.7%)	3 (1.1%)
Street name and number (bilingual Chinese-English)	0	3 (2.4%)	17 (15.2%)	20 (7.6%)
Street name and number (English only)	0	2 (1.6%)	22 (19.6%)	24 (9.2%)
Street number only	0	1 (0.8%)	25 (22.3%)	26 (9.9%)
Total	26 (100%)	124 (100%)	112 (100%)	262 (100%)

(equalling the proportion of English-only signs in Area 1, the token example in our data being the above mentioned, upmarket Manhattan Heights building in Sai Wan), and a fair amount of English-only monolingual signs (13%), as well as a small but intriguing number (five tokens) of uses of languages other than English and Chinese: French, Spanish and Italian. In our sample, there is also one token of a Chinese-Other bilingual sign in Area 2: the Mid-levels 'Casa Bella'/ '寶華軒' Po Wah Hin (Precious Flourish Study Room).

The use of French, Spanish and Italian (or Italian-sounding) names such as 'Chateau Vivienne', 'La Noblesse' (see Figure 9.3), 'La Hacienda' or 'Kelleteria' (derived from the local place name Mt. Kellet) does not seem at all random in the areas of greatest affluence (where we also find a relative paucity of Chinese-only signs). These languages, being associated with some of the most powerful, Western-European nations and popular tourist destinations (for wealthy Hong Kongers), connote not only wealth but also, as suggested above, 'high' culture, sophisticated, good taste and design, and a relaxed lifestyle. Alongside the use of English, a handful of these prestigious 'foreign' languages seem to position the affluent residents of Hong Kong as globally connected particularly through associations with the former colonial 'center' as well as Europeaness, invoking a sense of opulence, aristocratic tradition and land ownership.

Discursive Frames for Residential Signage

Interpretive frames are conceived by Goffman (1974: 8) as situational resources deployed by social actors when faced with the question 'What is it that's going on here?'. Goffman admits that the question is somewhat troublesome as different social actors may have different points of view in approaching the 'same' event. Therefore, frames are our definitions of situations that are built up in accordance with the conventional principles organizing social situations and our subjective involvement in them – in other words, our attention structures (cf. above). What Goffman (1974: 27) refers to as the 'primary frameworks of a particular social group' are the group's belief systems, naturalized interpretations of 'situations', 'given' meanings of objects, typically displaying an isomorphism 'between perception and the organization of what is perceived, in spite of the fact that there are likely to be many valid principles of organization that could but don't inform perception' (Goffman, 1974: 26). This is in contrast to 'social frameworks' that appear to introduce 'corrective' interpretation typically involving the understanding of motive and intent. Social frameworks provide understanding for events by orienting to the agency of the 'doer' while simultaneously apprising his/her action 'based on its honesty, efficiency, safety, elegance, tactfulness, good taste, and so forth' (Goffman, 1974: 22). For Goffman, our reactions to 'astounding' events, when we normally expect that a 'simple' or 'natural' explanation can or will be found is guided by our primary framework. Likewise, 'exhibition of stunts', bodily and communication breakdowns ('gaffes'), chance or accidental events, interpersonal 'tension' or joking, all require background understanding beyond the 'natural' or expected (primary framework) as they involve actors' 'guided doings' opening up events to multiple interpretations.

Social frames are subject to further transformations through '(re-)keying', i.e. 'set conventions by which a given activity, one already meaningful in terms of some primary framework, is transformed into something patterned on this activity but seen by the participants to be something quite different. As an example, the process of transcription can be called keying. A rough musical analogy is intended' (Goffman, 1974: 43–44). In this sense, key is not 'merely' the mood or tenor of the utterance (cf. Hymes, 1974), but a reconfiguration, or transformation of a primary activity (frame) into a new schema of interpretation, such as an instance of ordinary behavior transformed into a new activity, for example *work* into *play* ('play' being Goffman's chief example of (re-)keying behavior), or *fighting* into *contest* (i.e. ritualized and restricted displays of aggression). Other examples of keying include make-believe (e.g. scripted productions), ceremonials, technical redoings (demonstrations, exhibitions, illustrations, documentations, etc.), regroundings (insertion of the participant/performer into an activity outside his/her usual domain or activity, e.g. an ethnographer as participant-observer) and fabrications. Keying is then to be closely linked with the study of performance and recontextualization, although it opens up somewhat new possibilities to examine social interaction and its consequences, for example the relationship between primary frameworks and their transformed variants, and, consequently, the limits of acceptable behavior, allowable stances, boundaries between 'reality' and 'fantasy', encoding of ideologies, and so on.

In what follows, we analyze our data in terms of three discursive frames, with the caveat that, following Coupland and Garrett (2010), we do not see each frame as inherent to a particular set of emplaced texts. Rather, it appears that particular types of inscription (in terms of their style, materiality or language choice) can be shown to share certain interpretations. Besides, as Goffman (1974: 81–82) argues, adding another layer or *lamination* to an activity through re-keying does not simply obliterate the primary framework.

Our three frames for discussion of the residential signage in Hong Kong are *index*, *spectacle* and *brand*. Broadly speaking, these three frames can be linked to Halliday's (1978) three major communicative functions of linguistic utterances, extended to other modalities, e.g. visual communication (Kress & van Leeuwen, 1996): *ideational*, *interpersonal* and *textual*, respectively. The ideational function involves representation of facts and information, or what goes on in the world and in the mind. The interpersonal function constructs and defines social identities and relationships between social actors. The textual function is the capacity of language and other semiotic systems to form coherent texts and communicative events. Although for Halliday, all utterances simultaneously perform these three functions, we foreground each one as dominant in the three frames proposed here.

Index frame

According to Wikipedia,

An **address** is a collection of information, presented in a mostly fixed format, used for describing the location of a building, apartment, or other structure or a plot of land, generally using political boundaries and street names as references, along with other identifiers such as house or apartment numbers. Some addresses also contain special codes to aid routing of mail and packages, such as a ZIP code or post code. (< http://en.wikipedia.org/wiki/ Address_(geography) > , accessed 4 March 2010)

From this popular definition, it appears that the main function of addresses (inscribed in space of the built environment or, say, written on envelopes) is to pin-point or index specific locations, corresponding nicely to Halliday's ideational function. This is what we take to be Goffman's 'primary framework' of interpretation in the case of residential signage.

Figure 9.7 shows a typical municipal street sign in Hong Kong. The 'centrifugal force' (Scollon & Wong Scollon, 2003) of this mundane discourse dispersed throughout the city gives a rather democratic feel to all the streets and addresses in Hong Kong. The indexical frame of the sign, and all the others like it, is marked (or *keyed*) by the functionality of its design: the visibility and readability of the street names (in English and Chinese) and (optional) numbers is ensured by the 'no nonsense', modern, institutional, black sans serif typography in English and the formal, regular script of the Chinese characters on white background (cf. Jury, 2006).

Many signs on apartment blocks in less affluent areas such as Mong Kok, Tsuen Wan and Sai Wan (Figure 9.4), or on roads leading to some of the more exclusive houses in Victoria Peak (Figure 9.6) are also predominantly indexical. In Figure 9.4, the Chinese-only sign '龍旺大廈' (Lung Wong Dai Ha, 'Dragon Prosperous Building') uses a simple block

Figure 9.7 Street sign, Kowloon Tong, Hong Kong

font and it is placed directly over the entrance to the building's staircase. Although it is carefully designed with attention to equal spacing, symmetry and visual orderliness of the characters, using expensive and durable material (polished steel) on granite cladding, its appearance is decidedly functional and institutional. Elevated to the point that makes it visible only from a close distance, relatively small and without any stylistic pomposity, this sign is there predominantly to *inform* the passerby of the identity of the building out of hundreds of similar buildings in this area.

Even more modest, inconspicuous and barely ornamental street numbers alongside a road in Victoria Peak (Figure 9.6) point (in the case of number '54' with an arrow underneath) to houses completely hidden from view. Likewise, the street number '32' in Figure 9.8 is the only visible identifier of the walled house in the exclusive area of Kowloon Tong. This signage seems to fulfil the bare minimum of locating and pointing at the residences in the municipal space of Hong Kong.

In an interesting way, the indexical signage in Figures 9.4, 9.6 and 9.8 is prone to 'silencing', or ideological erasure (Irvine & Gal, 2000), albeit for different reasons and with different effects between the relatively poor and affluent areas. While many residential signs such as in Figure 9.4 are blocked from view or barely visible among the many other converging signs/discourses (forming 'centripetal' semiotic aggregates in Scollon and Wong Scollon's parlance; cf. Figure 9.1), the 'quiet' signs in the

Figure 9.8 Residential street ('No. 32'), Kowloon Tong, Hong Kong

affluent areas (Figures 9.6 and 9.8) seem deliberately to redirect the passerby's attention from their targets. These resulting silences or quietude of the indexical signs in our data appear to mark two extremes of the spatio-economic relations of Hong Kong, although, as has been stated, with different motives and consequences (cf. Wolfson's 1988 bulge theory, whereby the same speech forms are used in the opposite ends of the social spectrum).

While some of the less wealthy residents in Area 1 have their house signs 'obliterated' from view by crowded, aggressive conflation of the built area, traffic and other signage, for some residents in Area 3, clearly commanding the greatest economic capital, the manifestation of aspirational wealth through ostentatious signage may seem redundant and in 'bad taste' (though see below). This is compounded by the acoustic silence prevailing in the affluent streets, with little motorised and pedestrian traffic, exclusionary signs forbidding access to 'intruders' and the only non-wealthy people to be legitimately permeating the visible and invisible boundaries being the equally silent army of security guards and servants – domestic helps bringing in shopping (see Figure 9.8), nannies collecting children from schools, chauffeurs polishing or waiting in their owners' limousines and so on. The auditory silence of the street and the visual silence of the signage index the privileged lifestyle of the residents, and their anti-communication stance vis-à-vis other members of the public (cf. Thurlow & Jaworski, 2010).

Spectacle Frame

Drawing on Wikipedia once again, apart from their function to identify the location of a building, addresses also have a social function, i.e. 'someone's address can have a profound effect on their social standing'. Here, we find a neat correspondence with Halliday's interpersonal communicative function.

The neoliberal political doctrine that has dominated 'free market' economies since the 1980s has brought hitherto *public* assets such as utilities (e.g. water, transportation) and welfare provision (e.g. social housing, education, health care, pensions) increasingly under corporate control (Harvey, 2005). The extensive process of privatization and commodification of social housing in the UK (Harvey, 2006) as well as the progressive gentrification of inner cities (e.g. see Ley, 1996 on the process across six Canadian cities; Mills, 1993; Low, 2001) has led to a re-orientation of most housing from a utilitarian use-value good providing shelter to an exchange-value commodity and investment opportunity (for developers and individual home-owners alike). As the preserve of developers' trade, whether involving 'gentrification' of inner city areas or building new homes and gated communities in the suburbs, new housing projects are marketed as commodities offering more than a just a dwelling place, shelter or 'accommodation'. Rather, they provide their residents with a particular lifestyle, status and an identity resource based on class, ethnic and gender segregation (e.g. Low, 2003). Thus, following Debord (1994 [1967]: 32), we regard this commodifying transformation of housing as something of a consumerist *spectacle*.

Where the size of plots and/or buildings makes it possible, residential signage is often displayed in ways that surpasses the 'simple' indexical signage discussed above. Many modern apartment blocks and residential developments are indexed by highly prominent, lavish and extravagant signs re-keyed by their grandiose, over-the-top designs into spectacles of residential consumerism and as displays of social status. Alongside the unique architectural design of the buildings, where present, the signs' individualistic styles, their enormity, salience and opulence bestow each villa, apartment block or housing complex with a sense of authority, distinction and/or finesse. Typical stylistic resources include large, bold lettering (Figure 9.2) or carefully stylized running or cursive characters and typefaces often emulating 'handwritten' typography with elaborate ascenders and descenders (Figures 9.3 and 9.9); durable, expensive materiality, e.g. shiny golden, brass or silver finish (Figures 9.2, 9.3, 9.5 and 9.9); additional ornamentation, e.g. abstract or stylized floral patterns (Figure 9.9) or 'matching' street signs

Figure 9.9 Parc Oasis/又一居, Kowloon Tong, Hong Kong

(Figure 9.2); special or decorative lighting (Figure 9.9); elevated positioning (Figures 9.2 and 9.5); extravagant framing, e.g. large empty spaces surrounding the signs (Figure 9.5), borders (Figure 9.2) or specially designed gates, pillars and tablets displaying the names of buildings or residential estates (Figure 9.9).

In another (visual) link to Europeaness, the typography of the building's name 'Euston Court', the square logo made up of horizontal lines, and the decorative bars in the lower ground windows draw on the style of the Scottish architect Charles Rennie Mackintosh (Figure 9.5). As Jury (2006: 35) suggests, such grandly designed and presented words connote stability and power and 'cannot be read in haste'. Rather, they are to be contemplated, admired and in the case of the residents of such branded apartment blocks – appropriated as markers of 'distinction'.

The forecourts, entrances, hallways and reception areas to many of the residential buildings, especially in Area 2, reinforce the grandiose semantic and visual imagery of the signage. To take just one example of a building in Mid-levels, 'Centre Place', the relatively small area around its entrance, between the building itself and the busy street, is occupied by a small but carefully landscaped garden, fountains with two bronze sculptures: a representation of two galloping Pegasus horses, and a small frog with a 'golden' crown sitting on a large boulder. A large, glass, swinging door with a highly decorative wooden and metal handle, leads to a 'minimalist' reception area clad in white marble, with a large, bright abstract painting dwarfing one of the walls, and a large crystal chandelier hanging from the ceiling. At eye level, splashes of pink and red fresh flowers (e.g. red begonias on the concierge's desk) add a sense of luxury and appreciation of nature. In sum, the visual imagery of Centre Place draws on a number of diverse themes and somewhat chaotic discourses and design traditions, typical of postmodern cities (Harvey, 1989): 'cool' urban cosmopolitanism (minimalist design; abstract art), with the nostalgic romanticism and utopia of the mythical and fantastical (Pegasus; enchanted frog-prince), and the freshness, cleanliness and optimism of nature (for more on the 'semiotics of luxury', see Thurlow and Jaworski, submitted).

The sense of spectacle is heightened by the insertion into the space of residential Hong Kong intertextual links to other places, imagined and real, e.g.:

- Eden Gardens 怡翠花園, Yi Chui Fa Yuen (Pleasant Jade/Green Garden)
- Sussex Court 海雅閣 Hoi Nga Kok (Sea Elegant Pavilion/Court)
- The Mayfair 梅道一號 Mui Do (——)
- Euston Court 豫苑 Yi Yuen (Comfort[formal] Garden) (Figure 9.5)
- Yukon Court 殷豪閣 Yan Ho Kok (Abundant Hero Terrace)

Precisely because of the recognizable references to distant yet prestigious locations, these entextualizations or appropriations of other place-names become linguistic performances of distinction and prestige associated with refuge, sanctuary and safe haven (e.g. 'Eden Garden'), 'old' centers of colonial power (e.g. 'Sussex Court', 'The Mayfair', 'Euston Court') or just foreignness (e.g. 'Yukon Court'). Likewise, past values of the (European) aristocratic and royal splendour are appropriated and inserted into the space of Hong Kong through the mixing of English, Chinese and other European languages, creating a sense of exclusivity and taking an 'elitist stance' (cf. Jaworski & Thurlow, 2009) based on the idea of distant, secure and luxurious spaces, e.g.:

- La Noblesse 豪福軒 Ho Fuk Hin (Heroic Blessing Study Room) (Figure 9.3)
- Mountain Ville Court 景峰閣, King Fung Kok (View Peak Pavilion/ Court)
- Casa Bella 寶華軒 Po Wah Hin (Precious Flourish Study Room)

Similar references (linguistic and visual) to foreign, prestigious places are found in numerous advertisements for new housing developments scattered around the city, in estate agents' windows, billboards, MTR (underground) stations and on buses. For example, at the time of our data collection an advertising campaign for the Beverly Hills development featured numerous giant photographs of the model, Natalie Glubova, styled as a fairy-tale princess (an image not far off from that of her 'coronation' as Miss World 2005). Another advertisement for the Manhattan Hill development carried a caption 'Magic Happens' and featured a 'demand' image (i.e. an image in which the represented participant looks directly at the viewer's eyes; Kress & van Leeuwen, 1996) of a bejewelled female model in black evening dress striking an alluring pose in a richly decorated, 'palatial' swimming pool. In both advertisements, the female models were Caucasian, which 'removes' the images a step further from the more familiar sight of the majority of Asian women living in Hong Kong, adding to the models' objectification and epitomizing the Asian idealization and sexualization of Caucasian women (cf. Frith *et al.*, 2005). The concentrated entextualization of foreign place-names with their global appeal and high status (Manhattan as a financial and arts center; Beverly Hills as the home of many Hollywood stars), the glamorous styling of Glubova, the surreal and somewhat risqué styling of the other model, the reference to 'magic', and so on, are all *keyings* transforming the mundane, everyday (albeit elite and expensive) apartments into fantastical spectacles. The same transformation is achieved in the advertisements for the high-rise Bel-Air development featuring, somewhat intriguingly, photographs of the Bellagio Hotel in Las Vegas.

Finally, the keying of residential signage as spectacle with appeals to the past and traditional values is present in our data by the occasional use of archaic or formal register of Chinese characters (bolded), e.g.:

- Euston Court 豫苑 **Yi** Yuen (Comfort [formal] Garden) (Figure 9.5)
- Honor Villa **翰**庭軒 **Hon** Ting Hin (Imperial Exam Courtyard/ Family Study Room)
- Mountain Lodge/草廬 Cho **Lo** (Grass Cottage)

All such archaic forms appear in predominantly middle-class areas on upmarket buildings, suggesting that there is market value in using semiotic resources rooted in the past, perhaps drawing on the associations of nostalgia, authenticity and knowable sophistication. It appears then that spectacle here is keyed in by a combination of temporally and spatially distant references, coupled with flamboyant visual design, and possible admixture of a small, carefully selected linguistic code.

Brand frame

Our last interpretive frame for Hong Kong residential signage corresponds to Halliday's textual function. Although closely related to the spectacle frame, we see the brand frame as a further lamination of meaning of residential signage akin to giving the apartment block or housing complex 'textual' coherence. The main keying resource in this regard is the repetition and visibility of the brand (Klein, 2000: 45). In particular, together with the prominent display of the signs discussed above (especially salience and framing), in this brief section we pay attention to repetition that turns the building's name into a 'trade-mark' or 'logo'.

Figure 9.10 shows a detail of a large apartment block 'Cayman Rise'/ '加惠臺' in Sai Wan. Specifically, the image focuses on the glass door to the building's lobby 'branded' by a decorative yellow and blue strip (possibly also used for security reasons) with the Chinese and English names of the building running through its length. The inscriptions on the door match the fonts used for the building's names on its outer walls, reminiscent of the logo of other consumer products (cars, personal computers, etc.) with several movable and/or detachable parts, each one bearing the maker's name/logo. The repetition of the building's name is of course to be found in many other places: inside walls of the reception area, marquees over doorways, management/proprietor identification plaques, business cards of the management and so on.

The same branding transformation is exemplified in Figure 9.11, where the sign of a building's name '禮賢樓'/'Rhenish Mansion' with the building's street address ('84 Bonham Road') appears over a municipal, 'democratic' (see above) street sign with the same address

Figure 9.10 Cayman Rise/加惠臺, Sai Wan, Hong Kong

Figure 9.11 Street sign and Rhenish Mansion /禮賢樓, Mid-levels, Hong Kong

included. The building's own, relatively small but stylish sign with its brushed steel finish, polished steel framing, elegant and 'serious' typography appears in the 'ideal' position above the street sign, which assumes the 'real'/'down-to-earth' position (Kress & van Leeuwen, 1996). Whilst the street sign provides practical information about the location, 'merely' the street address in which all the buildings ranging from number 2 to 94 have the same 'value', the building's sign 'brands' 84 Bonham Road as a particular idea or idealization and its most salient aspect (see a similar contrast between the signs in Figures 9.7 and 9.9). With such branding of the buildings throughout, the corporatization of the residential/linguistic landscape of Hong Kong (and many other cities) is complete.

Discursive Construction of Identity in Urban Semiotic Landscape

In their study of the relationship between language and architecture, Markus and Cameron (2002) demonstrate how language (as written text and as visual image) influences the 'meaning' of buildings, with all the consequences for our perception, interpretation and use of built environment. Language/discourse creates buildings' functionality, power and symbolic value, or a sense of community or privacy; it transforms 'space' to 'place' (Harvey, 1989; Massey & Jess, 1995).With one of the largest population densities in the world, Hong Kong fits in the modern stereotype of many modern cities as an 'urban jungle'. In stark contrast to this metropolitan image, much signage of residential buildings appear to create a sense of the dwellers' aspirational identity (Thurlow & Jaworski, 2006) as occupants of idyllic, fantastical, almost utopian spaces. With their references to nature, beauty, cleanliness, good living, openness of space (the view!), past values of aristocratic and royal splendour and authenticity, Hong Kong appears as a lived space embodying the dreams and aspirations of its residents to be situated in an ideal, almost enchanted space. This particular style of residential signage seems to consistently run through all of Hong Kong's districts, suggesting that, regardless of their social class, ethnic background, wealth and the actual architectural design of their homes, Hong Kongers (and possibly the residents of most other large cities the world over) rely on linguistic/semiotic means to turn their dwelling spaces into idealized oases of tranquillity, Edens of happiness and pleasure, and castles of sovereignty.

Having said this, and in considering the styles of different signs – expressed through their emplacement, design, language choices, fonts, materiality, etc. – we do begin to notice a politics of *difference* (Bourdieu, 1984) shaping the residential space of Hong Kong through the process of 'textualization', or discursive representation and constriction of the social and economic processes (Fairclough, 2003) – the linguistic landscape of the city. Whether in the recently gentrified areas of relative deprivation or in the privileged and exclusive suburbs, signage is used to create a sense of luxury, elitism and power, marking off territorial boundaries, social segregation and limited access. Even places of material wealth and privilege rely on the symbolic resources of language and language design. The names invoking 'foreign' languages in the acts of code-crossing (Rampton, 1985), or intertextual references to distant, equally highly regarded geographical places, work as symbolic signs of *distinction*, despite creating *rupture* in the visual linguistic field (Yurchak, 2003), adding new, creative and unexpected elements to the city's iconosphere (Porebski, 1972; Chmielewska 2010; Gendelman & Aiello, 2010) and drawing on the linguistic and visual resources of 'global semioscape' (Thurlow & Aiello, 2007).

Wright (1985: 237) notes that different worlds typically occupy the same localities, an observation echoed in Mac Giolla Chríost's (2007) discussion of urban 'proximity of difference': 'Cities are evocative places, places where people are drawn into all kinds of proximate relationships, often by chance, often fleetingly and often on an unequal basis' (Allen, 1999: 85, quoted by Mac Giolla Chríost's, 2007: 22). The act of creating place is in part a semiotic process that minimally requires a deictic, or other indexical expression to anchor it socially (Hanks, 2001). These acts of anchoring space may be more or less visible, legitimate or authentic (authenticating), thus creating spaces of different accessibility, marked by different degrees of power, development and injustice (e.g. Harvey, 1989, 1996, 2006).

Mac Giolla Chríost (2007: 10) considers cities as 'mosaics of polarized geographies', linguistic marketplaces (Bourdieu, 1991), where language and discourse constitute part of the symbolic and material pool of resources in creating, upholding and contesting power relations. Just as graffiti is used to mark out the turf of competing gangs at its borders and to celebrate the gang and its exploits at the center (Ley, 1974, cited in Rose, 1995), the entextualization (Bauman & Briggs, 1990; Silverstein & Urban, 1996) of residential signage in the metadiscursive urban space, or the interpretive frames that they invoke, indicates 'the preferred way(s) of "reading" these texts' (Blommaert, 1999: 9) organizing communities into social categories, determining their relationships and political hierarchies (see also Stuart Hall, 1980 [1973] on 'preferred reading positions'). They become part of the 'scopic regime' (Jay, 1998) of the city available to some dwellers to create their sense of place, self-worth even, and to establish social difference and spatial boundaries around them. However, it must be borne in mind that much of this 'architectural spectacle' (Harvey, 1989) is led by the corporate efforts of maximizing profits and it is in this intense process of marketing, styling and promoting aspirational identities that citizens and residents become consumers. To draw on Bauman's (2007) observations on the consumerist culture of the late capitalist era, the fantastical names and rich signs of dwelling places invented and deployed by developers as *spectacles* and *brands* are aimed at the post-modern consumers of urban spaces in pursuit of immediate happiness and self-fulfilment, rather than long-term security, warmth and shelter.

Acknowledgements

We collected the data for this chapter while Adam was Visiting Professor at the Department of English, Hong Kong University, between January and April 2007. Adam wishes to thank all colleagues at the Department for their hospitality and stimulating atmosphere, and in particular Chris Hutton for useful discussions of the linguistic landscape of Hong Kong (including restaurant menus). An early version of this paper was presented at the Linguistic Landscape Workshop in Tel Aviv (January, 2008) organized by Elana Shohamy, Eliezer Ben-Rafael, Shoshi Waksman, Nira Trumper-Hecht and Efrat Marco. We are particularly grateful to Nik Coupland and Crispin Thurlow for their extremely useful and constructive criticism and comments on the first and penultimate drafts of the chapter, respectively. Last but not least, we are grateful to the editors and publisher for their support and patience.

References

Allen, J. (1999) Cities of power and influence: Settled formations. In J. Allen, D. Massey and M. Pyrke (eds) *Unsettling Cities: Movement/Settlement* (pp. 181–227). London: Routledge.

Amin, A. and Graham, S. (1999) Cities of connection and disconnection. In J. Allen, D. Massey and M. Pyrke (eds) *Unsettling Cities: Movement/Settlement* (pp. 7–47). London: Routledge.

Backhaus, P. (2006) Multilingualism in Tokyo: A look into the linguistic landscape. *International Journal of Multilingualism* 3, 52–66.

Bauman, Z. (2007) *Consuming Life*. Cambridge: Polity.

Ben-Rafael, E., Shohamy, E., Amara, M.H. and Trumper-Hecht, N. (2006) Linguistic landscape as symbolic construction of the public space: The case of Israel. *International Journal of Multilingualism* 3, 7–30.

Berger, J. (1972) *Ways of Seeing*. London: Penguin and BBC Books.

Blommaert, J. (1999) The debate is open. In J. Blommaert (ed.) *Language Ideological Debates* (pp. 1–38). Berlin: Mouton de Gruyter.

Bourdieu, P. (1984) *Distinction: A Social Critique of the Judgement of Taste* (R. Nice, trans.). Cambridge, MA: Harvard University Press.

Bourdieu, P. (1991) *Language & Symbolic Power* (J.B. Thompson (ed.); G. Raymond and M. Adamson, trans.). Cambridge: Polity Press.

Cenoz, J. and Gorter, D. (2006) Linguistic landscape and minority languages. *International Journal of Multilingualism* 3, 67–80.

Cheshire, J. and Moser, L-M. (1994) English as a cultural symbol: The case of advertisements in French-speaking Switzerland. *Journal of Multilingual and Multicultural Development* 15, 451–469.

Chmielewska, E. (2010) Semiosis takes place or radical uses of quaint theories. In A. Jaworski and C. Thurlow (eds) *Semiotic Landscapes: Text, Image, Space* (pp. 274–291). London: Continuum.

Cosgrove, D. (1985) Prospect, perspective and the evolution of the landscape idea. *Transactions of the Institute of British Geographers* 10, 45–62.

Coupland, N. (2010) Welsh linguistic landscapes 'from above' and 'from below'. In A. Jaworski and C. Thurlow (eds) *Semiotic Landscapes: Text, Image, Space* (pp. 77–101). London: Continuum.

Coupland, N. and Garrett, P. (2010) Linguistic landscapes, discursive frames and metacultural performance: The case of Welsh Patagonia. *International Journal of the Sociology of Language*, 205.

Crystal, D. (1995) *The Cambridge Encyclopedia of the English Language*. Cambridge: Cambridge University Press.

Entrikin, J.N. (1991) *The Betweenness of Place: Towards a Geography of Modernity*. Baltimore, MD: John Hopkins University Press.

Fairclough, N. (2003) *Analysing Discourse: Textual Analysis for Social Research*. London: Routledge.

Flowerdew, J. (2004) The discursive construction of a world-class city. *Discourse & Society* 15, 579–605.

Friedrich, P. (2002) English in advertising and brand naming. *English Today* 71, 21–28.

Gendelman, I. and Aiello, G. (2010) Faces of places: Façades as global communication in Post-Eastern Bloc urban renewal. In A. Jaworski and C. Thurlow (eds) *Semiotic Landscapes: Text, Image, Space* (pp. 256–273). London: Continuum.

Goffman, E. (1971) *Relations in Public*. New York: Harper and Row.

Goffman, E. (1974) *Frame Analysis: An Essay on the Organization of Experience*. New York: Harper & Row.

Hall, S. (1980 [1973]) Encoding/decoding. In Centre for Contemporary Cultural Studies (ed.) *Culture, Media, Language: Working Papers in Cultural Studies, 1972–79* (pp. 128–138). London: Hutchinson.

Haarman, H. (1989) *Symbolic Values of Foreign Language Use*. Berlin: Mouton de Gruyter.

Halliday, M.A.K. (1978) *Language as Social Semiotic*. London: Arnold.

Hanks, W.F. (2001) Indexicality. In A. Duranti (ed.) *Key Terms in Language and Culture* (pp. 119–121). Oxford: Blackwell Publishers.

Harvey, D. (1973) *Social Justice and the City*. London: Edward Arnold.

Harvey, D. (1989) *The Condition of Postmodernity: An Enquiry into the Origins of Cultural Change*. Oxford: Blackwell.

Harvey, D. (1996) *Justice, Nature and the Geography of Difference*. Oxford: Blackwell.

Harvey, D. (2005) *A Brief History of Neoliberalism*. Oxford: Oxford University Press.

Harvey, D. (2006) *Spaces of Global Capitalism: Towards a Theory of Uneven Geographical Development*. London: Verso.

Huebner, T. (2006) Bangkok's linguistic landscapes: Environmental print, codemixing and language change. *International Journal of Multilingualism* 3, 31–51.

Hymes, D. (1974) *Foundations in Sociolinguistics: An Ethnographic Approach*. Philadelphia, PA: University of Pennsylvania Press.

Irvine, J.T. and Gal, S. (2000) Language ideology and linguistic differentiation. In P.V. Kroskrity (ed.) *Regimes of Language* (pp. 35–83). Santa Fe, NM: School of American Research Press.

Jaworski, A. and Thurlow, C. (2009) Taking an elitist stance: Ideology and the discursive production of social distinction. In A. Jaffe (ed.) *Stance: Sociolinguistic Perspectives* (pp. 195–226). New York: Oxford University Press.

Jaworski, A. and Thurlow, C. (eds) (2010a) *Semiotic Landscapes: Text, Image, Space.* London: Continuum.

Jaworski, A. and Thurlow, C. (2010b) Introducing semiotic landscapes. In A. Jaworski and C. Thurlow (eds) *Semiotic Landscapes: Text, Space, Globalization* (pp. 1–40). London: Continuum.

Jay, M. (1998) Scopic regimes of modernity. In H. Foster (ed.) *Vision and Visuality: Discussions in Contemporary Culture* (pp. 3–23). Dia Art Foundation No. 2 and Seattle, WA: Bay Books.

Jones, R.H. (2005) Sites of engagement as sites of attention: Time, space and culture in electronic discourse. In S. Norris and R. Jones (eds) *Discourse in Action: Introducing Mediated Discourse Analysis* (pp. 141–154). London: Routledge.

Jones, R.H. (2010) Cyberspace and physical space: Attention structures in computer mediated communication. In A. Jaworski and C. Thurlow (eds) *Semiotic Landscapes: Text, Image, Space* (pp. 151–167). London: Continuum.

Jury, D. (2006) *What is Typography?* Hove: RotoVision.

Kallen, J.L. (2010) Changing landscapes: Language, space, and policy in the Dublin linguistic landscape. In A. Jaworski and C. Thurlow (eds) *Semiotic Landscapes: Text, Image, Space* (pp. 41–58). London: Continuum.

Kelly-Holmes, H. (2005) *Advertising as Multilingual Communication.* Basingstoke: Palgrave Macmillan.

Kress, G. and Van Leeuwen, T. (1996) *Reading Images – The Grammar of Visual Design.* London: Routledge.

Lanham, R.A. (1993) *The Electronic World: Democracy, Technology and the Arts.* Chicago, IL: The University of Chicago Press.

Lanza, E. and Woldemariam, H. (2008) Language ideology and linguistic landscape: Language policy and globalization in a regional capital in Ethiopia. In E. Shohamy and D. Gorter (eds) *Linguistic Landscapes: Expanding the Scenery* (pp. 189–205). New York: Routledge.

Lefebvre, H. (1991) *The Production of Space.* Cambridge, MA: Blackwell.

Ley, D. (1974) *The Black Inner City as Frontier Outpost: Images and Behaviour of a Philadelphia Neighbourhood.* Washington, DC: Association of American Geographers.

Ley, D. (1996) *The New Middle Class and the Remaking of the Central City.* Oxford: Oxford University Press.

Low, S.M. (2001) The edge and the center: Gated communities and the discourse of urban fear. *American Anthropologist* 103, 45–59.

Mac Giolla Chríost, D. (2007) *Language and the City.* Basingstoke: Palgrave Macmillan.

Markus, T.A. and Cameron, D. (2002) *The Words between the Spaces: Buildings and Language.* London: Routledge.

Massey, D. (2005) *For Space.* London: Sage.

Massey, D. and Jess, P. (eds) (1995) *A Place in the World: Places, Cultures and Globalization.* Oxford: Oxford University Press in association with The Open University.

Miles, M. (2007) *Cities and Cultures.* London: Routledge.

Mills, C. (1993) Myths and meanings of gentrification. In J. Duncan and D. Ley (eds) *Place/Culture/Representation* (pp. 149–170). London: Routledge.

Piller, I. (2001) Identity constructions in multilingual advertising. *Language in Society* 30, 153–186.

Porebski, M. (1972) *Ikonosfera*. Warszawa: PWN.

Shohamy, E. and Gorter, D. (eds) (2008) *Linguistic Landscape: Expanding the Scenery*. New York: Routledge.

Silverstein, M. and Urban, G. (1996) The natural history of discourse. In M. Silverstein and G. Urban (eds) *Natural Histories of Discourse* (pp. 1–17). Chicago, IL: University of Chicago Press.

Sperber, D. and Wilson, D. (1986) *Relevance: Communication and Cognition*. Oxford: Blackwell.

Rose, G. (1995) Place and identity: A sense of place. In D. Massey and P. Jess (eds) *A Place in the World?* (pp. 87–118). Oxford: Oxford University Press and Open University.

Scollon, R. and Wong Scollon, S. (2004) *Nexus Analysis. Discourse and the Emerging Internet*. London: Routledge.

Scollon, R. and Wong Scollon, S. (2003) *Discourse in Place: Language in the Material World*. London: Routledge.

Thurlow, C. and Aiello, G. (2007) National pride, global capital: A social semiotic analysis of transnational visual branding in the airline industry. *Visual Communication* 6, 305–344.

Thurlow, C. and Jaworski, A. (2003) Communicating a global reach: Inflight magazines as a globalizing genre in tourism. *Journal of Sociolinguistics* 7, 579–606.

Thurlow, C. and Jaworski, A. (2006) The alchemy of the upwardly mobile: Symbolic capital and the stylization of elites in frequent-flyer programmes. *Discourse & Society* 17, 131–167.

Thurlow, C. and Jaworski, A. (2010) Silence is golden: The 'anti-communicational' linguascaping of super-elite mobility. In A. Jaworski and C. Thurlow (eds) *Semiotic Landscapes: Text, Image, Space* (pp. 187–218). London: Continuum.

Thurlow, C. and Jaworski, A. (submitted) Elite mobilities: The semiotic landscapes of luxury and privilege. *Visual Communication*.

Wolfson, N. (1988) The bulge: A theory of speech behavior and social distance. In J. Fine (ed.) *Second Language Discourse: A Textbook of Current Research* (pp. 21–38). Norwood, NJ: Ablex.

Winchester, H.P.M., Kong, L. and Dunn, K. (2003) *Landscapes: Ways of Imagining the World*. London: Pearson Education.

Wright, P. (1985) *On Living in an Old Country*. London: Verso.

Yurchak, A. (2000) Privatize your name: Symbolic work in a post-Soviet linguistic market. *Journal of Sociolinguistics* 4, 406–434.

Chapter 10

Selling the City: Language, Ethnicity and Commodified Space

JENNIFER LEEMAN and GABRIELLA MODAN

Introduction

Material manifestations of language are an integral part of the urban public sphere: Cities are full of linguistic signs created by a panoply of public and private actors. Although linguistics research on space often speaks of language as located *within* a particular landscape, a landscape is not a container that holds objects like a picnic basket filled with lunch items. Instead, much as Reddy (1979) deconstructed the language-as-container metaphor, cultural geographers have emphasized that spaces are not merely holders for things that are in them. Rather, they are topographies that shape and are shaped by the items with which they are collocated (cf. Massey, 1999). Instead of functioning as distinct objects enclosed inside a territory, then, material manifestations of language in the built environment constitute key elements in shaping city *spaces* as urban *places* imbued with social meanings.[1] This is a dialectical relationship, however: the language that appears on city streets is shaped and constrained by other facets of the built environment, and – particularly in central city commercial areas – governed by municipal, regional or national linguistic and zoning regulations. These regulations are shaped not just by government bureaucrats, but also by a variety of interested parties, including civic organizations, NGOs, ethnic coalitions, developers and business owners. Because words on the street are part and parcel of the texture of urban landscapes, a full understanding of any urban linguistic landscape (LL) must be undergirded by in-depth knowledge of the ways in which cities themselves are shaped.

In this chapter, we propose a theoretical framework for thinking about the various political and economic interests that currently govern the development of urban spaces in North America and, increasingly, in urban centers throughout the world. We argue that in late modernity, much language in the urban landscape is both an outcome of, and a vehicle for, the commodification of space. Elsewhere, we have called for a contextualized approach to the LL (Leeman & Modan, 2009) and argued that the scholarship of cities can benefit from a consideration of the role of language (Leeman & Modan, 2010). Here, we draw on research from urban studies, sociology and tourism studies to propose an interdisciplinary approach for analyzing material manifestations of language specifically in the urban context. Our goal is to investigate how research on the social, political and economic landscapes of cities can offer new insights into the use of language in the built environment. Throughout the exposition of our theoretical framework, we provide illustrative examples primarily from Washington DC's Chinatown to demonstrate how minority languages are used as strategic tools in contemporary urban redevelopment initiatives and the construction of 'destination locations' for tourists and residents alike.[2] Material manifestations of language interact with other design elements in the built environment to construct commodified urban places – cities for sale.

A Contextualized Approach to the Linguistic Landscape

Most LL research has investigated commercial zones; although researchers include governmental and other non-commercial signs, they generally study areas with a large number of stores and restaurants, as these areas tend to display more material manifestations of language than primarily public sector or residential neighborhoods. Many LL studies implicitly assume that the ratio of languages in the landscape is a direct reflection of the relative status of various ethnolinguisitic groups within the community. In addition, with the exception of recent studies that have noted the use of English as an index of sophistication, cosmopolitanism or modernity (e.g. Cenoz & Gorter, 2006; Huebner, 2006; Ben Rafael *et al.*, 2006), many LL researchers seem to presuppose that the target audience of a given language consists largely of people who can read and/or understand that language.

We seek to expand the disciplinary boundaries of LL research and to break from the primarily quantitative tradition by adopting a contextualized interdisciplinary approach, one that attends to the linguistic and spatial contexts within which texts are located. In the case of a written street or store sign, the language on that sign gains its meaning from the extralinguistic phenomena such as the political and economic interests that led to its creation or its location in space (cf. Scollon & Scollon, 2003), as well from the language of the other signs around it. We illustrate the role of context in shaping the meaning of the language on signs by examining the Chinese and English signage on two Starbucks coffee shops, one in Washington DC and the other in Shanghai (see Figure 10.1).

Although both stores display 'Starbucks' written in both Chinese and English, the symbolic meanings of the Chinese and English writing are quite different. As we discuss below, Washington DC's Chinatown is a 'themed' shopping and entertainment district in which the city government has mandated the use of Chinese design elements. The

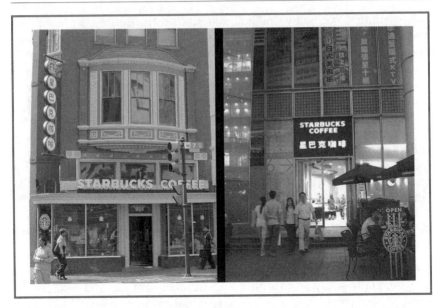

Figure 10.1 Left: Starbucks in DC's Chinatown (© Jennifer Leeman); right: Starbucks on Shanghai's Nanjing Rd. (© Hai Zhang)

English writing on this Starbucks shop functions to identify and brand the store as Starbucks to potential customers; because English is the dominant language in the US, its use in Washington DC is unmarked. By contrast, the Chinese writing on the DC store self-consciously references Chinatown, and reinforces the area as a themed ethnoscape. It is only within this landscape that the use of Chinese makes sense; were the sign located at a Starbucks outside of Chinatown, the presence of Chinese writing would be quite puzzling.

Both the Chinese and the English writing have very different symbolic meanings on the signage at the Shanghai Starbucks, which is located on Nanjing Road – Shanghai's '5th Avenue'. In this context, Chinese is the unmarked language, and it identifies the name of the shop. The English writing identifies a specific brand, much as it does in Chinatown, but it also constructs an air of cosmopolitan sophistication. This meaning is heightened spatially through the shop's location in a western-style shopping area. In terms of linguistic context, the distinction of 'Starbucks' in English is reinforced contextually through its location near other English-language signs in the vicinity, including the 'open' sign to the right.

As this discussion illustrates, a contextualized approach to the LL necessitates an explanation of both the extralinguistic and linguistic environments in which signs are located, as well as a consideration of the sociohistorical factors that have shaped their production (Leeman &

Modan, 2009). Our approach pays special attention to the symbolic functions of language and their role in the construction of *places* or social spaces (see also Shohamy & Waksman, 2008).

Symbolic Economies and Themed Environments

In the late 20th and early 21st centuries, there has been an international trend toward the commodification of culture and the commercialization of public space, a trend that has had a tremendous impact on urban environments and the LL. We stress the importance of acknowledging and problematizing the predominance of commercial language in the built environment, investigating the reasons for this predominance and analyzing the ways in which commercial interests influence material manifestations of language in urban places.

With the decline of Fordism – the system of large-scale standardized manufacturing production and mass consumption preeminent in industrialized economies through the mid-20th century – many cities have undergone a shift to service-based economies. In the US, this shift was accompanied by widespread outmigration of the middle class to the suburbs, a demographic movement promoted by the construction of a vast highway system and exacerbated by the urban riots of the 1960s. The growth of suburban shopping malls, which occurred during the same period, resulted in cities' loss of sales taxes as well as residents. In order to make up for lost revenue, cities have sought to attract suburbanites and out-of-town visitors alike via the 'symbolic economy', which Zukin (1995: 3) defines as 'the intertwining of cultural symbols and entrepreneurial capital'.

In the symbolic economy, cultural symbols play a significant role in the selling of products and services, and entrepreneurs invest in projects that rely on cultural symbols to attract consumers. Further, culture, products and services are bundled together and marketed as 'experiences'. For example, in addition to food and service, restaurants market a range of experiences; themed restaurants such as Hardrock Café surround patrons with rock and roll memorabilia, 'ethnic' restaurants provide diners with a taste of the 'authentic' or 'exotic', and restaurants showcasing locally grown or organic foods offer a sense of sophistication or cultural caché. Themed restaurants sometimes offer customers souvenir goods for sale (such as t-shirts and drinking glasses), with the experience of having eaten in the restaurant used to sell those products, just as the products and the theme are used to sell the restaurant. Along the same lines, retailers promote the concept of 'shopertainment', in which shopping is conceived of as a leisure activity, rather than a chore (Hannigan, 1998), and shopping malls commonly now include culture and entertainment spaces such as movie theaters, bowling alleys, art exhibits and sit-down restaurants among the shops and department stores.

This interweaving of culture, services, products and experiences, and the use of one to sell the others, is utilized in the marketing of all kinds of goods and services, as well as entire neighborhoods and cities. Urban developers deploy culture by pairing the 'retail experience' with unique physical settings, such as historic buildings or districts (e.g. the Old Post Office and Union Station in Washington, Faneuil Hall in Boston) or unique new construction (e.g. Harbor Place in Baltimore, Niketown and Apple stores). Although merchants have long used cultural artifacts to stimulate consumer desire, the development of shopping districts in historic or scenic locales takes this process to a new level, with urban spaces themselves entering the marketplace (Crawford, 1992). Because the transfer of qualities between culture and commodity is reciprocal, not only does culture provide added value to commodities, but those commodities also impute economic value to culture (Crawford, 1992). Urban areas that integrate historical preservation or other architectural themes with retail and entertainment intentionally aestheticize the city, turning it into a type of 'tableau' where tourists consume the built environment and the place, as well as the food and retail (Boyer, 1992). The commodification of culture and marketing of places, goods and services is mutually reinforcing and it takes place at multiple scales; when individual businesses, neighborhoods and cities sell products and experiences, they not only create a stream of revenue, they also enhance the touristic and leisure value of the places themselves.[3]

As post-Fordist cities have come to rely on commodified culture and experience to revitalize downtown neighborhoods, the symbolic economy has become a driving force behind urban policies around the world, many of which are supported by public/private partnerships between municipalities and entrepreneurs. Part and parcel of this trend is the growth of the travel and tourism industries, with cities increasingly carrying out marketing campaigns as they compete to attract local, national and international visitors. Cities put culture to use for economic development in a variety of ways; typical strategies include culture-based projects such as art museums and performing arts centers, as well as downtown arts districts with high concentrations of galleries and artists' studios. Many cities have also sought to draw visitors via the construction of convention centers and/or major league sports arenas, as well as through the creation of specialized retail and entertainment districts. Indeed, entertainment and spectacle have been a key part of this mix, with city planners working hard to convince suburbanites that 'cities are fun' (Hannigan, 1998).

Washington DC offers an illustrative example of this trend, with the city having developed a complex network of public-private partnerships devoted to attracting individual visitors and residents, as well as conventions, tradeshows and conferences. Created specifically to serve as the US national capital, Washington DC has always sought to attract visitors and tourists, in large part to promote public confidence in, and allegiance to, the new federal government (Luria, 2006). In the late 20th century, however, these efforts were ramped up, with the mayor and the municipal government working to increase revenues by counteracting the city's reputation as the 'murder capital of the US' and solidifying its status as a 'world class city' (Wheeler, 1986a). Promotional activities are conducted not only by the traditional government institutions, such as the Office of Planning and the National Capital Planning Commission, but by a whole array of economic development-geared city agencies, including the Clean City Initiative, the Sports and Entertainment Commission, Motion Picture and Television Development, the Washington Convention Center Authority and the Washington DC Convention and Tourism Corporation, as well as private and non-profit entities working in collaboration with the city government, such as Cultural Tourism DC and the Main Streets Initiative, which promote business development and tourism in a number of the city's mixed-use neighborhoods (Figure 10.2).

Figure 10.2 F St. NW, rechristened 'Fun Street' in Washington DC's redeveloped downtown (© Jennifer Leeman)

Selling Culture

Culture and cultural symbols have become key elements in the promotion of real estate development and commercial interests. However, as Zukin (1998) notes, culture is used not only to frame public space and to attract consumers of goods and services, but also to legitimate the appropriation of that space by private and commercial interests. The strategies employed by city planners to encourage economic development include using public funds for the construction of 'flagship' projects, providing special tax incentives or zoning exceptions and establishing Business Improvement Districts (BIDs). BIDs are non-profit entities whose goal is to create consumer-friendly urban spaces that attract visitors who might otherwise feel anxious about urban crime or dirt; the hallmark of BIDS are spaces that convey an urban feel through historic architecture and/or lively walkable streets, but that have a standardized and sanitized built environment designed to appeal to mass-market tastes and allay any fear of 'the urban' (cf. Mitchell, 2003). BIDs typically impose fees on all business owners and service providers in a district to enhance services normally offered by municipal governments, such as increased trash pickup and private security guards, and they mandate or regulate street banners, standardized trashcans and various types of signs. They therefore have a key role in shaping the LL.

The influence of the BID model is particularly clear in Washington DC, which has embraced the symbolic economy and BIDs in its efforts to draw suburbanites and tourists via a development plan promoting Downtown as a historical, cultural and entertainment zone. In addition to capitalizing on the area's 19th-century architecture, recent years have seen massive construction in the Downtown BID, including flagship commercial and civic buildings: two convention centers, a sports arena, a performing arts center, shopping complexes and upscale residential properties. A key component of these initiatives was the redevelopment of Chinatown, an area consisting of nine city blocks within the Downtown BID.

Although city leaders see public/private partnerships as crucial to the revitalization of cities, the extent to which these partnerships make urban planning dependent on private interests should not be overlooked. Moreover, because these models are based on the need to attract middle-class visitors, contemporary cities are less attuned to the needs of residents; rather than significantly investing in public transportation in non-tourist areas, healthcare, sewage systems, schools or neighborhood recreation centers, they instead devote enormous resources to promoting themselves as places for the middle class to play (Eisinger, 2000). Furthermore, special districts such as BIDs constitute a privatization of public space in which decisions are made by non-elected Boards of Directors, and in many cases, private security forces patrol city streets (cf. Christopherson, 1994; Mallett, 1994). Under these conditions, the line between public and private development is erased. As we discuss elsewhere (Leeman & Modan, 2009), this has important implications for research on the LL, which has often posited a strong dichotomy between public and private signage.

Ethnoscapes and the Symbolic Economy

Deploying symbols of ethnicity and national cultures to attract tourists is a common strategy on the part of urban municipalities. In cities the world over, neighborhoods once inhabited by persecuted ethnic minorities are now marketed as leisure and tourism destinations. For example, in Granada, Spain, the former Arab quarter has been reconfigured as a tourist attraction, 500 years after the forced conversion and expulsion of Muslims, while in Krakow, Poland, the Old Jewish Quarter is a major draw (Shaw *et al.*, 2004). So too, current or former immigrant neighborhoods like Little Italys or Greektowns are often targeted for touristic commodification. The cultural images and experiences that are marketed in these ethnic enclaves, however, are often 'safe, sanitized versions of the original' (Hannigan, 1998: 67), which mediate tourists' conflicting desires for the foreign and the familiar, the exotic and the safe. Around the globe, Chinatowns that were once considered dangerous and dirty have been reconfigured as themed exotic-yet-safe tourist destinations, reflecting changes in conceptions of ethnicity and diversity as well as of tourism (Santos *et al.*, 2008).

Washington DC's Chinatown is a prime example of this phenomenon. Business associations, ethnic institutions, corporations and the municipal government have joined forces, deploying culture to market Chinatown as an ethnic destination location. The economic value assigned to Chinese cultural symbols can be seen in the city's Comprehensive Plan (1984/1999): '[Chinatown's] role as a major regional and tourist attraction should be strengthened by... developing a stronger Chinese image in its building facades and street improvements, and by attracting new development to reinforce its economic viability' (Title 9 Section 900.27).

Developers of ethnic enclaves and downtown areas often manipulate the visual facade of the built environment to define the neighborhood via architectural preservation or innovation, or banners adorning the streets (Zukin, 1998). Historic neighborhoods tend to rely on visual images appropriated from the past, ignoring the human beings who built or inhabited those spaces and reshaping collective memory in order to offer the consumer a selective and conflict-free image of place (Boyer, 1992; Smith, 1992; Sorkin, 1992). Furthermore, as mentioned above, new development often overlooks the interests of current residents, focusing instead on building and environmental innovations that turn neighborhoods into themed urban spaces with spectacle used to sell places and goods (Crawford, 1992; Sorkin, 1992; Zukin, 1998). As Harvey (1991: 60) puts it, 'an architecture of play and pleasure, of spectacle and commodification, emphasizing fiction and fantasy, replaced that of function'. The architecture of spectacle is a staple of Chinatowns around the world, from Pagoda phone booths and '"double happiness" themed bike racks' in Victoria, Canada (City of Victoria, 2009), to the King's Birthday Celebration Arch in Bangkok (Dararai, 2002).

This pattern of visual theming can be seen clearly in Washington DC's Chinatown. Once the center of the Washington area's Chinese and Chinese American community, Chinatown underwent the outmigration and disinvestment typical of US urban neighborhoods in the 1960s and 1970s. Since then, two waves of redevelopment and gentrification have brought massive demolition and building, with row houses and family businesses (many of which were Chinese-owned) replaced by large-scale complexes, national and international chains, luxury apartment buildings and the MCI (now Verizon) sports arena. A key aspect of these public/private redevelopment efforts was the 'branding' of the neighborhood through Chinese-themed visual elements. This began in the 1980s with the construction of the Wah Luck House, a low-income publicly supported senior housing project exhibiting Chinese-style architectural features, the changing of the local Metro stop's name to include the word 'Chinatown' and the erection of the ornate Friendship Arch. In the 1990s, these were joined by such street ornamentations as Ming-dynasty inspired iron brackets holding banners that offer wishes of good health and happiness, and stylized Chinese lampposts (see Figure 10.3 and 10.4).

It is important to note that despite the symbolic economy's commodification of culture and authenticity, themed environments are valued by some precisely for their artificiality and consistency, as well as their referencing of leisure and entertainment. As Chinatown architect and developer Alfred Liu said, 'you create an image of "city." It's the theme park concept. People say it's fake, but they do enjoy it' (Fisher, 1995). Thus, while some urbanites disparage what they see as 'Disneyfied' cityscapes and simulated neighborhoods, others see them as fun places to visit, eat and shop.

Language is a key element in the creation of themed ethnic neighborhoods. Not only does language play a crucial role in the institutionalization of neighborhoods as places, such as in planning documents and municipal regulations, but it is also deployed in the commodified aestheticization of the built environment, as we discuss in the next section.

Figure 10.3 Friendship Arch at the intersection of Chinatown's two commercial corridors (© Jennifer Leeman)

Figure 10.4 Banners along Chinatown streets (© Jennifer Leeman)

Language and Ethnic Commodification

Language's status as a readily identifiable index of ethnicity and cultural authenticity casts it as a selling vehicle par excellence. For example, Heller (2003) has documented the use of French as a marker of authenticity in the marketing of heritage tourism in Ontario to

Francophone tourists. Souvenirs with writing in another language signal that one has been somewhere foreign, exciting or exotic, and thus serve as commodified markers of distinction as well as keepsakes of the experience. Further, the use of a 'foreign' language as a selling point is heightened when that language has a different orthography from the language of the target consumer. In such cases, language is valued primarily as an index of ethnicity and for its purely aesthetic qualities, rather than for its semantic content. Whereas a viewer unable to read a given orthography is aware at some level that the orthography conveys phonological or semantic meaning, she or he is less likely to instinctively process it as an encoding of linguistic information. Hence, for a viewer of an unfamiliar orthography, the linguistic valence of the writing system becomes backgrounded, and the aesthetic qualities become more salient. Mementos with 'your name in Chinese' or 'your name in Arabic' that are sold in themed ethnic neighborhoods are cases of the language itself being sold, rather than being used to sell another product (see Figure 10.5). The aesthetic nature of orthography can also be capitalized on through font design; consider the added exotifying function of Roman fonts designed to look like Chinese, Arabic or Hebrew, while still retaining comprehensibility to those unfamiliar with those orthographies (see Figure 10.6).

We argue that material manifestations of language can enhance particular commodities and, much like architectural elements, serve as vehicles to spatialize the commodification of culture; encountering a 'foreign' or minority language can give leisure visitors the sense of having visited an authentic place (rather than going to a mere 'tourist trap'). However, in many ethnic enclaves reconfigured as urban attractions, the actual, authentic histories are not part of the experience, for in many such places the speakers of minority ethnic languages have been forced out by resettlement, expulsion or genocide (cf. Jacobs, 1998; Shaw *et al.*, 2004), and, more recently, by rising rents and corporate-based economic redevelopment (cf. Lloyd, 2004; Mele, 2000). In such cases, material manifestations of minority languages work as sanitized visual references to cultural groups that neither rely on their actual presence, nor tell the full story of what happened to them. In the case of Washington DC's Chinatown, the massive development in the last decade of the 20th century led to a doubling of the neighborhood's total population (from 787 to 1470). Concurrently, the number of residents of Chinese birth or ancestry fell from 526 to 491 (US Census Bureau, 1990, 2000), and the center of Chinese commerce moved north to Rockville, Maryland (cf. Ly, 2006.). Thus, Chinatown's visual image became more Chinese at the exact moment when the Chinese residential and commercial sectors were shrinking.

Figure 10.5 'Your name in Arabic' for sale in the Arab Quarter of Granada, Spain (© Jennifer Leeman)

Aestheticizing Written Language

Material manifestations of language in contemporary urban themed environments are sometimes the direct consequence of intentional aestheticization and commodification of language, as when letter size, font style and sign colors are dictated in planning and zoning documents that standardize the visual qualities of the built environment. In Washington DC, for example, the Office of Planning stresses the aesthetic qualities of language in their guidelines for the development of new businesses in Chinatown, capitalizing on the exoticism of Chinese writing

Figure 10.6 Simulated Arabic fonts in Granada, Spain (© Jennifer Leeman)

to reconfigure the neighborhood as an enticing cultural destination. As the guidelines explain:

> Signage and Chinese characters are important design elements. Liberal use of Chinese characters in signage and decoration will provide needed Chinese ambiance in Chinatown (Section 6.91 Chinatown Design Review Guidelines, 1989: 42)

While the phrase 'Chinese characters in signage and decoration' implies signs written in Chinese, it is telling that the term 'characters', rather than 'language' is used. Whereas 'language' implies a coherent communicative system, 'Chinese characters' does not imply any semantic coherence; any random characters could be used to comply with these guidelines, regardless of whether or not they had a coherent meaning. The choice of the word 'characters' is consistent with the guidelines' description of Chinese characters as 'design elements' rather than as vehicles for communication. The guidelines thus cast the value and purpose of Chinese writing as solely aesthetic.

In keeping with the tenor of the guidelines, the Chinese-language elements of Chinatown's current LL overwhelmingly serve aesthetic functions: the vast majority of Chinese signs are name-signs[4] on chain stores and restaurants. In these establishments, Chinese is not used to communicate any semantic content that one might need in order to conduct a service encounter – and in the vast majority of these businesses, no workers speak Chinese. This is not to say that minority languages do not serve any communicative function in themed ethnic enclaves. In many cases, such languages are used in and by small businesses that are still owned by and cater to members of the ethnic communities in question. In addition, heritage tourism initiatives promote ethnic enclaves to visitors of the same ethnic background. Thus, themed ethnoscapes also include material manifestations of minority languages that go beyond the aesthetic to serve communicative functions. For example, small businesses are scattered among the mass-market sit-down restaurants and upscale cosmetics chains of Washington DC's Chinatown. In these small businesses, content-bearing signs such as menus and help-wanted ads are often written in Chinese – sometimes without complete translation into English – and service encounters may also be conducted in Chinese. For viewers who cannot read Chinese, such signs can also communicate cultural authenticity, intentionally or not. For example, Chinese-language menus posted on the walls of a restaurant add to the restaurant's 'Chinese ambiance' in addition to communicating information about the food available. These signs are thus polysemous – imparting different messages to different viewers.

The meanings of material manifestations of language are shaped by contexts operating at multiple scales. Thus, it is important to consider not only the micro-scale of their immediate settings, but also the meso-scale of the neighborhood, and the more macro-scales of the city, the nation and the global urban context. A multi-scalar analysis may reveal complex interactions of complementary and contradictory meanings. In Washington DC's Chinatown, the meso- and macro-scales heighten the symbolic meaning of many signs apparent at the micro-scale. For example, within the spatial context of the themed Chinatown environment, a handwritten flyer advertising an apartment for rent or a restaurant lunch menu posted on a door is part of a themed environment, and it takes on a symbolic value because it is interpreted within a commodified context. At the same time, because such signs communicate that there are Chinese people using the landscape to conduct daily life, they add an air of authenticity to the experience of visiting Chinatown; therefore they, too, contribute to the image of Chinatown as an exotic, exciting destination location. Thus, just as multiple scales of context shape their meaning, individual Chinese signs also have *effects* at multiple scales. At the micro-scale of an individual establishment, a Chinese sign adds value to the products or services offered. At the meso-scale of the neighborhood, the agglomeration of signs works in tandem with other Chinese-themed design elements of the built environment to enhance the neighborhood as a destination location. Finally, at the more macro-level of the city, Chinese signage ups the status of Chinatown as an interesting neighborhood in a 'city of neighborhoods' (one of Washington DC's current marketing slogans), thus helping Washington DC to compete against other cities for tourist, leisure and business dollars.

Conclusion

Not all neighborhoods are targeted for economic development, promoted as tourist destinations, or even paid much attention by public or private institutions or investors. Nonetheless, all cities and neighborhoods have a relationship with the municipal bodies that govern them. Whether that relationship is one of regulation, investment, suppression, negotiation or neglect, it has a bearing on the ways that social actors are encouraged or discouraged, desire, or are able to write (on) the landscape. To understand that writing, we need to know the backstory of how it came into being, and of the interests that constrained or enabled the form that the urban landscape ultimately takes.

In this chapter, we have stressed the role of socioeconomic and political forces shaping contemporary urban landscapes, and we have argued that material manifestations of language work in conjunction with other elements of the built environment to create particular kinds of urban places. As we have shown, language is a visual index of ethnicity that, when linked to various products, places and experiences, contributes to the commodification of culture typical of the symbolic economy. Inscribed on storefronts, for sale on souvenirs and hanging from ornamental banners that line the streets, written language is anchored to territory and becomes a vehicle both for the spatialization of culture and the commodification of space.

Acknowledgements

We would like to thank Hai Zhang for his Starbucks photograph, Aurelio Ríos Rojas for his help with Arabic translations, and Xu Huafang, Ben Kao, Hai Zhang and Weili Zhao for their help with Chinese translations.

Notes

1. For more on space and place theory, see Low and Lawrence-Zuñiga (2003) and Cresswell (2004).
2. For in-depth analyses of Chinatown's LL see Leeman and Modan (2009), Lou (2007 and this volume). The Chinatown examples included in this chapter are drawn from Leeman and Modan (2009), where details regarding data collection, coding and analysis are provided.
3. Although occasionally the products marketed are locally produced – such as local crafts or baked goods – more commonly the production sector where goods are produced is not part of the local economy. For example, the majority of Washington DC's tourist trinkets are made in China.
4. These may be translations or transliterations of a business's name, or a description of the products sold. In either case, they serve as a gloss for the store name.

References

Ben-Rafael, E., Shohamy, E., Amara, M.H. and Trumper-Hecht, N. (2006) Linguistic landscape as symbolic construction of the public space: The case of Israel. *International Journal of Multilingualism* 3, 7–30.

Boyer, M.C. (1992) Cities for sale: Merchandising history at South Street Seaport. In M. Sorkin (ed.) *Variations on a Theme Park: The New American City and the End of Public Space* (pp. 181–204). New York: Hill and Wang.

Cenoz, J. and Gorter, D. (2006) Linguistic landscape and minority languages. *International Journal of Multilingualism* 3, 67–80.

Christopherson, S. (1994) The fortress city, privatized spaces, consumer citizenship. In A. Amin (ed.) *Post-Fordism: A Reader* (pp. 409–427). Cambridge, MA: Blackwell.

City of Victoria (2009) Press release: New pagoda-style lamps to enhance Chinatown. April 17. On WWW at http://www.victoria.ca/contentmanager/press/090417_pr.pdf.

Crawford, M. (1992) The world in a shopping mall. In M. Sorkin (ed.) *Variations on a Theme Park* (pp. 3–30). New York: Hill and Wang.

Cresswell, T. (2004) *Place: A Short Introduction*. Malden, MA: Blackwell.

Dararai (2002) A walking tour in Chinatown: An old place with a new look. *Thaiways Magazine* 19 (17). On WWW at http://www.thaiwaysmagazine.com/thai_article/1917_bangkok_chinatown/bangkok_chinatown.html.

District of Columbia Office of Documents and Administrative Issuances (1999) District of Columbia Comprehensive Plan. *District of Columbia Register* 46 (8). Title 9, Sections 900.27 and 927. District of Columbia Office of Documents and Administrative Issuances. 1991/2000.

District of Columbia Office of Planning (1989) Chinatown design review guidelines. On WWW at http://planning.dc.gov/planning/frames.asp?doc = /planning/lib/planning/Chinatown_Design_Guidelines.pdf.

Eisinger, P. (2000) The politics of bread and circuses: Building the city for the visitor class. *Urban Affairs Review* 35 (3), 316–333.

Fisher, M. (1995) 'If the price is right, we sell': The last days of Chinatown. *The Washington Post Magazine*, 29 January.

Hannigan, J. (1998) *Fantasy City*. London: Routledge.

Harvey, D (1991) The urban face of capitalism. In J.F. Hart (ed.) *Our Changing Cities* (pp. 50–66). Baltimore, MD: Johns Hopkins University Press.

Heller, M. (2003) Globalization, the new economy, and the commodification of language and identity. *Journal of Sociolinguistics* 7 (4), 473–492.

Huebner, T. (2006) Bangkok's linguistic landscapes: Environmental print, codemixing and language change. *International Journal of Multilingualism* 3, 31–51.

Jacobs, J.M. (1998) Staging difference: Aestheticisation and the politics of difference in contemporary cities. In R. Fincher and J.M. Jacobs (eds) *Cities of Difference* (pp. 252–278). New York: Guilford.

Landry, R. and Bourhis, R.Y. (1997) Linguistic landscape and ethnolinguistic vitality: An empirical study. *Journal of Language and Social Psychology* 16, 23–49.

Leeman, J. and Modan, G. (2009) Commodified language in Chinatown: A contextualized approach to linguistic landscape. *Journal of Sociolinguistics* 13 (3), 332–362.

Leeman, J. and Modan, G. (2010) Trajectories of language: Orders of indexical meaning in Washington, DC's Chinatown. In M. Guggenheim and O. Söderström (eds) *Re-Shaping Cities: How Global Mobility Transforms Architecture and Urban Form* (pp. 167–188). London: Routledge.

Lloyd, R. (2004) The neighborhood in cultural production: Material and symbolic resources in the new bohemia. *City and Community* 3 (4), 343–372.

Lou, J. (2007) Revitalizing Chinatown into a heterotopia: A geosemiotic analysis of shop signs in Washington, DC's Chinatown. *Space and Culture* 10, 170–194.

Low, S. and Lawrence-Zuñiga, D. (eds) (2003) *The Anthropology of Space and Place: Locating Culture.* Malden, MA: Blackwell.

Luria, S. (2006) *Capital Speculations: Writing and Building Washington DC.* Lebanon, NH: University of New Hampshire Press.

Ly, P. (2006) MoCo's [Montgomery County's] Chinatown. *The Washington Post,* 9 April, p. M8.

Mallet, W. (1994) Managing the postindustrial city: Business improvement districts in the United States. *Area* 26 (3), 276–287.

Massey, D. with the collective (1999) Issues and debates. In D. Massey, J. Allen and P. Sarre (eds) *Human Geography Today* (pp. 3–21). Malden, MA: Polity Press.

Mele, C. (2000) *Selling the Lower East Side: Culture, Real Estate, and Resistance in New York City.* Minneapolis, MN: University of Minnesota Press.

Mitchell, D. (2003) *The Right to the City: Social Justice and the Fight for Public Space.* New York: Guilford.

Pang, C.L. and Rath, J. (2007) The force of regulation in the land of the free: The persistence of Chinatown, Washington DC as a symbolic ethnic enclave. In M. Lounsbury and M. Ruef (eds) *The Sociology of Entrepreneurship (Research in the Sociology of Organizations 25)* (pp. 191–216). New York: Elsevier.

Reddy, M.J. (1979) The conduit metaphor – A case of frame conflict in our language about language. In A. Ortony (ed.) *Metaphor and Thought* (pp. 284–324). Cambridge: Cambridge University Press.

Santos, C.A., Belhassen, Y. and Caton, K. (2008) Reimagining Chinatown: An analysis of tourism discourse. *Tourism Management* 29, 1002–1012.

Scollon, R. and Scollon, S.W. (2003) *Discourses in Place: Language in the Material World.* New York: Routledge.

Shaw, S., Bagwell, S. and Karmowska, J. (2004) Ethnoscapes as spectacle: Reimaging multicultural districts as new destinations for leisure and tourism consumption. *Urban Studies* 41, 1983–2000.

Shohamy, E. and Waksman, S. (2009) Linguistic landscape as an ecological arena: Modalities, meaning, negotiation, education. In E. Shohamy and D. Gorter (eds) *Linguistic Landscape: Expanding the Scenery* (pp. 313–331). New York: Routledge.

Smith, N. (2002) New globalism, new urbanism: Gentrification as global urban strategy. *Antipode* 34, 428–450.

Sorkin, M. (1992) See you in Disneyland. In M. Sorkin (ed.) *Variations on a Theme Park: The New American City and the End of Public Space* (pp. 205–232). New York: Hill and Wang.

US Census Bureau (2000) Census 2000, tables for census tract 58. On WWW at http://factfinder.census.gov.

US Census Bureau (1990) 1990 Census, tables for census tract 58, block groups 1, 2, and 5. On WWW at http://factfinder.census.gov.

Wheeler, L. (1986) Mixed blessing for Chinatown. *The Washington Post,* 12 July, p. E1.

Zukin, S. (1995) *The Cultures of Cities.* Malden, MA: Blackwell.

Zukin, S. (1998) Urban lifestyles: Diversity and standardization in spaces of consumption. *Urban Studies* 35, 825–839.

Chapter 11
Showing Seeing in the Korean Linguistic Cityscape

DAVID MALINOWSKI

Introduction

Since early 2009, a new means of visualizing urban scenes in South Korea has been steadily expanding across the capital Seoul and other city centers in this country of 48 million people, allowing virtual tourists to 'walk' up and down its roads, giving remotely located language learners access to millions of authentic texts embedded in lived urban spaces, and presenting the linguistic landscape researcher with an unimaginably vast storehouse of data. The internet portal website, Daum, has taken the lead on this front, launching a pair of new mapping services named 'Road View' and 'Sky View'[1] that integrate enhanced aerial photographs of cities with street-level imagery taken from pods of cameras mounted on automobiles, two-wheel Segway scooters and back-mounted frames for walking photographers (see Figure 11.1). Other companies are not far behind: Naver, the leading search portal in South Korea and the fifth most popular search engine worldwide, is leveraging its dominant position to promote and sell its own Road View-style service, while Paran, Yahoo and Google are also competing to deploy monetized and interactive visualization services for urban centers in South Korea (Kim, 2008a, 2008b, 2009).

As one small drop in the proverbial ocean of computing applications available in contemporary Korean society, where the high rates of internet usage are known worldwide (Townsend, 2008), and where the very word 'ubiquitous' has itself been made into something of a mantra with respect to the integration of mobile digital technologies into urban life (Choi & Greenfield, 2009), Daum's Road View may seem but a small addition. And, in comparison to resistance in several other countries against ongoing efforts of internet giant Google to similarly photograph and 'provide street views of the entire world',[2] concern over privacy rights in South Korea appears to be relatively subdued (Kim, 2009).

Yet, an exploration of the visual politics of online representations of the streets of Seoul seems particularly instructive in the interest of linguistic landscape studies in the present day. At the same time numerous scholars have made observations about the ready commoditization of the signed

Figure 11.1 Browser screenshot of Daum Road View imagery in downtown Seoul. On WWW at http://map.daum.net/. Accessed 30.6.09

landscape (cf. Ben-Rafael *et al.*, 2006; Huebner, 2009; Leeman & Modan, this volume), the South Korean capital presents a dramatic, though not unique, example of a centuries-old city whose sites and paths are being thoroughly remediated by new digital technologies of seeing. The intent behind this chapter, then, is to move toward what might be termed *applied linguistic landscape studies.* As a way of posing questions about the linguistic landscape as represented visually, it narrates the development of a website that uses images of the Korean-English linguistic landscape to aid learners of the Korean language at a US university. In so doing, the chapter picks up on the implicit call to attention in Shohamy and Gorter's (2009: 1) statement that 'technology [is] playing a major role in the growing attention to representations in public spaces'. Accordingly, the chapter begins by paying attention to questions of how language learners might read visual 'texts' – in this case, images of signs, billboards and posters that comprise the Korean-English linguistic landscape – and then expands its scope to the crucial visual and verbal politics of *contextualization* of multimedia images of the city and its linguistic landscape. I will argue that freely available, economically viable (from an institutional perspective) and personally compelling (from the user's perspective) technologies of contextualization for linguistic landscape imagery, represented in tools like Daum's Road View and Google's Street View, are one mechanism by which the linguistic landscape is *iconicized*, or rendered into a decontextualized and portable form, ready for commoditization. Further, the uncritical use of these technologies is seen as detrimental to authentic and agential engagement with the living city, just as it is inimical to the nuanced study of language. The chapter concludes its narrative by invoking the expanding field of visual culture as a necessary partner in dialog to linguistic approaches to the signed city. As the verbal-visual amalgamation 'linguistic landscape' suggests, processes of *reading* and *writing* can no longer be understood separately from processes of *seeing* the languages of the city.

Seeing Discovered: The Problem with an Educational Website on the Linguistic Landscape

Language learning and the linguistic landscape

Since at least the 1970s in the USA, literacy theorists and practitioners have recognized the importance of the 'environmental print' of billboards, food packages and street signs for the emergent reading skills of children and adults (cf. Goodman, 1984; Aldridge *et al.*, 1996). With respect to the educational applications of the 'linguistic landscape' in the growing body of literature that bears this title, a number of recent studies point to the linguistic, social and political importance of understanding the myriad inscriptions written into the urban environment. Gorter and Cenoz (2008: 274), for example, explore the relationship between public language and second language acquisition, identifying the former as 'authentic, contextualized input which is part of the social context' and suggest it may play a role in expanding students' pragmatic competence and literacy skills. Shohamy and Waksman (2009), drawing on Krasmch (2002) and other theorists of language ecology, argue for a more critical investigative stance to be taken by students of the linguistic landscape. In this view, students would use visible texts as '"tips of icebergs" to a deeper and more complex meaning which [is] embedded in histories, cultural relations, politics and humanistic inter-relations' (Shohamy & Waksman, 2009: 328). Meanwhile, in a longitudinal study of language awareness among elementary school children in Montreal and Vancouver, Canada, Dagenais *et al.* (2009) argue for the potential for young learners to cultivate a critical sociological awareness by reading the city as multilayered text. Pointing to the work of Louis-Jean Calvet and other French-language scholarship in sociolinguistics, they note that the diversity of representation in the linguistic landscape 'provides [students] with information about the population of their neighborhood, it signals what languages are prominent and valued in public and private spaces and indexes the social positioning of people who identify with particular languages' (Dagenais *et al.*, 2009: 254).

Clearly, the reading of the city as a body of interrelated and *lived* texts involves a set of competences that is much broader than the code-based linguistic competence of Chomskyan linguistics, or even the more pragmatically oriented communicative competence that emerged from Dell Hymes' ethnographies of speaking and the sociological orientation to language education in the 1980s and 1990s. In 2007, writing with an understanding of a 'late-modern world' in which national borders, learner identities and linguistic categories are fundamentally unstable, the Modern Language Association's Ad Hoc Committee on Foreign Languages asserted the need for a 'translingual and transcultural competence'. This version of competence stresses the ability to operate not just *in* the foreign or second language, but *between* languages, with facility in 'critical language awareness, interpretation and translation, historical and political consciousness, social sensibility, and aesthetic perception' (MLA Report, 2007: 5). As such, competence in *language* in the early 2000s may be broadly understood with respect to fields such as New Literacy Studies (cf. Gee, 1996; Lankshear & Knobel, 2003; Street, 1995) and Multiliteracies (cf. Cope & Kalantzis, 2000; Kress, 2003; New London Group, 1996), where fundamental differences between language and other modes of communication are being questioned. In particular, contentions such as Kress' (2003: 9) that 'the logic of the image now dominates the sites and the conditions of appearance of all "displayed" communication', draw attention to the computer screen as the site where language itself is being redefined in accordance with a visual mode of communication. Language educators – especially those concerned with the profoundly visual and spatial field of linguistic landscape – may be increasingly required to pay attention to the rhetoric of the online image as part and parcel of the rhetoric of the word.

Learning to see Korean in the city

The adaptation of investigative research methods to the multimodal linguistic landscape would seem not only to work toward the *general* goals of a translingual and transcultural competence through (among other things) readings of the city as text, but might fulfil a particular role in explicating the geopolitics of the visible Korean language for its learners. As one of the 20 most-spoken languages in the world, and as the language of a nation (South Korea) with the 11th largest economy, Korean has on occasion taken on the title of a 'world language'; it is more familiarly known as a 'national language' to some 70 million North and South Koreans and a 'heritage' or 'home' language to a diaspora of approximately seven million people (Silva, 2007). Within certain cities of China, the USA and Japan where the greatest numbers of this population find their homes, the Korean script *Hangeul* is often prominently displayed. Studies by Kim (2003) in the Ikuno district of Osaka and Backhaus (2007) in the Shin-Okubo area of Tokyo, for example, illustrate the historical and symbolic importance attached to the display of the Korean language in Japanese contexts. In the USA, meanwhile, where a so-called 'non-geographical' Korean American community has tended to gather around visible concentrations of ethnic businesses, debates over the display of the Korean language have been noted in places such as Flushing, New York, Bergen County, New Jersey and Los Angeles, California (Min, 1996; Andrew, 1997).

If learners of Korean outside of Korea, as with other foreign language learners, maintain some awareness as to the complexities of multi-lingualism in the linguistic landscape of their local environs, they might bring less of a critical eye to the diversity of voices and histories that populate the visible texts in the centers of Korea. The South Korean capital of Seoul, with over 10 million people and an additional 14 million people living in its suburbs, bears a tumultuous history of modernization and a legacy of either deprivileging or outright eradication of the display of the native *Hangeul* script (cf. Kang & Joo, 2002). Serving as the state capital for centuries before enduring Japanese colonial rule and violent urban 'respatialization' from 1910 to 1945, and then bearing the brunt of industrial reorganization for decades in the post-Korean War (1950–1953) era, the face of Seoul has, in the eyes of some, undergone a 'sudden and destructive process' over the past century (Pai, 1997: 105; cf. Henry, 2007). Along with the disappearance of the 'traditional urban fabric' (Pai, 1997: 104) of the city, recent years have seen a rise in the visibility of English in Seoul's linguistic landscape, a result (in part) of Korea's long-standing alliance with the USA and equation of economic globalization with ideologies of English as a global language (Nunan, 2003). In this context, new visual technologies such as Daum's Road View or Google's Street View – with their promise to produce imagery from the most out-of-the-way residential districts as well as international centers of commerce – appear to offer the language learner, as the urban geographer, one of the most comprehensive visions of the city: signs both large and small, mass-produced and hand-drawn, written in stylish English lettering and traditional Chinese characters, all transparently revealing (or so it would seem) the linguistic landscape as index and actor in Korean society.

Seeing Seoul online

Increasing calls in the foreign language teaching profession for a nuanced, historical and multimodally aware approach to language study,

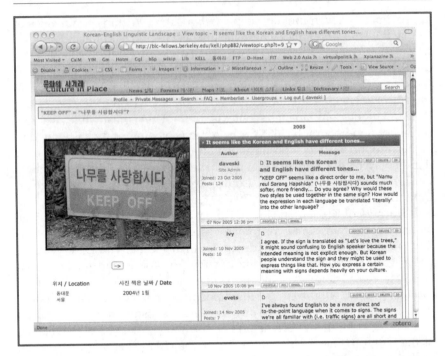

Figure 11.2 Browser screenshot of *Culture in Place* discussion forum. Accessed 30.6.09

as well as the author's own work as a Korean language teaching assistant, led in 2005–2006 to the development of a prototype online discussion forum based on linguistic landscape images (see Figure 11.2).

Named *Culture in Place*, this web-based project brought approximately 50 beginning and intermediate Korean learners at the University of California at Berkeley into dialog with each other and a handful of Korean students of English from Suwon University, located just south of Seoul. Featuring about 100 photographs of monolingual and bilingual Korean-English signs taken by the author in South Korean and Californian cities, and allowing for users to post questions and comments next to the photographs, the *Culture in Place* project was designed with the following goals:

(1) To foster learners' abilities to read and discuss how linguistic, cultural and social meanings are both indexed and created in multiple modes through the linguistic and other semiotic resources employed in material signage.

(2) To develop learners' fluency in the target language (TL) as they interact with fluent speakers.

(3) To create a context for motivation as language is linked to real places and activities in the TL. (Malinowski, 2006: 7)

Initial project results were mixed: about 230 paragraph-or-longer posts were written in English or Korean, with some students demonstrating curiosity and taking initiative to research unknown words, place names, legal codes and other unknowns indexed in the linguistic landscape. One example of this was found in several discussion threads concerning a simple-looking bilingual sign located on a foot path behind a shopping complex in Seoul's commercial district of Dongdaemun: the sign is divided in half horizontally, with Korean *Hangeul* reading 'LET'S RESPECT THE TREES' against a white background on top, and capital-lettered English reading 'KEEP OFF' against an orange background at the bottom (see Figure 11.2). Responding to their teachers' and the researcher's discussion prompts, approximately 30 students remarked on the social and pragmatic implications of this sign's phrasing, translation conventions, coloring, placement and other factors. One comment in English by a student in a second-year Korean language class in Berkeley demonstrates his emergent sense of the pragmato-political relations linking the language of his classroom to the geography of a city 6000 miles away. In a post dated 24 November 2005, the student wrote,

> In America there are many signs that say "KEEP OFF" or tell us what not to do or where not to go. In Korea, I believe there are signs just like America that say "KEEP OFF" but the fact that this sign is in [*Dongdaemun*], where there are MANY people who come only on special occasions, the city of Seoul may want to keep a "happy" sign to keep the people's moods happy. If the sign were in a neighborhood, it would probably have the tone "STAY OFF!" in korean [sic] as well, but it's in an area with lots of new people so it changes everything.

Just as often as this forum elicited thoughtful and engaged responses from students motivated by the internet-mediated immediacy of the linguistic landscape, however, many US students admitted to posting in the forum 'just to receive extra credit' in their Korean class, or complained about the lack of user-centered content on the site. And, more relevant to the concerns of the translingual and transcultural competence called for by the Modern Language Association, the few participants in Korea articulated a critique of the *Culture in Place* site itself that raised a much larger question. Remarking on the foreignness of Seoul in the Mapquest and Google maps that were used to 'anchor' the photographs of Seoul in place, they said simply, 'This site looks too American' (Figure 11.3).

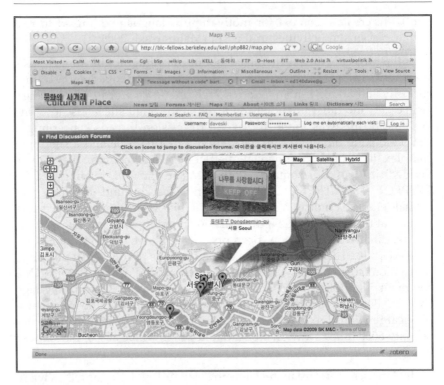

Figure 11.3 Browser screenshot of *Culture in Place* image of bilingual sign in Seoul geo-tagged to Google Map. Accessed 30.6.09

This critique, and the discussions that followed, helped to spawn a revision of the pedagogical principles and representational technologies upon which the *Culture in Place* project was founded. To the present day, revision of the website and use by subsequent groups of students have awaited the answer to a vexing question, the partial explication of which is the goal of this chapter as well: namely, what are the culturally situated practices of seeing 'real places' online, practices that underpin the vision of foreign cities as familiar to strangers, while at the same time rendering them strange to their own residents?

Visual Disruptions in Real and Virtual Cities

The Korean university students' remark about the *Americanness* of 'the Korean linguistic landscape' attached to a Google map of Seoul appeared, among other things, to turn on the questions of *location*: the relationship between photographic *sight* and the historical, geographical *sites* that inform the situated knowledge of those who try to read images. On the surface, to contest the reality of an image of the linguistic landscape seems to contravene the basic nature of the photograph, a seemingly unmediated *analogon* of reality, or what appears to be, in the words of the semiotician Roland Barthes (1977: 20), a 'message[s] without a code'. Yet, as Barthes later points out, even (or perhaps especially) photographs of 'other places' and 'other cultures' are amenable to perceptual, cognitive and ideological 'connotation procedures' (Barthes, 1977: 29), the imposition of culturally specific meanings that depend more on what the viewer already knows than on what she/he sees. Linked to an online map, and part of an incessant stream of imagery generated by an indiscriminate photographer-machine, the linguistic landscape image might lose the very historical ground that guarantees its authenticity to the foreign language learner, becoming a mere simulacrum of *the foreign*, interpretable according to a familiar set of visual and cultural coordinates.

Here it may be worthwhile revisiting the image of the Daum Sky View map of Seoul with its blue grid showing the presence of Road View imagery (Figure 11.1) and pose the question, 'What visual subjectivity might allow this image to be seen as Seoul?' Daum's Road View 'pictures', dynamically linked to the blue grid on this map, are unlike most images, film or digital: they are taken from *lines*, and not points, as is evident as one virtually travels with the car that was used to photograph them. They are not images of a particular scene, from a particular angle, taken in order to capture a specific person, thing or event. Indeed, these Road View pictures are, in conjunction with the enhanced satellite Sky View images that give them order, among some of the closest contemporary realizations of Jeremy Bentham's architectural panopticon, generalized in its principle of control through permanent visibility by Foucault (1977), and now *mobilized*.[3]

Juxtaposed against a history that includes attempts at hierarchized control of the urban public in Seoul, the contemporary fascination in online chatrooms with scenes of deviance captured by the cameras of Daum, Google, Naver and other online content providers seems but a logical outcome.[4] In his survey of the 'respatialization' of Seoul in the initial period of Japanese colonial occupation (1905–1919), Todd A. Henry writes that the Japanese were the first to attempt to impose a comprehensive vision of gridded order upon the streets of Seoul, after they did the same in occupied Taipei (Taiwan). Henry notes that urban planning was carried out in conjunction with measures for land use control and outright confiscation, and writes,

> By superimposing a grid system of straightened, widened, and clear streets over these preexisting roads, colonial officials hoped to create a well-organized and prosperous urban infrastructure in which Koreans, along with their Japanese counterparts, could efficiently

carry out their duties as diligent colonial subjects, while making a profit at the same time. (Henry, 2007: 27)

The Japanese efforts were only partially successful, Henry writes, as they were confounded by sedimented urban practices and acts of resistance, the most notable of which was undoubtedly the popular reclaiming of the city on 1 March 1919. Still, more than two decades after liberation, South Korean president Park Chung Hee's consolidated regime of economic development and political control was reported to bring similar changes upon the landscape of Seoul. Kim Hyeong-ok, mayor of Seoul from 1966 to 1970, was heard to remark simply, 'The city is lines,' a comment to the effect that the 'denaturalization' of modernizing Seoul was visible in the 'straight wires and streets [that] started to replace traditional winding roads' (Choi & Greenfield, 2009: 22).

Yet, considering the ubiquity of tools such as Daum's Sky View, methods of control and knowledge production engendered by strategies such as gridding may be said not to belong to any one regime more than the other. Indeed, they are almost second nature in their portability and scalability across context, and function much like the 'visualisable, organisable spaces' of virtual worlds that geographer Mike Crang (2000: 311) critiques for imposing 'closed realms of shared assumption' and a 'monologue of form representing function' to their viewers/users.

A New Imperative? 'Showing Seeing' in the Linguistic Landscape

Kramsch and Andersen's (1999: 40) dictum that 'the power and the complexity of multimedia technology increases the need to contextualize the texts and textualize the contexts presented on the screen' seems as pertinent for the layman's reading of images of the linguistic landscape as it does for foreign language learners in the technology-enabled classroom. While the complexity of the linguistic landscape may help explicate the multiscalar and emergent nature of multilingual phenomena in society generally (Hult, 2009), and while the ability of the linguistic landscape to perform both institutional and individual identities is understood to derive from the simultaneous indexical and symbolic sign relations of language (Backhaus, 1997; Ben-Rafael *et al.*, 2006; Scollon & Scollon, 2003; Spolsky & Cooper, 1991), the *iconic* power of the linguistic landscape seems to operate in a domain (at least partially) beyond the scope of language altogether. Indeed, as the applied linguist Leo van Lier (2000: 258) writes, referring to the tripartite *icon-index-symbol* semiotic relationship posited by C.S. Peirce: 'the iconic plane remains very much a vital force, even though it appears to run underground and often defies verbalization'. Crucially, however, the conversion of vital landscapes into marketable commodities, as in

Leeman and Modan's (e.g. 2007; this volume) studies of Chinatown in Washington, DC, would appear to turn precisely on the ability of institutions of power to naturalize iconic relations between urban scenes and the essentialized values they are held to represent.

In order to approach the complex questions of how people *see* Seoul's streets and other linguistic landscape 'scenery' visible online, embedded into representational grids such as interactive satellite-based maps, and iconized in multimedia pedagogical tools like Berkeley's *Culture in Place*, the growing field of visual studies (cf. Jay, 2005; Mirzoeff, 2002a; Mitchell, 1995) seems well-suited. Since about the time of Mitchell's (1995) *Picture Theory*, an overriding focus of this area of study, drawing from art history, aesthetics, media studies and other fields, has been exposing the very practices and politics of seeing, or, in Mitchell's (2002) words, 'showing seeing'. In particular, with respect to the discussion above on how top-down mapping schemes can provide a new paradigm for seeing (dis)order in the city, Rogoff (2002: 31) asserts that the very 'traditions of Western post-Enlightenment scientificity' are over-reliant on the gaze – what she describes as 'an apparatus of investigation, verification, surveillance and cognition', which 'becomes a neutral field in which some innocent objective "eye" is deployed by an unsituated viewer'. Significantly, the all-seeing power of the modern, disembodied eye is found to be as important for the purposes of aestheticized pleasure as it is for domination and control. Here, Rogoff invokes the words of Walter Benjamin, who was himself taken with the figure of Baudelaire's flâneur, the wanderer of the Parisian streets:

> To be away from home, yet to feel oneself everywhere at home; to see the world, to be at the center of the world, yet to remain hidden from the world – [are] a few of the slightest pleasures of those independent, passionate, impartial natures which the tongue can but clumsily define. (Quoted by Benjamin in *Arcades*, 443)

Regardless of the institutional position occupied by the seer, however, the adoption of particular technologies of representation cannot but raise questions of viewing subjectivities and viewed objecthoods – a problem that, in its most pernicious manifestations, must link even the language classroom to critiques of Orientalist colonialism (cf. Said, 1978; Mitchell, 1992).

In response to the conundrum posed by the unitary gaze implicated in representational media like geo-tagged photographs of the linguistic landscape, visual culture scholars argue for 'double vision' or 'multiple viewpoints' in simultaneity as a basic principle for creating difference, dissonance and discursive space for the emergence of dialog and relativizing of power. In the essay, 'The Subject of Visual Culture', Mirzoeff (2002b) argues for the replacement of the gaze with 'transverse glances', a manner of *seeing* that is akin to the speaking practices of those who struggle to reconcile irreconcilable meanings in the power-laden 'contact zone' between languages (cf. Pratt, 1999). Mirzoeff (2002b: 18), visually invoking a term also used by Pratt in the domain of language, writes that the goal of decentered practices of looking should be *transculture*, or 'the product of an encounter between an existing culture or subculture and a newly arrived migrant culture that violently transforms them both and in the process creates a neo-culture that is itself immediately subject to transculturation'. Perhaps the linguistic landscape, in which all visual signifiers derive from the diverse, historically rich, and yet readily accessible material reality of everyday life, provides an ideal platform for such an encounter. Rogoff suggests as much when she notes that

> Visual culture opens up an entire world of intertextuality in which images, sounds and spatial delineations are read on, to, and through one another, lending ever-accruing layers of meanings and of subjective responses to each encounter we might have with film, TV, advertising, art works, buildings or urban environments. (Rogoff, 2002: 24)

Conclusion and Coda

Rogoff's point above that a focus on the visual ought to open up an intertextual dialog with sound and spatial delineations through sub-jective encounters appears particularly important as 'real' living urban environments are sampled, classified and represented in online media that follow the increasingly visual logic of the screen. In this context, where the multiple, overlapping and sometimes contradictory histories, presents and futures that the city sustains move to the background of a reality mapped along X/Y coordinates in Euclidian space, to be an uncritical consumer of geo-referenced linguistic landscape images is to risk an alienation and loss of ability to differentiate geographic place from cyberspace. Paul Virilio warns as much when he writes:

> With the screen interface of computers, television and teleconfer-ences, the surface of inscription, hitherto devoid of depth, becomes a kind of "distance", a depth of field of a new kind of representation, a visibility without any face-to-face encounter in which the *vis-à-vis* of the ancient streets disappears and is erased. In this situation, a difference of position blurs into fusion and confusion... distinctions of *here* and *there* no longer mean anything. (Virilio, 1997: 382–383)

In this sense, the critical engagement with *representations* of signs – and the contextualization of these representations – by language learners and others ought to enable them to discover media and the very processes of remediation as important, and too often hidden, sites of knowledge production (cf. Iedema, 2003).

Yet, how is this to happen?

Within a year and a half of the launch of its road-level photography and mapping application Street View in May 2007, Google announced it had attained 'full coverage of all large and most medium-sized urban areas and most major highways and connecting arteries throughout the 48 contiguous states', and soon faced protests over privacy rights that led it to blur faces and license plates in all its imagery. In the summer of 2008, Google began taking pictures in France, Italy, Australia, Spain, England, Holland, New Zealand, Australia and Japan. Governments in Canada and Germany have lodged protests with Google; in Greece, the government has stopped the high-tech company from taking more pictures until it has further explained the relevant privacy issues, and residents in one English village are reported to have physically chased the Google car out of its streets. Google, for its part, contends that 'This imagery is no different from what any person can readily capture or see walking down the street' (quoted in Weeks, 2007).

But the case of Japan, where citizen groups, lawyers, professors and journalists have demanded that Google stop the service altogether, raises questions that are most relevant to possible objections in the Korean linguistic landscape, and to the purpose of this chapter more generally: IT professional Osamu Higuchi's 'Letter to the people at Google', published on 8 August 2008 on his blog *higuchi.com*,[5] asserted that fundamentally different conceptions of private and public space were operative in Japan and in Google's home country, the US. Residential streets, which Google and other mapping services are busy photograph-ing around the world, 'feel more like a part of one's own living space', Higuchi argued (Salzberg, 2008). The very act of looking, in his view and that of the many protesters, is politically and culturally charged, with deep ramifications for both the online subjects and offline objects of the technologized gaze. And, as of mid-2009, Google is reported to be re-filming all its Street View data in Japan from a lower, 'less conspicuous' angle; the company's website notes that it 'wished to provide the new service in a way that is socially acceptable in Japan' (Canwest News Service, 2009).

The case of Daum's Road View and similar technologies of seeing the linguistic and urban landscape in Korea remains open, yet there would seem to be ready paradigms for the 'transverse glances' of Mirzoeff's (2002b) visual culture and the critical literacy approach of Dagenais *et al.* (2009), Shohamy and Waksman (2009) and others. In their 2002 book, *Seoul Essay: A Portrait of Modernity, Traversing Seoul*, Kang Hong-bin (Director of the Seoul Museum of History) and photographer Joo Myung-duck uncover the history of the city in a series of reflective photo essays. They do not follow the lines of a pre-given map, but in essence create their own, moving from past and present seats of power along Sejong-ro street in the north, to the historical interface between media organizations, government entities and the people along Taepyung-ro street off to the south, into districts of contested identities in Seoul's popular market Namdaemun, past the still present 'warchild' of modern history in the US army base in Yongsan, and beyond. As long-time residents of the city of Seoul, Kang and Joo's approach to the landscape is through the trope of the *kihaeng*, or 'journey', a critical defamiliarization of the familiar that they enact through camera, pen and a commitment to uncovering multiple and conflicted pasts whose traces remain in the present (Kang & Joo, 2002: 10). Bringing to mind cultural geographer Tuan's (1977) sense of *places* as accretion of social and personal *value* and Hayden's (1995) communal reading of urban landscapes as public history, Kang and Joo assert,

> If the social, economic, cultural, and political power and processes that dominate at any period in time are what make places, they are also, by the same token, re-made by places. In this way, if people's daily lives and lifeworlds are held to be as important as the grand spatial structures and systems of an era, then "places" must be as important as these grand structures.
>
> *Han shidae reul jibae haneun sahoe, gyungje, munhwa, jeongchijeokin him gwa gwajeong eun jangso reul saengsan hago yeok euro jangso sogeseo jaesaengsan doenda. Geureomeuro ilsang saenghwal gwa saenghwal segye ga geodae han gujo wa chegye e motchi ankhe jungyo hadamyeon, jangso ddo han geodae han gonggan gujo mankeum jungyo hada.* (Kang & Joo, 2002: 13; author's translation)

Acknowledgements

Special thanks to the Academy of Korean Studies and UC Berkeley's Center for Korean Studies for support that enabled this research.

Notes

1. 'Sky View' and 'Road View' are transliterated, and not translated, English expressions in Korean as well.
2. See Conclusion for discussion.
3. Foucault writes of the 19th-century European origins of this principle as (he argues) it appeared in prisons, schools, hospitals and other redesigned spaces,

> in order to be exercised, this power had to be given the instrument of permanent, exhaustive, omnipresent surveillance, capable of making all visible, as long as it could itself remain invisible. It had to be like a faceless gaze that transformed the whole social body into a field of perception:

thousands of eyes posted everywhere, mobile attentions ever on the alert, a long, hierarchized network. (Foucault, 1977: 214)

4. Perusal of online forums tracking the progress of the Daum Sky View photographers, as with the Google cars in other countries, reveals a fascination with the social deviance these continuous images reveal: someone has been captured urinating in public, a male CEO is seen at a club with his arm around a young woman, a teenager is 'caught' spray-painting a school wall.

5. The letter can be found on WWW at http://www.higuchi.com/item/385.

References

Aldridge, J., Kirkland, L. and Kuby, P. (1996) *Jumpstarters: Integrating Environmental Print Throughout the Curriculum* (2nd edn). Birmingham, AL: Campus Press.

Andrew, R.P. (1997) Sign language: Colonialism and the battle over text. *Loyola L.A. Ent. Law Journal* 17. On WWW at http://ssrn.com/abstract=887434.

Backhaus, P. (2007) *Linguistic Landscapes: A Comparative Study of Urban Multilingualism in Tokyo.* Clevedon: Multilingual Matters.

Barthes, R. (1977) *Image, Music, Text.* New York: Hill and Wang.

Ben-Rafael, E., Shohamy, E., Hasan Amara, M. and Trumper-Hecht, N. (2006) Linguistic landscape as symbolic construction of the public space: The case of Israel. *International Journal of Multilingualism* 3 (1), 7–30.

Canwest News Service (2009) Google to reshoot Japan Street views. On WWW at http://www.canada.com/news/national/Google+reshoot+Japan+Street+views/1596123/story.html.

Choi, J.H-j. and Greenfield, A. (2009) To connect and flow in Seoul: Ubiquitous technologies, urban infrastructure and everyday life in the contemporary Korean city. In M. Foth (ed.) *Handbook of Research on Urban Informatics: The Practice and Promise of the Real-time City* (pp. 21–36). Hershey, PA: IGI Global.

Cope, B. and Kalantzis, M. (2000) *Multiliteracies: Literacy Learning and the Design of Social Futures.* London: Routledge.

Crang, M. (2000) Public space, urban space and electronic space: Would the real city please stand up? *Urban Studies* 37 (2), 301–317.

Dagenais, D., Moore, D., Sabatier, C., Lamarre, P. and Armand, F. (2009) Linguistic landscape and language awareness. In E. Shohamy and D. Gorter (eds) *Linguistic Landscape: Expanding the Scenery* (pp. 253–269). New York: Routledge.

de Certeau, M. (1984) *The Practice of Everyday Life.* Berkeley, CA: University of California Press.

Foucault, M. (1977) *Discipline and Punish: The Birth of the Prison.* New York: Vintage Books.

Gee, J. (1996) *Social Linguistics and Literacies: Ideology in Discourse.* London: Taylor & Francis.

Goodman, Y. (1984) The development of initial literacy. In H. Goelman, A. Oberg and F. Smith (eds) *Awakening to Literacy* (pp. 102–109). Exeter, NH: Heinemann.

Gorter, D. and Cenoz, J. (2008) The linguistic landscape as an additional source of input in second language acquisition. *International Review of Applied Linguistics in Language Teaching* 46, 267–287.

Hayden, D. (1995) *The Power of Place: Urban Landscapes as Public History.* Cambridge: MIT Press.

Henry, T.A. (2007) Respatializing Choson's royal capital: The politics of Japanese urban reforms in early colonial Seoul, 1905–1919. In T.R. Tangherlini and S. Yea (eds) *Sitings: Critical Approaches to Korean Geography* (pp. 15–38). Honolulu, HI: University of Hawai'i Press.

Huebner, T. (2009) A framework for the analysis of linguistic landscapes. In E. Shohamy and D. Gorter (eds) *Linguistic Landscape: Expanding the Scenery* (pp. 70–87). New York: Routledge.

Hult, F.M. (2009) Language ecology and linguistic landscape analysis. In E. Shohamy and D. Gorter (eds) *Linguistic Landscape: Expanding the Scenery* (pp. 88–104). New York: Routledge.

Iedema, R. (2003) Multimodality, resemiotization: Extending the analysis of discourse as multi-semiotic practice. *Visual Communication* 2 (1), 29–57.

Jay, M. (ed.) (2005) The state of visual culture studies. Themed issue of *Journal of Visual Culture* 4 (2). London: Sage.

Kang, H-b. and Joo, M-d. (2002) *Seoul Essay: A Portrait of Modernity, Traversing Seoul.* Seoul: Youlhwadang.

Kim, M. (2003) Gengo keikan kara mita nihon no taminzokuka [The Increase in Japan's Ethnic Diversity as Seen from the Linguistic Landscape]. In H. Shoji (ed.) *Kokusai imin no jizon senryaku to toransunashonaru nettowaku no bunka jinruigakuteki kenkyu* [*Cultural-ethnological Research About International Immigrants' Strategies of Independent Existence and Transnational Networks*] (pp. 175–190). Osaka: National Museum of Ethnology.

Kim, T-h. (2008a) Daum plans eye-catching map service. *The Korea Times.* On WWW at http://www.koreatimes.co.kr/www/news/biz/2008/11/123_345 01.html/.

Kim, T-h. (2008b) Internet portals competing for digital map marketing. *The Korea Times.* On WWW at http://www.koreatimes.co.kr/ www/news/tech/2009/ 05/133_36003.html/.

Kim, T-h. (2009) Daum map is impressive, but privacy concerns loom. *The Korea Times.* On WWW at http://www.koreatimes.co.kr/www/news/biz/2008/ 11/123_34501.html/.

Kramsch, C. (2002) Introduction. In C. Kramsch (ed.) *Language Acquisition and Language Socialization: Ecological Perspectives* (pp. 1–30). London: Continuum.

Kramsch, C. and Andersen, R.W. (1999) Teaching text and context through multimedia. *Language Learning & Technology* 2 (2), 31–42.

Kress, G. (2003) *Literacy in the New Media Age.* London: Routledge.

Lankshear, C. and Knobel, M. (2003) *New Literacies: Changing Knowledge and Classroom Learning.* Maidenhead: Open University Press.

Leeman, J. and Modan, G. (2007) Commodified ethnicity in Chinatown: A discourse approach to linguistic landscape. Presentation at the International Society for Language Studies Conference, Honolulu, Hawaii.

Malinowski, D. (2006) Making culture in place: The creation of an online Korean-English forum to discuss the offline linguistic landscape. *Language Teaching at Berkeley* 21 (2), 7–9.

Min, P.G. (1996) *Caught in the Middle: Korean Merchants in America's Multiethnic Cities.* Berkeley, CA: University of California Press.

Mirzoeff, N. (ed.) (2002a) *The Visual Culture Reader.* London: Routledge.

Mirzoeff, N. (2002b) The subject of visual culture. In N. Mirzoeff (ed.) *The Visual Culture Reader* (pp. 3–23). London: Routledge.

Mitchell, T. (1992) Orientalism and the exhibitionary order. In N. Dirks (ed.) *Colonialism and Culture* (pp. 289–300). Ann Arbor, MI: University of Michigan Press.

Mitchell, W.J.T. (1995) *Picture Theory: Essays on Verbal and Visual Representation.* Chicago, IL: University of Chicago Press.

Mitchell, W.J.T. (2002) Showing seeing: A critique of visual culture. *Journal of Visual Culture* 1 (2), 165–181.

Modern Language Association (MLA) Ad Hoc Committee on Foreign Languages (2007) Foreign languages and higher education: New structures for a changed world. On WWW at http://www.mla.org/flreport/. Accessed 29.4.09.

New London Group (1996) A pedagogy of multiliteracies: Designing social futures. *Harvard Educational Review* 66, 60–92.

Nunan, D. (2003) The impact of English as a global language on educational policies and practices in the Asia-Pacific region. *TESOL Quarterly* 37 (4), 589–613.

Pai, H. (1997) Modernism, development, and the transformation of Seoul: A study of the development of Sae'oon Sang'ga and Yoido. In W.B. Kim, M. Douglass and S-C. Choe (eds) *Culture and the City in East Asia* (pp. 104–124). Oxford: Oxford University Press.

Pratt, M.L. (1999) Arts of the contact zone. In D. Bartholomae and A. Petrofsky (eds) *Ways of Reading* (5th edn) (pp. 582–596). New York: Bedford/St. Martin's.

Rogoff, I. (2002) Studying visual culture. In N. Mirzoeff (ed.) *The Visual Culture Reader* (pp. 24–36). London: Routledge.

Said, E. (1978) *Orientalism.* New York: Pantheon.

Salzberg, C. (2008) Japan: Street view and public space. *Global Voices Online.* On WWW at http://globalvoicesonline.org/2008/10/07/japan-street-view-and-public-space/.

Scollon, R. and Scollon, S.W. (2003) *Discourses in Place: Language in the Material World.* London: Routledge.

Shohamy, E. and Gorter, D. (eds) (2009) *Linguistic Landscape: Expanding the Scenery.* New York: Routledge.

Shohamy, E. and Waksman, S. (2009) Linguistic landscape as an ecological arena: Modalities, meanings, negotiations, education. In E. Shohamy and D. Gorter (eds) *Linguistic Landscape: Expanding the Scenery* (pp. 313–331). New York: Routledge.

Silva, D.J. (2007) Issues in Korean language teaching in the United States: Recent facts and figures. *Korean Language in America* 12, 106–125.

Spolsky, B. and Cooper, R.L. (1991) *The Languages of Jerusalem.* New York: Oxford University Press.

Street, B. (1995) *Social Literacies: Critical Approaches to Literacy in Development, Ethnography, and Education.* London: Longman.

Townsend, A. (2008) Public space in the broadband metropolis: Lessons from Seoul. In A. Aurigi and F. de Cindio (eds) *Augmented Urban Spaces: Articulating the Physical and Electronic City* (pp. 73–91). Aldershot: Ashgate Publishing.

Tuan, Y-f. (1977) *Space and Place: The Perspective of Experience.* Minneapolis, MN: University of Minnesota Press.

van Lier, L. (2000) From input to affordance: Social-interactive learning from an ecological perspective. In J.P. Lantolf (ed.) *Sociocultural Theory and Second Language Learning* (pp. 245–259). Oxford: Oxford University Press.

Virilio, P. (1997) The overexposed city. In N. Leach (ed.) *Rethinking Architecture* (pp. 381–390). New York: Routledge.

Weeks, C. (2007) Google's detailed streetscapes raise privacy concerns. On WWW at http://www.nationalpost.com/news/story.html?id=9e53df0f-3211-4cde-837c-90a6bb4d561d&k=49986/.

Part 4

Perceptions of Passers-by

Chapter 12

Multilingual Cityscapes: Perceptions and Preferences of the Inhabitants of the City of Donostia-San Sebastián

JOKIN AIESTARAN, JASONE CENOZ and DURK GORTER

Introduction

Public space in urban commercial areas contains many different types of signs: street names, shops signs, outdoor advertisements, graphics, digital prints, promotional material, specialty displays, etc. Most of the signs have some text. But how much are the inhabitants of this linguistic landscape aware of the language(s) that surrounds them? The average passer-by may not notice the presence of the language used on fire alarm signs or rubbish containers, even if the signs on these and other common objects are plentiful. Billboards and store fronts with advertisements for products may attract some attention as they try to persuade costumers to buy the products. Tourists may be expected to pay more attention to signs, such as street names or direction signs, which provide them with relevant information. The public space will be experienced differently by different groups and individuals whose history or social positions differ (Lefebvre, 1991). The knowledge of languages and attitudes toward different languages may mediate in the way different groups perceive the linguistic landscape (Landry & Bourhis, 1997: 25). Here, we will also use the term linguistic landscape, although it is in urban areas by far that the highest density of signs is found and thus 'multilingual cityscape' could be used just as well (Gorter, 2006).

This chapter will focus on perceptions of languages on signs and the stated preferences of the local inhabitants of the city of Donostia-San Sebastián. It will also discuss the non-market value of the linguistic landscape in terms of the willingness to pay for the preferred way of having language on the signs. An innovative approach derived from environmental economics was employed to study the linguistic landscape (Cenoz & Gorter, 2009).

219

Sociolinguistic Context: The City of Donostia-San Sebastián and the Basque Country

The city of Donostia-San Sebastián has around 185,000 inhabitants. The city is located on the coast of the Gulf of Biscay, 20 km from the border with France in the Basque Country in Spain. The whole of the Basque Country, 'Euskal Herria', extends over an area of approximately 20,700 km^2 in the North of Spain and the South of France. The Basque Country has three million inhabitants, but the territory is not governed as one administrative unit. The population of the Basque Autonomous Community is 2.1 million and the rest is in the Community of Navarre and in the North Basque Country, Iparraldea in France.

The Basque language (or Euskara) is completely different from Spanish or French since it is not a Romance language and is not part of the Indo-European family. Basque is spoken on average by about 30% of the population. Recent survey results show that the number of Basque-speaking bilinguals in the Basque Autonomous Community is slowly increasing (Eusko Jaurlaritza, 2008). Yet, Spanish is the dominant language that all inhabitants are competent in, except in the North Basque Country in France, where French is the dominant language. The Basque Government actively encourages Basque as the medium of instruction and at present, 83% of primary schoolchildren use Basque as the language of instruction (see also Cenoz, 2009). Different studies conducted in the Basque Country show that the first language (L1) has a significant effect on attitudes toward Basque and Spanish (Etxeberria, 1995; García, 2001) as well as toward English (Cenoz, 2001; Sagasta, 2000; Lasagabaster, 2005). In fact, one can distinguish between two language groups, Basque speakers and Spanish speakers, creating a social division that will be taken into account in our exploration of perception of the linguistic landscape. The bilingual sign in Figure 12.1 displays the two languages, Basque and Spanish, in a market context; it also reveals the substantial linguistic distance between both languages.

Language policy

Language policy can have an impact on the way the linguistic landscape is regulated and arranged. Over a period of 30 years, the government of the Basque Autonomous Community has developed a strong language policy of 'normalization' (i.e. recuperation and revitalization) of the Basque language. The emphasis of language policy has been primarily on education, culture and the media, although a wide spectrum of measures has been developed. The language policy can be characterized as robust compared to other minority languages in Europe. Despite this, UNESCO (2009) lists Basque under the category of 'unsafe' and considers it to be an endangered language.

Figure 12.1 Bilingual Spanish-Basque sign ('serve yourself')

The language policy includes explicit measures with regard to the use of Basque in the linguistic landscape. Government signage in the Basque Autonomous Community is in both official languages, Basque and Spanish.

At the same time, the English language constitutes part of the linguistic landscape almost everywhere around the globe. The spread of English as the language of wider communication has been well documented (Edwards, 2004; Huebner, 2006). Rosenbaum *et al.* (1977) used the term 'snob appeal of English'. Similarly, Piller (2003: 175) states that, 'English has become a general symbol of modernity, progress and globalization'. Factors such as immigration, tourism and the revitalization of minority languages have led to increased use and exposure to English, but also to an increase in multilingualism (Cenoz & Gorter, 2008).

Shohamy (2006: 110) observes that 'the public space is a most relevant arena to serve as a mechanism to create a de facto language policy'. The choice of languages used on signs in the public space can be of great symbolic importance, in particular in bilingual or multilingual countries or regions. For instance, the language used to indicate place names has been a regular issue of linguistic conflict in many areas (Puzey, 2007).

The policy of 'normalization' in the Basque Country has an important influence on governmental signs, and to a much lesser extent, on the way commercial firms or private persons choose to put their signs in the public domain. The official government policy is bilingual, and even though the whole population can read Spanish, the Basque version is considered useful.

In the Basque Autonomous Community, there have been several campaigns to encourage the use of Basque in shops. In many towns and villages, campaigns led by local councils were organized to Basquisize the linguistic landscape. For example, the city council of Donostia-San Sebastián, in which this study was conducted, includes the promotion of Basque in private companies and commercial establishments in its strategic plans to support the language. The council offers aid toward the cost of putting signs outside shops in Basque or in Basque with Spanish, providing for 30% of the cost to set up monolingual Basque signs, and 15% to set up bilingual signs. A recent decree by the Basque Government (2008) states that Basque must have a presence in public institutions, in services of general interest (such as transport, utilities and communications) and also in large private commercial establishments. Smaller businesses also opt for English next to Basque, as is clear from Figure 12.2.

Figure 12.2 Bilingual Basque-English sign

Earlier Studies about the Linguistic Landscape of Donostia-San Sebastián

The study of the linguistic landscape is particularly interesting in bilingual and multilingual environments, where language contact and conflict take place (Cenoz & Gorter, 2006). Therefore, the study of the linguistic landscape can be considered an additional source of information about the sociolinguistic context, along with censuses, surveys and interviews. It is claimed that people process the visual and linguistic information that comes to them, and the language in which signs are written can influence their perception of the status of the different languages, their attitudes toward them and it can even influence their language use in either a positive or a negative way. For example, the increased use of the Basque language in the linguistic landscape of the Basque Country may influence the use of the minority language in society.

In a first exploratory study, Cenoz and Gorter (2003) analyzed the linguistic landscape of one street in Donostia-San Sebastián, the 'Calle de Escolta Real'. The study found that the linguistic landscape of the street was multilingual and that it reflected the use of language in society: Spanish as the dominant language, Basque as the minority language and English as an international language. It became clear that language policy does have an impact, as could be illustrated by the example of this one street.

In a follow-up study, Cenoz and Gorter (2006) investigated the linguistic landscape of Boulevard, one of the central shopping streets of Donostia-San Sebastián. The language use on the signs was compared to that of the Nieuwestad in Ljouwert-Leeuwarden, the capital of Friesland, a bilingual province in The Netherlands. There, Frisian is the minority language used side by side with Dutch, the dominant language, and English, the international language. The spread of English on the signs was more prominent in Ljouwert-Leeuwarden than in Donostia-San Sebastián. However, the outcome that English is used on 28% of all signs shows that English is no longer marginal in this city either.

The main difference between the two cities was the use of the minority language on the signs. There were more signs in Basque than in Frisian and this clear difference may provide evidence for the effect of a strong language policy. Figure 12.3 is a clear example of the effect of the government's bilingual policy.

Besides the quantitative studies of the 'objective' linguistic landscape, Gorter and Cenoz (2004) also investigated the more 'subjective' side of the linguistic landscape. An explorative study was carried out among a group of Basque students who study English at university and Frisian students in a teacher training college. The students ($n = 191$) completed a questionnaire about their language attitudes, perception and awareness of the linguistic landscape and the possible use of the linguistic

Figure 12.3 Top-down governmental sign: Basque-Spanish bilingual (pedestrian zone)

landscape for language learning. The conclusions showed that students in the Basque Country favored more multilingual and bilingual signs; the Frisian students, on the other hand, were about equally in favor of monolingual (Dutch) signs or of Frisian/Dutch bilingual signs. This preliminary study showed for both places a moderate awareness of the signs when walking along the streets. The students' answers also indicated that the linguistic landscape has a certain potential, even if limited, for language learning because the texts constitute a certain amount of input. This theme of language learning was further explored in Cenoz and Gorter (2008). Another topic of the analysis was the 'added value of multilingualism'. In collaboration with some economists, the data of the 'objective' linguistic landscape were re-analyzed using econometric techniques (Nunes *et al.*, 2008). The analysis focused on language choice and individual and social preference structures. The economic angle on the linguistic landscape was developed further in Cenoz and Gorter (2009). The study proposed to analyze the linguistic landscape by looking at the different use and non-use values by means of contingent valuation, a method that has been applied previously in the study of environmental economics (Nunes & De Blaeij, 2005). This chapter provides outcomes of a new study carried out with a sample of the local inhabitants of Donostia-San Sebastián.

Research Questions and Methodology

The specific research questions of the current study were as follows:

(1) What is the perception of the languages used in the linguistic landscape of speakers of Basque as L1 vs. Spanish as L1?
(2) What is the preferred way to have signs in the linguistic landscape for speakers of Basque as L1 vs. Spanish as L1?
(3) What is the economic commitment of speakers of Basque as L1 vs. Spanish as L1 to the use of languages in the linguistic landscape?

In order to obtain data on these questions, interviews were held with local passers-by in the streets of Donostia-San Sebastián. The respondents were randomly selected and the street interviews were carried out on different days and at different times, all in the central part of the city. Most persons approached were willing to participate in a short interview about 'the use of different languages in the city'. The interviews lasted on average around 5–10 minutes. All interviews were carried out by the same male interviewer.

A total of 303 successful interviews were accomplished over a period of three months. There was some oversampling of females as they constituted 57% and males were 43%. Although age was not asked directly, but estimated, the average was calculated at 36.5 years. This was somewhat on the young side, but the sample was not intended to be representative of the whole population of Donostia-San Sebastián. It is clear that the sample is limited because it contains only people that were present during the daytime in one of the shopping streets.

The questionnaire consisted of ten closed questions on one page. The first half were about the background of the respondent: (1) where they live in the city, (2) means of transport used to come to the city center, (3) first language, (4) other languages spoken and (5) occupation. The next five questions were about the linguistic landscape: (6) overall perception of the linguistic landscape, (7) observed frequency of each language (possible answers: never, occasionally, sometimes, often or very often), (8) preference structure: how many languages to be used, plus a specification for each language and whether the languages should be represented at the same level. The last two questions were more elaborate. First, a scenario was presented in which the respondents were asked to allocate an amount of 100 Euros over five possible alternatives, including the linguistic landscape. The literal wording of the question was:

> In order to assess and rank your priorities, we kindly ask you if you were given 100 Euros, how would you allocate this amount of money among the following activities? The following choices were provided: a) having the signs the way you want them, b) having clean, public

toilets in the city centre, c) having more parking space in the city centre, d) having more playgrounds for children and e) having a better public transport system.

The final question related to the respondent's answer and being asked directly for their 'willingness to pay' for the signs in the way preferred by them. The question was formulated as 'imagine that some local authority asks for your financial assistance. How much would you be willing to pay to implement this program?' As possible answers amounts of 10, 20, 30, 40 or 50 Euros were given.

Main Results

Perception

The first issue is about the perception of the linguistic landscape. The question was about perceiving 'the most commonly used language'. The answers are presented in Table 12.1, where a distinction is made according to the language background of Spanish speakers vs. Basque speakers (it is important to note that all L1 speakers of Basque are also proficient in Spanish).

Based on the answers presented in Table 12.1, it is clear that most of the local inhabitants of Donostia-San Sebastián who participated in the study see Spanish as dominating the linguistic landscape. The differentiation according to language background makes clear that the Basque mother tongue speakers think that Spanish predominates more than the Spanish speakers do. Among the Spanish speakers there is a somewhat higher proportion (22%) that assumes both languages to be present more or less to the same degree because they give 'Basque and Spanish' as an answer. Statistically, the difference between the two language groups is not significant. The multilingual shop sign is an exception because of the large number of languages; yet Spanish dominates (Figure 12.4).

The next question concerns more specifically the frequency with which different languages are perceived by the local inhabitants. The frequency with which the four different languages – Basque, Spanish, English and French – are noticed was asked in terms ranging from

Table 12.1 Overall perception: Most commonly used language on the signs (in percentages)

	Spanish	*Basque and Spanish*	*Basque*	*n*
Spanish L1	66	22	12	183
Basque L1	78	15	8	119

$p = 0.80$ (not significant)

Figure 12.4 Multilingual shop sign, with Spanish dominant and word 'sales' in over 10 other languages

Table 12.2 Perceived frequency: Noticing languages (averages from scores 1 to 4)

	Basque	*Spanish*	*English*	*French*
Spanish L1	3.17	3.77	0.90	0.70
Basque L1	2.76	3.73	0.96	0.59
t-Test	4.059/**	0.698/n.s.	0.512/n.s.	1.216/n.s.

**Significant at the $p < 0.01$ level

(1) never, (2) occasionally, (3) sometimes, (4) often, to (5) very often. The results are shown in Table 12.2.

The results in Table 12.2 do not indicate big differences between the speakers of Basque and those of Spanish. Yet, both groups agree that Spanish is seen most often. An important exception is the frequency with which the minority language, Basque, is observed on the signs. The Spanish speakers see it more often (3.17) than the Basque speakers (2.76), which turned out to be a statistically significant difference. It seems that

Basque speakers perceive an under-representation of their own language while Spanish speakers do not perceive this in the same way regarding their L1. In other words, the minority language stands out; it is the 'marked language' in terms of absence or presence, whereas Spanish is the dominant or unmarked language in the linguistic landscape. English and French are perceived as having low frequencies, somewhere between 'occasionally' and 'never', with a slightly higher average score for English. The outcomes are in agreement with the earlier studies that documented the actual frequency of the signs themselves (Cenoz & Gorter 2006).

Preference

The next question was more normative, as the local inhabitants were asked to give their opinions on the number of languages they want displayed on the signs on the streets of their city. A remarkable outcome was that only very few respondents (2%, i.e. 7 out of 303 respondents) had a preference for monolingual signs. A large majority of both the Basque and the Spanish language groups agreed to have more than one language on the signs. This outcome implies that the inhabitants of Donostia-San Sebastián agree with the language policy of the local government where there are at least two languages on the signs. However, in Table 12.3 it also becomes clear that there is an important difference between both groups on the issue of having two languages or having more languages on the signs. Thus, the Basque speakers are equally divided among themselves about a preference to have bilingual or multilingual signs. By contrast, the Spanish speakers clearly have a stronger preference for multilingual signs with more than two languages. The difference is almost statistically significant ($p = 0.053$).

One could conclude that the current 'objective' linguistic landscape, as measured by counting signs from digital pictures, does not reflect the preference structure of the local residents. The number of signs with only one language that was observed in earlier studies (Cenoz & Gorter, 2006: 72) is much higher, around 45%, than what is indicated here as the most preferred number of languages on signs. This poses interesting questions about the way the linguistic landscape is experienced by its

Table 12.3 Preference structure: Number of languages on the signs (in percentages)

	One	*Two*	*More than two*	*n*
Spanish L1	2	39	59	184
Basque L1	3	49	48	119

'inhabitants'. Obviously, people obtain only a superficial impression of the distribution of languages on signs. They do not walk around counting languages. The fact that there are many monolingual Spanish signs (36% of all signs) plus a good number of monolingual signs in Basque (12%) and, moreover, almost a quarter of all signs are bilingual in Basque and Spanish (22%) seems to give an overall impression of a bilingual, or even multilingual linguistic landscape.

The question about the preferred number of languages on the signs was logically followed by a question about *which* languages should be used. It turned out that both language groups had a strong preference for their own language. Thus, the few that chose a monolingual option only chose their own language. Those that opted for a bilingual solution (on average 43%) almost unanimously chose both Basque and Spanish. More important differences occurred between the choice of three languages (Basque, Spanish and English) or four languages (Basque, Spanish, English and French). The Spanish speakers more often chose a trilingual solution and the Basque speakers more often chose the four-language option. Other combinations, e.g. without Basque or without Spanish, were also chosen, but only by a small minority (less than 10%). The fact that French was mentioned relatively often in Donostia-San Sebastián should not come as a surprise, knowing that the French border is only 20 km away.

Looking at these results in another way, an additional analysis was done for the Spanish speakers and the Basque speakers separately, to check if they always included their L1 in their choice of preferred languages on the signs. It turned out that 99% of the Spanish speakers chose to have at least Spanish on the signs (one respondent indicated he wanted to have three languages without Spanish). All Basque speakers (100%) selected Basque as one of the languages to be displayed on the signs. Furthermore, 96% of the Basque speakers also wanted Spanish on signs and fewer chose English (46%) or French (19%). The Spanish speakers showed a similar pattern, where 93% included Basque in their preferences, 55% English and 23% French.

Figure 12.5 reflects the use of Basque, Spanish and English. It is cleverly designed in that it uses the term 'WiFi' as the central item, which is the same in all three languages. It also stands out because it uses Braille, which is not very common.

Although the respondents do agree, to a substantial degree, to include both official languages of the Basque Country on signs, the issue remains open whether the two languages should be represented equally prominent. A follow-up question on the issue of equality had only a yes or no answer. It turns out that two thirds of the Spanish speakers and less than half of the Basque speakers prefer an equal level of the languages on the signs. This is a substantial (and statistically highly significant, $p < 0.01$) difference between both groups. Probably the

Figure 12.5 Multilingual sign in Basque, Spanish and English (using the international abbreviation WiFi as the central item); it also uses Braille

Basque speakers prefer a more salient place for their own language and the Spanish speakers more often prefer both languages side-by-side.

Payments

In order to find out more about the importance the respondents attach to the languages on the signs, a scenario was presented to the respondents in which they were asked to distribute an amount of 100 Euros among five different options. These options were related to improving the facilities in the city center: better public transport, more parking spaces, clean public toilets and more playgrounds for children. The last option was to change the signs in the way the respondent had indicated he or she preferred them. The results are shown in Table 12.4.

As the results indicate, improvement of public transport was granted on average the largest share of the money the respondents were willing to donate. It is interesting to see that the Spanish and Basque speakers agree on most of these items and the differences were not significant. The difference becomes highly significant for the amount donated to the signs. The Spanish speakers score on average much lower than the Basque speakers. For the Basque speakers, the signs in the preferred way score similar to children's playgrounds and clean public toilets.

Table 12.4 Payment: ranking of five options

	Public transport	Parking space	Clean toilets	Children playgrounds	Signs in preferred way
Spanish L1	28.45	22.46	20.51	18.87	9.28
Basque L1	30.29	20.42	16.83	16.18	16.12
t-Test	−0.602	0.701	1.440	1.048	−4.155**

**Significant at $p < 0.01$ level.

Table 12.5 Willingness to pay (WTP)

	Average amount	s.d.	t-Test	Significance
Spanish L1	12.00	1.390		
Basque L1	16.70	1.673	−2.658	0.008

Overall, the signs in the preferred way scored the lowest of the five options, which is perhaps not surprising. This is related to the earlier results where a majority of the respondents had already indicated that the current situation of the signs is in agreement with their preferences.

The final question about the signs was in regard to a possible contribution to a program of having the signs the preferred way. In that way, their 'willingness to pay' was measured (Nunes & De Blaeij, 2005). Table 12.5 has the results for this question.

After all the foregoing outcomes, it does not come as a surprise that the Basque speakers on average are more ready to contribute to a program where the signs are changed in the way they want them. The 'willingness to pay' of the Basque speakers for the signs in the linguistic landscape is significantly higher than the 'willingness to pay' of the Spanish speakers. This is probably related to the perception that their own language is less well represented and their stated preference to always include Basque in the signs.

Conclusion

In this chapter, we investigated the perceptions and preferences about the languages on the signs in the urban space of Donostia-San Sebastián in the Basque Country, Spain. The local inhabitants were questioned in street interviews about these issues as well as about their 'willingness to pay' to get the signs the way they prefer them.

Overall, the inhabitants agree that Spanish, the dominant language, has a higher presence on the signs than Basque, the minority language.

This outcome is in agreement with earlier studies about the 'objective' linguistic landscape as measured by a quantitative approach by means of coding digital pictures. The L1 speakers of Basque see on average even less Basque in the signs than the L1 speakers of Spanish, although they agree more or less on the amount of Spanish or the much smaller amounts of English or French they perceive. Both language groups also agree that they prefer bilingual or multilingual signs over monolingual signs, although this might refer more to signage in general, thus the linguistic landscape as a whole, than to each individual sign. The Spanish speakers have a stronger preference for at least three languages on the signs, where more Basque speakers are satisfied with two languages. Furthermore, Basque speakers would give substantially more prominence to Basque and less to Spanish, whereas Spanish speakers would give similar prominence to both languages.

The outcomes for the economic commitment show that Basque speakers rank the importance of the signs in the city in the way they want them higher than the Spanish speakers, although both groups put the option of the signs at the bottom of the five different options given. It probably shows that the way languages are used in the linguistic landscape is not a major issue for the locals. On average, Basque speakers are ready to pay a higher amount for their preferred way of having the signs than the Spanish speakers. As members of the minority group, the Basque speakers are probably more aware of the 'risks' their L1 is exposed to. They seem to have a greater commitment for reversing language shift. The members of the dominant group do not have to worry about the use of their language in all kinds of domains in society or about the presence of their language in the urban surroundings. Even if Basque receives a lot of support through a strong language policy, the Spanish speakers are aware that their language is not threatened. It is remarkable though that very few of the Spanish-speaking inhabitants of Donostia-San Sebastián support a monolingual urban linguistic landscape. They seem to prefer a multilingual cityscape over an all Spanish surrounding. Perhaps this can be interpreted as a tacit acquiescence with the current status, but it could also be an expression of support for the efforts to safeguard the minority language and a more positive view of multilingualism.

Further research is necessary to find out more about the attitudes of the Basque and the Spanish speakers. Future studies of the linguistic landscape can help to clarify such differences of opinion between the different language groups. In particular, the seeming contradiction between the stated preference for the number of languages on the signs and the 'objective' measurement of the number of languages on individual signs can be approached in a more holistic way. This chapter reports only on the local inhabitants of the city, but the project that is currently taking place also includes interviews with tourists. Because of their temporary stay in the city, their beliefs and opinions can throw another light on the perceptions, preferences and willingness to pay for the urban linguistic landscape.

Acknowledgements

This study was carried out in the framework of SUS.DIV (Sustainable Development in a Diverse World), a European Network of Excellence (Contract No. CIT3-CT-2005-513438), see www.susdiv.org and was supported by the University of the Basque Country [grant number G7 U09/35].

References

Basque Government (2008) Decree about Linguistic Rights of Consumers and Users, dated 1 July 2008, 123/2008. On WWW at www.industria.ejgv.euskadi. net/r44-2252/es/-contenidos/informacion/normativa_consumo/eu_norma/ adjuntos/decreto_dchos_ling.pdf. Accessed 12.3.09.

Cenoz, J. (2001) Three languages in contact: Language attitudes in the Basque Country. In D. Lasagabaster and J.M. Sierra (eds) *Language Awareness in the Foreign Language Classroom* (pp. 37–60). Zarautz: University of the Basque Country.

Cenoz, J. (2009) *Towards Multilingual Education: Basque Educational Research in International Perspective*. Bristol: Multilingual Matters.

Cenoz, J. and Gorter, D. (2003) The linguistic landscape of Erregezainen/Escolta Real. Paper presented at the Third Conference on Third Language Acquisition and Trilingualism, Tralee Ireland, 4 September.

Cenoz, J. and Gorter, D. (2006) The linguistic landscape and minority languages. *International Journal of Multilingualism* 3 (1), 67–80.

Cenoz, J. and Gorter, D. (2008) Linguistic landscape as an additional source of input in second language acquisition. *IRAL, International Review of Applied Linguistics in Language Teaching* 46, 257–276.

Cenoz, J. and Gorter, D. (2009) Language economy and linguistic landscape. In E. Shohamy and D. Gorter (eds) *Linguistic Landscape: Expanding the Scenery* (pp. 55–69). New York/London: Routledge.

Edwards, V. (2004) *Multilingualism in the English-speaking World*. Hoboken, NJ: John Wiley and Sons.

Etxeberria, M. (1995) Competencia y actitudes lingüísticas en la Comunidad Autónoma Vasca. In *Actas del simposi de demolingüística/III trobada de socio-lingüistes* (pp. 119–125). Barcelona: Generalitat de Catalunya.

Eusko Jaurlaritza (2008) *Fourth Sociolinguistic Survey 2006*. Vitoria-Gasteiz: Servicio Central de Publicaciones del Gobierno Vasco. On WWW at www.eus kara.euskadi.net/r59738/en/contenidos/informacion/inkesta_soziolinguisti koa2006/en_survey/adjuntos/IV_incuesta_en.pdf. Accessed 12.3.09.

García, I. (2001) Euskararen erabileran eragiten duten prozesu psikosozialak: identitate etnolinguistikaren garrantzia. PhD thesis, University of the Basque Country.

Gorter, D. (2006) Further possibilities for linguistic landscape research. In D. Gorter (ed.) *Linguistic Landscape: A New Approach to Multilingualism* (pp. 81–89). Clevedon: Multilingual Matters.

Gorter, D. and Cenoz, J. (2004) Linguistic landscape and L2 users in multilingual contexts, Eurosla-14. Conference of the European Second Language Association in San Sebastian/Donostia, 8–11 September.

Huebner, T. (2006) Bangkok's linguistic landscapes: Environmental print, code mixing, and language change. *International Journal of Multilingualism* 3 (1), 31–51.

Landry, R. and Bourhis, R.Y. (1997) Linguistic landscape and ethnolinguistic vitality: An empirical study. *Journal of Language and Social Psychology* 16 (1), 23–49.

Lasagabaster, D. (2005) Attitudes towards Basque, Spanish and English: An analysis of the most influential variables. *Journal of Multilingual and Multicultural Development* 26 (4), 296–316.

Lefebvre, H. (1991) *The Production of Space*. Oxford: Blackwell.

Nunes, P. and De Blaeij, A. (2005) Economic assessment of marine quality benefits: Applying the use of non-market valuation methods. In F. Maes (ed.) *Marine Resource Damage Assessment* (pp. 135–163). Berlin: Springer.

Nunes, P., Onofri, L., Cenoz, J. and Gorter, D. (2008) Language diversity in urban landscapes: An econometric study. Milan: FEEM-working papers, No. 199. On WWW at http://www.bepress.com/feem/paper199. Accessed 15.3.09.

Piller, I. (2003) Advertising as a site of language contact. *Annual Review of Applied Linguistics* 23, 170–183.

Puzey, G. (2007) Planning the linguistic landscape (A comparative survey of the use of minority languages in the road signage of Norway, Scotland and Italy). MSc by Research Scandinavian Studies (II), The University of Edinburgh.

Rosenbaum, Y., Nadel, E., Cooper, R.L. and Fishman, J.A. (1977) English on Keren Kayemet Street. In J.A. Fishman, R.L. Cooper and A.W. Conrad (eds) *The Spread of English: The Sociology of English as an Additional Language* (pp. 179–194). Rowley, MA: Newbury House.

Sagasta, M.P. (2000) La producción escrita en euskera, castellano e inglés en el modelo D y en el modelo de inmersión. Unpublished PhD dissertation, University of the Basque Country.

Shohamy, E. (2006) *Language Policy: Hidden Agenda's and New Approaches*. New York: Taylor & Francis.

UNESCO (2009) UNESCO Interactive Atlas of the World's Languages in Danger (Ch. Moseley, editor in chief). On WWW at www.unesco.org/culture/en/endangeredlanguages/atlas. Accessed 12.6.09.

Chapter 13

Linguistic Landscape in Mixed Cities in Israel from the Perspective of 'Walkers': The Case of Arabic

NIRA TRUMPER-HECHT

Introduction

The present linguistic landscape (LL) study focuses on the visibility of Arabic as it is perceived by Arab and Jewish residents in mixed cities in Israel. 'Mixed cities' refers to Israeli urban localities in which Arabs and Jews reside under the same municipal jurisdiction. Mixed cities, of which there are about seven in Israel, present a unique opportunity to examine the vulnerable relationship that exists between the Jewish majority and the Arab minority in Israel. This chapter focuses on the case of Upper Nazareth through the eyes of its residents, and analyzes Jews' and Arabs' perceptions and attitudes toward the visibility of Arabic in their mixed city's public space. Unlike Jaffa, Acre, Lod or Haifa, which were Arab cities that became mixed after the establishment of the state of Israel in 1948, Upper Nazareth was built as a Jewish city in 1957, and became a mixed city when two decades later Arabs from Nazareth and neighboring villages started settling there (Figure 13.1).

In this chapter, I shall present and analyze the diverse perceptions, preferences and attitudes held by Upper Nazareth's Arab and Jewish residents regarding the visibility of Israel's two official languages: Hebrew and Arabic.

The questions examined in this study are:

(1) How do Jewish and Arab residents perceive the LL in their city, and how does the image they have of the LL compare with the actual LL as it was documented by camera in previous studies? (Ben Rafael *et al.*, 2006; Trumper-Hecht, 2009)

(2) What are the linguistic preferences of Arab vs. Jewish residents regarding the two official languages (Hebrew and Arabic) in the LL of their city?

(3) What are the attitudes of Arab vs. Jewish residents toward the representation of Hebrew and Arabic in the public space of their own mixed city as well as in the country as a whole?

Figure 13.1 Mixed cities in Israel

Data were collected in the summer of 2006 by telephone question-naires answered by 300 Jewish and Arab residents in Upper Nazareth, Jaffa and Acre. The subjects, Arab and Jewish residents aged 25 to 65, were randomly sampled. An attempt was made to include the same number of women and men, but more women (both Arab and Jewish) eventually took part in the study.

Although the focus of this chapter is on the case of Upper Nazareth, a few of the findings about the mixed city of Jaffa will also be discussed in order to shed light on the case of Upper Nazareth.

Theoretical Background: Adding a Third Dimension to Linguistic Landscape Studies

In *The Production of Space* (1991), Lefebvre defines landscape as the visual aspect of space. As such, it inevitably changes from one social context to another, according to the specific characteristics of each society. According to Lefebvre, the landscape embodies social relations, and, at times, serves as the locus of struggle between groups over their respective place in a given social order. Following Lefebvre (1991), linguistic landscape, a salient visual aspect of urban landscape today, can be defined in the same way if one looks at language facts that mark the public space as 'social facts' (Ben Rafael, 2009).

Studies in Israel and around the globe have shown that the LL has indeed become the locus of power struggles between ethnolinguistic groups looking to either maintain their dominance in the public space, or gain some visibility in it. Previous LL studies have also shown that in those social contexts where 'power relations' is the main 'structuration principle' of the LL (Ben Rafael, 2009), a careful empirical examination of the representation of languages on signs can mirror a given balance of power between groups. This is especially true in contexts where language serves as a symbol of social, national or ethnic identity.

Lefebvre's (1991) conceptualization of space includes three interconnected and ever-evolving dimensions: 'spatial practice', 'conceived space' and 'lived space'. The spatial practice of a given society is, according to Lefebvre, human action whose results in the physical space one can empirically study. The second dimension, 'conceived space', refers to space as it is conceptualized by technocrats, planners, politicians and other policy makers. The third analytical dimension of space, 'lived space', is the space of 'inhabitants'. It is the space that is experienced by the people who live their everyday life in it and who experience that space through symbols and metaphors that appear in its landscape. Following Lefebvre, we suggest that the LL as a sociolinguistic-spatial phenomenon be studied by looking at these same dimensions and the ways in which they are interrelated. We see Lefebvre's 'spatial practice' as the 'physical' dimension of the LL, that is, the actual distribution of languages on signs that can be observed and documented by camera. We see his 'conceived space' as the 'political' dimension of the LL as it is represented by views and ideologies held by different policy makers whose policies mold the LL. Finally, we regard Lefebvre's 'lived space' as the 'experiential' dimension of the LL as it is presented by 'inhabitants'. The latter, which is the focus of this chapter, can be explored from the inhabitants' point of view. Their attitudes and perceptions about the LL may teach us something about the ways in which the LL is experienced by its 'inhabitants' or 'users', if to use Lefebvre's own terms. We believe that in order to arrive at a deeper theoretical understanding of the LL as a sociolinguistic-spatial phenomenon, as well as gain a more comprehensive insight into the LL in specific contexts, a study of all three dimensions and the ways in which they may be interrelated is required.

Previous LL studies of the mixed city of Upper Nazareth (and of other cities in Israel) looked at the 'physical' and the 'political' dimensions of the LL (see Ben Rafael et al., 2006; Trumper-Hecht, 2009). In the present study, the 'experiential' dimension of the LL is added to the analysis in order to learn how the LL is experienced by Jews and Arabs living in Upper Nazareth.

Findings of the present study show, for example, that the LL is perceived very differently by Arab and Jewish residents of Upper Nazareth, and also that members of the two national groups have different attitudes regarding the visibility of Arabic in their city's LL as well as in the country as a whole.

In order to examine the ways in which the three dimensions of the LL may be interconnected, we compared, for example, the LL as it was perceived by residents (the 'experiential' dimension) with the reality on signs as it was documented by camera (the 'physical' dimension). This comparison enabled us to learn to what degree residents notice the LL, or in other words, to what degree residents notice 'language facts' in the urban space they live in. A comparison of residents' perceptions and attitudes about the LL (the 'experiential' dimension) with local policy makers' views and consequent LL policies (the 'political' dimension), taught us a great deal about the forces that work to mold Upper Nazareth's LL and thus influence the city's identity.

Why Upper Nazareth?

Upper Nazareth, as mentioned earlier, is one of the only mixed cities in Israel, which was established as a Jewish city after independence and became mixed in the early 1980s when Christian Arabs from the neighboring villages and from Nazareth moved to the city. While Jews see the founding of the Jewish city in the midst of an area historically populated by Arabs as a legitimate manifestation of Zionism, Arabs see the founding of the city as an incursion into their territory (see Rabinowitz, 1997; Trumper-Hecht, 2009). Today, 50 years after its founding, the population of Upper Nazareth consists of approximately 50,000 residents; half are Russian Jews who immigrated from the CIS in the 1990s and approximately 20% are Christian and Muslim Arabs. The resentment many Jews in Upper Nazareth feel toward the increasing number of Arab residents in the city is clearly reflected in the data collected for the present study. In a previous LL study focusing on the physical dimension of the LL (Ben Rafael et al., 2006), findings showed that in Upper Nazareth, an officially mixed city, Hebrew, the majority language, appeared on all signs; 66.7% of all monolingual signs and another 30% of bilingual 'Hebrew-English' signs. By contrast, Arabic, the language of a growing proportion of the city's population, had a negligible presence (less than 4% of all signs). Five years after the completion of that study, a repeat study we conducted in Upper Nazareth showed that despite the Supreme Court's decision (issued in 2002) that Arabic be included on all public signs in mixed cities in Israel, there had been hardly any change in the presence of Arabic in the city's LL (Trumper-Hecht, 2009). The analysis of the 'political' dimension of the LL showed how different policy makers, like local politicians and entrepreneurs, worked to shape Upper Nazareth's LL to suit their ideologies, as well as serve their electoral and economic interests.

Findings

Walkers' perceived linguistic landscape ... and the real picture in mixed cities

The first question we asked related to residents' perception of the LL in their city and its relation to the actual 'physical' reality of the LL. The first part of this question examined Arabs' and Jews' image or perception of the LL in the public space they share on a daily basis. The second part examined the possible gap between residents' perceived LL and the real picture of the LL as it was documented by camera.

Lefebvre (1991) contended that the public space (the street, shopping center or square) is experienced differently by groups and individuals whose history or social status is different. Bauman (1996) goes further in this direction, claiming that the public space only exists as an abstraction that cannot be experienced directly. Bauman claims that we understand or experience the public space through pre-conceived ideas that we have developed in order to 'map' the diverse relations we have with others. Following Lefebvre and Bauman, I assumed that given Jews' and Arabs' different historical collective experience and their different social status in Israeli society, they would have different perceptions of the LL. The findings show that this is indeed the case. Findings also show that both Jews and Arabs (as Bauman would have predicted) do not generally see what really exists in the LL, but what they assume is in the LL based on how members of each national group perceive their relations with the other group. As a consequence, a gap exists between residents' perceptions of the LL and the linguistic reality on signs. Specifically, the findings show the following.

Private signs: Walkers' perceptions of commercial linguistic landscape in Upper Nazareth

Looking at the findings, one learns that more than 98% of all respondents believe that Hebrew, the majority language, is present on all private signs. Moreover, both Jews and Arabs believe that Hebrew is also the most salient language on private signs. In Upper Nazareth,

Table 13.1 Walkers' cognitive map: The image Arabs and Jews in Upper Nazareth have of the LL on commercial signs

	Jews (N=5)				Arabs (N=60)				
		Salience				Salience			
P	Presence (%)	Most	Half	Very little	Presence (%)	Most	Half	Very little	Language
>0.05	98.1	80.8	19.2	0	98.3	74.6	20.3	5.1	Hebrew
<0.00	32	17.7	29.2	52.9	90	65.4	21.8	12.8	Arabic
<0.00	56.6	53.4	20	26.7	46.7	14.3	7.1	78.5	Russian
<0.03	26.4	28.5	28.5	42.9	58	2.9	37.1	60	English

80.8% of the Jewish respondents and 74.6% of the Arab respondents think that most commercial signs are in Hebrew.

While there is a consensus among Upper Nazareth's Arabs and Jews as to the dominance of Hebrew on private signs, there is a significant difference between the two national groups regarding Arabic, the minority language. Specifically, while 90% of Arab respondents believe that their language is present on private signs in Upper Nazareth, only 32% of Jews do (see Table 13.1).

Walkers' perceptions of commercial linguistic landscape and the real picture

If one compares Upper Nazareth's residents' perceived LL with the linguistic reality on signs, it is possible to see that the image that both Arabs and Jews have regarding the presence of Arabic in the LL in their city does not reflect the reality on signs. Interestingly enough, this is not the case where Hebrew is concerned. As we have seen, in Upper Nazareth, both Jews and Arabs believe that Hebrew is the dominant language in the LL of their city, and indeed it appears on 75% of all commercial signs and on 100% of all public signs. Yet, with regard to Arabic, there is a big gap between the image that Jews and, more so, Arabs, have of the presence of the minority language in the LL and its actual representation on signs. A surprisingly high percentage of Arab respondents (90%) think that Arabic is present on private signs, and more than 65% of them believe that Arabic appears on more than half the signs. Yet, the reality of the LL proves that only 5.8% of all commercial signs and *none* of the public signs in the mixed city of Upper Nazareth include Arabic. By contrast, only 32% of the Jewish respondents think that Arabic is present on commercial signs, and add that if it is present, it's on very few of the signs if at all. As we can see from this data, there exist significant differences between the Arab residents, who greatly overestimate the presence of Arabic in Upper Nazareth's LL, and Jewish residents, who mostly believe Arabic has no presence at all on private signs in the city.

Public signs: Walkers' perceptions of linguistic landscape in Upper Nazareth

The Supreme Court's decision from 2002 to include Arabic on all public signs in mixed cities was met with resistance on the part of the Jewish leadership in Upper Nazareth. With this publicized controversy in the background, we assumed that residents would be aware of the reality on public signs in their city. However, findings show that this is not the case. Looking at the image Arabs and Jews have of Arabic's presence on public signs, one can even more clearly see the gap that exists between people's perception of the LL and the physical reality on signs.

Because of Upper Nazareth's mayor's objection to the Supreme Court decision from 2002, there is to date, no Arabic on public signs in this mixed city (Trumper-Hecht, 2009). Still, 77% of Arab respondents (and 21% of Jews) believe Arabic *is* present on public signs in their city (see Table 13.2).

Hence, as far as Arabic's visibility is concerned, there exists a clear gap between Arabs' and Jews' perception of the LL, as well as a gap between the two groups' perception of the LL and the real picture on signs. This is not the case, however, where Hebrew is concerned. The vast majority (more than 93%) of both Arabs and Jews believe that Hebrew is the dominant language on public signs in their city, which is indeed the case. Well aware of the existing imbalance of power between Arabs and Jews in Israel, both groups' perceived LL is one in which Hebrew has a clear prevalence in the mixed city in which they live.

Table 13.2 Walkers' cognitive map: The image Arabs and Jews have of the LL on public signs

P	Jews (N =53)				Arabs (N =60)				
	Presence (%)	Salience			Presence (%)	Salience			Language
		Most	Half	Very little		Most	Half	Very little	
>0.05	92.5	87.8	10.2	2	93.3	87.5	8.9	3.6	Hebrew
<0.027	49	26.9	46.2	26.9	55	33.4	15.2	51.5	English
<0.008	21	27.3	18.2	54.5	77	67.4	19.6	13	Arabic

Walkers' preferences regarding the linguistic landscape in their mixed city

The second question investigated in the present study focused on the language preferences of Arab vs. Jewish residents regarding the representation of Arabic and Hebrew in the public space of mixed cities. Previous research on language attitudes (Ben Rafael, 1994; Kopelewitch, 1992; Shohamy & Donitsa-Schmidt, 1998; Spolsky & Shohamy, 1999) found an asymmetry between Jews' and Arabs' attitudes regarding language learning, for example. While Arabs hold positive attitudes toward learning Hebrew, the majority language, most Jews hold negative attitudes toward learning Arabic, the minority language. As a result, the Arab community in Israel is bilingual and bicultural while the Jewish majority in most cases doesn't speak Arabic nor is it interested in learning about Arab culture. The present study shows that this asymmetry also exists with regard to the LL preferences of the two national groups living in mixed cities. The most extreme case is that of Upper Nazareth.

Findings show that Upper Nazareth's Jewish residents (78.3%) prefer the bilingual 'Hebrew-English' pattern for the LL in their city. By contrast, most Arab residents prefer either the 'Hebrew-English-Arabic' trilingual pattern or the bilingual 'Hebrew-Arabic' LL pattern (82.9 and 72.7%, respectively). Thus, there is a significant difference between Jews' and Arabs' LL preferences (see Table 13.3). It is interesting to note, though, that despite continuous efforts to marginalize Arabic in Upper Nazareth (see Trumper-Hecht, 2009), an unexpectedly high percentage (40.9%) of Jewish residents also mention the trilingual 'Hebrew-English-Arabic' pattern as their preferred LL pattern for the city. Moreover, despite the

Table 13.3 Walkers' linguistic preferences regarding the LL in their city: Upper Nazareth

	Jews (N = 23)			*Arabs (N = 35)*			
P	*Most prefer*	*So, So*	*Not at all*	*Most prefer*	*So, So*	*Not at all*	*LL pattern*
<0.05	70.8	16.7	12.5	37.9	48.3	13.8	Hebrew only
<0.01	4.3	8.7	87	48.3	34.5	17.2	Arabic only
>0.05	9.5	38.1	52.4	13.3	46.7	40	English only
<0.05	78.3	13	8.7	37.9	34.5	27.6	Hebrew and English
<0.01	23.8	23.8	52.4	72.7	24.2	3.0	Hebrew and Arabic
>0.05	40.9	18.2	40.9	82.9	5.7	11.4	Hebrew, English and Arabic
<0.05	27.3	27.3	45.5	0	34.5	65.5	Hebrew and Russian

fact that half of Upper Nazareth's residents are Russian speakers, only 27.3% of Jews chose 'Hebrew-Russian' as their preferred LL pattern for the city's public space (compared with the 40.9% who favor a pattern that includes Arabic). Still, while the majority of Arab residents prefer a bilingual LL that includes both Hebrew and Arabic, the majority of Jewish residents prefer an LL that excludes the minority language.

In order to find out whether Jewish residents who show a preference for the trilingual 'Hebrew-English-Arabic' pattern hold a positive emotional attitude toward Arabic, we asked both Arabs and Jews if they liked to look at shop signs in Arabic/Hebrew. Findings show that while most of the Arab respondents (85%) state that they like to see Hebrew on shop signs, most of the Jewish respondents (74.5%) *dislike* seeing Arabic on shop signs in their city. Therefore, we may conclude that Jewish residents' choice that shop signs in their city include Arabic does not necessarily indicate that they have positive attitudes toward the minority language. Arab residents on the other hand, seem to hold positive attitudes toward the majority language.

When Upper Nazareth residents were asked to mock-design the LL of an imaginary future shopping center, most Arab residents (66.7%) chose Hebrew to be the most visible language next to Arabic while Jews chose English (60.4%) or Russian (39.6%) rather than Arabic as the additional languages. Only 15% of Jewish respondents said that they would want to include Arabic in the LL of a new shopping center in their city if they were to design it.

In summary, we found a clear asymmetry in the language preferences of Jews and Arabs regarding the LL in their city. While Upper Nazareth's Arab residents favor a public space in which Hebrew is dominant, but aspire for a greater balance between the two official languages, most Jewish residents prefer that the LL in their city exclude the minority language.

Walkers' attitudes regarding Arabic in Israel's linguistic landscape

The asymmetry observed regarding Jews' and Arabs' linguistic priorities was found also with regard to their attitudes toward the visibility of Hebrew vs. Arabic in the LL. While the question about residents' LL preferences focused on the LL of their city only, the question about residents' language attitudes focused on both the LL of their city and the LL of the country as a whole.

Based on previous research on language attitudes (Ben Rafael, 1994; Kopelewitch, 1992; Shohamy & Donitsa-Schmidt, 1998; Spolsky & Shohamy, 1999), we hypothesized that the same asymmetry found between Jews and Arabs regarding language learning, attitudes toward multilingualism, linguistic stereotypes etc., will be found concerning LL attitudes. Still, we wondered whether life in a mixed city had any positive influence on Jewish resident' attitudes toward the visibility of Arabic in Israel's urban public space.

Walkers' attitudes regarding commercial linguistic landscape

Local decision makers fought against Arabic in Upper Nazareth's commercial LL (Pinto, 2006; Trumper-Hecht, 2009), and openly objected to the 2002 Supreme Court ruling to include Arabic on public signs (Trumper-Hecht, 2009). We wondered whether Upper Nazareth's Jewish residents' attitudes matched those of local officials on this issue.

Findings show that this is indeed the case (see Table 13.4). There exists a significant difference in the importance Arabs and Jews give to the

Table 13.4 Upper Nazareth's residents' language attitudes: Commercial LL: **Statement a:** 'It is important that the language appears on all signs in my city' **Statement b:** 'It is important that the language appears on all signs in Israel'

P	Arabs (N=60)		Jews (N=53)		Degree of consent	Language
	My city	*Israel*	*My city*	*Israel*		
<0.01	70	76.7	96.2	98.1	Agree completely	Hebrew
	26.7	23.3	3.8	1.9	Agree	
	3.3	0	0	0	So, So	
	0	0	0	0	Disagree completely	
<0.01	80	70	13.2	13.2	Agree completely	Arabic
	16.7	21.7	11.3	13.2	Agree	
	3.3	8.3	18.9	26.4	So, So	
	0	0	56.6	27.2	Disagree completely	
>0.05	15	13.3	13.2	11.3	Agree completely	Russian
	25	30	35.8	18.9	Agree	
	20	26.7	22.6	35.8	So, So	
	40	30	28.3	34	Disagree completely	
>0.05	39	44.8	28	32	Agree completely	English
	35.6	34.5	44	52	Agree	
	20.3	13.8	24	12	So, So	
	5.1	6.9	4	4	Disagree completely	

representation of Arabic in the commercial LL in all three mixed cities. However, the most extreme gap between Jews and Arabs is found in Upper Nazareth. There, almost all Arab respondents (96.7%) think it is important that Arabic (alongside Hebrew) be represented in the commercial LL in the city and in Israel as a whole (91.7%). By contrast, most Jewish respondents in Upper Nazareth (75.5%) think it is *not* important that Arabic be represented in the commercial LL in their city, and more than half (53.6%) believe the same should be true for the commercial LL in Israel as a whole (see Table 13.4).

As we can see, both Arabs and Jews agree that Hebrew should appear on all commercial signs. But, while there is a clear consensus regarding Hebrew, the majority language, there clearly exists a sharp disagreement between the two national groups regarding the place Arabic should occupy in the mixed city of Upper Nazareth and in the country as a whole.

Walkers' attitudes regarding public signs

Findings show (see Table 13.5) that most Jewish respondents in Upper Nazareth (77.3%) think that public signs need to be in Hebrew and English, while most Arabs object to this idea. The vast majority of Arab residents (95%) think that public signs need to be in Hebrew and Arabic while most Jewish residents (64.2%) object to this idea.

It is interesting to note that both Jews (67.3%) and more so Arabs (75.3%) disagree with the idea that in neighborhoods populated mostly by Arabs, street signs should appear in Arabic only. This rare agreement, however, stems from very different reasons: Arabs' need for inclusion in Israeli society, symbolized by Hebrew, and Jews' fear of losing Hebrew dominance.

In sum, findings show that in Upper Nazareth, local decision makers' attempts to restrict the use of Arabic in the commercial LL in the city (Pinto, 2006) indeed match Jewish residents' attitudes toward the question of representation for Arabic in their city as well as in the country as a whole. Upper Nazareth's mayor's reluctance to comply with the Supreme Court decision to include Arabic on all public signs in his city can thus be explained by his attempt to please his Jewish voters.

Discussion and Conclusions

Walkers' perceived linguistic landscape: The 'cognitive maps' of the linguistic landscape

The fact that there are significant differences in Jews' and Arabs' perceptions of the LL in their city, may be explained by Bauman's (1997) claim that the public space is experienced indirectly through pre-conceived ideas that people form in order to 'map' their relations with

Table 13.5 Public signs: Upper Nazareth's residents' language attitudes

P	Jews (N=53)	Arabs (N=60)	Degree of consent	Statement
<0.0	22.6	78.3	Agree completely	9.1: All street signs in the city need to be in Hebrew and Arabic
	13.2	16.7	Agree	
	20.8	3.3	So, So	
	43.4	1.7	Disagree completely	
<0.04	41.5	40	Agree completely	9.2: Arabic should be added only in Arab neighborhoods
	15.1	25	Agree	
	13.2	13.3	So, So	
	30.2	21.7	Disagree completely	
<0.0	49.1	13.3	Agree completely	9.3: In Jewish neighborhoods signs should be in Hebrew only
	17	23.3	Agree	
	11.3	21.7	So, So	
	22.6	41.7	Disagree completely	
>0.05	23.1	13.7	Agree completely	9.4: In Arab neighborhoods signs should be in Arabic only
	9.6	11	Agree	
	19.2	20.5	So, So	
	48.1	54.8	Disagree completely	
<0.0	54.7	6.7	Agree completely	9.5: All street signs in the city have to be in Hebrew and English
	22.6	25	Agree	
	11.3	25	So, So	
	11.3	43.3	Disagree completely	

others. Despite its growing Arab population and official status as a mixed city, Jews in Upper Nazareth view their city as a Jewish city (Rabinowitz, 1997). As a result, they experience the LL in their city as one in which Hebrew is dominant and Arabic, a language symbolizing Arab identity, is non-existent. As one of Upper Nazareth's Jewish residents told me in answer to my question of why Arabic does not appear on public signs when 20% of the city's residents are Arab, he replied, 'Arabic belongs *there* (in Arab Nazareth and the Arab villages). *This* is a Jewish city' (his emphasis). Arab residents, aware of the power the Jewish majority enjoys both nationally and locally, perceive Hebrew as the dominant language in Upper Nazareth's LL. Strangely enough, though, they also believe that Arabic enjoys a high presence in Upper Nazareth's LL.

An interesting question to be asked is: 'Why do Arab residents living in Upper Nazareth have this misperception of the LL when in reality only 5.8% of signs include Arabic, and when the balance of power between the two groups in the city point to the opposite?' Is it possible that Upper Nazareth's Arab residents are blind to LL dynamics, or maybe something else is at play here?

To answer this question, we need to borrow the notion of 'cognitive maps' from cultural geography. Cognitive maps, which are invisible, subjective and personal or interpersonal, must be distinguished from cartographic maps, which are visible and objective. Each person or group has a mental representation of their geographic surrounding, and as Portugali (1996) shows, the members of a cultural or ethnic group may have similar cognitive maps that enable them to construct a distinct representation of the space they share with another group. Thus, while Upper Nazareth's Jews' collective cognitive map informs them that the mixed city they live in is in fact a Jewish city with a Hebrew dominant LL, the city's Arab residents' collective cognitive map of the same space tells them a different story. Upper Nazareth, founded a decade after the establishment of the state of Israel, is still seen by Arabs in this area of Galilee as an incursion into their territory. Thus, many of them prefer to see the Jewish city they chose to move into as a type of suburb of historic Arab Nazareth. It is likely, therefore, that Arab residents perceive the urban space of Arab Nazareth and that of Upper Nazareth as one urban space. The cognitive map by which they live the space dictates, as Portugali (1996) would have argued, the different perception Arabs and Jews have of the LL in their city. Therefore, Jews believe that Hebrew and Russian are the dominant languages in the city they see as a Jewish city, while Arab residents believe Hebrew and Arabic to be the dominant languages in Upper Nazareth's LL. De Certeau (1980) identifies the practices of everyday life as strategies that enable walkers to challenge existing power relations. In this light, one may see Upper Nazareth's Arab residents' definition of the urban space they live in as defiance against the formal division of that space into two cities: a Jewish city and an Arab one.

A somewhat different explanation of the gap between the LL as it is perceived by residents and the LL as it was documented by camera has to do with the different ways in which the two groups lead their everyday lives. While much of Jews' everyday life takes place in Upper Nazareth, most of Arabs' daily life takes place outside the city, in Arab Nazareth and Arab villages in this region. In most areas of everyday life, such as work, business, shopping, culture and religion, the daily lives of

Upper Nazareth's Arab residents are carried out in Arab Nazareth, where they also send their children to school (Rabinowitz, 1997). As King-Irani (2008) explains, 'given its proximity to Naasira (i.e. Arab Nazareth), it is hard to say whether Upper Nazareth's non-Jewish inhabitants are residents or commuters since most Palestinians who purchase or rent homes in the various neighborhoods of the hilltop Jewish development town continue to work, play, study, socialize, worship, and get married and buried in Naasira'.

Since the LL in Arab Nazareth and the neighboring villages enjoys a high presence of Arabic (alongside Hebrew), Upper Nazareth's Arab residents may be referring to their 'lived space' when asked about their perceptions of the LL in their city. Hannerz (1980) directs our attention to relational and sociological definitions as opposed to geographical or demographic definitions of the city. It may be that we are mistaken in assuming that our respondents will go by the official geographical definition of the city when asked to report their perceptions of its space. Our findings seem to indicate that LL perceptions are influenced by the way in which the space is 'lived' and experienced by each of the groups in everyday life.

Walkers' linguistic landscape preferences

Aside from the asymmetry found in this study between Jews' and Arabs' LL preferences, another key finding is the difference between cities. A comparison with the mixed city of Jaffa will help shed light on the case of Upper Nazareth discussed here. One could place Jaffa and Upper Nazareth at two extremes of a tolerance continuum regarding Jewish residents' LL preferences. While Upper Nazareth Jews clearly resent the idea that Arabic be visible in their city's public space, Jaffa Jews seem to favor the visibility of Arabic in the LL. The question is, of course: 'How can this difference be explained, and what (if at all) can be learnt from this comparison about the conditions required for coexistence in mixed cities in Israel?' One possible explanation for the differences we found between Jaffa and Upper Nazareth has to do with the history of the two cities. While Jaffa was a thriving Arab city prior to 1948, Upper Nazareth was established as a Jewish city overlooking ancient Nazareth a decade after the establishment of the state of Israel. Jaffa was greatly depopulated during the war of independence, and immediately repopulated by Jewish immigrants. Still, despite the complete reversal in population proportion between Palestinian veterans and Jewish immigrants, and the attempt to turn it into a Jewish city, Jaffa did not become a Jewish city in people's consciousness, but remained Palestinian in the minds of both Palestinians and Jews (Rabinowitz & Monterescu, 2007). Upper Nazareth, by contrast, was established as a Jewish city, and remained so in the minds of its Jewish residents even after Palestinian infiltration (starting in the 1980s) turned it (*de facto*) into a mixed city.

Fear of the Arab minority is another way to explain the difference in the language preferences of Jews in Jaffa and in Upper Nazareth. In a paper dealing with the question of trust between Jews and Arabs, Rabinowitz (1992) claims that in the conflict-ridden relationship that exists between the two groups, the *ad hoc* trust established in mixed cities on an interpersonal level does not seem to work on the group level. In Upper Nazareth, where Jews are a majority in their city but a minority in that area of Galilee, the presence of Arabic in what they see as 'their' public space is automatically perceived by Jewish residents as a threat. In Jaffa, on the other hand, the presence of Arabic may be more tolerated by Jews not only because they are aware of the Arab history of the city, but also because Arabs today constitute a very small and weakened minority in an area that is predominantly Jewish. In Jaffa itself, 25% of the population is Palestinian, but in the Tel-Aviv metropolitan area they constitute only 4% of the population. The reverse is true of Upper Nazareth, where Jews constitute a minority in that area of Galilee.

Even though Jaffa Jews seem to be more tolerant toward the visibility of Arabic in the public space, there still exists a clear asymmetry in the language preferences of Jews and Arabs. Therefore, we may conclude that, as Saban and Amara (2004) argue, achieving equal representation for Arabic on public signs through litigation (as is the case in Jaffa), does not guarantee change in Jews' LL preferences regarding the minority language in mixed cities or outside of them.

A significant change in the LL; one that would reflect a greater balance between Hebrew and Arabic on both commercial and public signs, could take place once Jewish residents' language preferences and attitudes have changed.

Walkers' linguistic landscape attitudes

A collective emotion orientation of fear dominates societies involved in intractable conflicts (Bar Tal, 2001). In Israel, as long as peace seems out of reach and violence rules the scene, it is difficult to replace this orientation with a collective emotion orientation of hope. As a political psychologist, Bar Tal (2001) suggests that we study collective emotion orientation to explain individual as well as societal functioning. It is my contention that because of its great symbolic value for the two national groups, the case of the LL in Israel requires such an examination. The consistent asymmetry in Jewish and Arab walkers' attitudes in mixed cities seems to be telling us that while Arabs living in mixed cities in Israel live according to a collective emotion orientation of hope, their Jewish neighbors tend to be dominated by a collective emotion orientation of fear. Further research on what lies behind Arabs' positive attitudes toward bilingualism in the LL and Jews' resistance to Arabic in the LL is needed in order to determine what conditions are needed for a more symmetrical and hopeful coexistence. As the example of Upper Nazareth shows us, Jews' fear of becoming a minority in their city, and local as well as national political endeavors to control the city's national identity, are well reflected in Jewish residents' attitudes toward Arabic in the LL. Jewish residents' negative attitudes toward the question of visibility for Arabic, is symbolic of their refusal to see Upper Nazareth as a mixed community. The example of Jaffa may indicate that when Jewish residents do not feel demographically threatened, and the Arab identity of the city is kept alive, one can expect a more tolerant attitude toward minority language visibility in the LL. An example of this relative tolerance is manifested both by Jaffa's Jewish residents' LL attitudes toward Arabic and the Tel-Aviv-Jaffa municipality swift compliance with the Supreme Court decision to add Arabic onto all public signs in the city. In light of this comparison, one wonders whether state intrusion in Upper Nazareth meant to control social and political life in the city (Torstrick, 2000) doesn't help limit the social relationships that may have otherwise developed within the mixed community of Upper Nazareth. Thus, an important question to be asked in this context is: 'How much freedom do Jews and Arabs possess to develop mixed communities in which Hebrew and Arabic can "float freely" in the shared public space?'

In summary, the present study shows that when one attempts a comprehensive analysis of the LL as a sociolinguistic-spatial phenomenon in specific cities, one still cannot generalize about the LL of nations as cities add to the complexity of analysis. However, the analysis of the LL in specific urban settings enriches our understanding of these particular contexts, and enables us to look more closely at the ways in which the LL operates both as a reflection of the sociopolitical reality and as a scene of social action.

References

Bar-Tal, D. (2001) Why does fear override hope in societies engulfed by intractable conflicts as it does in the Israeli society? *Political Psychology* 22, 601–627.

Bauman, Z. (1997) *Postmodernity and its Discontents*. New York: University Press.

Ben-Rafael, E. (1994) *Language, Identity and Social Division: The Case of Israel*. Oxford: Clarendon Press.

Ben Rafael, E. (2009) A sociological approach to the study of linguistic landscapes. In E. Shohamy and D. Gorter (eds) *Linguistic Landscape: Expanding the Scenery* (pp. 40–54). London: Routledge.

Ben-Rafael, E., Shohamy, E., Amara, M. and Trumper-Hecht, N. (2006) Linguistic landscape as symbolic construction of the public space: The case of Israel. *International Journal of Multilingualism* 3 (1), 7–30.

De Certeau, M. (1984) *The Practice of Everyday Life*. Berkley, CA: University of California Press.

Hannertz, U. (1980) *Exploring the City*. New York: Columbia University Press.

King-Irani, L. (2007) A nixed, not mixed, city: Mapping obstacles to democracy in the Nazareth/Nazareth Illit conurbation. In D. Rabinowitz and D. Monterescu (eds) *Mixed Towns, Trapped Communities: Historical Narratives, Spatial Dynamics, Gender Relations and Cultural Encounters in Palestinian Israeli Towns* (pp. 179–200). Farnham: Ashgate.

Kopelewitz, I. (1992) Arabic in Israel: The sociolinguistic situation of Israel's Arab minority. *International Journal of the Sociology of Language* 98, 29–66.

Landry, R. and Bourhis, R.Y. (1997) Linguistic landscape and ethnolinguistic vitality: An empirical study. *Journal of Language and Social Psychology* 16 (1), 23–49.

Lefebvre, H. (1991) *The Production of Space*. Oxford: Blackwell.

Pinto, M. (2006) Language rights, immigration and minorities in Israel. *Mishpat Umimshal Law and Government, Univ. of Haifa Law Review* 10 (1), 223–269.

Portugali, Y. (1996) *Implicate Relations: Society and Space in the Israeli-Palestinian Conflict*. Dordrecht: Kluwer Academic.

Rabinowitz, D. (1992) Trust and the attribution of rationality: Inverted roles amongst Palestinian Arabs and Jews in Israel. *Man* 27 (3), 517–537.

Rabinowitz, D. (1997) *Overlooking Nazareth: The Ethnography of Exclusion in Galilee*. Cambridge: Cambridge University Press.

Rabinowitz, D. and Monterescu, D. (2007) *Mixed Towns, Trapped Communities: Historical Narratives, Spatial Dynamics, Gender Relations and Cultural Encounters in Palestinian Israeli Towns*. Farnham: Ashgate.

Saban, I. and Amara, M. (2004) The status of Arabic in Israel: Reflections on the power of law to produce social change. *Israel Law Review* 36 (2), 5–39.

Shohamy, E. and Donitsa-Schmidt, S. (1998) *Jews vs. Arabs: Language Attitudes and Stereotypes*. Tel Aviv: The Tami Steinmetz Center for Peach Research. Tel Aviv University.

Spolsky, B. (2004) *Language Policy*. Cambridge: Cambridge University Press.

Spolsky, B. and Shohamy, E. (1999) *The Languages of Israel: Policy, Ideology and Practice*. Clevedon: Multilingual Matters.

Supreme Court (2002) 4112/99 Adalla versus Tel Aviv Jaffa and other mixed cities.

Torstrick, R. (2000) *The Limits of Coexistence: Identity Politics in Israel*. Ann Arbor, MI: The University of Michigan Press.

Trumper-Hecht, N. (2009) Constructing national identity in mixed cities in Israel: Arabic on signs in the public space of Upper Nazareth. In E. Shohamy and D. Gorter (eds) *Linguistic Landscape: Expanding the Scenery* (pp. 238–252). London: Routledge.

Chapter 14

Responses to the Linguistic Landscape in Memphis, Tennessee: An Urban Space in Transition

REBECCA TODD GARVIN

This chapter focuses on individual cognitive and emotional responses to the linguistic landscape (LL) in urban communities of Memphis, Tennessee. With a population of approximately 650,000, Memphis is the eighteenth largest city in the USA, located in the mid-south region, and is an urban space in transition due to heavy flows of transnational migration to the area. A phenomenon so recent that it is not currently reflected in official census reports, this international migration trend is manifested by shifts in public language use that are visible and salient in the LL throughout the city. With interviews conducted onsite during 'walking tours' of specifically chosen areas, this qualitative study explored self-reported understandings and visual perceptions of public signage – the multiple languages, images and icons marking multi-lingual urban communities.

Introduction

Descriptions of the scope and phenomenon of language behavior and linguistic interactions in urban contexts are not possible to accomplish fully without a workable frame of reference (Goffman, 1963). Such framing provides a focus for research and a manageable space for linguistic exploration. Barton and Hamilton (2005) maintained that we live in a textually mediated world elucidated and framed by literacy events that are situated, enacted and understood in specific contexts. Referring to these mediational texts or signs as they are physically placed in the world, Scollon and Scollon (2003: introduction, p. x) wrote: 'Everywhere about us in our day-to-day world we see the discourses which shape, manage, entice, and control our actions'. Studies of signs in public spaces have been documented since the 1960s (see chart in Backhaus, 2007: 56), but it was not until a study to investigate perceptions of ethnic group vitality based on the presence or absence of minority languages on public signage in Canada by Landry and Bourhis (1997) that the LL was framed as the study of concrete languages on signs and billboards in public places. Since then, a growing number of applied linguists and language scholars have creatively and systematically applied this approach to the study of multilingualism in areas throughout the world. With growing enthusiasm, brought about by a richness of data in terms of sociolinguistic information embedded in the LL, linguistic landscape scholars, in a mode of critical reflexivity, are now questioning the boundaries of the frame and coalescing to articulate the field and scope of LL studies, with particular focus on the multilingual urban landscape.

According to Coulmas (2009), written language coincided with the development of urbanization laying the foundation for the conception and management of the public sphere – public signs, marking and defining centers of human habitation, have been around for a long time. He stated that urban landscapes should logically be the focus of LL study. In *Linguistic Landscape: Expanding the Scenery*, editors Shohamy and Gorter (2009) opened a dialogue to expand the focus of the LL beyond concrete language inscriptions to include icons and images and other multimodal literacies present in the public sphere. This work grounded the emerging field of LL study with theories based on language choice (Spolsky, 2009), sociological approach (Ben-Rafael, 2009), economic approach (Cenoz & Gorter, 2009), genre theory with varied norms of interpretation (Huebner, 2009) and ecological orientation (Hult, 2009). Nonetheless, Huebner (2009: 70) maintained that for him, there are still 'problems of selection, classification, and linguistic analyses of artifacts found in the LLs' as well as the ways a variety of readers are observing LL items.

Since 1997, according to Gorter and Cenoz (2008: 343) the majority of LL studies have focused primarily on the 'description and analysis of written information' in the LL. Increasingly, researchers (e.g. Ben-Rafael, 2009; Cenoz & Gorter, 2009; Gorter, 2006, 2009; Huebner, 2009; Shohamy & Gorter, 2009; Spolsky, 2009) are calling for interpretations of the LL that take into account not only the intended meanings of the sign makers, but also the psychological and visual perceptions of the sign readers. Spolsky (2009: 33), for example, alluded to the risks of misinterpretation about the status of language activity and a tendency toward 'organized language management' when the sign-maker is out of touch with the sign-reader. In *Reading shop windows in globalized neighborhoods*, Collins and Slembrouck (2007: 335) noted 'how they [public signs] are read [by passersby] is a question rarely addressed'. In a recent study with school children in Canada, Dagenais *et al.* (2009) posited that relatively few studies have been conducted to examine ways in which individuals interact with the LL text. To promote language awareness in children, Dagenais *et al.* (2009: 256–257) argued that the 'LL serves as a research tool to stimulate children's observations of texts, multilingualism and language diversity'. Not enough is known about the ways individuals interact with the LL or its role in the negotiation of thoughts, feelings, actions and identity formations.

This chapter presents a new methodology designed to investigate the cognitive and emotional verbal responses elicited and triggered by close physical proximity and explicit reference to the LL. Utilizing postmodern interviewing methodology (Gubrium & Holstein, 2003), this dissertation study (Garvin, 2010) explored self-reported understandings of the LL and the psychological, emotional impact of *migrant cityscaping*, the act of signing the urban LL to reflect the needs and identities of migrant populations (Garvin & Hanauer, 2007). The questions posed are: In what ways do individual residents understand, interpret and interact with the LL in their communities? What are their thoughts and feelings about multilingualism or changes in the LL? In what ways does the LL connect residents to their social and psychological identities? By addressing issues of readership of the LL in urban spaces in transition, the researcher attempted to address a gap in LL research and accept Malinowski's (2009: 124) challenge to LL scholars 'to situate and contextualize our studies in the lives of those who read, write, and conduct their lives amongst the signs of our field'. The theoretical framework for this qualitative ethnographic study can be described as a critical postmodern interview inquiry with a LL approach. Starting with a discussion of methodology aspects such as the use of the LL as both text and tool, the 'walking tour' interview, the site, and participants, the remainder of this chapter will present the results and conclusions drawn that demonstrate the psychological and emotional impact of migrant cityscaping on the participants as they interacted with and responded to the LL in their communities.

The Linguistic Landscape as Text and Tool

Like a snapshot of one moment in time, the LL presents a concrete text of actual language use in a particular time and place. It is a text created and bounded by geography and human habitation in a particular location. In urban communities, the LL reflects the complex patterns of communicative life in an urban space and indexes language practices, ethnic cultures, values and the history of a community. Perhaps in this way, the gestalt of the LL text (Ben-Rafael, 2009) is holistically experienced as it embodies situated linguistic practices, in particular, the phenomenon of language contact, choice and change often constrained by local ideologies, practices and government language policy (Spolsky, 2009). Hanauer (2009: 13) stated 'the beauty of the linguistic landscape is that it is a living entity that evolves and reflects the "here and now" of discursive positioning and the power relations within a social arena'. As such, the urban LL text is not fixed. It is dynamic and multilayered, constantly changing to represent the values, needs, resources, institutions, restrictions, contestations, cultures, languages and dreams of its multiple authors who are positioned and actively positioning themselves within a geographical space.

In addition to providing an authentic text of actual situated language use (Scollon & Scollon, 2003; Gee, 2005), the LL has potential as a powerful research tool in its function as a *stimulus text* during interviews. In qualitative interviewing, researchers often employ techniques to encourage participants to talk, techniques that include use of stimulus texts. Pavlenko (2003) conducted a study to examine second language influence on Russian first language speakers using films as stimuli to elicit narratives. In *Emotions and Multilingualism*, Pavlenko (2005) presented a list of cross-linguistic decoding studies that used recordings as stimuli. In other instances, interviewees have been asked to interpret pictures, to draw, to write stories, to complete sentences, to respond with one word 'free' associations and to watch movies. This is not new. However, Törrönen (2002) stated that research needs to explore and include more discussion on how these texts are internalized and the ways they are used during the interview. Functioning as externalized reference points, in a study on alcohol use in Finland, Törrönen (2002) maintained that stimulus texts can be used as clues (references), as microcosms (symbols of groups or cognitive associations) or as provokers (emotional triggers) in the production and analysis of interview texts. As explained above, the LL in the current study functioned as both text and tool in that it embodied the phenomenon under investigation as well as stimulated and focused the interviews that were conducted onsite during the 'walking tours'.

'Walking Tour' Methodology

Embracing postmodern interviewing sensibilities, a 'walking tour' methodology was designed to investigate the dynamic processes of interaction and the co-construction of knowledge mediated and stimulated by the LL. With long-standing and migrant residents of Memphis, the researcher explored the ways the LL text focused and stimulated the conversation during the interview while mediating a sense of place and space. The LL reflects the communicative life in an urban space. Through systematic observation of the LL during 'walking tour' interviews, this communicative life was brought to the conscious attention of local participant-readers. The interviews were recorded and analyzed to explore ways that participants interacted with the LL and how meanings and understandings were constructed through dialogue enacted within the discursive aesthetic experience of moving in the landscape (Tuan, 1993). Pennycook (2009: 309) cited and elaborated de Certeau's (1990) thoughts that, 'The act of walking in the city is what brings to life, a spatial realization of place'. Blommaert *et al.* (2005: 206) maintained that 'neighborhoods are often the kind of real material and symbolic space in which people anchor a dense complex of symbolic and material practices and to which they refer in performing these practices'. This study also draws from Farrell's (2006) work in reflective practices, which built on Schön's (1983) process of reflection-in-action, suggesting that being in the body, reflecting in action, at the moment of seeing, sharpens the senses and brings to the surface thoughts and emotions that are often socially constrained or suppressed by time.

Memphis: The Site

To outsiders, the city of Memphis is often perceived as a racially divided southern city known for its unique styles of music, barbeque cook-offs and high crime rates. However, this urban area is also the home of the National Civil Rights Museum, Elvis Presley's Graceland, Federal Express and Holiday Inn Corporations, as well as known for being the largest cargo hub in North America – a bustling intersection of major highways, railroads, river barge traffic and commercial airways.

> Memphis is a city in black and white, a vibrant city with a divided heart. It is a city of contrasts and contradictions where southern charm and elegance meet southern tension and violence. For much of its history, Memphis has been inhabited by and divided by two peoples who share a common place and history but are separated by the social and political differences ascribed to race. (Bond & Sherman, 2003: 7)

In 2007, the total population of Memphis was recorded as 649,443 (US Census Report, American Community Survey, 2007). Of that number, 32.8% were white and 63.1% were African American, accounting for almost 96% of the total population. With 91.8% speaking English only, the public sphere in Memphis has been, for the most part, monolingual. However, in the past five years, substantial transnational flows of migrants 'have complicated this simple binary of black and white' (Bond & Sherman, 2003: 7), diffusing this dyadic stronghold of racial segregation. Bond and Sherman (2003: 7) stated, 'The newest migrants to Memphis include an estimated half-million Latinos, Asians, Africans, and people from the Middle East'. Peck (2007), editor of *The Commercial Appeal*, reported that the Hispanic population is estimated at well over 100,000 – three times the number published in the latest census reports (US Census Report, American Community Survey, 2007). Multilingual signs are now widespread throughout the LL of this urban area (e.g. see Figures 14.1 and 14.2), thus reinforcing Barni and Bagna's (2009: 126)

Figure 14.1 Billboard seen from the Interstate 240 by-pass (photographed October 2007)

Figure 14.2 On Getwell Rd (photographed October 2007)

assertion of the importance of the LL in the mapping of 'linguistic diversity in multilingual contexts'.

The Study

The overall purpose of this study was to collect and analyze the self-reported emotional understandings and visual perceptions of residents of Memphis, Tennessee, concerning migrant or minority language discourses in the LL. Taking a bottom-up approach described by Ben-Rafael *et al.* (2006), the study focused on unofficial public commercial signage and billboards within the city limits. While official government signs, such as street names and highway markers, were written in English, the codes enforcement policy in Memphis had no restrictions on language choices used on commercial signs (see Figures 14.3 and 14.4). In 2007 and 2008, ten individual onsite 'walking tour' interviews were conducted with residents of Memphis to collect their self-reported, emotional understandings of the LL. Communities with a high frequency of multilingualism on public signs were selected for the study and photographed. Figure 14.5 is a map of Memphis (google.earth.com) showing the street sites and areas selected for the 'walking tour' interviews.

These streets are major traffic arteries of the city and were selected due to the high frequency of multiple languages present on public signage.

Figure 14.3 On Summer Ave (photographed October 2007)

Figure 14.4 On Getwell Rd (photographed October 2007)

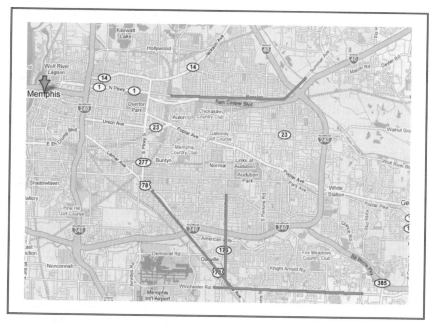

Figure 14.5 Map of Memphis (google.earth.com) with 'walking tour' street sites

Table 14.1 Description of languages of commercial place signs on 'walking tour' street sites

Streets	Number of businesses	English only	Multilingual/ other language	Multilingual/other language signs (%)
Lamar Ave	140	128	12	8.5
Getwell Rd	139	120	19	13.6
Winchester Rd	249	213	36	14.5
Summer Ave	280	231	49	17.5
Total	808	692	116	14.3

Prior to the 'walking tour' interviews, these sites were digitally photographed for later reference. In the areas designated for the 'walking tours', unofficial community/commercial business name signs were counted. Table 14.1 shows the total number of businesses and the number with percentages of business name signs containing multilingualism or languages other than English.

The data collection was conducted in the following phases: (1) the selection of the sites, photographing and describing of 'walking tour' sites; (2) selection of the participants, initial contact with prospective participants through flyers circulated in public offices with a brief interview; (3) conducting the postmodern 'walking tour' interviews; (4) recording of field notes and transcription of the interviews; and (5) conducting a follow-up meeting to ensure validity of data by giving the participants copies of their interview transcripts and an opportunity to continue the dialogue and add, clarify and provide any other thoughts and feelings about their responses.

The Participants

The selection of participants was initiated through flyers with information about the study that were distributed in public offices, non-academic institutional settings. After an initial meeting with each consenting participant, dates and times were scheduled for individual 'walking tours'. The participants were purposefully selected to reflect the demographic diversity of the current population in Memphis. The group of participants represented both long-established and migrant residents; half had lived in Memphis all their lives while the other half had migrated to the area. The participants were purposefully selected to reflect the demographic diversity of the current population in Memphis. There were five males and five females between the ages of 20 and 80. Of the group, seven reported that English was their first language while the other three, one born in Ethiopia, one born in Mexico and one in Cambodia, reported Amharic, Spanish and Khmer (C'mai) as their first languages. Five were self-described as white/Caucasian, two as African American/Black, one as Ethiopian, one as Hispanic and one as Asian. All the participants held jobs in areas of public service in the city of Memphis.

The following questions were posed to the participants during the 'walking tours':

- How do you feel when you see signs in languages other than English?
- When was the first time you noticed new languages present on signs in this area?
- What was your initial thought or reaction to the linguistic changes?
- Do you feel at home visiting or shopping in this area? If yes, why? Or, if not, why so?
- Do you go into stores and shops that advertise in languages other than English?
- Does or did this place have a special meaning or memory for you?
- What do you think the languages on the signs say about the people groups in this area?

Interacting with the Linguistic Landscape in Urban Spaces

Results obtained from the study showed, as Huebner (2009) suggested, that the ways individuals are reading, interpreting and responding to these texts are complex and not easily generalized. In *Ways of Seeing*, Berger (1997) stated the moment of seeing is integrated with our expectations and previous experiences of meaning, which cannot be separated from the context or physical setting in which they are observed. Berger (1997: 8) stated that making meaning of visual texts, or any form of art or literacy, is very much dependent on 'what we know and what we believe'. Individuals approached this text as historical bodies with a variety of backgrounds, discourses, languages and experiences – everything came into play at the moment of seeing.

Identity and the linguistic landscape

The findings in this study indicated that the LL as a stimulus text and 'walking tour' as a methodology elicited from participants a series of self-positioning statements. These self-positioning statements changed from one participant to another participant and at times even within the same participant as different identities were accessed. At approximately the same location in the 'walking tour' and near the beginning of each tour, the participants were asked a similar question, 'How do you feel when you see signs in other languages?' Results showed that 30% responded positively to multilingual signs; 20% indicated negative feelings about the presence of migrant discourses; and 10% expressed mixed emotions about current linguistic changes. Although the remaining 40% stated that they were neutral or had not noticed, their positions shifted as interviews progressed. From the two excerpts that follow, one can begin to understand how the LL connects individuals to the environment as they negotiated their identities and self-positioned themselves.

Extract 1: Participant 2, multilingual male, originally from Ethiopia
Interviewer: When you are looking at signs in other languages, how do you feel? (pause) Would you not go into a place if you saw a language that you did not understand?
P2: It depends. For example, if I plan to go to a Chinese restaurant, and there is a Chinese sign, that doesn't deter me. But if I am looking, for example, for car maintenance, to buy some item, and the description is written only in Spanish it doesn't make sense to me; unless there is no other option, I don't go there. But if I want to eat Mexican food and the sign is written in Hispanic, it doesn't matter to me.

This participant's responses indicated a pragmatic, detached position in relation to the LL. Impressing the researcher with a cosmopolitan-like attitude, he was not deterred by unknown languages, if he had a purpose or use for services or businesses even though they were inscribed with unfamiliar languages, he would go in. His final comment in this excerpt 'it doesn't matter to me' reinforced the distant position he chose to maintain in relation to the migrant discourses on the signs he was observing. This participant's identity as a highly educated professional was accessed during the interaction in contrast to the participant in extract 2 that follows:

Extract 2: Participant 6, bilingual female, originally from Mexico
Interviewer: Well, how do you feel when you see Spanish on signs?
P6: Uhmm...well, I mean it makes me realize that our population is growing because before you would never really see a Mexican restaurant especially like in Spanish. And now most restaurants they already have them in Spanish when before they used to kind of have it to where the people would understand it like 'The Mexican Restaurant' or something like that.
Interviewer: Yeah.
P6: It's changed. Now they do have a certain name, you know, the name that they want to put on the restaurant.

In contrast to Participant 2, Participant 6 positioned herself within the migrant Hispanic community commenting that 'our population is growing'. At the end of this excerpt, she also shifted slightly in this position by referring to Hispanics as 'they'. Not yet confident in this interaction, she indirectly acknowledged changes in the community now allowing Hispanics freedom to express their identities instead of catering to the dominant language group. It was interesting to note that as the interview progressed and she realized the extent of the Hispanic population in Memphis, her confidence grew and expressions of her Hispanic identity became more bold and enthusiastic. This seemed to indicate that individual ethnic vitality is boosted by the presence and frequency of personal minority language in the LL (Landry & Bourhis, 1997).

Connections of culture and ethnicity

On Winchester Avenue, the third street site on the 'walking tour', one of the most emotionally provocative literacy objects in the LL was observed. The multiple responses and meanings the participants reported and ascribed to the impact of this visual representation substantively showed the diversity in the ways individuals make sense of icons and literate objects based on their own culture, values, ethnic backgrounds and experiences (Shohamy & Waksman, 2009). Standing boldly on the property of the World Overcomers Church, at the corner of a busy intersection, was a modified replicate of the Statue of Liberty (see Figures 14.6 and 14.7). In this version, the statue lifted in her right hand a cross – instead of a torch. Resting in the curve of her left arm, was not just a book, but what appeared to be a portion of the Bible. At the base of the statue were the words, 'America Must Return to Christ'. In the background were rows of international flags. Below are responses from five different participants when asked what they thought about this site:

P2 (male/Ethiopia):   Sometimes I think they are trying to show that they are international. But sometimes I don't understand it because when they have four or five flags, how come they selected just those flags?

P5 (male/white/Memphis):   Well, there was a lot of controversy. Some thought it was a violation of church and state.

P8 (male/black/Memphis):   The Statue of Liberation. . . .people were saying they were so sick of things, in Memphis, that had signs and things that were negative in the Black community. And the church decided to put up the Statue of Liberty and said because we want to say that we are American and America needs to follow its path back to Christ.

P9 (female/Cambodia):   I remember what we're here for, why we're here.

P10 (male/white/Memphis):   I don't like it! It's just too in your face.

Figure 14.6 Statue located at Winchester and Kirby (photographed November 2007)

Figure 14.7 International flags displayed behind the statue on Winchester Ave

The responses to the icons as shown in Figures 14.6 and 14.7 emphasized Berger's claim that in the moment of seeing the interpretation of text, images and icons are integrated with the viewer's background and experiences. The statue and flags triggered strong emotions but had different, multiple meanings for each participant. Interestingly, this data also showed the lack of interdependence between word and text to create meaning. Kress and Van Leeuwen (1996: 17) maintained that the semiotic components of a visual text are 'an independently organized and structured message—connected with the verbal text, but in no way dependent on it: and similarly the other way around'. Most participants reacted to the written text and visual components independently, not as a unified text. The message in the written text was often subdued by the icons.

Connecting responses to the linguistic landscape with political and social discourses

Stimulated by the LL and the conversation during the 'walking tours', participants spontaneously introduced a variety of topics and relevant social issues. For example, some interesting topics discussed in the interviews, triggered by responses to the LL, were race, religion, segregation, illegal immigration, Ebonics/African American Vernacular, poverty, economic development, personal cultural traditions and family values. In each instance, in the analysis of interview texts, the researcher was able to trace specific wider discourses influencing the participants' responses as in the following extract.

Extract 3: Participant 3, monolingual female from Memphis
Interviewer: When did you start noticing things like that (pointing) and languages present in this area in Memphis?
P3:   This widespread, I would say about six years ago. It has really mushroomed. It was always spread out more; it has been fairly recent and fairly fast.
Interviewer: How does it make you feel?
P3:   Well, I mean, the whole illegal immigrant thing, you know, gives it a different light to me. At first, it was just, OK, these are Mexican people and it didn't register with me that, you know, the Hispanics are here and, OK, they're working and minding their own business and they seem to be nice and stuff until all the political controversy came out about them being illegal and, you know, that kind of stuff. That has drawn my attention more to it and maybe changed my view a little bit.

One of the most interesting observations in this excerpt was how clearly this demonstrated the influence of a wider discourse, triggered by the LL, beyond this conversation and interaction. Although not explicitly stated, this participant positioned herself as legal resident in opposition to the Mexican community, symbolically referenced in the signage. The data in this section shows that the LL is never a neutral context. It is always a point of reference for self-positioning. Accordingly, there is always some form of psychological response to the LL.

Co-constructing knowledge of place and space

The following portion of the interview with Participant 9 exhibits how the interviewer and participant together discursively constructed a space that allowed conversation to flow naturally and, as a result, produced complex multilayered understandings of the LL text that did not previously reside in one individual. During the interview, as distance in the perceived status of interviewer and participant decreased and the roles blurred, conversation was enhanced, understandings that were co-constructed would not have been as rich and meaningful without their social interaction in concert with the material, multimodal text.

Extract 4: Participant 9, bilingual female, originally from Cambodia
P9:   (pointing) Is that the Vietnamese temple?
Interviewer: Yeah, we need to turn... I've taken pictures of this one.
P9:   The Vietnamese temple. They were telling me about it. I was going to drive by one day. So this is it.
Interviewer: Uh huh.
P9:   (pointing to a large flag) You know that's a religious flag, don't you?
Interviewer: No. I didn't know that. I need a picture of it. Really, I didn't know that.
P9:   Each color represents a different thing that Buddha gave up his life for Vietnamese, uh, they.... Gah, this is big! (Walking over to a statue)
Interviewer: It is big.
P9:   I'm surprised they don't have signs. The one, the one on...
Interviewer: They did before. I took a picture of the sign before. It looks like they remodeled.
P9:   (pointing to another statute). That's Sray Daene. You see a lot of pendants with her on it.
Interviewer: What was her name again?
P9:   I know in Cambodian. We call it Sray Daene. They say she like Moses. She went up to heaven though she did not die. If you have any connection with her that you see her in your meditation. You see a lot of pendants in jade with her image on them.
Interviewer: Her image on them. Wow.

In this excerpt, that creative, safe space sought for in postmodern interviewing, is evident in that the tone of the conversation and the empathy between the researcher and participant resembled that of friends. Upon arrival at this site (see Figure 14.8), near the end of the 'walking tour', with the first pointing gesture, the participant assumed the role of teacher and the researcher became a genuinely eager student. Again, icons in the LL at this site elicited strong emotional responses. Participant 9's expression 'Gah, this is big!' was so expressive, ethnic and natural and was accompanied by gestures to show surprise or awe. The researcher's impression of the scene recorded in field notes indicated that there was an absence of conscious social performance at this place. The personal identity, that aspect of identity described by Harré and Van Langenhove (1998) as how we are known to ourselves, was perceived, freely and bodily expressed. The participant's actions to increase the researcher's understanding of the relevancy of the cultural icons and images enhanced the knowledge and meanings of the icons that were observed at this site. Making meaning of the LL marking this place grew out of discursive interaction and co-construction of knowledge in a space created within the 'walking tour' interview.

Figure 14.8 Statue at Vietnamese Temple off Winchester (Photographed October 2007)

Conclusion

The postmodern 'walking tour' interview methodology described in this chapter offers researchers in the LL, and in applied linguists in general, a tool for exploring cognitive and emotional understandings played out in response to the LL in urban settings that surround them. Results showed that the LL served as a catalyst or stimulus text mediating understandings of public space while eliciting emotional and psychological statements of belonging and identity in time and place. The LL text was never neutral. Owing to the diverse backgrounds and experiences of the participants, interpretations and responses to the LL were varied and deeply connected to their own personal and professional identities as well as individual ethnic, linguistic and cultural orientations. These results substantiated Hanauer's (2003, 2006) assertion that meanings are not fixed, but reside within the individual who is in the center of competing and imposed social discourses. With this research tool, attention to the complexities of public language use, and the multiple meanings and individual interpretations of the LL was possible. However, more systematic data collection procedures should be developed to enable the researcher to compare and synthesize the responses for broader understandings.

In addition to the stimulus of the LL to trigger emotional responses, findings from this study illuminated a dynamic process of negotiation and co-construction of meanings through the interactions between the interviewer, the participant and the LL. Maintaining a critical dialogic approach, processes of meaning construction were identified and analyzed to provide the researcher with a system to track internalized thoughts – represented in self-reported statements triggered by explicit focus on the LL – as they were externalized and shaped through the dialogic interaction. While analyzing discursive processes proved to be very challenging, the current study's focus on the dynamic interactions provided rich layers of complexity for understanding the cognitive and emotional responses to the LL. Further development of this analysis approach is needed in order to more fully answer the questions posed in future studies investigating readership of the LL.

As for limitations, the participants in this particular study represented only a small sampling of the residents in Memphis and the selected sites provided only a partial picture of the linguistic diversity present in multilingual signage and multimodal literacies so widely dispersed throughout this urban space. As with many modern urban areas in the USA, Memphis is in linguistic transition and deserves a more thorough study of the LL. Nonetheless, 'walking tours' that focus on the LL in selected areas will provide the researcher with opportunities to open dialogue about this transition, to raise awareness to the potential benefits and resources embedded in multilingual communities and to take an active role in promoting and preserving multilingualism one individual at a time. To that end, it is important to continue assiduous investigations that explore local feelings and attitudes about multilingualism and linguistic changes in our urban communities, as local attitudes can either create obstacles or establish bridges for a global society.

References

Backhaus, P. (2007) *Linguistic Landscapes: A Comparative Study of Urban Multilingualism in Tokyo*. Clevedon: Multilingual Matters.

Barton, D. and Hamilton, M. (2005) Literacy, reification and the dynamics of social interaction. In D. Barton and K. Tusting (eds) *Beyond Communities of Practice: Language, Power, and Social Context* (pp. 14–35). New York: Cambridge.

Barni, M. and Bagna, C. (2009) A mapping technique and the linguistic landscape. In E. Shohamy and D. Gorter (eds) *Linguistic Landscape: Expanding the Scenery* (pp. 126–140). New York: Routledge.

Ben-Rafael, B. (2009) A sociological approach to the study of linguistic landscapes. In E. Shohamy and D. Gorter (eds) *Linguistic Landscape: Expanding the Scenery* (pp. 40–54). New York: Routledge.

Ben-Rafael, E., Shohamy, E., Amara, M. and Trumper-Hecht, N. (2006) Linguistic landscape as symbolic construction of the public space: The case of Israel. In D. Gorter (ed.) *Linguistic Landscape: A New Approach to Multilingualism* (pp. 7–30). Clevedon: Multilingual Matters.

Berger, J. (1972) *Ways of Seeing*. London: Penguin Books.

Blommaert, J., Collins, J. and Slembrouck, S. (2005) Polycentricity and interactional regimes in 'global neighborhoods'. *Ethnography* 6 (2), 205–235.

Bond, B. and Sherman, J. (2003) *Memphis in Black and White*. Charleston, SC: Arcadia Publishing.

Collins, J. and Slembrouck, S. (2007) Reading shop windows in globalized neighborhoods: Multilingual literacy practices and indexicality. *Journal of Literacy Research* 39 (3), 335–356.

Coulmas, F. (2009) Linguistic landscaping and seed of the public square. In E. Shohamy and D. Gorter (eds) *Linguistic Landscape: Expanding the Scenery* (pp. 13–24). New York: Routledge.

Dagenais, D., Moore, D., Sabatier, C., Lamarre, P. and Armand, F. (2009) Linguistic landscape and language awareness. In E. Shohamy and D. Gorter (eds) *Linguistic Landscape: Expanding the Scenery* (pp. 253–269). New York: Routledge.

Farrell, T. (2004) *Reflective Practice in Action*. Thousand Oaks, CA: Corwin Press.

Garvin, R. (2010) Emotional responses to the linguistic landscape in Memphis, Tennessee: Visual perceptions of public spaces in transition. PhD dissertation, Indiana University of Pennsylvania.

Garvin, R. and Hanauer, D. (2007) Migrant cityscaping: A visual essay of the linguistic landscape in Markham, Ontario, in the Greater Toronto Area. Paper presented at the Pennsylvania Canadian Studies Consortium at Indiana University of Pennsylvania. Indiana, PA.

Gee, J.P. (2005) *An Introduction to Discourse Analysis: Theory and Method* (2nd edn). New York: Routledge.

Goffman, E. (1963) *Behavior in Public Places*. New York: The Free Press.

Gorter, D. (2006) Further possibilities for linguistic landscape research. In D. Gorter (ed.) *Linguistic Landscape: A New Approach to Multilingualism* (pp. 81–89). Clevedon: Multilingual Matters.

Gorter, D. and Cenoz, J. (2008) Knowledge about language and linguistic landscape. In J. Cenoz and N.H. Hornberger (eds) *Encyclopedia of Language and Education* (2nd edn) (pp. 343–355). New York: Springer.

Gubrium, J.F. and Holstein, J.A. (2002) From the individual interview to the interview society. In J.E. Gubrium and J.A. Holstein (eds) *Handbook of Interview Research: Context and Method* (pp. 1–32). Thousand Oaks, CA: Sage.

Hanauer, D. (2003) Multicultural moments in poetry: The importance of the unique. *The Canadian Modern Language Review/La Revue canadienne des langues vivantes* 60 (1), 69–87.

Hanauer, D. (2006) Narrative, multiculturalism and migrants: A proposal for a literacy policy. In D. Schram, J. Hakemulder and A. Raukema (eds) *Promoting Reading in a Multicultural Society* (pp. 164–175). Utrecht, Netherlands: Stichting Lezen.

Hanuaer, D. (2009) Transnationalizing and historicizing contested place: Graffiti at Abu Dis partially in the municipality of Jerusalem. Paper presented at the Siena Linguistic Landscape Workshop. University for Foreigners of Siena, Italy.

Harré, R. and Van Langenhove, L. (1999) *Positioning Theory.* Oxford: Blackwell Publishers.

Huebner, T. (2009) A framework for the linguistic analysis of linguistic landscapes. In E. Shohamy and D. Gorter (eds) *Linguistic Landscape: Expanding the Scenery* (pp. 70–87). New York: Routledge.

Hult, F. (2009) Language ecology and linguistic landscape analysis. In E. Shohamy and D. Gorter (eds) *Linguistic Landscape: Expanding the Scenery* (pp. 88–104). New York: Routledge.

Kress, G. and Van Leeuwen, T. (1996) *Reading Images: The Grammar of Visual Design.* London: Routledge.

Landry, R. and Bourhis, R.Y. (1997) Linguistic landscape and ethnolinguistic vitality: An empirical study. *Journal of Language and Social Psychology* 16 (1), 57–76.

Malinowski, D. (2009) Authorship in the linguistic landscape: A multimodal-performative view. In E. Shohamy and D. Gorter (eds) *Linguistic Landscape: Expanding the Scenery* (pp. 107–125). New York: Routledge.

Pavlenko, A. (2003) 'I feel clumsy speaking Russian': L2 influence on L1 in narratives of Russian L2 users of English. In V. Cook (ed.) *Effects of the Second Language on the First* (pp. 32–61). Clevedon: Multilingual Matters.

Pavlenko, A. (2005) *Emotions and Multilingualism.* New York: Cambridge University Press.

Peck, C. (2007, 6 May) Say hello to our Hispanic future. Newspaper editorial. *The Commercial Appeal*, Memphis, TN.

Pennycook, A. (2001) *Critical Applied Linguistics: A Critical Introduction.* Mahwah, NJ: Lawrence Erlbaum Associates.

Pennycook, A. (2009) Linguistic landscapes and the transgressive semiotics of graffiti. In E. Shohamy and D. Gorter (eds) *Linguistic Landscape: Expanding the Scenery* (pp. 302–312). New York: Routledge.

Schön, D. (1983) *The Reflective Practitioner: How Professionals Think in Action.* London: Temple Smith.

Scollon, R. and Scollon, S. (2003) *Discourses in Place: Language in the Material World.* London: Routledge.

Shohamy, E. and Gorter, D. (2009) *Linguistic Landscape: Expanding the Scenery.* New York: Routledge.

Shohamy, E. and Waksman, S. (2009) Linguistic landscape as an ecological arena: Modalities, meanings, negotiations, education. In E. Shohamy and D. Gorter (eds) *Linguistic Landscape: Expanding the Scenery* (pp. 313–331). New York: Routledge.

Spolsky, B. (2009) Prolegomena to a sociolinguist theory of public signage. In E. Shohamy and D. Gorter (eds) *Linguistic Landscape: Expanding the Scenery* (pp. 25–39). New York: Routledge.

Spolsky, B. and Cooper, R. (1991) *The Languages of Jerusalem.* Oxford: Clarendon Press.

Törrönen, J. (2002) Semiotic theory on qualitative interviewing using stimulus texts. *Qualitative Research* 2 (3), 343–362.

Tuan, Y.F. (1993) *Passing Strange and Wonderful: Aesthetics, Nature and Culture.* Washington, DC: Island Press.

US Census Bureau (2007) American Community Survey: Memphis, Tennessee. On WWW at http://www.census.gov/acs/www/index.html.

Part 5

Multiculturalism in Linguistic Landscape

Chapter 15

Linguistic Landscape and Language Diversity in Strasbourg: The 'Quartier Gare'

FRANÇOIS BOGATTO and CHRISTINE HÉLOT

Introduction

The aim of this chapter is to propose a first empirical study of the linguistic landscape (LL) of the French city of Strasbourg. We have chosen to explore the notion of multilingualism in this specific urban space using two approaches: (1) linguistic landscape (Landry & Bourhis, 1997) and (2) urban sociolinguistics (Calvet, 1994; Bulot & Messaoudi, 2003). We know that the linguistic diversity in cities is forever changing, and the city of Strasbourg, although officially monolingual, is no exception and cannot be impervious to the process of language contact. Indeed, as in most cities in the world, different linguistic varieties, either endogenous or exogenous, coexist in this given space. In the present study, we attempt to explore this aspect of multilingualism as it manifests itself through examples of 'urban writing', and to analyse the relationships of power both at the social and symbolic level between the different languages displayed. Like other researchers before us (Shohamy & Gorter, 2009: 3), we assume that language in the environment is not arbitrary and random; 'rather there is a goal to understand the system, the messages it delivers or could deliver, about societies, people, the economy, policy, class, identities, multilingualism, multimodalities, forms of representation and additional phenomena'.

In our attempt to analyse what written signs might say about Strasbourg, we were first faced with the problem of sampling (Gorter, 2006) and decided to limit our research to the analysis of one component of the LL, i.e. commercial signs on shop fronts in one specific area known as 'Quartier Gare'. This quartier[1] presents interesting particularities for our study: it is an old area, with a multi-ethnic population of mixed socio-economic status; according to the census figures of 1999 (INSEE), among the 12,000 inhabitants, almost 1,700 are foreigners (13.5%). The quartier includes many small shops run by people belonging to immigrant communities as well as small businesses linked to the railway station (hotels, restaurants, cafés and employment agencies). Many commuters and tourists pass through this area everyday to reach the city centre.

As part of a corpus of bottom-up signs, these commercial signs will be envisaged as examples of individual discourses from the point of view of both their production and perception, thereby meeting particular objectives within a specific space. Thus, we will question the different ways in which these examples of urban writing reveal and express various forms of linguistic and cultural diversity, and whether their production and display can be envisaged as individual strategies of demarcation, identification and appropriation of the space concerned.

Theoretical Perspective

The specificity of urban contexts

When studying examples of urban writing such as commercial shop front signs, it is essential to take into account the specificity of the context in which they are displayed because it is the context that gives rise to their production and their perception. This is the reason why some researchers insist on the importance and particularity of the urban context in its relationship to the social dimension. For example, Sautot and Lucci (2001: 29) remind us that, 'alongside with the present expansion or urban spaces, contemporary urban centres are seeing the growing emergence of numerous written signs [...] produced in order to be read by one person or many people'.[2]

Therefore, because of the specificity of the urban context and notwithstanding all the possible definitions given to the notion of 'city', we believe it is still necessary to start from one minimal definition. Our approach is twofold: firstly it stresses the complexity and heterogeneity inherent in urban spaces and secondly, the double dimension of cities. If we take into account the distinction Lefebvre (1968: 92) made between 'habitat' and 'to inhabit' (in the sense of 'to live in'), the city can only be studied as an entity referring to two kinds of reality: 'on the one hand, a city is static, somewhat constrained, as least circumscribed for a certain period within material limits; on the other hand, a city is dynamic, composed of its inhabitants and of groups which relate to one another' (Stébé & Marchal, 2007: 9). Such a definition, even if minimal, stresses the social dimension, 'as far as it [the city] always produces and/or imposes some forms of identity in the same way as it creates necessary differentiations' (Bulot & Dubois, 2005: 3). This said, its inhabitants, administrators and other agents are aware that they belong to 'an entity which is uniform although complex, but which can be circumscribed' (Bulot, 1999: 21). This is the reason why urban identities or, more precisely, the means, strategies and motivations to express such identities or to display them through written signs, can be defined 'in relation to a quasi dialectical process between conjunction (the relationship to the community) and disjunction (the relationship to otherness)' (Bulot, 1999: 21).

From urban sociolinguistics to the study of the linguistic landscape

Since the beginning of the 1990s, some researchers in France have been developing a new domain of research close to the sociolinguistics of discourse, which is referred to as 'urban sociolinguistics'. For them, the city is more than a place of study, it is a complex, heterogeneous and social entity that demands to be problematised as such. We owe the first publications in this area to Calvet (1990, 1994), who studied multilingualism mainly in African cities, and later on to Bulot (1999, 2001, 2003), who theorised this kind of research further when he studied the two French cities of Rennes and Rouen. Urban sociolinguists analyse the linguistic practices of speakers in cities, the way they use their languages, and how the languages in question are distributed in the urban space as well as how they construct and define borders within the city. In a somewhat similar approach, a recent study by Barni (2008) looked at the way migrant group languages in Italy enter into the Italian LL and the effect they have on this linguistic space; she explains: 'The relationship with the physical territory is thus not only one of support or surroundings, a simple panorama in which the immigrant languages can be seen, but is itself a factor in the construction of the significance of these languages'.

Because this domain of research insists on taking into account the complexity of the urban context, we would argue it is relevant for our study in Strasbourg. Therefore, we do not envisage the city solely as a space where languages are spoken, but also as a space where languages are displayed or more specifically written for a potential reader. As explained by Backhaus (2007), this implies a double dimension of production (LL by whom) and of reception (LL for whom), which means that urban signs are to be considered as discourses marked by practices, which in return mark these discourses as well. However, at this stage of our research we propose to focus mainly on the dimension of production and we can only suggest a first interpretation of a few signs from the reception point of view.

In order to analyse the diversity and heterogeneity of Strasbourg through the numerous examples of urban writings it offers, we also chose to investigate our context from the point of view of LL research and, like many other researchers, to start our analysis with Landry and Bourhis's (1997: 25) definition: 'The landscape of public road signs, advertising billboards, street names, place names, commercial shop signs, and public signs on government buildings combines to form the LL of a given territory, region or urban agglomeration'.

From the first studies (Rosenbaum *et al.*, 1977) to the more recent ones (Gorter, 2006; Backhaus, 2007; Shohamy & Gorter, 2009), specific attention has been paid to officially multilingual cities and regions and to the potential linguistic conflict linked to asymmetrical language varieties (e.g. Ben-Rafael *et al.*, 2006). Alongside these studies, others tend to look at officially monolingual cities such as Tokyo (Backhaus, 2007), Bangkok (Huebner, 2006), Basel (Lüdi, 2007), etc. We hope to contribute to this body of research with the present study on the French city of Strasbourg.

It is interesting to note that the research carried out in the domain of LL has not had much of an echo with scholars in France, even if studies on the way linguistic signs mark the public space are not totally absent. As mentioned above, Calvet (1990, 1994) studied what he calls 'the graphic environment' of cities like Paris and Dakar, and more recently in Alexandria (Calvet, 2003). Then, Lucci *et al.* (1998) studied the city of Grenoble, Lajarge and Moïse (2005) studied Montpellier and Gonac'h (2007) focused on how the street names in the town of Vitrolles in the South of France were changed after the National Front won the municipality (see also Blackwood in this volume for LL research on regional minority languages in France).

Methodological Considerations and Data Collection

The city of Strasbourg is situated in the North East of France, on the left bank of the river Rhine. The main administrative bodies of the Alsace region are based there. Strasbourg is a border city with Germany, it has been the seat of the Council of Europe since 1949, of the European Parliament since 1992 (with Brussels) and it holds the title of Capital of Europe. With a population of 272,500 in 2005, it is placed seventh in population size in France. Its surface covers 78 km^2. Although officially monolingual the Strasbourg urban space is the site of much language diversity and contact between endogenous linguistic varieties (French, Alsatian and to a lesser extent German) and exogenous languages (languages of immigrant communities, English, etc.).

According to the last census carried out by the national census bureau (INSEE, 2001), the city consists of 12.9% immigrants; this figure is much higher than the national figure, which amounts to 5.6%, and the regional percentage of 7.2%. These immigrants originate primarily from North Africa (25%), Turkey (13%) and Germany (10%). As opposed to the 1960s when Italians immigrants were the most numerous, today few migrants come from countries such as Spain, Italy, Portugal and Algeria. Since 2000, most migrants in Alsace come from Turkey, Morocco and Germany.

As a micro context of cultural, social and linguistic mixing, the *Quartier Gare* lends itself particularly well to an analysis of linguistic diversity and the possible spatial delimitations, appropriation and construction linked to the production and display of urban written signs.

Based on Gorter's (2006) distinction between top-down and bottom-up signs, we chose to restrict our analysis to one component of the LL of Strasbourg, i.e. commercial or shop front signs. As opposed to top-down signs, which are the product of powerful institutions, we would like to argue that shop front signs as instances of individual discourses can help us to understand the individual strategies of social actors, in our case shop owners. Indeed, apart from very ordinary shops and services, written signs often give material clues to some expressions of identity, either local or global. To quote Guillorel (1999: 71): 'by naming a particular place or space, one makes it one's own and consequently one creates a territory'.

Moreover, Gorter (2006: 8) insists on the double dimension of these signs, which can have both informative and symbolic value. Indeed, one of the specificities of shop front signs is to constantly mix references to the products and/or services offered with some information about the identity of the author or owner, whether real or imagined (Malinowski, 2009). This is the reason why Lucci (1998: 169) considers shop front signs as paradoxical instances of writing: 'Any author, when s/he writes, must at the same time give information and introduce him/herself, thus identifying messages are interdependent to referential messages'. This ambivalent or paradoxical dimension of shop front signs has remained the focus of our attention for the analysis of the *Quartier Gare* in Strasbourg, because we believe it can provide us with some clues on how to study the way this urban area is marked.

The corpus of our study comprises an exhaustive collection of photographs of 'signs', which can be read from the street. It includes the 'signs' of the shop fronts in the 21 streets of the *Quartier Gare* as well as the area in front of the station and the corpus comprises a total of 272 photographs. In some cases, we have taken several photographs of the 'signs' on the same commercial unit, which means that for our analysis these photographs had to be categorised in 'units of analysis'. We did exclude some principles of categorisation based on the work of Backhaus (2007), and chose to follow the methodological approach used by Cenoz and Gorter (2006: 71), who explained that for their study: 'It was decided that in the case of shops and other businesses each establishment but not each sign was the unit of analysis, that is, it was considered "one single sign" for the analysis'. Following this principle, we ended up with a corpus of 170 'signs' on which we propose to base our analysis.

Analysis of the Shop Front 'Signs' in the 'Quartier Gare'

In order to illustrate the linguistic diversity that is displayed on shop front signs in the *Quartier Gare*, we approached the LL from the point of view of the various languages present. We considered both mono- and multilingual signs and apart from French, which unsurprisingly is clearly dominant, we found instances of the following languages: Alsatian, German, English, Arabic, Mandarin, Thai and Turkish. Rather than adopting a detailed quantitative approach (Ben-Rafael *et al.*, 2006), we focussed our analysis on more qualitative issues such as strategies of demarcation, identification and appropriation of space by the written sign.

A clear dominance of the French language as an expression of a local and global identity

It is not surprising to discover that the dominant language is French, which can be read on 87% (148 signs) of both mono- and multilingual signs. We see the dominance of French as a distinct expression of identification since, as explained above, shop front signs are a type of discourse, which holds specific referential values (Lajarge & Moise, 2005). Some of the shop front signs in our corpus clearly show through their denomination that their 'authors' (Malinowski, 2009) chose to refer to the local area. For example one sign, *Bazar de la Gare (sic)*, refers explicitly to the station area. Other marking strategies were used in shop signs where a clear reference was made to the street or area where it was located. We found eight examples illustrating this strategy: *Délice de la laiterie* (referring to the former milk factory), *Grill national* (referring to the boulevard, i.e. Faubourg national), *Pharmacie Sainte Aurélie* (referring to the nearby square and Church), *Optique du Faubourg* (referring again to the name of the boulevard), *Pressing Saint Jean* (referring to the local church), *Épicerie de la Bibliothèque* (grocery shop situated in front of the city library), *Restaurant Bar le 9* (situated at number 9 in the rue de la Course), *Brasserie La Course* (in the street of the same name rue de la Course) and *À la ville d'Andlau* (situated in a street called rue d'Andlau). This type of local and spatial identification of shop front signs can also express a regional or national reference, but always in terms of more or less proximity: for example *Hôtel du Rhin* refers to the Rhine River, *Hôtel des Vosges* refers to the Vosges Mountains nearby and *Garage du Midi* to the South of France.

It is interesting to notice that the French language is also used to express a reference to global spaces and more widely to cultural identity. For example, five signs refer to geographical items such as cities, countries and continents and clearly define the cosmopolitan identity of the *Quartier Gare*: *Restaurant L'Anatolie*, *Restaurant Le gourmet d'Afrique*, *Bolywood Bazar (sic)*, *Délices d'Asie*, *Bosphore*, *La boutique antillaise*, *Restaurant Ô Liban*, *Hôtel Bruxelles*, *Restaurant Le Cappadoce*. Many cultural and symbolic references can also be found as in *Restaurant Gandhi*, *Pizzeria Le Vésuve*, *Le sable d'or [the Golden Sand]* and *Bar Perestroika*.

The power of a proper noun

In order to identify and to distinguish themselves from other businesses in the area and for the purpose of marking their territory, some shop owners/authors resort to using either their family name or their first name. We consider this type of strategy as a direct expression of identity, whether real or imagined. The first objective of a proper noun is to identify a person, to distinguish him or her, to create a feeling of uniqueness and specificity. Lajarge and Moïse (2005: 109) remind us that a proper noun with no special signification begs the question of who we are. This strategy of identification can be found in ten signs in our corpus, all of them monolingual: *Annie coiffure, Boucherie Scherrer, Laura cosmétique, Raphaël coiffeur, Serrurerie centrale Scherer, Pâtissier-chocolatier Heiligenstein, Boulangerie-pâtisserie Jean-Philippe, Jade esthétique, Restaurant chez Michel* and *Restaurant au Hohwald/Chez Martine et Patrick*. We noticed that all the shops concerned here are small local businesses and we believe that the dominant display of first names suggest more proximity and a potential complicity. In this case, it would be interesting to carry out further research linking the production and the reception of such signs and to investigate whether the affective dimension expressed does play a part in the reception of such signs. More specifically, a linguistic approach would question the syntax of the sign whether the first name is placed first or second and how the order of the elements in the sign could reveal a preference for the identity of the owner/author or for the nature of the shop.

Puns, the apostrophe, shortening of words and elision: Towards a personal appropriation of language

Because shop front signs use specific syntactic structures in order to be different from one another, they offer examples of further linguistic strategies such as puns, creative use of the apostrophe or the shortening of words. These strategies are somewhat similar to those used in advertising and 'then the shop front sign becomes unique; it attracts the eye through the display of its uniqueness and thus its identity' (Sautot & Lucci, 2001: 30).

Although it is not very present in our corpus, language puns (Pires, 2001) are particularly interesting to analyse. We found only five examples of word play in monolingual signs and in signs with structures where borrowings from other languages, mostly English, appear. Examples of language puns in monolingual signs need to be explained: *Infinitif Coiffure* (Hairdresser's, the pun is in the word *infinitive* and its ending in *tif*, which means *hair* in French slang); *Bar atteint* is a very nice example of linguistic creativity (*atteint* means *reached* and the two words pronounced together mean to chat, to sweet talk, to spoof); *Raj Mahal* (an Indian restaurant, the pun being on *Raj* and its pronunciation in French meaning *rage*); *Disque tu veux* (a record shop, a phonetic pun using the word *disque* and meaning '*say what you want*'). Apostrophes, shortening of words and elisions can also be found in seven signs: *Italmod* (tailor), *Chez P'tit Gros* (restaurant), *Salon Coiff'tous* (hairdresser's), *Styl'Coiff* (idem), *Le p'tit break* (fastfood), *L'actif's bar* (bar) and *Troc'afé* (bar) (Figures 15.1 – 15.3).

Figure 15.1

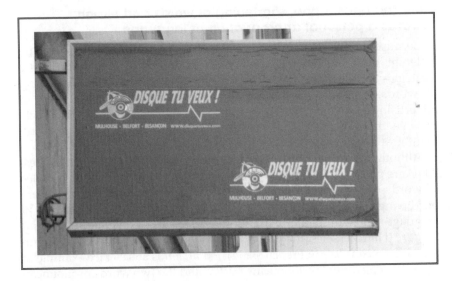

Figure 15.2

Figure 15.3

The specificity of these word plays and puns is that they give rise to different meanings that are ambiguous and where the different interpretations are produced not only at the linguistic, but also at the semiological level. Such puns can also be interpreted as examples of perfomativity: the authors of messages make their signs singular through the appropriation of language, in order to inscribe their own singularity in the urban space and in this way contribute to its structure. Moreover, we agree with Harris (1993) who explains that shop front signs should be envisaged at the intersection between the author's production (LL by whom) and the competences of the readers (LL for whom).

The place of the regional language

The regional language in Alsace is very commonly referred to as 'the dialect' or Alsatian. Nowadays, the different language varieties spoken in Strasbourg and in Alsace are envisaged along a linguistic continuum that spreads from standard French to standard German (Bothorel-Witz, 1997). We need to stress here that we are referring to examples of written signs in Alsatian as specifically different from standard German. In the same way as Lüdi (2007: 7) in Switzerland, studying the Basel LL said, 'Swiss German in Basel is not only spoken but written as well', we felt we could not analyse the LL of Strasbourg without taking into account the regional language, despite those who argue that Alsatian is not a written language (Huck *et al.*, 2008: 50). Therefore, as part of our study of an area where different languages are present, we believe the regional language should not be considered separately from other languages.

We found five examples of signs where Alsatian was displayed: '*A la ville d'Andlau Bierstub*' (meaning restaurant), '*S'Duwacklaedel*' (meaning tobacco shop), '*Le Schnokeloch*' (Brewery), '*Winstub Wynmuck*' (restaurant and brewery) and '*S'Zwilling Stuebel*' (restaurant). As a first remark, we note that the use of Alsatian in shop front signs is directly linked with the kind of service offered, since four out of the five signs refer to restaurants and more specifically to restaurants serving Alsatian specialities. The strategies underlying these signs are obviously linked to identity in the way the language is used, and in one case where it states explicitly a linguistic competence: e.g. one sign reads '*Mir rede Elsassisch*' meaning '*We speak Alsatian*' (Figure 15.4).

Even if the present study only takes into account shop front signs as examples of bottom-up signs, it is important to explain that next to the French language, Alsatian is the only regional language present on

Figure 15.4

top-down signs, as in street names, for example, in our area of study. Such signs are always bilingual and French always figures on the top part. As Blanchet (2005) explains, this is not a unique case since from the 1990s there has been a marked increase in road signs in regional languages in Provence, the Basque Country, Corsica and Brittany (see also Blackwood, 2008). Thus, it would be interesting to investigate further written signs in Alsatian, and to compare and confront the different strategies used to produce and to interpret these messages, both at the institutional and the individual level.

The German language in urban signs

Although Strasbourg is situated directly on the border with Germany and for obvious historical reasons German has long been part of the social life of Alsace, the presence of this language in our corpus was very limited, quantitatively and functionally. This argues for a further study of the LL in Strasbourg, which would include a larger area of the city than in the present study.

German could be found in four signs in our corpus and we noted that these signs were all multilingual: *Snack **Imbiss** Nemrut* (fast-food restaurant), *Brasserie Snack MOKA **Imbiss** Rapid* (brewery), *Le Muguet II **Imbiss-Snack*** (fast-food restaurant) and *Allmilmö **die phantastische Küche*** (a shop selling kitchens). Apart from the last example, the presence of German on restaurant signs can be explained by the strategy of 'LL for whom', meaning that it is intended for German tourists, all the more so since these three signs can be found in the same street, which goes from the station to the historic city centre. Therefore, we would like to argue that such a strategy has nothing to do with the authors of the signs ('LL by whom') wanting to mark or identify the given space, but rather simply by wanting to give some information to German-speaking foreigners visiting the city.

The English language

It is no surprise to find that English is very present, at least quantitatively in the LL of the shop front signs in Strasbourg. Indeed, after French, English is the second most present language. In other words, Strasbourg is no different from other cities such as Basel studied by Lüdi (2007), and many others. Even if the place and role of English has not been approached in the same manner in various studies, it is important to stress that the quantitative dominance of English in Strasbourg is not an isolated case.

We counted 26 signs where English was visible; among them only three were monolingual. Within our corpus, English does not seem to be used primarily for information purposes, it is easy to understand and used more with a connotative function. As Piller (2003: 174) writes: 'The audience can recognise that the message is in English and this activates values such as international orientation, future orientation, success, sophistication or fun'. Indeed, we know that English brings up images of modernity and a sense of being fashionable, therefore it is not surprising to find it in shops selling clothes or mobile phones, as well as in bars. Five signs referred to clothes (*Sportwear Kayshop, Feeling, General Store, Urban street* etc.), eight signs to restaurants/bars (*Dream's, Oriental Lounge, Jo and Jimmy's club*) and two signs to shops selling phones or offering photocopies and new technological appliances (*Call phone, Top print,* etc.).

The languages of immigration: Languages from Asia and Arabic

Languages from Asia, i.e. Mandarin and Thai and Arabic are present on six multilingual signs and more precisely on five restaurants and one Asian supermarket. Arabic is present on three signs (two grocery stores and a phone shop). In such cases, Lucci and Millet (1998) make a distinction between a knowledgeable and a non-knowledgeable public and such a distinction can help to understand the strategies used to mark, identify and appropriate one's space. For the non-knowledgeable public who do not have the necessary linguistic competence to decode

Figure 15.5

the message, the presence of languages from Asia or of Arabic holds a more decorative function, since the main name of the shop does appear in another language; however, the use of these languages can also be deictic and simply meant to incite customers. Therefore, it is not the content of the message, which is important, but rather its presence that brings to mind distant lands and a certain exoticism, all the more since it is always made explicit by meta discursive language, e.g. *Traiteur chinois, Spécialités thailandaises, Téléboutique, Boucherie Traiteur Alimentation*, etc. But when these messages are meant for a knowledgeable public, meaning people who know the language concerned, the strategy is to make the link to the community visible through the shop front sign or one of its components (Figure 15.5).

The case of Turkish or the power of the family name

As we explained above, proper names and more specifically family names are used first and foremost to identify and distinguish one person from another. Whether the family name corresponds or not to the real identity of the shop owner, because they appear 'to conform to a set of representations, connotations and associations which are shared by a social group' (Lucci, 1998: 172), they are noteworthy examples of marking and appropriating a given space. This is how the presence of the Turkish community could be identified through 11 signs in our

Figure 15.6

corpus, not through the display of a message in the Turkish language, but indeed through the use of the family name and its intended impact on the LL. This is particularly relevant to our study because it could be one of the specificities of the *Quartier Gare*, since this expression of identity through the display of Turkish names seems to be clearly assumed, whereas in other areas in Strasbourg it is not rare for Turkish shop owners to hide under less stigmatised identities such as a Greek one for example (Figure 15.6).

Conclusion

At this stage of our research, it is difficult to propose some clear concluding remarks. What we attempted to do in this study was to approach an example of urban multilingualism in one area in the city of Strasbourg, through instances of written language displayed on shop fronts. We decided to limit our study to one given area and to commercial shop front signs purposely. We tried to describe the LL of the *Quartier Gare* in as far as it could reveal the linguistic diversity of one part of the city and what it could signify for its inhabitants. We consider the specific area we chose as part of a complex and heterogeneous urban space where linguistic and cultural diversity could be displayed even in an officially monolingual context. Not only did we find a number of linguistic varieties displayed, but our corpus also contained a substantial number of multilingual signs, illustrating the growing underlying linguistic diversity of the city as well as different modalities of contact.

Even if our study argues for shop front signs to be envisaged as a form of individual discourse produced by an 'author', in our case a shop owner, and received by a reader, we are aware of Malinowski's (2009: 123) point that 'any readings of territorial or other far-reaching symbolic intent from code choice and positioning on signs may result as much from the *agency of landscape* as they do from the intent of any individual or group of people'.

As we hope to have shown, the production and display of such messages are in no way trivial or insignificant. On the contrary, they are used to mark a given space even if only symbolically, to make oneself out as different from others or to express one's identity in various ways and through different processes.

Obviously, our approach would need to be more comprehensive and should be followed by a comparative study looking at both institutional and non-institutional signs, as well as at both the production and reception of these various types of written signs without forgetting that they can include physical objects giving rise to multiple readings and interpretations. We should also undertake a study of the LL in other parts of Strasbourg and compare our data with that gathered in the *Quartier Gare*, in order to uncover the varying degrees of visibility of languages in the city as a whole. In the French context, a study of the LL in Strasbourg could bring a new understanding of the dynamic structure of this urban space – languages being part of this structure – and ultimately help us to go beyond the borders of these political, geographical and partly social entities referred to as *quartiers*. We would also need to further analyse the presence or absence, the concentration or dispersal of languages across the city, on the basis of urban writings as concrete manifestations of asymmetrical language contacts.

Finally, because the presence of languages cannot be separated from the context of their display, we feel it is necessary to approach the LL from the viewpoint of its impact on the urban space while recognising that the urban space also constructs the LL, at least in parts. This is the reason why we chose to cross our approach of the LL with some of the theories of urban sociolinguistics.

Notes

1. The notion of *'quartier'* in French is difficult to translate into English. It refers to a specific area within a city, clearly delimited by certain streets, e.g. the Latin Quarter in Paris. The city of Strasbourg is officially divided into 14 *'quartiers'* for administrative management.
2. Our translation of: 'Les centres urbains contemporains se caractérisent par l'émergence – qui va croissant avec l'extension urbaine contemporaine – de nombreux écrits... conçus pour être lus par une ou plusieurs personnes, dans un contexte urbain'. All further quotes from French or Swiss German authors are also translated by us.

References

Backhaus, P. (2006) Multilingualism in Toyo: A look into the linguistic landscape. *International Journal of Multilingualism* 3 (1), 52–66.
Backhaus, P. (2007) *Linguistic Landscapes: A Comparative Study of Urban Multilingualism in Tokyo*. Clevedon: Multilingual Matters.
Barni, M. (2008) Mapping immigrant languages in Italy. In M. Barni and G. Extra (eds) *Mapping Linguistic Diversity in Multicultural Contexts* (pp. 217–244). New York: Mouton de Gruyter.
Ben-Rafael, E., Shohamy, E., Amara, M.H. and Trumper-Hecht, N. (2006) Linguistic landscape as symbolic construction of the public space: The case of Israel. *International Journal of Multilingualism* 3 (1), 7–30.
Blackwood, R.J. (2008) *The State, The Activists, The Islanders: Language Policy on Corsica*. Amsterdam: Springer.
Blanchet, P. (2005) Usages actuels du provençal dans la signalétique urbaine en Provence: motivations, significations et enjeux sociolinguistiques. *Revue de l'Université de Moncton. Signalétiques et signalisations linguistiques et langagières des espaces de villes (configurations et enjeux sociolinguistiques)* 36 (1), 255–287.
Bothorel-Witz, A. (1997) Nommer les langues en Alsace. In A. Tabouret-Keller (ed.) *Le nom des langues, I. Les enjeux de la dénomination des langues* (pp. 117–142). Louvain-La-Neuve: Peeters.

Bulot, T. (ed.) (1999) *Langue urbaine et identité. Langue et urbanisation linguistique à Rouen, Venise, Berlin, Athènes et Mons.* Paris: L'Harmattan.

Bulot, T., Bauvois, C. and Blanchet, P. (eds) (2001) Sociolinguistique urbaine (Variations linguistiques: images urbaines et sociales). *Cahiers de Sociolinguistique 6.* Rennes: Presses Universitaires de Rennes 2.

Bulot, T. and Dubois, L. (2005) Avant-propos. *Revue de l'Université de Moncton. Signalétiques et signalisations linguistiques et langagières des espaces de villes(configurations et enjeux sociolinguistiques)* 36 (1), 3–7.

Bulot, T. and Messaoudi, L. (eds) (2003) *Sociolinguistique urbaine (Frontières et territoires).* Cortil-Wondon: Editions Modualires Européennes.

Calvet, L.-J. (1990) Des mots sur les murs. Une comparaison entre Paris et Dakar. In R. Chaudenson (ed.) *Des langues et des villes (Actes du colloque international à Dakar, du 15 au 17 décembre 1990* (pp. 73–83). Paris: Agence de coopération culturelle et technique.

Calvet, L.-J. (1994) *Les voix de la ville. Introduction à la sociolinguistique urbaine.* Paris: Editions Payot & Rivages.

Calvet, L.-J. (2003) Le plurilinguisme alexandrin. In T. Bulot and L. Messaoudi (dirs.) *Sociolinguistique urbaine (Frontières et territoires)* (pp. 15–53). Cortil-Wondon: Editions Modulaires Européennes.

Cenoz, J. and Gorter, D. (2006) Linguistic landscape and minority languages. *International Journal of Multilingualism* 3 (1), 67–80.

Gonac'h, J. (2007) Pratique de redénomination des rues à Vitrolles. In G. Cislaru, O. Guérin, K. Morim, E. Née, T. Pagnier and M. Veniard (eds) *L'acte de nommer. Une dynamique entre langue et discours* (pp. 101–112). Paris: Presses Sorbonne Nouvelle.

Gorter, D. (2006) Introduction: The study of linguistic landscape as a new approach to multilingualism. *International Journal of Multilingualism* 3 (1), 1–6.

Guillorel, H. (1999) Toponymie et politique. In S. Hakim (ed.) *Noms et re-noms: ladénomination des personnes, des populations, des langues et des territoires* (pp. 61–91). Rouen: Publications de l'Université de Rouen.

Harris, R. (1993) *La sémiologie de l'écriture.* Paris: Presses du CNRS.

Huck, D., Bothorel-Witz, A. and Geiger-Jaillet, A. (2008) L'Alsace et ses langues. Eléments de description d'une situation sociolinguistique en zone frontalière. In A. Abel, M. Stuflesser and L. Voltmer (eds) *Aspects of Multilingualism in European Border Regions* (pp. 14–100). Bozen-Bolzano: EUR.AC Research.

Huebner, T. (2006) Bangkok's linguistic landscapes: Environmental print, codemixing and language change. *International Journal of Multilingualism* 3 (1), 31–51.

Lajarge, R. and Moïse, C. (2005) Enseignes commerciales, traces et transition urbaine. Quartier de Figuerolles, Montpellier. *Revue de l'Université de Moncton. Signalétiques et signalisations linguistiques et langagières des espaces de villes (configurations et enjeux sociolinguistiques)* 36 (1), 97–127.

Landry, R. and Bourhis, R.Y. (1997) Linguistic landscape and ethnolinguistic vitality: An empirical study. *Journal of Language and Social Psychology* 16, 23–49.

Le Calonnec, V. (2001) Les étrangers en Alsace. On WWW at http://www.insee.fr/fr/insee_regions/alsace/themes/cpar04_2.pdf. Accessed 30.8.09.

Lefebvre, H. (1968) *Le droit à la ville.* Paris: Editions Anthropos.

Lucci, V. (1998) En quête d'une identité. In V. Lucci (dir.), A. Millet, J. Billiez, J.-P. Sautot and N. Tixier (eds) *Des écrits dans la ville. Sociolinguistique d'écrits urbains: l'exemple de Grenoble* (pp. 166–217). Paris: L'Harmattan.

Lucci, V. (dir.), Millet, A., Billiez, J., Sautot, J.P. and Tixier, N. (1998) *Des écrits dans la ville. Sociolinguistique d'écrits urbains: l'exemple de Grenoble.* Paris: L'Harmattan.

Lüdi, G. (2007) Basel: einsprachig und heteroglissisch. *Zeitschrift für Literaturwissenschaft und Linguistik* 148, 132–157.

Malinowski, D. (2009) Authorship in the linguistic landscape. A multimodal-performative view. In E. Shohamy and D. Gorter (eds) *Linguistic Landscape Expanding the Scenery* (pp. 107–125). New York, London: Routledge.

Piller, I. (2003) Advertising as a site of language contact. *Annual Review of Applied Linguistics* 23, 170–183.

Pires, M. (2001) Leçons de Gramm'hair: fonctions de l'apostrophe dans l'onomastique commerciale. *Langage et Société* 91, 59–86.

Rosenbaum, Y., Nadel, E., Cooper, R.L. and Fishman, J.A. (1977) English on Keren Kaymet Street. In J.A. Fishman, R.L. Cooper and A.W. Conrad (eds) *The Spread of English* (pp. 179–196). Rowley, MA: Newbury House.

Sautot, J.P. and Lucci, V. (2001) Lire dans l'espace urbain: les paradoxes des enseignes commerciales. *Langage et Société* 96, 29–44.

Shohamy, E. and Gorter, D. (eds) (2009) *Linguistic Landscape. Expanding the Scenery.* New York, London: Routledge.

Spolsky, B. and Cooper, R.L. (1991) *The Languages of Jerusalem.* Oxford: Clarendon Press.

Stébé, J.M. and Marchal, H. (2007) *La sociologie urbaine.* Paris: Presses Universitaires de France.

Chapter 16

Marking France's Public Space: Empirical Surveys on Regional Heritage Languages in Two Provincial Cities

ROBERT J. BLACKWOOD

There are many different perspectives that research into France's linguistic landscape (LL) can take, given the State's long history of an explicit language ideology privileging the national standard language over various (real or perceived) rivals, including the regional heritage languages (RHLs) and English. The long-standing and well-documented pursuit of language management strategies to manipulate language practices in favour of French has meant that France has distinguished itself as, in Spolsky's (2004: 83) words, 'the paradigmatic case for strong ideology and management'. Through various reigns, revolutions and renaissances, France repeatedly commits itself to ensuring the hegemony of the standard language over all comers, meaning that, throughout the 20th century, language management strategies were pursued to govern the use of language in and beyond the public space.

Language Ideology

The backcloth on which all LL research in France is projected is the 20th-century legislation that, effectively, criminalises public language practices that defy this ideology (see, e.g. Adamson, 2007: 26–29; Blackwood, 2008: 74–76; Judge, 2007: 28–30). The Toubon law of 1994 was presented as providing protection for French in public life, including work and employment, education, research, the media and advertising (Adamson, 2007: 27), requiring the use, primarily, of French in these domains, wherever possible. Although the Toubon law was glossed as targeting the insidious threat posed to the position of French by English, Judge (2000: 75) notes that it 'made no concessions to the regional languages', of which France boasts several. Despite the fact that the actual number of these languages is not without controversy, France's centre-right government proposed a change to the country's constitution, which acknowledged the RHLs as part of the national heritage of France. This passed into law in July 2008, without specifically naming the actual languages. It is generally accepted that there are seven principal RHLs in

European France: Flemish, Alsatian, Occitan, Corsican, Catalan, Basque and Breton.[1] The opportunities offered by the LL for evaluating the vitality, the presence and the use of the RHLs in the cities most closely identified with them needs to be considered in the context of this long history of an explicit ideology privileging the national standard language, and of sustained language management strategies to change the practices (and beliefs) of the different ethnolinguistic communities. Using data collected from a study of the LL in France, this chapter will examine the relationship between the city and the RHL of the region.

The interest in the city from the perspective of research into the LL lies in the acknowledgement of the city as a space for linguistic diversity. Dorier-Apprill and van den Avenne (2002: 151) reason that 'The city, a place of heterogeneity and the existence of different languages, is in fact the privileged space in which to observe daily multilingual language practices, above all through the observation of social practices'. The existence of historical ethnic communities in France, despite the State's assertions to the contrary,[2] persists and is posited on a number of factors, enumerated by Mac Giolla Chríost (2007: 153): 'Its key features are the ascription of a collective proper name for the group, a myth of common ancestry, shared historical memories, various peculiar elements of common culture, an association with a homeland and a sense of solidarity'. In addition to these characteristics, we can add a bond, of varying strength, between the group and the RHL, thereby creating an ethnolinguistic community. This project sets out, therefore, to establish the extent to which the two ethnolinguistic communities in France – the Bretons and the French Catalans – mark the public space of their cites in order to evaluate their position and status as discrete groups or communities.

Rennes and Perpignan: A Case Study

The research project discussed here analyses the LL of two French provincial cities, each at the heart (in practice, if not in terms of official recognition) of a region strongly identified with a RHL. In the context of France, the term 'region' should be handled with caution, since it is a legal entity created in 1972 (and reshaped in 1982) to refer to an administrative area with an elected chamber with limited powers. Henceforth, we shall use the term 'region' to refer to this kind of administrative area. In the north-west corner of France, Rennes, with a population of approximately 212,000 inhabitants (according to INSEE, France's national institute for statistical information), is the principal city of the region of Brittany. In the south-west of France, Perpignan (population: 105,096) is the cultural centre of French Catalonia, whereas the capital of the region in which the Catalan-speaking community lives, Languedoc-Roussillon, is Montpellier, within the boundaries of a different ethnolinguistic area.

To use cities identified with France's RHLs for LL research, it is necessary to acknowledge the differences in the statuses and profiles of these locations in the context of the related ethnolinguistic communities. From the outset, it must be acknowledged that data on language practices in cities are not available; the French State does not permit official surveys of speaker numbers. The data on speaker numbers and actual language practices offered by researchers are usually a projection based on a sample survey, and refers to entire ethnolinguistic communities, rather than subsets of them. As such, there are no data on the number of Breton speakers living in Rennes, or the use of Catalan by the residents of Perpignan. However, this obstacle does not prevent the analysis of the LL of French cities identified with a RHL. For this study, the city of Perpignan is relatively straightforward to exploit since, in French Catalonia, it is unquestionably the principal city of the Catalan ethnolinguistic community, as described above. Its history has seen the city anchored in a notional greater Catalonia, with close cultural links to the Spanish autonomous region of Catalunya. Perpignan is France's thirty-first largest city and, in 2008, it enjoyed the accolade of being Capital of Catalan Culture. Perpignan's industry centres on agriculture, although the rate of unemployment is above the national average. The surveying of Rennes, however, is more complex: Rennes is the principal town of the region of Brittany in the political-administrative terminology, but its link to the Breton language is, in historical terms, more tenuous, despite its acceptance nowadays as the centre of the Breton-language revival. Historically, Rennes has been in a different linguistic zone, where Gallo, dismissed by some (according to Judge, 2007: 118) as a patois or as 'deformed French', was traditionally the RHL. Gallo, a Romance language with far fewer estimated speakers than Celtic Breton, and suffering from its relative closeness to standard French, does not enjoy the same status as Breton. Rennes is France's eleventh largest city, with a significant student population, where the average monthly wage is marginally above the national average.

Based on fieldwork developed by others, notably Backhaus (2007) and Ben Rafael *et al.* (2006), we developed a methodology for collecting data from the LL in mixed environments (namely, rural as well as urban centres), which is outlined in full in Blackwood (forthcoming). For this cities project, 10 survey sites were selected in the cities of Rennes and Perpignan. In Rennes, we counted a total of 5081 signs, whereas we recorded 4912 signs in Perpignan. In terms of commonalities, the national standard language dominated in both corpora. French appears on 4449 signs (91%) in Perpignan, of which 4403 (89% of the total number of signs) are monolingual in French, whereas in Rennes, French was recorded on 4749 signs (93%), of which 4697 (92% of the total) are monolingual. Given the context for the LL of France, namely, the 'strong ideology and management' identified by Spolsky (2004: 83), it is hardly surprising that French predominates in the public space. Although they are cities within areas identified with ethnolinguistic groups, Perpignan and Rennes both present themselves as French cities, with the national standard language featuring as the sole language in more than nine of every ten signs. From this perspective, the LL attests the widespread use of French, reflecting in practice the ideology of the French State as stated in the introduction to this chapter.

The Regional Heritage Languages in the City

This chapter, however, seeks not to analyse the visibility of French in peripheral cities, but to evaluate the presence of the RHLs, namely, Breton and Catalan, from the perspective of both monolingual and multilingual signs featuring the RHL. In Rennes, Breton features on a total of 33 signs (in the corpus of 5081 signs recorded in 10 sites), or 0.65% of the total number of signs recorded. In Perpignan, the total number of signs that include Catalan is 98, or 2% of all signs in the survey. The second shared attribute that can be inferred from this project is, therefore, that the RHLs barely figure in the LL of the two cities surveyed. If we contrast the extent of the presence of Breton and that of Catalan based on the 10 survey sites in both cities, it can be noted that Catalan appears proportionally twice as frequently as Breton. We will examine some of the key differences below.

The trends in the presence of the two RHLs in the LL are not identical. On the one hand, in Rennes, Breton is twice as likely to appear in a sign with French as it is on its own. On the other hand, Catalan is more than twice as likely to appear on its own in a sign as it is to appear alongside the national standard. This point requires further analysis, which requires the reinterpretation of the data using models proposed by others, to which we return below. To summarise the crude position of the RHLs in their respective cities, 66% of signs featuring Catalan are only in that language, whereas the proportion for monolingual Breton signs is 30% of signs featuring the RHL.

One of the aims of the wider project of which this is a part is to compare signs featuring only the RHL in France's cities. As part of this wider LL project, we devised a categorisation of signs, grouping all signs into one of nine divisions. We identified these nine categories in the light of Landry and Bourhis' (1997) two-function, five-category classification (on the one hand, communication, which is sub-divided into information, instruction and persuasion, and, on the other hand, symbolic function, either to declare ownership or express linguistic dominance), and sought to expand

Table 16.1 Monolingual signs in the RHL

Category of sign	Perpignan	Rennes
Business names	4	0
Business signs	3	0
Graffiti	0	0
Information	14	3
Instructions	0	4
Labels	0	1
Legends or slogans	35	1
Street signs	4	1
Trademarks	5	0

the categories to cover the different functions of signs recorded whilst limiting them to the fewest possible number of divisions for ease of use. The nine categories are enumerated in Table 16.1. In Perpignan, of the 65 monolingual signs, 4 were business names, 3 were business signs, 14 were signs conveying information, 35 were legends, 4 were street signs and 5 were trademarks.

In Rennes, of the 10 monolingual signs in the RHL, 3 were classed as conveying information, 4 were instructions, 1 was a label, 1 was a legend and 1 was a street sign. Given the raw data, it is possible to interpret these signs and the comment they make on the RHLs in the public space. However, as brut figures, their significance is limited.

Top-down vs. Bottom-up Signs

At this stage, it is pertinent to reinterpret the data from a different perspective, namely, the model proposed by Ben Rafael *et al.* (2006), which seeks to evaluate the signs based on whether they are classed as top-down or bottom-up. In other words, if we re-examine monolingual Breton and Catalan, we can discern patterns in the management of the RHLs in the LL of Rennes and Perpignan. Ben Rafael *et al.* (2006: 14) reason that there are conflicting forces at work in the governance of the urban public space, and that this tension can best be understood as contrasting top-down with bottom-up language management. This project uses the definitions offered by Ben-Rafael *et al.* (2006: 14): 'The "top-down" LL items included those issued by national and public bureaucracies – public institutions, signs on public sites, public announcement and street names. "Bottom-up" signs, on the other hand, included those which were issued by individual social actors – shop owners and companies – like the names of shops, signs on businesses and personal announcements'. These definitions allow the researcher to evaluate differing motivations in the marking of the city, with a view to extrapolating across the wider ethnolinguistic areas.

If we look first at the monolingual signs in Rennes, top-down signs account for 70% of the 10 signs in Breton. The majority of these signs appear in 1 of the 10 survey areas, namely, the railway station in Rennes, and were put in place by the public transport company, STAR. These signs are three pieces of information and three instructions. The remaining monolingual sign in Breton is a street sign. The bottom-up signs in Breton are one label on a product, one legend (a sticker identifying the shopkeeper with the Diwan schools system) and one instruction on the door of a bank. In Perpignan, this proportion is reversed, with 89% of the monolingual signs in Catalan classified as bottom-up, and 11% of the 65 signs being top-down. The bottom-up signs include four business names, three business signs, 13 pieces of information, 33 legends and five trademarks. The signs that can be considered as top-down are four street signs, one piece of information and two legends, publicising Perpignan's status as Catalan Capital of Culture 2008. Although we are considering small corpora, which requires caution when drawing conclusions, it can be inferred that Catalan appears on its own in the public space more often because of the decisions and actions of 'individual actors' (Ben Rafael *et al.*, 2006: 14), rather than thanks to the language practices of public agencies, whereas this tendency is reversed in Rennes, where it is publicly owned bodies who are largely responsible for Breton's limited presence.

This method of evaluating signs does not only hold for monolingual signs, and we can approach those signs that feature both the national standard language and the RHL from this perspective. In Rennes, 21 signs that feature French and Breton were recorded, of which two are business names, two were labels and one was a piece of information, meaning that 24% of the bilingual French-Breton signs are bottom-up. The remaining 76% of signs, namely, 16 signs conveying information – again produced by the regional transport authority – are top-down. In Perpignan, there were 29 bilingual French-Catalan signs, of which over half (52%) are street signs erected by the city council, thereby qualifying as top-down. Furthermore, the city council is responsible for the logo for the city of Perpignan, which it produces in both French and Catalan, and 11 of these signs appear in this corpus. Only one bilingual sign can be considered to be bottom-up, and that is the sign outside a travel agency in Perpignan, giving the business name in Catalan but the business sign in French.

Bilingual Signs and a Language Ideology

Acknowledging the potential difficulties of seeking to identify wider trends from relatively small corpora, we suggest that bilingualism in the LL is sustained to a greater extent from a top-down perspective in both cities, although the statistics are more striking in Perpignan than in Rennes. In Rennes, as noted above, 76% of the bilingual signs are top-down, whereas this proportion rises to 97% in Perpignan. There is a greater tendency in Perpignan on the part of 'public bureaucracies' (Ben Rafael *et al.*, 2006: 14) to produce signs in both the RHL and the national standard language. In so doing, the city authorities conform to the much-publicised language ideology of the French State, namely, that the primacy of the prestigious national standard language must be assured, but that, as permitted by the Toubon law of 1994, other languages may appear alongside French. This officially sanctioned bilingualism in the LL merits closer examination, especially in Perpignan, given that there is very little evidence of bilingualism in French and Catalan being sustained by any private citizens in the city. In looking at this use of bilingual signs, the question of language ideologies and the LL must be considered. Sloboda (2008: 175) examines this issue in the context of Belarus, Slovakia and the Czech Republic, and notes that ideology can be controlled to a greater extent in signs than in speech. In Perpignan, we see the management of ideology by the public authorities with the representation of the city as an ethnolinguistic construct anchored in both a French and a Catalan sphere. This is illustrated by the sign used by the city authorities to represent Perpignan (Plate 16.1).

Plate 16.1 The official logo for the city of Perpignan

This sign, which appears 11 times in the survey area (and therefore constitutes 38% of the bilingual French-Catalan signs recorded in the city), identifies Perpignan as a Catalan city, first by the choice of colours. Red and yellow are widely recognised as the colours of Catalunya, and not only appear as the regional flag of the Spanish autonomous region, but are adopted in Perpignan to identify with a notional Catalan cultural area, as well as serving as the colours for Perpignan's rugby union team, USAP. In terms of the use of language, the focus of this chapter, the city's motto 'Perpignan, the Catalan' appears both in French and in Catalan, confirming Perpignan's double identity as a French and a Catalan city, although this sign must be considered in its wider context, namely, that of an overwhelmingly French city, where a majority of signs (89%, as stated above) are monolingual in French. There might well be investment on the part of the public authorities to represent Perpignan in signs as a bilingual city, but in terms of the citywide LL, this position is the exception rather than the rule. In terms of language practices, the majority of the city presents itself as francophone.

However, the positioning of the two languages is hierarchical and reflects the French State's ideology. At this point, it is important to consider the 'code preference system' devised by Scollon and Scollon (2003: 120). Considering elements such as position in the sign, as well as font (size, shape and colour), a hierarchy of languages can be established in multilingual signs. Given the State's commitment to the primacy of French, the sign produced by the 'civic bureaucracy' in Perpignan conforms to France's stated code preference. This places French, the national standard language, in the dominant, upper position, with Catalan in the secondary, lower position. This language ideology is reflected in 97% of all the bilingual French-Catalan signs, including the one bottom-up sign found outside a travel agency, which placed the business sign in French (albeit in a slightly smaller font) above the business name in Catalan. In this small corpus, the only sign to reverse this ideology is the business name on the wall outside the European Union office for the Euroregion of Catalunya, Languedoc-Roussillon and Midi-Pyrénées (Plate 16.2), which was the only EU-made sign encountered in French Catalonia.

Therefore, it can be reasoned that the State ideology for code preferences in multilingual signs is reflected in the small sample in Perpignan, except for the sign produced by the supranational body, the European Union, which places Catalan above (and, elsewhere in the sign, before) French.

In Rennes, the majority of the bilingual signs recorded (almost exactly three-quarters of this sub-corpus) are produced by the city's regional transport company, STAR (Plate 16.3). That these 16 signs are to be found in one location is, in itself, significant. At no other location in the

Plate 16.2 The plaque outside the European Union office

survey was there such a pattern for bilingual signs as in the underpass that links the national railway station with the city's underground train network.

Further research, not part of the formal surveying of the 10 sites in the city for this project, confirms that at none of the other metro stations is bilingualism in signage as consistently presented. It is clear, therefore, that in one metro station a decision was taken to make signs bilingual in both the RHL and in French. In these signs, the hierarchy adopted is comparable to that found in Perpignan, namely, that the position of the RHL is consistently subordinate to French as the national standard language. Moreover, unlike the sign that serves as the emblem for the city of Perpignan, these bilingual signs use a smaller font for the Breton language than for French. Here, therefore, the language ideology is represented in stronger terms, with the national standard not only placed in the dominant position, but the size of the font for Breton reinforces its secondary position.

For the bottom-up signs, namely, the two business names, the two labels and the one piece of information, the State's language ideology is not represented consistently. The business name in question here (Plate 16.4), which appears twice on one premises, is found outside a restaurant. The restaurateur places the Breton name for the business,

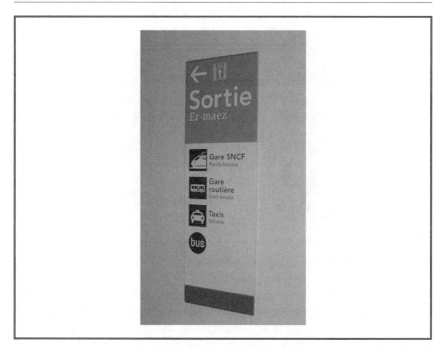

Plate 16.3 A sign in the underpass of Rennes' main railway station

Ouzh Taol, in the dominant central position of the sign, and in a considerably larger font than the French translation.

Moreover, the position of the French text is significantly minorised, running up the right-hand side of the sign. In terms of the visual aspect of this sign, the prominence of Breton is unquestionable, although we must be cautious if we choose to understand this prominence as a reflection of the power relationship between Breton and French. The Breton text here is a proper name, in that it is the name of the restaurant, and therefore its significance is possibly not as striking as it initially appears. Furthermore, although French has been relegated to a minorised position on the sign, its existence is important since it is the translation of the main text, as if it were a reference or a footnote. There are two possible explanations to infer from this footnote in French. First, the translation into French might be used to comply with the language ideology enacted in laws, such as the Toubon law, which requires the use of French where possible and/or necessary. Second, however, it might be argued that this translation is necessary in order to explain the text in Breton, suggesting that Breton, despite its significance in the local cultural identity, cannot – without the gloss in French – be understood by a majority. Under these circumstances, whilst Breton is visually dominant, French is functionally dominant,

Plate 16.4 The business name of a pancake restaurant in Rennes

in that Breton is communicatively subjugated to French. Such an interpretation is supported by the fact that the nature of the establishment, the business sign (explaining that the business is a pancake restaurant) is in French, further diminishing the significance and importance of the firm's proper name in Breton.

In terms of discerning trends, it is possible to note that there is a division in the presentation of languages in bilingual signs, with top-down signage conforming to the State ideology of privileging French above all other languages, even the regional heritage language that is indexed by the area in which the signs appear. Given that the majority of signs within this sub-corpus of bilingual signs in French plus the RHL are designed, produced and/or erected by civic bureaucracies, be they the city authorities or the regional transport system, it is possibly unsurprising that they conform in spirit and in practice with the ideology that French is the primary language of France and that, where multi-lingualism is tolerated, the position of French must be retained. However, this pattern is not uniformly followed by the bottom-up actors in the LL, who are, statistically, more likely to place the RHL in the prized dominant position.

Social Representation and the Linguistic Landscape of Cities

To conclude this examination of the position of France's RHLs in comparison with French in the LL of Rennes and Perpignan, it is useful to consider the application of social representation theories. Moscovici (2001) is most frequently identified with social representation, and he seeks to examine the individual through their social, cultural and collective surroundings. This theory is particularly pertinent for the examination of the LL and the interaction between the LL and those who engage with the city, either as residents, workers or passers-by. Augoustinos *et al.* summarise social representation theory thus:

> It attempts to understand how social processes impinge upon and influence the social functioning of individuals and groups. Social representation theory, however, does not separate the individual and society, but, rather, sees both in a dialectical relationship, in which the individual is both a product of society (its conventions, norms and values) and an active participant who can effect change in society. (Augoustinos *et al.*, 2006: 36)

It is not difficult to see how social representation theory can help inform our understanding of the LL. In this dialectical relationship, those who inhabit (or even merely pass through) the LL develop as individuals and communities partly in response to the city in which they find themselves. At the same time, these inhabitants, shopkeepers and workers manage the LL as an urban space on which to project and through which to reflect themselves, something that is facilitated by cities given their high density of individuals using the space for many different purposes.

In terms of the present study into the LL in two peripheral cities of France, we can exploit social representation theory to evaluate the LL of Rennes and Perpignan. We noted above how these two cities have differentiated themselves from each other in terms of the LL. Although both unquestionably francophone cities, an individual is twice as likely to encounter Catalan in the LL of Perpignan than Breton in Rennes. When discussing ways in which these cities present themselves, it is important to recall that cities are not animate entities, in that they do not act of their own volition. The LL reminds us that the urban space is manipulated by those who inhabit it, or who work there, or who administer the city, or who own property there. As such, the city appears as these individuals and groups make it appear, be that voluntarily, collectively, willingly or reluctantly. This management of the LL is one half of the dialectic relationship that underpins social representation theory, namely, that the urban space reflects the actions of those who can, for whatever reason, control the areas of a given city. This also allows us to examine whether cities, especially those identified with a RHL, express the LL in different ways, not only between themselves, but also in contrast to a wider national context.

To this extent, the fact that Rennes and Perpignan are overwhelmingly francophone cities, according to the findings outlined here, echoes the language practices and the language beliefs of those who manage the public space. These managers include shop-owners, graffiti artists, the local and national authorities, banks and major industries, as well as the residents who not only manage their own homes, but also participate in electing the civic bureaucracies that act on the voters' behalf. Therefore, the innumerable managers of the LL in Rennes and Perpignan choose to present their cities first and foremost as francophone spaces. These choices might well be motivated by the explicit State ideology of France, outlined above. However, through social representation theory, Augoustinos *et al.* (2006: 38) reason that this kind of representation is 'determined by tradition and convention'. Although French Catalonia and Brittany became part of France at different stages in the country's history, they – like other parts of France – have been subject to pressure to become French. The tradition and convention noted by Augoustinos *et al.* have privileged French and all its connotations, especially since the Revolution at the end of the 18th century.

The other side of the dialectic relationship is the changing of the public space by the very same managers outlined above who have reinforced the projection of the public space as profoundly French. Here, based on the evidence from the research into the LL of Rennes and Perpignan, we can detect another form of social representation in the form of the ethnolinguistic identities of the two heritage communities in these cities. In both cities, there are actors, from individual shop-owners up to the city authorities, who present Rennes and Perpignan as multilingual spaces. It should be noted, given the extent to which we have recorded the presence of the two RHLs in their respective LL, that this representation of multilingualism featuring French plus either Breton or Catalan, is very much the minority position. At the same time, this presentation of multilingualism is not uniform, and the cities differ in the extent to which the various managers of the public space use the RHL in addition to the national standard language.

From a top-down perspective, we have seen how the civic authorities in Perpignan seek to represent the city as a bilingual Franco-Catalan centre. Although the supremacy of French is maintained by granting the important, dominant space in the sign to the national standard language, the RHL is included. This is not the case for Rennes, which only presents the city name in its logo. There are reasons for this difference, not least the fact that Rennes, in the area described as Upper Brittany, has been historically a Gallo-speaking area, and the RHL for the city would have been Gallo. However, this is not reflected in the signage of the city, where we find Breton in use. Rennes is the principal city of Brittany and decisions have been made by the managers of the public space to identify Rennes with Breton, rather than Gallo. In this respect, the fact that Breton appears at all in the city's LL is striking, given that Breton is the RHL of a neighbouring area. What is equally noteworthy is that the regional transport agency, STAR, which operates in the greater Rennes area, chooses to place French-Breton bilingual signs in the underpass that links Rennes main railway station with its metro station. In the name of the civic authorities, STAR produces and erects both bilingual French-Breton and monolingual Breton signs, representing the wider public space beyond the metro station as both francophone and bretonnant.

The second element of the dialectical relationship that governs social representation is one that calls for diachronic research into the LL in these two cities. One method by which scholars can investigate the extent to which the individual is, in this context, a product of the conventions and traditions of the city, is to repeat this kind of survey work in Rennes and Perpignan some years hence, and again after a second interlude. This kind of longitudinal study would allow the LL to suggest the extent to which language practices change as a result of the representation of the RHL in the two cities. Future research questions include an evaluation of the extent to which the representation of Perpignan as a bilingual city encourages increased use of Catalan in the public space, as well as analysing trends in using Breton in a linguistic zone traditionally identified with another RHL.

Acknowledgements

The British Academy and the University of Liverpool Research Development Fund financially supported the fieldwork discussed in this chapter, for which I am particularly grateful. I would also like to record my thanks to Joan-Lluís Marfany, Paul O'Neill and Diana Cullell at the University of Liverpool for their assistance with the texts in Catalan, and to Ian Press for his advice on Breton. Finally, I am grateful to Marián Sloboda for his suggestions for the nuancing of some of the points made here.

Notes

1. At the end of the 20th century, the government-commissioned Poignant Report (Poignant, 1999) found that there were 20 languages spoken in mainland France, including some non-territorial languages, and a further 55 in France's overseas territories, hence the clarification that this chapter will focus on those languages spoken in European France.
2. See Blackwood (2008: 74) for a summary of the decision by France's Constitutional Council to rule against the acknowledgement in law of any communities in France other than 'the French'.

References

Adamson, R. (2007) *The Defence of French: A Language in Crisis?* Clevedon: Multilingual Matters.
Augoustinos, M., Walker, I. and Donaghue, N. (2006) *Social Cognition: An Integrated Introduction* (2nd edn). London: Sage.

Backhaus, P. (2007) *Linguistic Landscapes: A Comparative Study of Urban Multilingualism in Tokyo*. Clevedon: Multilingual Matters.

Ben-Rafael, E., Shohamy, E., Amara, M.H. and Trumper-Hecht, N. (2006) Linguistic landscape as symbolic construction of the public space: The case of Israel. In D. Gorter (ed.) *Linguistic Landscape: A New Approach to Multilingualism* (pp. 7–30). Clevedon: Multilingual Matters.

Blackwood, R. (2008) *The State, the Activists and the Islanders: Policy on Corsica*. Dordrecht: Springer.

Blackwood, R. (forthcoming) The linguistic landscape of Brittany and Corsica: A comparative study of the presence of France's regional languages in the public space. *Journal of French Language Studies*.

Dorier-Apprill, E. and van den Avenne, C. (2002) Usages toponymiques et pratiques de l'espace urbain à Mopti (Mali) – la toponymie entre linguistique et géographie. *Marges Linguistiques* 3, 151–158.

Judge, A. (2000) France: 'One state, one nation, one language'? In S. Barbour and C. Carmichael (eds) *Language and Nationalism in Europe* (pp. 44–82). Oxford: Oxford University Press.

Judge, A. (2007) *Linguistic Policies and the Survival of Regional Languages in France and Britain*. Basingstoke: Palgrave Macmillan.

Landry, R. and Bourhis, R.Y. (1997) Linguistic landscape and ethnolinguistic vitality: An empirical study. *Journal of Language and Social Psychology* 16 (1), 23–49.

Mac Giolla Chríost, D. (2007) *Language and the City*. Basingstoke: Palgrave Macmillan.

Moscovici, S. (2001) Why a theory of social representations? In K. Deaux and G. Philogène (eds) *Representations of the Social: Bridging Theoretical Traditions* (pp. 8–36). Oxford: Blackwell.

Poignant, B. (1998) *Langues et Cultures Régionales. Rapport au Premier Ministre*. Paris: La Documentation Française.

Scollon, R. and Scollon, S.W. (2003) *Discourses in Place: Language in the Material World*. London and New York: Routledge.

Sloboda, M. (2009) State ideology and linguistic landscape: A comparative analysis of (post) communist Belarus, Czech Republic and Slovakia. In E. Shohamy and D. Gorter (eds) *Linguistic Landscape: Expanding the Scenery* (pp. 173–188). Abingdon and New York: Routledge.

Spolsky, B. (2004) *Language Policy*. Cambridge: Cambridge University Press.

Chapter 17

Linguistic Landscape as Multi-layered Representation: Suburban Asian Communities in the Valley of the Sun

GERDA DE KLERK and TERRENCE G. WILEY

In this chapter, we present a case study of two suburban shopping communities in two cities that are contiguous with Metropolitan Phoenix in Arizona, USA. Metro Phoenix is also known as The Valley (of the Sun), and more technically refers to Maricopa County, the most densely populated and urbanized county in the desert state.

The purpose of our study is to (1) demonstrate the presence, use and vitality of minority languages in the linguistic landscape (LL) of a state where English is the official language, bilingual education in public schools is severely restricted and anti-immigrant policies are promoted; (2) present a broad and dynamic notion of the LL to capture through environmental print and artifacts the fluid, pragmatic and functional language use at our research sites; and (3) show how mapping the larger language environment surrounding our units of analysis can help us interpret how our data may be linked with communities of speakers in a policy environment hostile to the use of languages other than English.

Theoretical Approach

Given the multiple linguistic aspects we wanted to capture, and the interactions among these elements we were trying to uncover, we chose an approach to the LL that goes beyond studying signage in the urban landscape, but includes 'any sign or announcement located outside or inside a public institution or a private business in a given geographical location' (Ben-Rafael *et al.*, 2006: 14) as elements of the landscape. We framed our research drawing on Shohamy and Waksman's (2009) theoretical orientation that views the LL as a form of meaning construction in public spaces. Key to this approach is that multiple modes in the LL come together to construct such meaning. Shohamy and Waksman (2009: 318) add multiple modes to the baseline of eye-level public signage, such as 'clothing, fashion, architecture, industrial designs, food and cinema,... interfaces... as well as "people"... integrated into all

307

those modes'. In our study, we pay particular attention to product packaging, as well as to print materials circulating through the sites, making the print environment highly dynamic.

Cenoz and Gurter (2006) argue that the study of the LL can provide particularly useful information about the sociolinguistic context in which speakers of minority languages find themselves in a multilingual society. Findings can be compared with official language policies, as well as with language use as speakers of minority languages report it in surveys. Such comparisons can inform the understanding of the symbolic use of language in the LL and the power relations and negotiations between minority and majority cultures. In our study, we assess the vitality of minority languages in a region where language and immigration matters are highly contested and take on great symbolic value.

Background to the Research

This study developed out of our work on factors that contribute to the maintenance, vitality and visibility of heritage languages (HL). A number of socio-economic and political factors may be considered in assessing the linguistic vitality of community languages. These include: (1) number and density of speakers; (2) supply/re-supply through immigration; (3) closeness of homeland and ease of communication with homeland; (4) attitude toward the homeland and rate of return; (5) stability of immigrant community: growth/decay; (6) economic stability of the group; (7) socio-economic mobility of the group; (8) economic utility of mother tongue; (9) level of education in the mother tongue; and (10) intensity of group identity with mother tongue even in the face of discrimination. Among these, high-density urban clustering of HL speakers has been regarded traditionally as crucial to HL vitality (Baker, 2006). We can also expect these factors to influence the visibility of languages other than English in areas frequented and utilized by immigrants. And it is important to consider the disposition of the majority toward minorities, particularly at specific minority groups.

In 2000, Arizona voters passed 'English for the Children' (Prop. 203), which restricted bilingual education in public schools. In 2006, Arizona became the 28th state enacting English as the 'Official' Language, at the same time the state made it illegal to teach English to adult undocumented aliens in publicly funded adult English as a Second Language programs. Undocumented aliens (largely Spanish speaking) are estimated to make up 10–12% of the state workforce. Nevertheless, the state signed into law (effective January 2008) tough penalties for businesses knowingly or intentionally hiring undocumented workers, despite protests from the business community against this legislation. The state also has a 17-year-old court case, *Flores v. Arizona*, in which the Spanish-speaking plaintiffs charge that the state department of education does not provide enough funds to teach English to minority children in public schools.

Thus far, Spanish speakers, who are the largest minority group, have encountered the brunt of this xenophobia. Anti-immigrant sentiment has been directed at Mexicans who cross Arizona's common border with Mexico, who also experience class prejudice, as immigrants from Mexico generally have a much lower socio-economic status than any other immigrant group in the state. Interestingly, however, most of the attempts to restrict the use of Spanish have been directed at schools and not print in public spaces – although one may find letters to the editor complaining about the Spanish option in automated telephone systems. There have been no efforts to control non-English language signs, product packaging or other uses of environmental print, and strong use of Spanish signage along with English in high-density Latino neighborhoods persists. Likewise, there does not seem to be an effort to restrict non-English signs in stores, restaurants and other commercial spaces that are frequented by Asian immigrant groups, as was the case in California, in the 1980s when Asian minority communities there started to become more visible (Crawford, 1992; cf. Wiley, 2004), and New Jersey during the 1990s when Korean immigrants settled in the state in large numbers, and ordinances banning signs in shop windows in languages other than English were enforced only against stores with Korean signs (Andrew, 1997).

The small and dispersed presence of Asian immigrants in Arizona may contribute to maintaining the status quo of tolerance regarding public signage. Historically, multilingual signage representing minority languages has been common in high-density ethnic enclaves and ghettos, particularly in the case of Chinatowns in the USA and other countries. As Spolsky (2007: x) notes, 'Downtown areas it seems, can vary in their preferred languages (how else do we recognize a Chinatown in an American city?)'. This pattern was the case, and still is to some extent, for urban Chinese immigrant communities, in San Francisco, Los Angeles, New York, Chicago, to name a few. But a closer inspection of these high-density communities generally reveals that they are also hubs for other Asian immigrant groups, including Vietnamese or other ethnic Chinese minorities from Vietnam. Environmental print artifacts within shops and businesses in high-density Chinatowns often incorporate languages other than Mandarin Chinese or English. In a sense, these 'Chinese' urban spaces have served as multi-ethnic, multilingual hubs for Chinese immigrants and for other Asian immigrants as well.

More recently, however, with increased immigration among Asians into the USA, and secondary migration of Chinese and other Asian immigrants within the country, there is a more diffused suburban settlement of people of Asian origin. This is particularly the case in the greater Phoenix metropolitan area, where the first Chinese settled in the late 1860s, and except for the period between the mid-1870s and 1915 when a Chinatown existed in the downtown area, Chinese immigrants have been dispersed over the Valley, with an acceleration of this dispersion after WWII (Luckingham, 1994). One of the reasons Chinese immigrants initially moved into Arizona was because they did not experience in Arizona the violent treatment many Chinese suffered elsewhere in the American west. However, just as Mexican Americans in Arizona, they were regarded as second-class citizens, and experienced discrimination, segregation and exclusion from mainstream life in Phoenix. This changed after WWII, both because economic conditions improved, and because Mexican Americans and Chinese Americans had been part of the war effort. Even though discrimination and prejudice did not disappear, minority communities in Phoenix became more integrated into mainstream society. This increasing acceptance from the mainstream majority made it easier for a small community of immigrants like the Chinese to disperse over the Valley, whereas Mexican Americans, because of their numbers and longer presence had already carved out larger sections of the cities as ethnic enclaves (Luckingham, 1994).

General Strategy

Our focus is on ethnically oriented suburban commercial centers in the Phoenix metropolitan area that are hubs for linguistic social networks. We started this project by documenting aspects of the LL of the Chinese Cultural Center, a 'planned' ethnic site, self-consciously Chinese, and located near the international airport and major hotels, in a semi-industrial area. The center promotes its restaurants, market and ethnic arts shops as a site for a cultural experience and cultural events. Chinese characters are used along with traditional architecture to create the feeling of an ethnic cultural space. By contrast, there are more 'organic', commercial centers (that were established more naturally through market forces and not planned and then constructed) in the Phoenix metropolitan area that are hubs for linguistic social networks, and are located in more suburban areas. These 'organic' sites present a more fluid and vibrant linguistic picture than the Cultural Center does, and here we report on two such sites.

Lee Lee Supermarket in the city of Chandler (see Figure 17.1) was established in 1992, and is owned by a Cambodian Chinese immigrant. The store specializes in Asian, South Asian, Latin American, African, Caribbean and other ethnic foods, spices, artifacts and herbal medicines,

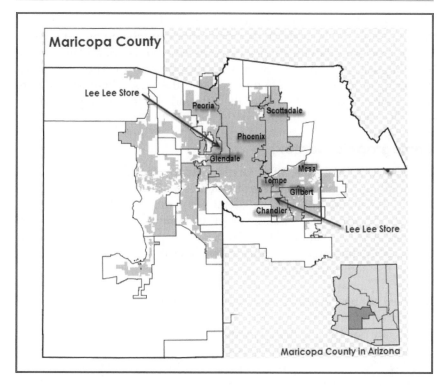

Figure 17.1 Maricopa County, where the majority of Arizona's population live. Adapted from Wikimedia Commons

from about 30 different countries. Inside the store, Chinese products and language dominate, but the clientele is a mix of various minority groups, and also includes Caucasian monolingual English speakers. A new Lee Lee store opened in May 2008 in the City of Peoria, 33 miles (53 km) northwest of the original Lee Lee, and also in a suburban area.

We use the two Lee Lee stores as 'anchors' or 'reference points' for sketching the landscape of interest. Each Lee Lee store is situated in a strip mall at the corner of a busy intersection. One key enterprise such as Lee Lee, as the major strip mall tenant, serves as a magnet for other ethnically focused enterprises, all of which become part of a functional network of HLs. The unit of our analysis is the *gestalt* (see Ben-Rafael, 2009) of the strip mall, seen from the street, seen from close-up inside the mall, and also at the micro level inside the store.

As described earlier, we believe that paying close attention to the distribution and density of speakers of HLs in relation to the sites under investigation (rather than just providing aggregate demographic information for a city or region) is necessary to gain more reliable insight into what the LL of a site suggests about relations among minority communities, and between these communities and the dominant culture. This is true especially in studies like ours where it is not apparent if the multilingual environment of a site corresponds to any residential clustering of minority communities around the sites, where we compare similar sites in different parts of the city, and where we are planning to study the sites longitudinally.

Demographic Context

Phoenix is now the fifth largest city in the USA. Phoenix and surrounding communities are located in Maricopa County, where 61.64% (3.7 million) of Arizona's total population of 6.04 million reside. Collectively, with Phoenix, these desert communities are euphemistically referred to as the 'Valley of the Sun'. Like other large metropolitan areas in the USA, this area is linguistically diverse even though English is clearly the dominant language.

Despite a rapid increase over the last decade in Arizona of the numbers of speakers of Asian languages, these speakers are still a small proportion of the total population. The purpose of this research is to investigate how visible these languages are, and how they are used, if at all, in public spaces where there is a presence of mainly Chinese, but also Tagalog, Vietnamese and Korean people, institutions and establishments.

Through the decennial US Censuses, as well as through the annual American Community Surveys (ACS) of the US Census bureau, language data are collected for the population aged five years and older.[1] According to the most recent (2007) of these data, Arizona has 5.7 million people aged five years and older, of which 3.6 million live in Maricopa County. In Arizona, 27.8% of this population speaks a language other than English at home, and in Maricopa County, 27.5%. The largest language groups in the state are Spanish, Navaho, German and other North American Indian languages (see Table 17.1). Demographic shifts in the state have led to speakers of Asian and Middle Eastern languages beginning to outnumber speakers of German, French and North American Indian languages. The four largest Asian languages in the state are Chinese (referring here to those who identified their language in the ACS survey as any of Chinese, Cantonese or Mandarin),[2] Tagalog, Vietnamese and Korean.

Chinese, with 74% of its 21,300 speakers residing in the Valley, is, after Spanish, the biggest minority language in Maricopa County, and the one that will be the main focus of our analysis. In addition, 66% of the estimated 16,000 Tagalog speakers in the state, 77% of the estimated 15,400 Vietnamese speakers in the state and 59% of the estimated 8,400 Korean speakers in the state, live in Maricopa County and these

Table 17.1 Estimates of speakers of 10 largest languages other than English for population five years and older, Arizona and Maricopa County, 2007

Arizona		*Maricopa County*	
(1) Spanish	1,233,306	(1) Spanish	771,060
(2) Navaho	85,658	(2) German	12,879
(3) German	23,377	(3) Chinese	12,194
(4) Other specified North American Indian languages	17,154	(4) Vietnamese	11,805
(5) Chinese	16,942	(5) Tagalog	10,706
(6) Tagalog	16,184	(6) French	9,639
(7) French	15,985	(7) Navaho	9,199
(8) Vietnamese	15,435	(8) Arabic	8,897
(9) Apache	11,473	(9) Hindi	6,256
(10) Arabic	10,828	(10) Polish	5,991

Note: Data based on sample. Estimates may vary from actual values due to sampling errors. As a result, the numbers of some languages shown may not be statistically different from the number of speakers of languages not shown. For the same reason, small differences in numbers of speakers of some languages may not be statistically different from each other
Source: 2005–2007 American Community Survey 3-Year Estimates micro data

languages are also included in our analysis. The total number of speakers of these four Asian languages in Maricopa is about 43,000, which makes up about 1.2% of the Maricopa population aged five years and older.

Geospatial Context

In order to establish the spatial relation of the HL communities in question in relation to the two Lee Lee stores, we used demographic data from the ACS, and some simple search and mapping techniques. To determine density and spread of speakers of Asian HLs, we used the ACS 2005–2007 raw data. The smallest spatial unit in the ACS is the Public Use Microdata Area (PUMA), each of which has a minimum population of 100,000. Typically, counties with large populations are subdivided into multiple PUMAs, as is the case for Maricopa County, which is made up of 22 PUMAs.

We combined speakers of Chinese, Vietnamese, Korean and Tagalog into one group, 'speakers of Asian languages', and found the highest density of these HL speakers in PUMAs 116, 120 and 121 (roughly corresponding to the cities of Tempe, Chandler and Mesa). Otherwise, the density distribution of speakers of the four languages above is similar to the density distribution for the Maricopa total population. Even though Tempe, Chandler and Mesa have relatively high concentrations of speakers of Asian languages compared to other parts of the Valley, these speakers still only make up a small section of the general population for those cities. PUMA 120 (Chandler) contains 13.4% of all speakers of Asian languages in Maricopa County; however, that is only 3.5% of the total population of the Chandler area. PUMA 121 (Mesa) contains 8.2% of all Asian language speakers in Maricopa County, which is 2.6% of the total population of the Mesa area; and PUMA 116 (Tempe) contains 6.1% of all speakers of Asian languages in Maricopa County, and these Asian HL speakers make up 2.3% of the total population of the Tempe area.

Lee Lee Peoria is diagonally across the Valley from the Chandler store, almost in the center of the area made up of PUMA 103 (roughly corresponding to the city of Peoria) and PUMA 104 (roughly corresponding to the city of Glendale). PUMA 103 contains 6.6% of all the Asian language speakers in Maricopa County, and those HL speakers make up 1.4% of the total population in the Peoria area; the Glendale area (PUMA 104) contains 3.4% of speakers of Asian languages in Maricopa County, and those make up 0.8% of the total population of PUMA 104 (see Figure 17.1).

In addition to establishing residential density, we also mapped locations where HL speakers were likely to congregate regularly. With Google Earth, we mapped ethnic-specific establishments by doing a simple search using Lee Lee Chandler first, and then Lee Lee Peoria, as reference point. For instance, for Chinese we mapped Chinese churches, community schools and traditional medicine services provided by individuals that could be identified as ethnically Chinese.

Geospatial Findings

There is some clustering of speakers of Asian languages, and Chinese establishments, in Chandler and Mesa, which is where Lee Lee Chandler is located. The density of both Chinese population and establishments is too low for this area to constitute an ethnic enclave. There is no clustering (yet) around the Peoria Lee Lee store.

Other than the higher density in the Chandler and Mesa areas, speakers of Asian languages are fairly evenly distributed through most of the remaining 19 PUMAs that make up Maricopa County and their distribution generally follows that of the general population. The northeast Valley and southwest Valley are densely populated, but here the density distribution of Asian language speakers dips slightly below the trend for the general population. The Chinese institutions we mapped are spread out across a broad band that cuts southeast to northwest across the Valley. Based on residential density, and the sites of institutions and establishments, Asian HL speakers, and Chinese speakers in particular, are dispersed over the Phoenix Metropolitan Area, even within the broad band that shows a relatively higher density of these communities. Traditionally, such urban dispersion has been considered detrimental to the maintenance and vitality of the HL and culture.

Data Collection and Organization

Our interest in collecting data at these sites started through casual observations when shopping at Lee Lee Chandler. We were struck by the increasing presence of multilingual signage as one entered the mall from the surrounding linguistically and architecturally bland suburban landscape. Signage around the mall is in English, and most establishments are franchises of national chains. The residential area around the mall can best be described as 'MacSubdivision', a clone of any lackluster, recently built, suburban housing development in any growing city in the USA.

We started our formal data collection by sketching a rough diagram of Lee Lee Chandler on which we made notes about the locations, types of languages and scripts of the signage. After getting permission to take pictures with a digital camera, we took wide exterior shots of the mall and stores, and on the inside of Lee Lee we photographed aisles, shelves, individual products and media and notices around the entrances. We did not conduct any interviews, and where we needed background data (e.g. circulation numbers) we contacted the relevant establishment via e-mail or telephone with an information request.

From our notes and observation, we had already formed a rough coding system for our data, and then coded our photographs accordingly. First, we delineated four levels of analysis (eye-levels) from macro to micro for our data (see Table 17.2, first column). Then we recorded for each level and sub-level ('Areas' in Table 17.2) if the signage originated internally or externally in relation to the site (the latter classification corresponding to Ben-Rafael *et al.*'s (2006) notion of bottom-up versus top-down flows in LLs). Since our core interest was in the interplay of HLs with English, we noted where signage fell on a spectrum of language use: from English only, through bilingual or multilingual use, to HL only use. We repeated this process for the Lee Lee store in Peoria, compared data for the two stores at each eye-level, noted the flow (external or internal) of signage at each level and the location of such signage on the spectrum of language use. Table 17.2 illustrates how these components relate to one another.

Table 17.2 Lee Lee supermarket (reference point) and Strip Mall linguistic landscape

	Areas	Signage	Origin (external or internal to unit of analysis)	Language
Level of analysis				
City	Public use microdata areas (PUMA)			HL speakers dispersed, very small proportion (0.04–3.5%) of total PUMA population
Street view	View from cross streets	Store names, marquees	External – city regulations and conventions	English and HL, English dominant
Strip mall	Business establish-ments	Storefront windows	Internal – individual stores	English, HL, bilingual, depending on store
Store interior	Customer service area	Banners, posters	Internal – community and local entrepreneurs	Bilingual, HL more dominant
	Aisles	Names of sections	Internal – store owner/manager	English and Chinese – planned
		Labels on shelves	Internal – store owner/ manager/staff	English and HL – *ad hoc*, sometimes handwritten
		Product packaging	External – multinational corporations	Multiple languages, multiple scripts, often more than two languages or scripts
Store entrance	Community notice board	Handwritten or home-printed notices	Internal – customers	Multiple languages, multiple scripts, code switching and code mixing
	Newspaper distribution bins	International, national, local ethnic community-oriented media	External – publishers	HL, English or bilingual in HL and English

Signage Findings

Street view

Major signage visible from the highway is in English or bilingual. At the Chandler location, signage for Lee Lee supermarket, CVS pharmacy and McDonald's stand out from a distance. From this level there is not much distinction in representation between newer ethnically oriented and other more established stores (Figure 17.2).

Strip mall view

Most of the remaining stores in the mall at the Chandler location are ethnically focused. Signage in storefront windows is more likely to be bilingual or in languages other than English, and used for commercial advertising or informal advertising. At the Peoria location, at the time of

Figure 17.2 Approaching Lee Lee supermarket from the highway

writing (July 2009), there are no other obviously ethnically oriented establishments in the mall. In December 2008, there was no HL signage on storefront windows, except for some very unobtrusive Vietnamese phrases on the storefront window of an insurance company. By June 2009, two more stores were displaying HL signage on portable A-frames outside the store entrance.

Store interior

Within Lee Lee and the surrounding stores, HL or bilingual signs are part of formal business advertising networks. In the Lee Lee customer service area – which includes a travel agency and a cell phone vendor – the walls are covered with banners and posters advertising the services of local entrepreneurs. In December 2008, the customer service area at the Peoria Lee Lee store had bare walls, and all the signage was in English. By May 2009, three banners with Vietnamese signage covered some of the wall space (Figure 17.3).

Figure 17.3 Customer service area at new Lee Lee store, and banners in customer service area in older Lee Lee store

Figure 17.4 A small sample of what is on the shelves

Aisles are marked clearly with Chinese/English bilingual signs. Some shelves have notices providing translations for the name of an item; this is the case especially in the produce and frozen foods sections. The direction of translation could be either way for English and HL, depending on the language of the packaging, and sometimes the notices are handwritten, creating the sense of an *ad hoc* and real time attempt at making the environment functionally bilingual and bi-scriptal to accommodate different customers. The two Lee Lee stores stock the same products. In most cases, packaging signage is multilingual and in multiple scripts. Even though food aisles are loosely organized by country or region, instances of cultural and linguistic crossover are found in all the country sections (Figure 17.4).

Store entrance area

Signage on the cork notice boards at both Lee Lee stores is similar, and serves as a hub for informal advertising of goods and services. These include cosmetology services, goods for sale, accommodation needed

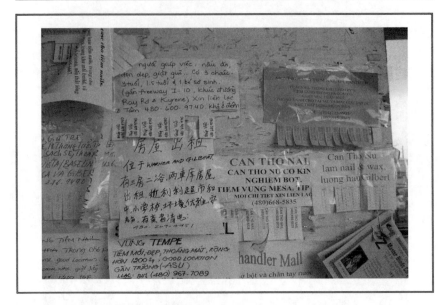

Figure 17.5 Community notice board outside Chandler store

and offered notices, and home maintenance services. Notices are hand-written or printed out from a computer. Here we find HL signage, code mixing and a variety of scripts. The only difference between signage on the notice boards at the two sites is that English is used more often at Lee Lee Peoria, i.e. a greater number of the signs are in English, or for any bilingual notice the larger surface area is in English (Figure 17.5).

The entrance at each Lee Lee store is lined with bins containing ethnic newspapers. Lee Lee serves as a hub for information networks that can connect local Chinese communities to source country news through the distribution of these newspapers. They include US editions of Taiwanese and PRC-Hong Kong publications in HL; the *Korean Arizona Times* and the *Arab Voice*, published bilingually, or in HL only, or in the case of the *Filipino Times*, English only.

The *Asian American Times* is published locally, twice a month, in Chinese and English. The current owner is a Taiwanese immigrant, who runs the paper out of her house in suburban Mesa, from where she distributes it with the aim to reach every Chinese person in Arizona. Given its key role in social networks in the Chinese community, we singled out this newspaper for more detailed study. News copy is either in Chinese or in English, with no mixing of languages. About half of the paper is made up of local advertisements. These offer rich data on language use in social networks among local Chinese people. In an analysis of a sample of 215 advertisements published between January and August 2008, we categorized language usage in the advertisements as English only, English with token Chinese, mainly English, 50/50 both languages, mainly Chinese and Chinese only. The content of these newspaper advertisements partially mimicked those on the community notice boards at both Lee Lees (e.g. services, accommodations, items for sale). However, in the newspaper advertisements, services offered would be those of university-educated professionals (e.g. lawyer), rather than those of cosmetologists, for instance. Accommodations would be apartments or condos, not rooms for rent as on the notice boards. Maintenance services tend to be small businesses, rather than a single contractor. Advertisements in the newspaper are much more English oriented than the notice boards, as can be expected of edited printed language. There is no code mixing. The newspaper advertisements that leaned toward the English side of the spectrum were mostly for upscale accommodations and professional services, whereas the ones on the Chinese side of the spectrum were for establishments (e.g. a video store and a spa) geared toward the local Chinese community.

Trends

From the findings presented in Table 17.1, the following trends can be identified. As we move down from macro to micro level ('Areas' in column 2), we find less English, less standard language use, less formal language use and less partitioning of languages, but more code switching. There is also a degree of register shift from the street level, which tends to be formal, to the window level, which is more functional, to the notice board level, which is eclectic and even *ad hoc*.

The signage at the older establishment (Lee Lee Chandler) displays HLs more often than at the new establishment (Lee Lee Peoria). However, it appears there is a shift underway at the new establishment toward using more HL, both proportionally as well as numerically. An example of the former would be more wall space covered in banners and posters in HL, an example of the latter would be that recently the stores for the first time started stocking South African products, which means Afrikaans has been added to the landscape.

At the macro level end of the spectrum, signage of external origin is more likely to be in English. However, at the micro level (aisles and distribution bins), even external origin signage becomes more multilingual. For instance, the signage on packaging originates from multinationals that may not even be based in the USA, but the language used in the packaging is multilingual and informal. On the other hand, while the newspapers use HL extensively, language is more formal and standardized; to be expected since they have large distribution networks.

Signage on the notice board is functional, informal, and code switching and code mixing are very common.

Concluding Remarks

We started out by noting that Arizona has a political and regulatory climate that sees English engaged in a zero sum game against HLs, makes possible punitive anti-immigrant laws and condones negative attitudes toward immigrants. The LL of our sites visible from the road always includes, or even prioritizes, English. This could be because of local requirements and standards for commercial properties; store owners wanting to blend in and keep a low profile; owners wanting to attract a broad audience, or any combination thereof.

Signage through which we attempt to uncover social networks, i.e. notice boards and classified advertisements, renders a similar caution and conscious design at the macro level. The prevalence of English in newspaper advertisements for professional services, hiring and more up-market accommodations, may indicate that these advertisers want to reach out to the general population, in which advertising in English is necessary, while – in the case of using token Chinese – still signaling their membership of a specific ethnic community. The prevalence of job advertisements in English may signal an employer preference for employees who perform in English, or possible concern about getting into trouble because of Arizona language regulations if employees are not fluent in English. The use of more Chinese in advertisements for restaurants, ethnic medicine and movies, may indicate that these establishments are mainly interested in advertising to people in the local community. The more monolingual HL orientation of notice board advertisements indicates a similar smaller and more intimate reach for these advertisements. People who put up these notices may not be fluent enough in English to feel confident to post a note that also includes English; or the language use may be a screening system to attract clientele from the same ethnic or language group.

Regardless of the reasons, the *gestalt* of the Lee Lee environment provides a constellation of language combinations and linguistic scaffolding that does not presume any particular linguistic competence. Thus, any customer or client can enter at some level of the landscape and participate in the network, independent of their language capabilities. Although ethnic enclaves may contribute to exclusion and segregation, an ethnically oriented hub like Lee Lee becomes inclusive by artfully balancing English and HLs to adapt to the suburban environment and its inhabitants. Whereas some forms of HL and functional multilingual signage at the micro level signal a certain familiarity with, or preference for the very local, HL and multilingual signage at the micro level of food and products connects individuals with the world at large. At this level, language use is fluid and 'authentic', and languages (and even cultures) are not delineated, but hybridized.

Over the last few decades, some scholars (see Phillipson, 1992) and activists have argued that globalization will lead to a McDonaldization of cityscapes and English will overwhelm other languages as it dominates the global economy. The LL inside Lee Lee, however, seems to indicate the opposite – multinational corporations diversify language use as they trade globally, which can help keep or make cityscapes distinct and diverse. And those who are functionally multilingual may have an advantage over English-only speakers when it comes to participating in global economic and social networks.

The LL described in this chapter also illustrates multilingualism as an attribute of a community, not an individual. Looking at the packaging of an entire section – rather than individual products – we see how languages overlap in much the way they do in multilingual communities of speakers. A South African product with labeling in Afrikaans and English, for example, can be found next to a South African product (aimed at export to Europe) with English, French and Spanish labeling, which may be next to a Latin American product with labeling in Spanish and English, which may be next to a product with Chinese and English labeling, which in turn could be next to a product with Chinese and Japanese labeling. In this way, one can get from Afrikaans to Japanese without breaking the chain. Real world multilingualism in ethnically diverse communities does present in the same way with people having different sets of language skills, but without communication ever breaking down.

Even though Lee Lee is Chinese oriented, it is frequented by an ethnically diverse clientele, including English, monolingual, suburban, Americans. In a recent article in the local daily (Chan, June 2009) about Lee Lee Supermarket, the reporter writes:

> The store has become more than just a place to buy food and ethnic products – it's a place where both immigrants craving food from home and connoisseurs of global cuisine can feel part of an international family.

Although the notion of an international family may be somewhat of a cliché, our findings do indicate that even though the Arizona Asian population is dispersed, they have a number of strategies for staying connected over distance, and for keeping their languages vibrant and relevant. Commercial endeavors and trading of goods and services, as illustrated by our LL, play an important role here. Despite the absence of any official attempts to promote HLs in Arizona, and in an often hostile English-dominant environment, HLs seem to have remarkable resilience.

It is unclear if this resilience can provide the critical mass to maintain HLs among new generations. This case study looks at one type of site, ethnic markets. Community language schools, churches, community associations, health establishments and other places where language minorities gather are also sites worthy of similar investigation into language vitality and maintenance. We know that in the Valley there has been a steady increase in the number of churches using HLs, and in the number of HL community schools, especially Mandarin language schools. It is possible that if this growth continues, these different endeavors may bolster one another to contribute to HL maintenance or at least to slow the shift to English over the next generations of local Asian-origin populations. However, given the heady mix of languages, scripts and interactions we have seen so far, it may also be possible that neither HL maintenance nor English assimilation prevails, but that a new and hybrid use of language and literacies is established over the long term.

Acknowledgements

This research project was conducted in affiliation with the UCLA National Heritage Language Resource Center, US Department of Education. The findings and opinions expressed here do not reflect the positions or policies of the Department of Education. All photographs were taken by Gerda de Klerk and Terrence G. Wiley between April and December 2008.

Notes

1. The most current reliable data regarding language demographics in Arizona can be found in the US Census Bureau's American Community Survey (ACS) 2007 surveys (released in 2008 and 2009). The ACS collects information every year instead of every 10 years, with a questionnaire equivalent of the Census long form. We used 2005–2007 ACS 3-Year Estimates rather than 2007 ACS 1-Year Estimates, since the former produce more accurate estimates for small populations.
2. Data source: 2005–2007 American Community Survey 3-Year Estimates microdata. Language questions in US Census surveys ask about levels of fluency in English; whether respondents speak a language other than English at home, and if yes, what that language is.

References

Andrew, R.P. (1997) Sign language: Colonialism and the battle over text. *Loyola L.A. Ent. Law Journal* 17, 625.

Baker, C. (2006) *Foundations of Bilingual Education and Bilingualism* (4th edn). Clevedon: Multilingual Matters.

Ben-Rafael, E. (2009) A sociological approach to the study of linguistic landscapes. In E. Shohamy and D. Gorter (eds) *Linguistic Landscape: Expanding the Scenery* (pp. 313–331). New York: Routledge.

Ben-Rafael, E., Shohamy, E., Amara, M.H. and Trumper-Hecht, N. (2006) Linguistic landscape as symbolic construction of public space: The case of Israel. *International Journal of Multilingualism* 3 (1), 7–30.

Cenoz, J. and Gorter, D. (2006) Linguistic landscape and minority languages. *International Journal of Multilingualism* 3 (1), 67–80.

Chan, A. (June 29, 2009) Ethnic bounty. *Arizona Republic, Section D*, p. 1–2.

Crawford, J. (1992) *Hold Your Tongue: Bilingualism and the Politics of 'English Only'*. Reading, MA: Addison-Wesley.

Luckingham, B. (1994) *Minorities in Phoenix: A Profile of Mexican American, Chinese American, and African American Communities 1860–1992*. Tucson, AZ: The University of Arizona Press.

Phillipson, R. (1992) *Linguistic Imperialism*. Oxford: Oxford University Press.

Shohamy, E. and Waksman, S. (2009) Linguistic landscape as an ecological arena: Modalities, meanings, negotiations, education. In E. Shohamy and D. Gorter (eds) *Linguistic Landscape: Expanding the Scenery* (pp. 313–331). New York: Routledge.

Spolsky, B. (2007) Foreword. In P. Backhaus (ed.) *Linguistic Landscapes: A Comparative Study of Urban Multilingualism in Tokyo* (pp. ix–x). Clevedon: Multilingual Matters.

US Census Bureau. 2005–2007 American Community Survey 3-Year Estimates. Microdata.

Wiley, T.G. (2004) Language policy and English-only. In E. Finegan and J.R. Rickford (eds) *Language in the USA: Perspectives for the Twenty-first Century* (pp. 319–338). Cambridge: Cambridge University Press.

Chapter 18

Diaspora and Returning Diaspora: French-Hebrew and Vice-Versa

ELIEZER BEN-RAFAEL and MIRIAM BEN-RAFAEL

Theoretical Considerations

This chapter focuses on the linguistic landscape (LL) of two urban spaces. The first, Sarcelles-Pletzel, is a French Jewish (FJ) space in the surroundings of Paris and in Paris itself; the second, Natanya, is an Israeli city that has recently absorbed thousands of FJ immigrants 'returning home'. We want to delve into this case of 'returnees' by comparing them to their original diasporan setting: does 'return' make any difference in terms of diasporan experience – as far as linguistic studies may tell?

The study of the LL has expanded recently. One of the earliest works in this area was Spolsky and Cooper's (1991) investigation of public signs in the city of Jerusalem, which discussed the relation between the informational and symbolic dimensions of LL items. Bourhis and Laundry (2002) have further related the study of the LL to the notion of linguistic vitality, applying this perspective in Montreal, Canada. A later work is a study by E. Ben-Rafael *et al.* (2006) about the LL in Israeli cities. In that study, the LL was viewed as the symbolic construction of the public space, and accounted, from this perspective, for different LL models of multilingualism. As elaborated elsewhere (E. Ben-Rafael, 2008), LL studies may serve the investigation of major societal issues. Accordingly, in this chapter, we present research of a relatively limited scope aimed, within this perspective, at exploring new directions for investigation and reflections. We compare the LLs of a Jewish community in France with an Israeli setting where FJ immigrants have settled in large numbers. This investigation relates to the wider phenomenon of returning diasporas, which is a basic feature of our globalizing era.

Globalization implies flows of resources and migrants on a global scope (Appadurai, 2002). What is unprecedented today with respect to migration movements is that they take place in a world of direct communication, rapid means of transport and in real-time, omnipresent media coverage. In this context, a transnational diaspora refers to immigrant groups that, unlike in the past, insert themselves in new societies without necessarily disengaging from their societies of origin – or from fellow-diasporans settled elsewhere. Moreover, they are benefiting from the opportunities offered by welfare states and democratic regimes: these immigrants build communities where original linguistic and cultural resources may continue to be of use (Tambiah, 2002). This does not preclude these immigrants from also acquiring languages and symbols pertaining to their new environment, but they are able to develop a sense of 'dual homeness', indicating that they relate to two societies simultaneously as 'theirs'.

This kind of group is designated by the notion of transnational diaspora, which contemporary scholars view as a major factor of today's multiculturalism (Fludernik, 2003). In this perspective, the old concept of 'integrating society' becomes outdated by the notion of 'insertion', which makes do with asking about the patterns by which migrants assert their presence in society, without assuming that groups always tend to assimilate and 'disappear into the crowd'.

Insertion in society, unlike integration or, better, assimilation, represents cultural and social acculturation without necessarily implying total disengagement from former legacies and symbols. In other words, insertion means some kind of 'hybridization', i.e. the mixing in one set of symbols of patterns stemming from different sources (Pieterse, 2000; Glick Schiller, 1999).

This cultural hybridization should be readable in the group's markers and, above all, its linguistic markers. Such markers may consist of a fully fledged vernacular retained for generations, or of sparse linguistic tokens (M. Ben-Rafael, 2001). This use of two or more codes does not only depend on migrants' attitude toward their language; it may also be conveyed by educational institutions, temples, newspapers or radio stations operated by, or at the intention of, diasporans.

The distinction we want to focus on in this chapter specifically concerns 'returning diasporas' that represent a particular category of diasporas, which is multiplying today concomitantly with the multi-plying of transnational diasporas. A returning diaspora consists of people who emigrated in the past to a new country and decided, even generations later, to 'go back' to their original country. Now, however, these people carry prints of their diasporic endeavour and when they settle in what Herzl (1904/1941) called *'Altneuland'* (old-new homeland), may well find themselves distinct from, and distinguished by, their fellow nationals. All the more so when they valorise the resources they acquired in the diaspora and aspire to re-constitute communities on this basis. Well-known cases of such developments include ethnic Germans 'returning' from the Soviet Union (*aussiedlers*) to Germany (Dietz, 2000), the 'repatriated' French from Algeria (the *pieds noirs*) of the 1960s (Naylor, 2000) or the Brazilian Japanese in Japan (studied by Yashita, 2009).

The literature still lacks works that focus in the context of today's globalizing reality, on 'coming home' from the viewpoint of returnees' relation to their previous diasporic setting, with respect to that insertion or re-insertion. This is the goal of this chapter, which elaborates on the impact in this respect of the situational shift from 'Jewish Frenchness in France' to 'French Jewish Israeliness in Israel'. The newness of the topic should elicit some aspects not yet discussed of the experience of transnational diasporas. LL analysis, we found, is an appropriate methodology for this kind of investigation. All the more so because returning diasporas, like contemporary diasporas in general, tend to settle in urban spaces that, in this era of globalization, often constitute transglobal units made up of communities, sharing but little common cultural resources and symbols.

In this context, we may ask whether returning diasporas do strengthen the common ground – if any – of these transglobal units that make up the most vivid forces of the national society, or do they only add to the incoherence and chaotic aspects of these cosmopolitan areas. In this perspective, returning diasporas become an important field in the study of contemporary urban LLs.

Linguistic Landscape Investigation as Methodology

The LL, as we know, refers to all linguistic objects that mark the public space. As such, the LL responds to Durkheim's notion of 'social fact', which actors encounter in social reality independent of their will (Durkheim, 1895/1982). From a sociology-of-language perspective and as elaborated in previous studies (E. Ben-Rafael *et al.*, 2006; M. Ben-Rafael & E. Ben-Rafael, 2009), LL items that mark the public space may be seen as generated by structuration principles – actors' presentation of self, expectations regarding the rationality of potential clients, power relations between groups of actors over the predominance of given registers, and collective identity. The latter principle should be of special relevance in the present context, as it refers to items that signal an *a priori* relation between agencies and a given population group (Hall, 1990).

Though, and as explicated by the notion of hybridization, we also know that a diaspora – whether conventional or returning – carries features that associate it with different sources of influence. By this, immigrants remain 'different' from others around them, while also becoming 'different' from what they were in the past and from their fellow ethnics who remained behind. A transnational diaspora thus constitutes a factor of twofold heterogenization – of both societies and diaspora entities.

In light of the distinction between kinds of diasporas, several questions now arise: does 'coming back' make a difference regarding the ways diasporans insert themselves in society? Do the symbols of collective identity change when individuals endeavour the 'nationalization' of their previous ethnic identity? Do they still illustrate continuity when their previous national tokens become markers of what is at best a secondary allegiance? Above all, is 'returning home' a negation of, and an exit from, the diaspora condition? It is in this context that we delve into the LLs of two urban spaces: Sarcelles in France which, from a Jewish point of view, is a diasporic setting, and Natanya in Israel which is, in the same perspective, Jews' original homeland. In Sarcelles, one finds a FJ community typical of a large part of French Jewry, while in Natanya one finds concentrations of recent French Jewish immigrants (RFIs).

From French Jews to Recent Immigrants

FJs number 500,000–600,000 people, concentrated mainly in France's large cities. For centuries, they lived in France as a discriminated minority. While the 1789 Revolution emancipated the Jews, anti-Jewish feelings have never disappeared from France. In the late 19th century, the Anti-Semitic League of France operated openly, while the Dreyfus affair was upsetting the country. Between the two world wars, Jewish immigration from Eastern Europe strengthened French Jewry, but during WWII the Vichy government made the persecution of Jews an official policy, in support of the Nazis. After 1945, FJs found more comfortable circumstances. In the 1960s, Algerian Jews who left their country following its independence mostly settled in France where they were joined by thousands of Moroccan and Tunisian Jews. Many of the newcomers were more traditionalist than the veteran FJs and re-invigorated French Jewry. Many felt quite uncomfortable with the official republicanism that opposed public displays of community particularism.

Moreover, De Gaulle's anti-Israeli policy in the late 1960s pushed FJs into a difficult position. Since the 1970s, the ever-growing Moslem population aggravated FJs' conditions by arousing anti-Israeli and anti-Jewish feelings (Cohen, 2007). Under these circumstances, together with the renewed vitality of Jewish life in France, Jewish immigration to Israel has increased since the mid-1990s. In the 2000s, this new wave of immigrant numbers approximately 30,000–40,000 – in addition to the 100,000 longer-established Israelis of French origin who arrived in earlier years.

The evolving of the FJ group in Israel is to be viewed in the context of the definition of this land by Judaism as the Jews' 'original' homeland. The Zionists who concretized this tenet brought about the revival of Hebrew, as the national language and the cradle of a new culture (Myhill, 2004). Nonetheless, Israeli society's development has transformed it into a Western-like society in which sociocultural communities multiplied

(Spolsky & Shohamy, 1999). Among the groups that nowadays surround the non-ethnic middle class that upholds secular Zionism, one can count the ultra-Orthodox, the national-religious settlers of the West Bank, low-class communities populated by Jews of Middle-Eastern and North African origins, Russian-speaking Jews from the FSU, Ethiopian immigrants and Israel's Arab community (whose language, Arabic, is Israel's second official language, after Hebrew). These groups have acculturated at varying degrees into the Hebrew culture (on the Russian and French communities, see: M. Ben-Rafael & Schmid, 2007) and Israel's democracy has enabled them to achieve increasing recognition on the political scene. In addition, Israel's participation in globalization due to its strong relations with the USA and its orientation toward international markets has given English an important role as both a resource for worldwide communication and a status symbol among nationals.

FJs' insertion Israel does not proceed without any difficulty. Their history has made them feel fully 'French' at the same time that they have always seen themselves a part of the 'Jewish world' (Cohen, 2007). Hence, Hebrew is taught as the first language in all Jewish schools and FJs visit Israel regularly. On the other hand, FJs who decide to immigrate to Israel may still feel close to the country they left and to its culture. Moreover, mostly from middle-class milieus and North African origin, they often contrast with veteran middle-class Israelis by their religious or traditionalist orientation and affinities to French culture. Most middle-class Israelis, indeed, are secular, of European origin and culturally close to the English-speaking world. These contrasts increase the interest of our research about the ways FJs insert themselves in Israel and become different from FJs who remain in France.

Linguistic Landscape in France vs. Israel

Sarcelles lies 15 km north of Paris; it numbers 60,000 inhabitants. The largest part of the city was built in the 1950s. About 15,000 inhabitants are Jews who settled in specific neighbourhoods where community organizations and synagogues are numerous. Because of this Jewish presence, the city is often tagged as 'France's Jerusalem'. In this work, we attach to the Sarcelles data the quarter of Paris known as 'Pletzel', one of the city's oldest Jewish areas. Only a few thousand Jews still live there today, but Jewish institutions remain numerous. The LL items that we found in the Pletzel area yield a similar picture to that in Sarcelles.

Natanya lies by the Mediterranean Sea, 40 km north of Tel-Aviv, and numbers 170,000 inhabitants of whom tens of thousands were born in North Africa. This has always given a special flavor to the city. It is also a resort for vacationers. During the 1990s, the city absorbed about 50,000 immigrants from the Former Soviet Union, which made Russian the most overheard language on the street after Hebrew. In the second half of the 1990s, about 10,000 FJs immigrated to the city and again altered the coloration of the city.

The LL items pertaining to these two settings were collected by means of photographs taken in the main streets of the two cities. These pictures covered more than half of all items of the spaces investigated. This methodology ensured the representativeness of the data. Moreover, our focus was on the languages and their combinations displayed on the LLs. Table 18.1 presents the major languages and their various combinations that we found in the two settings; in total, 13 combinations using from one to three languages, some of which included non-linguistic markers.

In Sarcelles-Pletzel, we find that in accordance with the official 'republican' attitude toward the public space, French effectively has overwhelming importance in the LL. It stands alone as well as in a variety of combinations, in nearly 95% of all LL items. Yet, in a manner that deviates from republican guidelines, in the Jewish quarter French is often joined by Hebrew words, whether in French or in Hebrew characters: these combinations hold the lead among LL items. The total of the combinations where Hebrew participates (in Hebrew or French characters) amounts to about half of all items. This figure reaches about 75% when one adds up LL items that make use of non-Hebrew Jewish or Israeli non-linguistic markers – the Star of David, a candlelight, names that are unmistakably Jewish (*Goldenberg*) or Israeli (*Yoram*), and even Hebrew religious tokens such as *Mashiah* (Messiah). Another type of marker that belongs here consists of connoted specifications, such as *importation d'Israël*. On the other hand, we find here little use of other

Table 18.1 The languages and language combinations in LL[a]

French (F)	*French +Asian language[b] (F-As)*
Hebrew (H)	French + Hebrew + Russian (F-H-R)
French words in Hebrew characters (Fh)	French + Hebrew + Heb words in F char. (F-H-Hf)
French + Hebrew words in Fr char (F-Hf)	French + Hebrew + Arabic (F-H-Ar)
French + Hebrew (F-H)	French + Hebrew + English (F-H-E)
French + English (F-E)	French + English + Russian (F-E-R)
Hebrew + English (H-E)	Markers attached to LL items

[a] The initials in brackets designate their use of the table's elements in Tables 18.6 and 18.7
[b] An Asian language may be Thai, Chinese or Japanese

languages; English itself accounts for less than 10% under all possible combinations (Figure 18.1).

In brief, in Sarcelles-Pletzel there is a high degree of homogeneity in terms of language representation of its LL – this means the predominance of French, followed by Hebrew and Jewish markers. As far as LL shows, Sarcelles' FJs live simultaneously in two different spheres: Frenchness and Jewishness-Israeliness. Interestingly enough, one also finds here a number of plaques commemorative of the historical experience of the Jewish community – memorials of mass arrests of Jewish children by Nazis and the French police, and of terrorist attacks against Jewish institutions. In their way, these LL items signal the continuity and vicissitudes of the Jewish community's presence on French soil (Table 18.2).

In Natanya, where as previously noted, FJ immigrants are especially numerous, similar to Ashdod or some neighborhoods of Jerusalem, the importance of French is definitely asserted in the LL, as shown in the findings of Table 18.3. And indeed, we discover in the city's center an LL generally unknown in Israel. This refers to the appearance of French monolingual signs in one-fifth of all LL items that we photographed, together with other languages in nearly all other LL items. Among these data, one observes items with Hebraized French (like 'La Bohème' in Hebrew characters) or, in a variety of ways – such as combinations with French, Hebraized French, English or Russian. French and Hebrew combined is the most popular pattern that accounts for about one third of all LL items. Even when items do not feature any French, they may emphasize their link to French in some way: a restaurant, for instance, specifies, in Hebrew and English, that its cuisine is French (Figure 18.2).

French appears in Natanya's LL not as the language of an enclave, but on the contrary, as one of the major languages used in the city center, in conjunction with other languages. This in itself shows openness toward the environment as also discernible in the conjunction with Hebrew and Russian,[1] Israeli Jewish society as a whole (Hebrew) and the world at large (English).

Sarcelles-Pletzel and Natanya Compared

The common denominator of Natanya's and Sarcelles-Pletzel's LLs consists of the large use of both French and Hebrew. Hebrew is important as a minority language in Sarcelles-Pletzel, where it is combined in a variety of models with French; French is important as a minority language in Natanya, where it is combined in a variety of ways with Hebrew. French and Hebraized French combinations hold the lead in Sarcelles-Pletzel; Hebrew-French combinations lead in Natanya (Table 18.4). This common denominator is further strengthened by the

Figure 18.1 All items in Sarcelles-Pletzel

Table 18.2 Sarcelles-Pletzel ($N = 70$)

Languages and combinations of languages	%
French + Hebrew words in French characters	26.5
French + markers	23.8
French	18.5
French + Hebrew + Hebrew words in French characters	9.5
Hebrew words in French characters	6.5
French + English + markers	4.6
Hebrew	3.1
French + English	1.5
Hebrew + English	1.5
French + Hebrew + English	1.5
French + Hebrew + Arabic	1.5
French + Asian language	1.5
Total	100.0

Table 18.3 LL in downtown Natanya ($N = 42$)

Languages and language combinations	%
French and Hebrew	35.6
French	21.4
French + Hebrew + Hebrew words in French characters	16.6
French + Hebrew + Russian	7.2
French + Hebrew + English	4.8
French + English	4.8
French + Hebrew words in French characters	2.4
Hebrew + English	2.4
French in Hebrew characters	2.4
French + English + Russian	2.4
Total	100.0

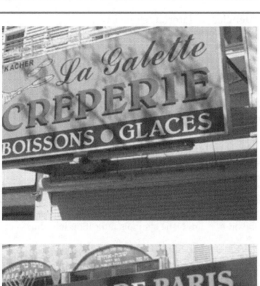

Figure 18.2 All items in Natanya

Table 18.4 Frequencies of languages in LL items[a]

	Natanya (N = 42)	*Sarcelles-Pletzel* (N = 70)
French	97.8	93.0
Hebrew/Jewish or Israeli markers[b]	71.6	79.2
English	14.4	10.7
Russian	9.6	
Arabic/Asian languages		3.0

[a] Numbers indicate the percentage of items in each LL that carry the various languages, whether alone or in combination with other languages
[b] By markers are meant non-linguistic symbols indicating Jewishness or Israeliness

role of markers in Sarcelles-Pletzel that find their counterpart in the plain use of Hebrew in the Israeli-Jewish context of Natanya.

On the other hand, the major difference between the two cities lies in the fact that, in Natanya, French and Hebrew are often attached to English and Russian, expressing implantation of the multicultural context and influences of globalization. In Sarcelles-Pletzel, one rarely finds any additional language in the LL, which may illustrate the overlooking of, or lack of reference to, wider multilingual or multicultural diversity (see Table 18.4).

Languages of Domains

In this analysis, we also considered an additional dimension of the LL, namely, the domains of use of the different codes. We wanted to specify thereby, and in a comparative perspective, the meanings of the use of these languages. And, indeed, we found additional divergences and convergences between the two settings. Table 18.5 shows the categorization of types of domains that we used in our analysis.

In Sarcelles-Pletzel (Table 18.6), the domains of activity reflected in the LL show that restaurants hold the first place among places designated by LL items – though they are not too numerous. They are followed by top-down commemorative plaques of Shoah events and other signs that attest to the presence and status of French Jews in the public space. Following this category of LL items, we find grocery stores and religious and public institutions as well as agencies of cultural goods. The rather restricted range of categories shows that these places pertain to non-central quarters in the urban space, and thus do not compete with downtown area for the diversity of services that they offer.

Table 18.5 Categories of LL items according to domains

1	Public billboards, graffiti, street plates
1'	Commemorative stones or plaques referring to events, figures or places of symbolic-historical community importance
2	Food (grocery, butchery, bakery, fruit and vegetables, etc.)
3	Animal health center, vets, pet shops
4	Financial services and real-estate (including banks and exchange offices)
5	Office supplies and communications (phone shops, photo services, travel agents)
6	Cultural goods (libraries, book shops, print shops, music, art)
7	Supermarkets and salerooms
8	Clothing (including leather shops, shoes, underwear, sport equipment, dry-cleaning)
9	Home (furniture, dishes, kitchen equipment, bathrooms)
10	Public and religious institutions (synagogues, public libraries, schools, official agencies)
11	Luxury goods – jewellers, watch shops, chocolate, flowers, lace, perfumeries, specialties
12	Catering and restaurants (including cafés, tearooms, pubs, dancing halls)
13	Health and aesthetic centers (beauty salons, medical clinics, pharmacies, hairdressers clubs)
14	Road and traffic signs
15	Services (garage mechanics and the like)

In Natanya as well, as Table 18.7 indicates, restaurants come first for the use of French in the LL. LL items comprising French are more numerous than in Sarcelles-Pletzel, and the use of French concerns more LL domains. It is noteworthy that financial and real-estate agencies in Natanya have far greater importance than in Sarcelles-Pletzel. In Natanya, the LL appears to address people in the process of settling into their new environment. So while the LL in Sarcelles-Pletzel reflects a 'regular' daily community life that shares and memorizes its historical experience, in Natanya, one may speak of the insertion of a new group of great vitality turned toward its environment (see Table 18.7).

While these aspects point to divergences between FJs in France and Israel, another factor appears that indicates convergence. This refers to

Table 18.6 Sarcelles-Pletzel: LL items according to languages and combinations of languages (N = 70)[a]

It[b]	F	F*	H	Hf	F-Hf	F-E	F-E*	H-E	H-E*	F-As	F-H-Hf	F-HE*	F-H-Ar	Total
1	3.1	1.5	1.5	3.1	7.7						3.1			15.4
1'	6.2	1.5	1.5						3.1	1.5		3.1	1.5	21.5
2	1.5	6.2			3.1						1.5			12.3
3														
4														
5	1.5						1.5							3.1
6	1.5	1.5			1.5						3.1			7.7
7														
8	1.5	3.1												4.6
9														
10				1.5	1.5									3.1
11		1.5			1.5									3.1
12		7.7		1.5	9.2	1.5	1.5	1.5			1.5			24.4
13	1.5	1.5												3.1
14	1.5													1.5
15					1.5									1.5
Total	18.5	23.8	3.1	6.2	26.2	1.5	3.1	1.5	3.1	1.5	9.2	1.5	1.5	100+

[a] F = French; H = Hebrew; Fh = French; Fh = French words in Hebrew characters; F-H = French + Heb characters; F-Hf = French + Heb. Words in Fr characters; F-E = French + English; H-E = Hebrew + English; F-As = French + Asian language; F-H-R = French + Heb + Russian; F-H-Hf: French + Heb + Heb words in French characters; F-H-Ar: French + Heb + Arabic; F-H-E: French + Heb + English; F-E-R: French + English + Russian; (*) = markers attached to LL items
[b] See domains of items in Table 18.5

Table 18.7 LL in downtown Natanya $(N = 42)^a$

Categories items[b]	F	Fh	F-H	F-Hf	F-E	H-E	F-H-R	F-H-E	F-H-Hf	F-E-R	Total
1	4.8		4.8	2.4							12.0
2						2.4			2.4		4.8
4	12.0		16.7	2.4					4.8		35.7
5	2.4									2.4	4.8
6									2.4		2.4
10			2.4	2.4					2.4		7.2
12		2.4	9.6			2.4	2.4	2.4	4.8		23.8
13	2.4						2.4	2.4			7.2
14			2.4								2.4
Total	21.4	2.4	35.7	2.4	4.8	2.4	7.2	4.8	16.7	2.4	100+

[a] See Tables 18.1 and 18.6 for the names of the languages and combinations that the initials used here stand for
[b] See categories of items in Table 18.5

the presence in both places of synagogues and religious institutions where Hebrew and French are used conjunctively. This phenomenon raises questions. The presence of Hebrew in FJ religious institutions in France is, of course, self-evident considering the role of Hebrew in Judaism. The role of French on signs of similar institutions in Israel is much less obvious, since French has no status in relation to Judaism. The interpretation may be that this finding reveals continuity between FJs in the two countries regarding the endeavouring of Jewishness. It is visible, for instance, in items topping the doors of synagogues in Natanya – like 'Synagogue Francophone' followed by names of famous French or North African rabbis. We found similar LL patterns on bookshops of religious literature in Natanya.

In other words, we find here a continuity not just of 'Frenchness' but also of 'Jewish Frenchness', meaning that Sarcelles-Pletzel's FJs and Natanya's still concretize – each in its own place – their belonging to a common FJ transnational entity. This assessment finds additional support in a 2009 research by E. Ben-Rafael and Sternberg, which cited the multiplication of internet sites,[2] internet television, magazines and bulletins common to FJs everywhere. These sites and publications are, as a rule, dedicated to the diffusion of cultural and religious contents as well as of information about Israel and French Jewry – in France and in Israel.

Conclusions

In conclusion, FJs have effectively created a *francophonie* of a new type in Israel; this kind of francophonie did not take root in Israel even when tens of thousands of francophone immigrants arrived in the 1950s and 1960s. At that period, the struggle for the supremacy of Hebrew was raging, while in the context of today's multiculturalism, FJs encounter no obstacle to using French in public. FJs in Israel appear to be moved by a transnational model and a notion of dual-homeness that are their own.

The parts endowed French and Hebrew in the LL of RFIs' setting point to an orientation asserting a Jewish future in Israel through the maintenance of an allegiance to French culture. The multiple uses of French signal a refusal to 'disappear in the crowd' – and, at the same time, velleities for insertion in society. This characterization of FJs in Israel converges with the results of the research mentioned above that also used an attitudes-survey methodology with a large sample of French-Israeli Jews (E. Ben-Rafael & Sternberg, 2009). This research found that respondents, especially recent arrivals, indeed insist on their Jewish identity, express satisfaction with the Israeli reality, identify with the country and see themselves as part of it. On the other hand, and as also discernible in Natanya's LL, they continue to use French in many respects of their social life, are appreciative of French culture and are often involved in French-Israeli community associations.

This characterization recalls similar developments in other transnational diasporas – the Muslims (Al-Azmeh, 1996), Hispanics (Davis *et al.*, 2002) and Chinese (Chee-Beng, 2004) in various countries. The difference is apparent when we juxtapose Natanya's data to those of Sarcelles-Pletzel. In Sarcelles-Pletzel, the uses of French that are conjunctive with Hebrew and Jewish markers, attest to insertion in French society in ways that ally Frenchness and allegiance to Judaism and Israel. The use of Hebrew and French in Natanya demonstrates continuity vis-à-vis Sarcelles-Pletzel. Hebrew used in France and French used in Israel mean that RFIs and FJs retain a convergent visibility in both places. The comparison of LLs also shows, however, that the primary role of Frenchness in the LL is inverted when one moves from Sarcelles-Pletzel to Natanya, where Israeli-Jewishness marked by Hebrew is granted the primary position. The marker of the previous ethnic identity is now the marker of national identity, materializing the significance of 'homecoming'.

What is not yet explained relates to the fact that the institutions and agencies tagged by LL items containing French in Natanya include those that refer to French Jewish practices in Israel. One would have expected instead a discontinuation of the use of French in cult and religious matters. The more so that Hebrew, which symbolizes Jewishness in France, is in Israel the language of all Jews. That FJs find it necessary to make use of French in this domain as well hints, we suggest, that for them, Jewishness remains associated with French, not only with Hebrew. This attitude may be accounted for by the far-reaching past of French Jewry and its legacies (including those imported from francophone North Africa). This should explain why FJs in Natanya aspire to continue to assert French-Jewishness concomitantly with their velleity to retain their Frenchness, on the one hand, and to endorse Israeliness, on the other. What is visible in this is how far this 'returning diaspora' still constitutes a diaspora which, despite the situational shift, sees some of the roots of its cultural and religious heritage elsewhere.

Hence, the very fact of 'returning' is not equated in this case with negation of the diasporic condition itself. Returnees – at least the first-generation ones – may well continue to exhibit in their old-new homeland a particularism that binds them to their communities of origin. This does not rule out that the 'return' and insertion in society will make them different in many respects from what they were on arrival, and from their fellow-diasporans left behind.

One major line of differentiation we already observe in our data – and this is their contribution to urban space's LL, and from there to the social fabric of this space – is that RFIs' French becomes allied both to English, which symbolizes and concretizes Israel's search for globalization, and Russian, which is indicative of this country's multicultural-ism. What we see in Natanya also applies to other places in Israel, like certain quarters of Ashdod, or Jerusalem where FJs settle in large numbers. It is probably also under their influence that French is tending to increase its imprint in LLs outside RFI settings. *Café Hillel* in Herzliya, *Café Noir* in Tel-Aviv, fashion boutiques *Comme il faut* and *La Folie* in Ramat Hasharon are all expressions of the impact of FJs on Israel's version of multiculturalism as they 'return' from the diaspora and continue, in some ways, to refer to it.

At the same time, the LL contours in Sarcelles-Pletzel, which can also be seen in other FJ communities like Creteil or Marseille, show more strictly the alliance of Frenchness with Hebrew. As in Sarcelles-Pletzel, the LL illustrates a more restricted notion of multiculturalism than in Israeli settings – even though, in their own ways, these communities tend to achieve a wider influence attested to by the recent appearance of Hebrew tokens outside Jewish quarters – a grocery named *Cash Kacher Naouri* in Levallois or a furniture store tagged *Tiv Taam Ameublement* in central Paris.

All in all, it appears that we see a tendency in the LL contributed by returnees – in urban areas that they directly mould or through their influence beyond these areas – to hyphenate different symbolic-linguistic systems that somehow contrast with the LL of their communities of origin.

These convergences and divergences bring French Jews and recent French immigrants both closer to, and more distant from, each other.

Notes

1. Since the large wave of Russian-speaking immigrants in the 1990s, Russian has become a major (though unofficial) language in the country, used in areas where people of this group concentrate – including Natanya (Ben-Rafael *et al.*, 2006).
2. The most important sites like *Akadem* and *Guysen* operate from both Jerusalem and Paris.

References

Al-Azmeh, A. (1996) *Islams and Modernities*. London: Verso.

Appadurai, A. (ed.) (2002) *Globalization*. Durham, NC: Duke University Press.

Ben-Rafael, E. (2008) A sociological approach to linguistic landscape. In E. Shohami and D. Gorter (eds) *The Linguistic Landscape: Expanding the Scene* (pp. 40–54). London: Routledge.

Ben-Rafael, E., Lyubansky, M., Gluckner, O., Harris, P., Israel, Y., Jasper, W. and Schoeps, J. (2006) *Building a Diaspora: Russian Jews in Israel, Germany and the USA*. Leyden and Boston: Brill.

Ben-Rafael, E., Shohami, E., Amara, M. and Hecht, N. (2006) The symbolic construction of the public space: The case of Israel. *International Journal of Multilingualism* 3 (1), 7–28.

Ben-Rafael, E. and Sternberg, Y. (2009) *La population franco-israélienne: Composition, disposition, structuration*. Tel-Aviv: Université de Tel-Aviv, Consulat général et Institut français de Tel-Aviv.

Ben-Rafael, M. (2001) Codeswitching in the immigrant languages: The case of Franbreu. In R. Jacobson (ed.) *Codeswitching Worldwide II* (pp. 251–307). Berlin: Mouton de Gruyter.

Ben-Rafael, M. and Ben-Rafael, E. (2009) The linguistic landscape of transnationalism: The divided heart of Europe. In E. Ben-Rafael and Y. Sternberg (eds) *Transnationalism: Diasporas and the Advent of a New (Dis)order* (pp. 399–416). Leyden and Boston: Brill.

Ben-Rafael, M. and Schmid, M. (2007) Language attrition and ideology – two groups of immigrants in Israel. In B. Kopke *et al.* (eds) *Language Attrition – Theoretical Perspectives* (pp. 205–225). Amsterdam: John Benjamins.

Bourhis, R.Y. and Landry, R. (2002) La loi 101 et l'aménagement du paysage linguistique du Quebec. In P. Bouchard and R.Y. Bourhis (eds) *L'Aménagement linguistique au Québec* (pp. 107–132). Québec: Publications du Québec.

Chee-Beng, T. (2004) *Chinese Overseas: Comparative Cultural Issues*. Hong Kong: Hong Kong University Press.

Cohen, E. (2007) *Heureux comme Juifs en France?* Jerusalem: Alkana et Ed. Akadem.

Davis, K.G., Fernfindez, E.C. and Mendez, V. (2002) *United States Hispanic Catholics: Trends & Works 1990–2000*. Scranton, PE: University of Scranton.

Dietz, B. (2000) German and Jewish migration from the Former Soviet Union to Germany. Background, trends and implications. *Journal of Ethnic and Migration Studies* 26 (4), 635–652.

Durkheim, E. (1895 [1982]) *Rules of Sociological Method*. New York: The Free Press.

Fludernik M. (ed.) (2003) *Diaspora and Multiculturalism. Common Traditions and New Developments*. Amsterdam: Rodopi.

Glick Schiller, N. (1999) Transmigrants and nation states: Something old and something new in the U.S. immigrant experience. In C. Hirschman, P. Kasinitz and J. DeWind (eds) *Handbook of International Migration, the American Experience* (pp. 94–119). New York: Russell Sage Foundation.

Hall, S. (1990) Cultural identity and diaspora. In J. Rutherford (ed.) *Identity, Community, Culture, Difference* (pp. 222–237). London: Lawrence and Wishart.

Herzl, Th. (1904 [1941]) *Old-New Land*. New York: Bloch Publishing Co. and Herzl Press.

Myhill, J. (2004) *Languages in Jewish Society: Towards a New Understanding*. Clevedon: Multilingual Matters.

Naylor, Ph. Chiviges (2000) *France and Algeria: A History of Decolonization and Transformation*. Miami, FL: University Press of Florida.

Pieterse, J.N. (2000) Globalization as hybridization. In F.J. Lechner and J. Boli (eds) *The Globalization Reader* (pp. 99–105). Oxford: Blackwell.

Spolsky, B. and Shohamy, E. (1999) *The Languages of Israel: Policy, Ideology and Practice*. Clevedon: Multilingual Matters.

Tambiah, S.J. (2002) Vignettes of present day diaspora. In E. Ben-Rafael and Y. Sternberg (eds) *Identity, Culture and Globalization* (pp. 327–336). Leyden: Brill Academic Press.

Yashita, A. (2009) Brazilian Japanese back in Japan. International Workshop of Linguistic Landscape, Siena, 14–17 January 2009.

Epilogue: The Theoretical Edge

Grosso modo, the empirical works presented in this volume offer support for our theoretization of linguistic landscape (LL) structural principles. These works refer to specific aspects and are relevant to both quantitative and qualitative research. In a quantitative-statistical perspective, what matters is the distribution of items, uses of languages, categories of designs and texts that unveil the relative impact of different structuration principles. Consideration of these works highlights issues such as the extent to which the norms and value-orientations underlying LL items originating in the ruling spheres – and reflected in the top-down flow of LL items – converge with the flow of bottom-up items originating in autonomous actors. The impacts of structuration principles may similarly be followed by replicating the same investigation in locations of different demographic composition – by class, ethnicity or the like – a comparative approach that is effectively illustrated by several chapters. As also shown by some of those works with other research instruments, LL hypotheses may also require qualitative LL research. We are thinking here, as illustrated by our chapters here and there, of content analyses of LL items revealing the values they stand for, perceptions of potential clients, how coercion or its rejection may be practiced in the LL and the kind of reasoning beneath tactics and strategies of getting 'close' to the public.

As a whole, these chapters show that each structuration principle discussed above can assume varied models, though all of them jointly create a quite coherent perspective on the chaotic reality revealed by observations at the surface. Theoretization, it is true, by no means constitutes a full-fledged LL theory, since it does not specify any precise expectation regarding how far, and in what manner, those structuring principles impact on the LL. We have no *a priori* assumption regarding which of those principles prevail, in what circumstances, nor their precise modes of intermingling. Still, it is our contention that using this approach, we may elicit hypotheses of general significance assisted by external bodies of knowledge. As illustrations of this assessment, we can state – in the vein of elementary marketing theory – that the subjective perception of the structuring of the LL would increase its weight in the formation of the LL, where LL actors are subject to stronger competition over clients, and where the goods proposed and advertised by LL items multiply. Indeed, the more numerous the alternate services and goods, the more important people consider them in making their choices – the more also LL actors would invest in their self-presentation in order to influence these choices. In the same circumstances, one may also expect the 'good-reason' principle to grow in importance: LL actors should then be more attentive than ever to capturing the rational considerations of their potential clients, and theorize about them.

On the other hand, where society is characterized by a higher degree of multiculturalism, the collective-identity principle should have a stronger presence. This tends to happen, we suggest – after following the literature dealing with contemporary transnational diasporas (Ben-Rafael, 2010) – when a larger number of diasporic communities exist in the society and tend to form distinct neighbourhoods. It also occurs where the prevailing culture – and therefore the major lines of official linguistic policies – does not make exaggerated use of its power supremacy to oppose open expressions of pluralism. Moreover, one cannot disregard the fact that LL items referring to a minority community may be particularly asserted in top-down LL items, expressing politicians' ambition to demonstrate tolerance for that minority.

These are just a few examples out of many that may be generated from this approach in that manner, i.e. by focusing on the relation of structuration principles and contextual societal variables. As a whole, such hypotheses concur in viewing the LL as a system, notwithstanding its notable anarchic-chaotic aspects. They point out patterns representing different ways in which people, groups, associations, institutions and public agencies cope with the game of symbols within common complex spaces. Through this confrontation, they aspire to take up the challenge of deciphering that *gestalt*, which we call the *linguistic landscape* and look down into its deep structures that generate the structuration of this space. A space, that carries emblematic meanings as the decorum of public life...a space which is not only 'chaotic' but also 'accountable'.

More generally, the analysis of the LL offers the opportunity of outlining how well-known principles of social life mould together a specific scene of major importance. What happens here cannot be entirely foreign to what happens on other scenes, and in this respect, the LL is but one more field of the shaping of social reality under diverse, uncoordinated and possibly incongruent structuration principles. In this, the LL illustrates processes expressing 'at the surface' the working of what Levi-Strauss (1958, 1977, 1978) would call 'deep structures' and which he elaborates on by emphasizing contradictory options they convey. It is a perspective that aspires to delve into the LL beyond its appearance as a jungle of jumbled and irregular items. In brief, this approach focuses on the variations of LL configurations, aiming to account for their constituting what is after all a quite 'ordered – and not so unusual – disorder'.

References

Ben-Rafael, E. (2010) Diaspora – Entry in *Sociopedia ISA*. Sage: http://www.sagepub.net/isa/resources/pdf/Diaspora.pdf.
Levi-Strauss, C. (1958) *Anthropologie Structurale*. Paris: Plon.
Levi-Strauss, C. (1977) *L'Identite : seminaire interdisciplinaire*. Paris: B. Grasset.
Levi-Strauss, C. (1978) *The Origin of Table Manners*. New York: Harper & Row.

Author Index

Adamson, R. 292
Aiello, G. 177
Al-Azmeh, A. 340
Aldridge, J. 201
Allen, J. 177
Amara, M.H. 249
Amin, A. 156
Andersen, R.W. 208
Andrew, R.P. 203, 309
Anisimov, A. 135, 142, 143, 144
Appadurai, A. 326
Arbel, R. 53
Arutiunian, A. 135, 142
Augé, M. 4
Augoustinos, M. 303, 304
Avraham, E. 58
Azaryahu, M. 60, 66

Backhaus, P. xii, xiii, 19, 20, 21, 23, 74, 92, 118, 131, 148, 163, 203, 208, 252, 277, 278, 279, 294
Bagna, C. 4, 5, 6, 7, 12, 33, 256
Bairoch, P. xii
Baker, C. 308
Barni, M. 3, 4, 5, 6, 7, 12, 33, 256, 277
Bar-Tal, D. 249
Barthes, R. 207
Barton, D. 252
Basque Government 222
Bauman, Z. 157, 177, 178, 239, 245
BBC News 30
Ben Zadok, E. 41
Ben-Rafael, E. xi, xv, xvii, xviii, 200, 208, 253, 254, 258, 278, 296, 307, 315, 326, 338, 339, 340, 342
Ben-Rafael, M. 327, 328, 330
Berger, J. 155, 261, 265
Besters-Dilger, J. 135, 148
Bhabha, H.K. 59
Bilaniuk, L. 135, 144, 145, 148
Blackwood, R.J. 278, 285, 292, 294, 305
Blanchet, P. 285
Blom, J. 22
Blommaert, J. 96, 105, 177, 256
Bogatyrev, P. 50
Bond, B. 256
Botes, L. 78
Bothorel-Witz, A. 282
Boudon, R. xvii
Bourdieu, P. 53, 176, 178

Bourhis, R.Y. xi, xii, 4, 15, 19, 38, 97, 219, 252, 263, 275, 277, 295, 326
Boyer, M.C. 186, 189
Breidbach, O. xvi
Bright, W. 129
Bulot, T. 275, 276, 277

Cabinet of Ministers of the Republic of Latvia 117
Calhoun, C. xviii
Calvet, L.-J. 201, 275, 277, 278
Cameron, D. 176
Canwest News Service 211
Caritas 3, 7, 8, 12, 16
Ceccagno, A. 10
Cenoz, J. 92, 118, 163, 183, 201, 219, 220, 221, 223, 224, 228, 253, 279, 308
Censis 14
Central Statistics Office 20, 23
Chan, A. 323
Chazak, H. 42
Chee-Beng, T. 340
Cheshire, J. 162
Childe, V. G. xiii
Chmielewska, E. 177
Choi, J.H-j. 199, 208
Chow, E.N. 97
Christopherson, S. 189
City of Fukuoka 20
City of Victoria 190
Cohen, E. 329, 330
Coleman, J.S. xvii
Collins, J. 253
Cooper, R.L. xi, xii, 19, 208, 326
Cope, B. 202
Cosgrove, D. 155
Coulmas, F. 71, 72, 253
Council of Europe 116, 117, 278
Coupland, N. 157, 162, 167, 178
Cowling, M. 81
Crang, M. 208
Crawford, J. 186, 190
Crawford, M. 309
Cresswell, T. 196
Crystal, D. 162
Cultural Tourism DC 97, 187
CWMG website 25

Dagenais, D. 201, 202, 211, 253

Dahan, Y. 52
Dararai 90
Davis, K.G. 340
De Blaeij, A. 224, 231
De Certeau, M. 50, 247, 255
De Mauro, T. 5, 6
De Mente, B.L. 30
Delanty, G. xiv
Dell'Aquila, V. 9
Department of Arts and Culture (DAC) 78, 79
Department of Environmental Affairs and Tourism (DEAT) 80
Department of Transport (DoT) 80
Dietz, B. 327
Donitsa-Schmidt, S. 242, 243
Dorier-Apprill, E. 293
Duncum, P. 38
Durkheim, E. xiv, 328

Edelman, L. 118, 131
Eder, K. xiv
Edwards, V. 221
Efrat, Z. 51
Eisinger, P. 188
Entrikin, J.N. 153
Etxeberria, M. 220
Eusko Jaurlaritza 220
Evans, J. 39
Evdokimova, A. 135, 138
Extra, G. 3, 4

Fairclough, N. 177
Fararo, Th. xvii
Farrell, T. 256
Fenster, T. 57, 71
Fisher, M. 190
Flowerdew, J. 162
Fludernik, M. 327
Fortuni, F. 14
Foucault, M. 207, 212, 213
Franklin, S. 135, 136, 137, 139
Friedrich, P. 162

Gal, S. 169
García, I. 220
Garrett, P. 157, 167
Garvin, R. 254
Gee, J.P. 202, 255
Gelber, Y. 60
Gendelman, I. 177
Giliomee, H. 75
Gillette, F. 97
Gleick, J. xv
Glick Schiller, N. 327
Goffman, E. xviii, 3, 104, 105, 155, 157, 166, 167, 168, 252
Gonac'h, J. 278
Goodman, Y. 201
Gorter, D. xi, xii, xxiv, 4, 5, 38, 92, 98, 118,

154, 163, 183, 200, 201, 219, 221, 223, 224, 228, 253, 275, 277, 279
Graham, S. 156
Greenfield, A. 199, 208
Greenspan, E. 59
Gubrium, J.F. 254
Guillorel, H. 279
Gumperz, J.J. 22

Haarman, H. 162
Habermas, J. xiv
Hall, S. 39, 177, 328
Halliday, M.A.K. 167, 168, 170, 174
Hamilton, M. 252
Hamm, M. 135, 136, 139, 140, 141, 142, 143
Hanauer, D. 42, 254, 268
Hanks, W.F. 177
Hannigan, J. 185, 186, 189
Harré, R. 267
Harris, R. 283
Harvey, D. 153, 154, 170, 172, 176, 177
Hatuka, T. 58
Hayden, D. 212
Heller, M. 203
Henry, T.A. 203, 207, 208
Holstein, J.A. 254
Horowitz, N. 52
Huck, D. 284
Huebner, T. 163, 183, 200, 221, 253, 261, 278
Hult, F.M. 208, 253
Hutchinson, J. xviii
Hymes, D. 166, 202

Iannàccaro, G. 9
Iedema, R. 211
Inoue, F. 21, 22, 23
Irvine, J.T. 169
Israel Central Bureau of Statistics 40

Jacobs, J.M. 192
Jakobson, R. 50
Jaworski, A. xii, 154, 155, 163, 170, 172, 173, 176
Jay, M. 177, 209
Jenkins, E. 74
Jones, R.H. 156, 157
Joo, M-d. 203, 212
Jost, J. xvi
Joubert, N. 79, 91
Judge, A. 292, 294
Jury, D. 168, 172

Kalantzis, M. 202
Kallen, J.L. 20, 23, 157
Kang, H-b. 203, 211, 212
Kelly-Holmes, H. 163
Khedama, Q. 82, 91
Kim, M. 203
Kim, T-h. 199
King-Irani, L. 248

Knobel, M. 202
Kögler, H.H. xiv
Konchakovskii, A. 135, 142
Kramsch, C. 208
Kress, G. 167, 173, 176, 202, 265
Krige, D.S. 21, 76

Lajarge, R. 278, 280, 281
Landry, R. xi, xii, 4, 15, 19, 38, 97, 219, 252,
    263, 275, 277, 295, 326
Lanham, R.A. 156
Lankshear, C. 202
Lanza, E. 21, 163
Lasagabaster, D. 220
Lawrence-Zuñiga, D. 196
Lee, K. 4
Leeman, J. 96, 97, 98, 112, 182, 185, 189, 196,
    200, 209
Lefebvre, H. 3, 37, 48, 57, 58, 153, 219, 236,
    237, 239, 276
Levi-Strauss, C. 345
Ley, D. 170, 177
Liber, G. 141, 143, 144
Lim, W. 108
Lloyd, R. 192
Loftus, W. 75, 81, 82, 85
Lotte website 32
Lou, J. 96, 97, 98, 112
Low, S. M. 154, 170, 171
Lubbe, J. 85
Lucci, V. 276, 278, 279, 281, 286, 287
Luckingham, B. 310
Lüdi, G. 285
Lufrano, F.L. 9
Lukowski, J. 135, 143
Luria, S. 187
Ly, P. 192

M'ethot, M. 58
Mac Donnacha, S. 23
Mac Giolla Chríost, D. 4, 14, 154, 156, 177, 293
Magocsi, P. 136, 138, 139, 140, 141, 143
Mahoko, L. 82, 90
Makarov, A. 135, 142
Malakov, D. 135, 142
Malinowski, D. 96, 99, 112, 205, 254, 279,
    280, 288
Mallet, W. 189
Marais, L. 91
Marchal, H. 276
Markus, T.A. 176
Marshall, C. 148
Martin, L.A. 20
Masenko, L. 144, 148
Mashkevich, S. 142
Massaro, B. 14
Massey, D. 156, 176, 182
Matiase, S. 82
McDonald, T. 58

McGuinne, D. 21
McQuire, S. 58
Mele, C. 192
Melnyk, S. 135, 148
Messaoudi, L. 275
Miles, M. 12, 156
Millet, A. 286
Mills, C. 154, 170
Min, P.G. 203
Mingozzi, V. 14, 15
Mishori, A. 47
Mitchell, D. 155, 188
Mitchell, T. 209
Mitchell, W.J.T 37, 38, 39, 209
Modan, G. 96, 97, 98, 112, 154, 155, 182, 185,
    189, 192, 200, 209
Moïse, C. 280
Mondada, L. 5
Monterescu, D. 61, 62, 248
Moore, D. 97
Moscovici, S. 302
Moser, L-M. 162
Mothekhe, M. 82
Municipality of Arezzo 14
Municipality of Ferrara 14
Municipality of Florence 13
Municipality of Prato 9, 11
Municipality of Rome 7
Myhill, J. 329

Naidoo, R. 82
Naylor, Ph. Chiviges 327
New London Group 202
Nikitenko, N. 135, 137, 139, 140
Nunan, D. 203
Nunes, P. 224, 231

Ó Cuív, B. 23
Ó Giollagáin, C. 23
Ó Riagáin, P. 23
Ozolins, U. 115, 116

Pacione, M. xiii
Pai, H. 203
Pang, C.L. 96, 97, 98, 112
Pavlenko, A. 143, 144, 148, 255
Peck, C. 256
Pelser, A. 78
Pennycook, A. 42, 255
Phillipson, R. 323
Pieterse, E. 76
Pieterse, J.N. 327
Pile, S. xiii
Piller, I. 163, 221, 286
Pinto, M. 244, 245
Pires, M. 281
Poignant, B. 305
Porebski, M. 177
Portugali, Y. 247

Pošeiko, S. 131
Pratt, M.L. 210
Press, I. 137, 139, 141
Puzey, G. 221
Pycroft, C. 75

Rath, J. 96, 97, 98, 112
Reddy, M.J. 182
Reh, M. 21, 24, 28, 29
Republic of Latvia 116, 117
Rēzeknes pilsētas dome 116
Rogoff, I. 38, 209, 210
Rose, G. 154, 177
Rosenbaum, Y. 221, 277
Rotbard, S. 61
Rozycki, W. 23
Rusina, O. 135, 139, 140

Saban, I. 249
Sagasta, M.P. 220
Said, E. 210
Salzberg, C. 211
Santos, C.A. 189
Sassen, S. xiii
Sautot, J.P. 276, 281
Schmid, C. 116
Schmid, M. 330
Schoeman, K. 75
Scholl, B.J. xiv
Schön, D. 256
Schuh website 28
Scollon, R. 14, 96, 97, 98, 99, 154, 155, 156,
    157, 168, 183, 207, 252, 255, 299
Segev, T. 62
Shakwane, T. 82
Shaw, S. 189, 192
Shepard, J. 139
Sherman, J. 256
Shilo-Cohen, N. 53
Shohamy, E. xi, xii, 5, 38, 62, 63, 71, 72, 92,
    96, 98, 112, 113, 155, 178, 185, 200, 201,
    211, 221, 242, 243, 253, 263, 275, 277, 307,
    330
Silva, D.J. 203
Silverstein, M. 157, 177
Slater, D. 38
Slembrouck, S. 253
Sloboda, M. 298, 305
Smith, A.D. xviii
Smith, N. 189
Smolij, V. 135, 136, 139, 140, 144
Snyder, T. 135, 136, 139, 140
Sorkin, M. 189, 190
Sperber, D. 157
Spolsky, B. xi, xii, 19, 208, 242, 243, 253, 254,
    292, 295, 309, 326, 330
Stébé, J.M. 276

Sternberg, Y. xviii, 339, 340
Street, B. 202
Subtelny, O. 140, 141, 144
Šuplinska, I. 116, 117

Tambiah, S.J. 327
Tanaka, K. 23
Tellini, B. 14
Thurlow, C. xii, 154, 155, 163, 170, 172, 173,
    176, 177, 178
Törrönen, J. 255
Torstrick, R. 250
Townsend, A. 199
Trumper-Hecht, N. 19, 62, 92, 178, 235, 238,
    239, 241, 242, 244
Tuan, Y.F. 212, 255
Tzfadia, E. 40, 41

UNESCO 220
Urry, J. xv

Van den Avenne, C. 293
Van Donk, M. 76
Van Langenhove, L. 267
Van Leeuwen, T. 162, 173, 176, 265
Van Lier, L. 208
Vartanian, I. 20
Venter, S. 75
Vertovec, S. 4
Villarini, A. 6
Virilio, P. 210
Visser, L. 91
Vlasto, A. 136, 137, 141

Waksman, S. 63, 71, 72
Weeks, C. 211
Wheeler, L. 187
Wiley, T.G. 309, 324
Williams, C. 4
Wilson, A. 136, 140, 141
Wilson, D. 157
Winchester, H.P.M. 154
Woldemariam, H. 21, 163
Wolfson, N. 170
Wong Scollon, S. 14, 96, 97, 98, 99, 154, 155,
    156, 157, 168, 183, 207, 252, 255, 299
Wright, P. 177

Yakobi, H. 57, 71
Yashita, A. 327
Yurchak, A. 177

Zalizniak, H. 148
Zawadzki, H. 135, 143
Zerubavel, E. 58, 66
Zochrot 69, 70
Zukin, S. 185, 188, 189, 190

Subjects and Places Index

Acre 235-6
Activity space 98, 109, 111-2
Aesthetics, aesthetic use of language 190-5
Albanian (language) 15
Alexandria 278
Alphabet 11, 22, 136, 142; *see also* script
Alsatian (language) 278-85, 293
Amsterdam 118, 131
Anxiety 125-30
Arabic (language) xxv, 15, 62-4, 69, 139,
    192-4, 235, 238-50, 280, 286-7, 313, 330-1,
    334, 336, 338
Arezzo 6, 14-5
Arizona xxvi, 307-10, 312-3, 320, 322-4
Armenian (language) 138, 140, 143
Asian languages 312-4, 336
Attention structures 156-7, 166

Basel 67, 278, 283, 285
Basque (language) xxiv, 220-32, 293
Belarusian (language) 136, 140, 143
Bergen County 203
Bilingualism, official 74, 79, 81-2, 86
Bloemfontein xxi, 74-92
Boston 186
Breton (language) xxvi, 293-305
Brussels 278
Bulge theory 170
Business Improvement District (BID) 188

Calendar systems 65-6
Catalan (language) xxvi, 293-99, 303-5
Centennial xxi, 57-71
Centrifugal force 168
Centripetal semiotic aggregates 169
Chaos xiv-xvii
Chicago xiv, 309
Chinatown xxi-xxii, 96-113, 155, 183-95,
    309-10
Chinese (language) xxii, 6-15, 20-22, 96-108,
    110-113, 155-8, 161-74, 183-4, 192-6, 203,
    262, 309, 312-5, 319-23, 331
Co-construction xxv, 255, 267-8
Codeswitching 22, 27
Cognitive maps 245, 247
Collective memory 68, 189
Commodification xxiii-xxiv, 155, 170, 182,
    185-96
Commoditization xxiv, 160, 199, 201

Corsican (language) 293

Dakar 278
Diaspora, returning xxvii, 326-41
Diaspora, transnational xxvii, 202, 326-41
Distinction 171-3, 177, 192
Donostia-San Sebastian 118, 219-32
Dublin 19-20, 25-6, 157

Emotional response 252, 267-8
English (language) xiii, xx, xxi, xxii, xxvi,
    xxvii, 11, 14, 20-34, 61-6, 74-92, 97-102,
    105-10, 116-30, 134, 145-9, 158-74, 183-4,
    195, 199, 203-6, 220-32, 238-46, 256-61,
    278-81, 285-9, 292, 307-24, 330-41
Entextualization 157, 173, 177
Ethnography, ethnographic approach 39,
    96, 112, 145, 154, 202, 254

Ferrara 6, 14-5
Flemish (language) 293
Florence 6, 13-4
Flushing 203
Font 19, 21, 24, 29, 34, 100, 169, 174, 176,
    192-4, 299-301
Frame analysis 157
French (language) xvi, xxvi, xxvii, 11, 20,
    119, 123, 125, 141-3, 161, 165, 191, 201,
    220, 226-9, 232, 275-89, 292-305, 323,
    331-41
French Jews, in France xxvii, 326-42
French Jews, in Israel xxvii, 326-42
Fukuoka 20-1, 30-1, 33

Galway 19-21, 24-6, 28
Gated communities 154, 158, 160, 169
Geosemiotics xxii, 96-103, 112, 154-5
Geospatial context 313-4
Gestalt xiv, xvi, 254, 311, 322, 345
Globalization, globalisation xiii, xiv, xviii,
    xx, xxv, xxvii, 22-3, 28, 31, 34, 52, 92, 128,
    203, 221, 323, 326, 328, 330, 336, 341,
Good reasons (perspective) xvii, xix, xxiii, 345
Graffiti xxi, 39, 42, 68-72, 124, 134-40, 148,
    177, 296, 304, 337,
Greek (language) xv, 136-40, 143, 288
Grenoble 278

Haifa 40, 235

Hapache (language) 313
Hebrew (language) xxv, xxvii, 60-71, 138, 143, 145, 192, 235, 238-50, 326-41
Hegemony (hegemonic) 37, 144, 292
Heritage Language xxvi, 96, 157, 202, 292-5, 302, 308, 324
Hindi (language) 15, 313
Hong Kong xxiii, 153-78
Hybridization 30, 327-8

Iconization (semiotics) xxiv, 201, 209
Identity xxi, xxii, xxv, xxvi, 9, 22-3, 37-40, 49, 51-2, 59-63, 71, 97, 102, 153-4, 169, 171, 176, 237-8, 247, 250-4, 261-2, 267-8, 276, 279-81, 284, 287-8, 299, 301, 308, 329, 340
Identity, aspirational 176, 178
Identity, collective xviii, xix, 66, 328-9, 345
Ideology, language 39, 292-301
Ideology, Zionist xxi, 60-6
Immigration xiv, xx, xxiii, xxvi, xxvii, 3-16, 22, 37, 40-2, 51-2, 57, 69, 97, 107, 112, 189, 221, 248, 265-6, 275, 279, 286, 308-10, 320, 322, 324, 326-30, 340, 342 Immigrant language xxvi, 3, 4, 6, 10, 13-6, 277, 279
Index, indexicality 23, 26, 28, 30, 34, 153, 155-78, 183, 191-2, 196, 203-8, 302
Index, linguistic vitality 12
Indexability 155
Interaction xii, xiv, xxiii, xxv, 3-5, 15, 97, 103, 133, 139-40, 145, 148-9, 154, 167, 195, 252, 256-68
Irish (language) 19-34

Jaffa 59-62, 66, 68, 235-6, 248-50
Japanese (language) 29-33, 119, 203, 207, 323, 331
Judaism 329, 339-40

Keying 166-7, 173-4
Kiev, Kyiv xxii, 134-149
Korean (language) 20-1, 200, 202-6, 211, 309, 312-3
Kufic (language) 139

Language (linguistic) attitude xxiii, xxv, xxvi, 16, 115-7, 125-30, 219-23, 232, 235-50, 269, 327, 340-1.
Language (linguistic) contact xxvi, 4-6, 154, 210, 223, 254, 275, 278, 288-9
Language (linguistic) crossing 177
Language (linguistic) diversity 16-7, 20, 23, 163, 201, 253, 258, 268, 275, 277-9, 288, 293, 336
Language (linguistic) education 130, 134, 141, 144, 149, 201-2, 307-9
Language (linguistic) learning 201, 224, 242-3
Language (linguistic) preference 78, 81, 235, 242-3, 249

Language (linguistic) prestige xxii, 91, 116, 123, 126, 128, 148-9
Language (linguistic) regime 74-92
Language (linguistic) visibility 148, 168, 203, 235-50, 289, 295, 308, 340
Language (linguistic) vitality xi, xviii, xx, xxii, xxv, xxvi, 3-16, 154, 307-8, 315, 324, 326
Language policy xxi, 20, 29, 75, 78-84, 90, 92, 115-6, 129-30, 154, 220-1, 223, 228, 232, 254
Latgalian (language) 115-9, 124-30
Latvian (language) xxii, 115-30
Legal hypercorrection xxii, 129-30
Linguistic landscape online 199-212
LL change xxi, 57, 62, 74-92, 134, 143, 147-8, 208, 249, 254,
Liouwert 118, 223,
Lod 235
Los Angeles 203, 309

Mapping 209-11, 258, 307, 313
Maricopa County 307-24
Marketing, language and culture in 25, 186, 191, 344
Melting pot 51-2
Memphis xxv, 252-69
Migdal ha-'Emeq 37-53
Migrant cityscaping 254
Minority language xxii, xxv, xxvi, 3-4, 115-9, 128, 183, 192, 194-5, 220-32, 240, 242-3, 249-50, 252, 258, 263, 278, 307-12, 332
Mixed cities xxv, 61, 235-50
Monterotondo 6, 12-3
Montpellier 278, 294
Montreal 201, 326
Multilingual cityscape xxiv, 219, 232
Multimodality 38, 98-9, 266, 275

Narrative xxi, 37-8, 40, 57-8, 68-72, 255
Natanya xxvii, 326-41
Navaho (language) 312-3
Nazareth 40, 235-6, 238-50
Newspapers 68, 144, 320-2, 327
New York city xiii, xiv, 57, 58-60, 71, 97, 309

Occitan (language) 293
Orthography, writing systems, *see also* alphabet, script 11, 21-6, 30, 34, 105, 192
Osaka 203

Packaging 30, 308-9, 316, 320-1, 323
Paris xvi, 278, 326, 330, 341
Peoria 311-20
Perception xvii, xviii, xix, xxiv, xxv, 58, 71, 121, 125, 156, 166, 176, 202, 219-33, 235-48, 252-53, 258, 276, 344
Peripheral town, city (periphery) xx, 39, 42, 52, 97, 294, 303

Perpignan xxvi, 293-305
Phoenix xxvi, 307, 310, 312, 315
Place, sense of 37, 41, 51-2, 153, 155, 177, 212, 255
Polish (language) 15, 115-9, 128, 130, 139-48, 313
Popular art 37, 45, 51
Postmodern interview 254-5, 267
Power relations xvii, xix, xxii, 92, 153-4, 156, 177, 237, 247, 254, 301, 308, 328,
Prato 6, 9-12, 16
Presentation of self xviii, xix, xxi, 328
Production (of LL) xii, xxvi, 12, 38-9, 103, 112, 184, 276-8, 281, 283, 288
Public/private partnerships 88, 186, 188

Quartier 275-89
Québec 118, 191

Reflection-in-action 256
Rennes xxvi, 277, 293-305
Representational space 153
Representational technologies 206, 209
Residential buildings, areas xxiii, 118, 123, 128, 153-177, 183, 188, 192, 203, 211, 315
Reversing Language Shift xxiv, 232
Rezekne 118-131
Ritual (artifacts) 43-51
Romanian (language) 6, 12-5, 143
Rome 3, 6-7, 9, 12, 16
Rouen 277
Russian (language) xxii, xxvii, 6, 14-5, 20, 115-30, 133-49, 240, 242-4, 247, 255, 330-2, 334, 336, 338, 341-2

San Francisco 97, 309
Sarcelles-Pletzel xxvii, 326, 329-41
Scale 186, 195
Scopic regime 177
Script 136, 141, 168, 203, 315
Seeing, practices of 206
Self-positioning 261, 266
Seoul xxiv, 199-212
Serbian (language) 143
Shanghai 183-4
Shop signs (signage) xi, xxii, 9, 11, 96-104, 111-2, 134, 226, 243, 277
Signs as branding 34, 162, 174, 176, 190
Signs (signage), bilingual xxi, 30, 83-4, 86, 88, 97-8, 105, 111, 119-20, 162, 165, 205-6, 220, 222, 224, 297-300, 302, 305, 318-9
Signs (signage), bottom-up xvii, xix, xxiii, 10, 75, 80, 87, 92, 258, 276, 284, 296-7, 299-300, 302, 315, 344
Signs (signage), commercial xi, xxiii, 20, 96-7, 105, 134-5, 137, 139, 142-5, 148-9, 156, 240, 244-5, 249, 258, 260, 275-7, 279, 288
Signs (signage), direction 82-3, 88-90, 219

Signs (signage), monolingual 84, 165, 228-9, 232, 238, 281, 296-7, 332
Signs (signage), multilingual 19, 21-2, 34, 228, 230, 232, 256, 262, 268, 280, 286, 288, 295, 299, 309, 315, 322
Signs (signage), municipal 82-5, 88
Signs (signage), non-commercial 183
Signs (signage), non-official 80, 85-7, 92, 258
Signs (signage), official xxiii, 20, 80, 86-7, 89, 92, 134-5, 139, 142, 144-5, 148-9, 258
Signs (signage), private xi, xxiii, 117, 122, 134, 137, 139, 143, 145, 148-9, 189, 239-41, 298
Signs (signage), public xi, xxi, 62, 80-5, 88-9, 91-2, 130, 134, 140, 142, 189, 239-41, 244-6, 249-50, 252-3, 258, 277, 296, 307, 309, 326
Signs (signage), top-down xvii, xix, xxi, xxii, xxvi, 9-10, 12-3, 75, 80, 92, 224, 279, 285, 296-8, 304, 315, 344-5
Signs (signage), trilingual 83-4, 90, 118, 120, 229, 242-3
Silence 170
Slavonic (language) 136-7, 139-40, 148
Social facts xiv, xvi, 237
Social networks 153, 310, 320, 322-3
Social representation 302-5
Space, lived 153, 176, 237, 248
Spanish (language) xxiv, 119, 122-3, 157, 161, 165, 220-32, 261-2, 294, 308-9, 312-3, 323
Status of language 253
Stimulus text xxv, 255, 261, 268
Strasbourg xxvi, 275-89
Street name signs 29, 62-6, 68, 71, 75, 81-3, 85-7, 120, 134-5, 141, 157-8, 161, 165, 167-8, 171, 174-6, 201, 219, 245-6, 258, 277, 285, 296-7
Surveillance 39, 209, 212
Symbolic economy xxiii, 185-6, 188-90
Symbolic meaning, symbolic use of language 183-4, 195, 308

Tagalog (language) 312-3
Tatar (language) 143
Tel Aviv-Jaffa xxi, 57, 59, 61-3
Temporal markers 58
Themed environments 185, 190, 193, 195
Tokyo xii, 20, 118, 203, 278
Tourism, tourism promotion xxiii, 14, 20, 22, 25, 91, 98, 123, 183, 186-7, 189, 191, 195, 221

Ukrainian (language) xxii, 6, 14-5, 116-7, 119, 133-4, 140-1, 144-9
Urban planning xxii, 71, 97-8, 105, 188. 207
Urban sociolinguistics 275, 277, 289
Urban space(s) xi, xii, xv, xx, xxi, xxiv, xxv, 3-5, 39, 57, 82, 96, 154, 177-8, 182, 186, 188, 190, 231, 238, 247, 252, 254-5, 261, 268,

275-8, 283, 289, 303, 309, 326, 328-9, 336, 341
Urban writing 275-7, 289

Vancouver 97, 201
Vietnamese (language) 312-3, 318
Visual culture xx, 37-40, 51, 201, 209-11
Vitrolles 278

Walking tour xxv, 72, 252, 254-5, 258-61, 263, 265, 267-8
Washington, DC 96-113, 154, 155, 183-96, 209

Yiddish (language) 60, 143

Zionism 67, 238, 330